MOTIVATING AND MANAGING PERFORMANCE

Compiled by Chris Lee
from articles that have been published in

TRAINING
THE MAGAZINE OF HUMAN RESOURCES DEVELOPMENT

LAKEWOOD BOOKS
50 South Ninth Street
Minneapolis, MN 55402
(612) 333-0471

Production Editor: Helen Gillespie
With special thanks to: Jeanne Dunlap, Brenda Owens and Wanda Stephenson

Second Printing

Lakewood Publications Inc. publishes TRAINING Magazine, The Training Directors' Forum Newsletter, Creative Training Techniques Newsletter, The Lakewood Report, Potentials In Marketing Magazine, Presentations Magazine, and other business periodicals and books. James P. Secord, president; Mary Hanson, Philip G. Jones, Linda Klemstein, Michael C. Miller, Jerry C. Noack, vice presidents.

ISBN 0-943210-20-8

TABLE OF CONTENTS

CHAPTER 2
MOTIVATING PERFORMANCE

REWARDING AND RECOGNIZING PERFORMANCE

THE NEW HRD LIBRARY

Contemporary training ideas, strategies and techniques for managers
and HRD professionals

Welcome to *The New HRD Library*. Before you read on, there are a few things you should know about this series of books and how it came into existence.

Each book in *The New HRD Library* contains articles originally published in *TRAINING Magazine, The Training Directors' Forum Newsletter, Creative Training Techniques, The Service Edge Newsletter* or *Front-Line Service Newsletter,* all Lakewood publications that explore contemporary human resources development issues, trends and ideas from different (although sometimes only slightly different) angles and perspectives. While there is some overlap among the books in the series, each of them stands on its own.

Our editors selected articles to illuminate a particular theme or subject area—from the dynamics of adult occupational learning, to managing and running a corporate training function, to designing cost-effective training programs, to training that ensures top-notch customer service. And more.

The pervasive style of the selected articles is that of magazine and newsletter journalism, opinion and commentary. In this accessible, nonacademic style, the authors address the real and immediate challenges you face as practicing HRD professionals or as managers and motivators of people.

The edited articles are contained between the covers of the books in *The New HRD Library*. Not, to repeat, as the definitive texts or final words on any one subject area, but as books that serve a different and (depending who you are) maybe even more useful purpose.

As the training profession evolves, it demands a solid understanding of the original ideas, theories and systems that shaped its development. Today's training professionals also must be prepared to absorb, assimilate and put into perspective an astonishing amount of new informa-tion. Like doctors, lawyers, bankers or other professionals, HRD professionals can never stop learning. Not if they want to be effective. Certainly not if they want to get ahead.

The publications that form the core of *The New HRD Library* have become among the most widely read and influential in the field because their editors have never forgotten that fundamental need. In addition to featuring the best writers, theorists and practitioners in HRD, each publication also meets the HRD professional's need to understand the newest techniques, strategies and approaches to tough workplace challenges *within* the context of the established body of HRD knowledge.

Thus, each publication I've discussed here is carefully balanced to appeal to relative novices in HRD as well as to seasoned professionals. And so are the books in *The New HRD Library*, which represents a comprehensive and systematic collection of current ideas and practical responses to meeting workplace challenges (in many cases, articulated by those who first formulated them) within the context of HRD's most enduring, time-tested fundamentals. In other words, these books manage to be both timeless and as relevant as the challenges you now face in the rapidly evolving American workplace.

Plus, the books in *The New HRD Library* are designed so you can find useful information *fast*. And with that information, you probably can meet a challenge, solve a problem or defuse a crisis right away. It's a fact that HRD changes constantly, especially today. But I think you'll find, due to the care with which the contents of these books were selected and to the editorial strengths of the publications in which this material first appeared, *The New HRD Library* series will be as useful many years from now as it is today.

Philip Jones
Lakewood Publications

INTRODUCTION

Geary Rummler, HRD Hall of Fame member, performance technologist and Summit, NJ-based consultant, is fond of saying, "Put a good performer up against a bad system, and the system will win every time." Memorable words. But how do you go about building a system that will support human performance instead of inhibiting it?

This volume focuses on a trio of interlocking factors that provide part of the answer to that question: performance appraisal and management, motivation techniques, and rewards and recognition.

The section titled Managing Performance examines performance-appraisal systems, a longtime bugaboo in many organizations, from a variety of angles. Designing a better form will not make your performance-appraisal system a winner, but using it to set goals and give feedback on a regular basis may make it a useful—if still uncomfortable—process.

But there's more to managing performance than appraising it. The competitive challenges of the '80s ushered in the era of employee involvement, a management philosophy that often produces spectacular results in organizations that dedicate themselves to it. Empowerment, teamwork, pushing responsibility down to employees on the front lines—these and a variety of other techniques that have changed the way we manage also are examined in this section.

Which segues directly into Motivating Performance. Theories on motivation abound, and you'll get a generous sampling of them here. But you'll also see how those theories are put into practice—and the results they can produce. There's a dark side, too, of course. If some management practices can turn employees on, others can turn them off. Several articles in this collection provide food for thought by taking a look at the impact on employees of traumatic changes such as mergers and layoffs.

We've long used the twin tools of rewards and recognition to motivate employees. Incentives may range from plaques commemorating a job well-done to Caribbean cruises to cash, but all are designed to confirm accomplishments and reinforce commitment. Do they work? Overwhelming evidence says they do—as long as the rewards and recognition are structured to be meaningful to employees. You'll find that Rewarding and Recognizing Performance holds a wealth of suggestions on how to create effective incentive programs and how organizations use them successfully.

Keep in mind Rummler's maxim as you peruse this collection. It will help you keep your perspective as you consider some of *TRAINING's* best thinking on managing and motivating performance.

Chris Lee
Managing Editor, TRAINING Magazine
November 1990

CHAPTER 1

MANAGING PERFORMANCE

IS PERFORMANCE APPRAISAL A PAPER TIGER?

Performance appraisals have long been accepted as a necessary, if unpleasant, fact of organizational life. But a rising chorus is voicing some serious doubts about whether they really work

BY RON ZEMKE

Performance appraisals are about as beloved as IRS audits. Managers hate giving them, subordinates dislike receiving them, and the personnel people who have to shovel the paperwork blizzard they generate often aren't crazy about them either.

But performance reviews are necessary, of course. You have to conduct them; you need some formal system for doing so; and, provided you have a "good" system, you achieve the desired results with it. That's axiomatic. Has been for years. Except. . .lately, even experts who have encouraged organizations to fight the good fight for systematic performance appraisal are having their doubts.

In short, despite the logical appeal of performance appraisal as a tool for increasing productivity, developing people and assessing the capacity of the organization's talent pool, evidence has been popping up to suggest that most performance appraisal systems are more noteworthy for the angst they create than the results they achieve.

Attacks on employee evaluation systems are nothing new, of course. The idea of formal performance appraisal no sooner came into vogue than the methods used to do the appraising began to draw fire. An army of consultants has staked out the ter-

ritory as a specialty, sending forth its soldiers to explain to exasperated executives why their systems don't work the way they're supposed to.

But almost always those explanations have focused on forms and procedures: Your system doesn't produce valid and reliable ratings of individual performers, for example, because your evaluation forms ask supervisors to rate their subordinates according to vague, subjective criteria such as "innovativeness" and "initiative." What you need instead is a behaviorally based or goal-oriented rating system that uses specific, observable, job-related criteria.

What is different about these latest rumblings of dissatisfaction is that critics are pointing to problems that seem to apply regardless of the rating system used. Tinkering with forms and procedures, they argue, becomes an expensive exercise in bolt-tightening that has little impact on some of the monkey wrenches inherent in the performance appraisal machinery.

In theory, performance appraisal systems make all the sense in the world. To be successful, the Industrial Relations 101 argument goes, an organization must make effective use of its human resources. In English that means:

• People who work in the organization must be able to do the work assigned to them in an effective and efficient manner.

• Managers must be able to predict who in the organization is able to take on different or more challenging work.

• Management, in the abstract sense, must be able to compare the current "skill pool" to future needs, and come up with ways to ensure that the two mesh properly when the time comes.

That is the basic rationale for having a performance appraisal system. But there's more. On top of the organizational benefits of systematic appraisal, advocates claim, there are personal and interpersonal benefits. A good performance review system increases employee motivation and job-related communications between subordinates and managers. It provides a vehicle for discussing current performance, determining an individual's developmental and training needs, and for talking about advancement desires and opportunities.

A third use of performance appraisal, one often discounted in the professional literature but of utmost import to appraisees, is the distribution of dollars. Determining salaries by merit is becoming an increasingly respectable practice as more and more organizations decide that pay should be directly linked to performance.

Indeed, a recent survey of 875 companies conducted by Sibson & Company, a Chicago-based compensation consulting firm, found 32% of respondents experimenting with some form of performance-based pay—an increase of 39% over the previous year. In a related study, this one conducted by New York-based Towers, Perrin, Forster & Crosby, half of the 462 senior human resource executives polled rated "relating pay to performance" their number-one priority.

Promise unfulfilled

The premise behind all this promise is that performance appraisal systems actually work—that is, that they provide the organization with valid and usable information about its people. It is this crucial supposition that has fallen open to growing doubt.

The assault on the efficacy of performance appraisal didn't begin yesterday. One of the earliest salvos was fired in a 20-page monograph released in 1977 by researchers Morgan

L. McCall Jr. and David W. De Vries of the Center for Creative Leadership in Greensboro, NC. They argued that most appraisal systems are not designed with the realities of organizational life in mind. Specifically, "the nature of managerial work, environmental demands and organizational characteristics generally clash with the internal structure of appraisal systems." In other words, they may work well in the lab, but. . . .

More recent reviews and reports have been equally if not more critical. Earlier this year, the American Society for Personnel Administration's (ASPA) Personnel Research Committee conducted a special, open workshop on performance appraisal and found, among other things, that "performance appraisal has become difficult because so much is asked of the people involved in the transaction. It has become the vehicle for reviewing behavior on the job, career development, announcing pay decisions and discussing remedial action. Neither the appraiser nor the appraised can be faulted for expressing frustration over having to cope with all those transactions during any one interview."

In the September 1985 issue of *Psychology Today*, contributing editor Berkley Rice reviewed the last 30 years' research on performance appraisal, interviewed some of the leading experts in the field, and came to many of the same conclusions as McCall, De Vries and the ASPA research committee. Rice also pointed out that opinion is beginning to jell around the idea that the problems in performance appraisal may extend far beyond bad systems and poor tools. "[Cognitive researchers] suspect that perceptual and cognitive differences among raters may affect their ratings as much as or more than the nature of the rating scale itself and may be impervious to any changes in the evaluation system or the structure of the rating scale."

In short, a number of people have begun to suspect that performance appraisal systems not only don't work but *can't* work. Or at least, they can't be made to do the things they're supposed to do in a reliable way.

Why not? Some common themes:

1. *People don't like to do it.* Managers don't like to give formal appraisals; subordinates don't like to receive them. This hasn't exactly been the world's best-kept secret for the last three decades, so perhaps the surprise is that it took this long for significant numbers of experts to focus on it as an iceberg that doesn't disappear when you change your procedures or evaluation forms.

Harry Levinson, of the Levinson Institute, Inc. in Cambridge, MA, attributes manager reluctance to "guilt about judging others and [discomfort] about being straightforward."

Dean Spitzer, of QuickSkills Learning Centers, Inc. in Menasha, WI, carries that theme further. "Managers are afraid of performance appraisal because they are afraid of their people. They are afraid to confront people, to tell them straightaway that they are doing a bad job. I've seen managers agonize for weeks over a performance review of a person everyone in the department knows to be incompetent."

Worse yet, some—dare we say many?—managers resent the insinuation that they even *should* do performance reviews. As one trainer confided, "I was doing the unit on performance appraisal and one of our VPs just floored me. 'Listen,' he said, 'if they don't know how they are doing without *me* having to tell them, they need their butts fired out of here. We don't need that kind of person in corporate lending.' I thought that attitude went out with Genghis Khan."

THE TROUBLE WITH PERFORMANCE APPRAISAL

In attempting to establish criteria to discriminate between "high and low performers" among their workers, U.S. businesses have become involved in what seems to be an increasingly intricate relationship between appraisal systems and the law.

"An ever-growing demand by government requires a formally documented and legally sound measure of work behavior," says Robert Laud, vice president of Drake Beam Morin, Inc., a New York-based management consulting firm. Last year, Laud's firm conducted a survey of *"Fortune* 1300" companies regarding their efforts to improve productivity through performance evaluation. His overall conclusion: It's not easy to do it well.

In the first place, Laud cites the U.S. Equal Employment Opportunity Commission's five-year-old *Uniform Guidelines on Employee Selection Procedures* as a potent force governing the content and procedures of employee-appraisal systems.

"In addition," he says, "performance-appraisal issues are closely tied to the Equal Pay Act of 1963, the Age Discrimination in Employment Act of 1967 and the Vocational Rehabilitation Act of 1973. Interestingly enough, the 'minority' or protected groups collectively comprise close to 75% of the labor force."

Even assuming adherence to the law, there is widespread resistance to performance-appraisal systems, Laud observes, and not only because the results often conflict with union-supported seniority systems (only about 25% of U.S. workers are unionized).

"Employees often believe that the appraisal information gathered is not objective and will not adequately reflect either ability or performance," says Laud. "Inappropriately high or low ratings may then lead to feelings of guilt or frustration. This type of selective distortion—or the perception of it—is an inherent and widespread problem."

According to Laud, American corporations are generally amenable to performance appraisal "focusing on mutual goal setting, accountability, awareness of contributions and self-reliance." The question that remains to be settled, he says, is not whether to implement an appraisal system, "but to what extent the system should be participative and collaborative?" And, of course, how do you design or select a system that works for you?

"Through the *Fortune* 1300 survey," says Laud, "it was found that a very large proportion (29%) of hourly workers are reported not to have a formal appraisal system at all." This suggests to him that "productivity concerns in America today might well be addressed through a review of the appraisal system at this level."

Laud recommends that managers give primary concern to "clarity of purpose" in designing performance-appraisal systems that will meet legal requirements and win support from working people and their managers. It helps, he says, to tie performance goals to the corporate "mission" so that everyone in an organization clearly understands what is expected.

Reprinted from TRAINING, April 1984

The worst part is that this guy is 31 years old, a senior VP with a Stanford MBA in finance. He's one of our stars!"

Levinson tends to dismiss such outbursts as symptoms of "managerial avoidance," but others do not. De Vries, for instance, argues that performance appraisal, because it requires careful planning, information gathering and an extensive formal interview, is antithetical to normal managerial work, which he says (relying on research by the University of Montreal's Henry Mintzberg) is characterized by activities of short duration, *ad hoc* meetings, non-routine behavior and a focus on current, rather than past, information.

2. *Performance appraisals are valued more by administrators than by managers and employees.* In a series of studies on the factors that affect managerial careers, Minneapolis-based Honeywell Corp. found that formal performance appraisals bring up the rear (see "The Honeywell Studies: How Managers Learn to Manage," TRAINING, August 1985). According to Honeywell researcher Sam Campbell, "It was near the bottom of a list of 24 impact items managers mentioned. About 4% of supervisors, 2% of managers and 1% of executives said performance appraisals had a positive impact on their careers."

De Vries is not surprised. "In most organizations, performance appraisals are something managers do at the insistence of the personnel department. The hammer is pay. No reviews turned in, no pay increases for you or your people."

In that same vein, De Vries questions the "pay-for-performance" link compensation theorists attach to performance reviews. "Managers are smart and they are human. They know that about one-tenth of 1% of the people are going to be *allowed* a maximum increase—say it's 5%—and to do that you have to give those people a nearly perfect, walk-on-water performance review. So there you are, a manager who has a single parent with two kids working for you. You know the person is struggling to make ends meet and at *best* you're going to be able to give that person a 5% increase. So you undermine the system to help that person out. It's not that unusual."

Brian Davis, a vice president with Personnel Decisions, Inc. (PDI), a Minneapolis-based developer of personnel systems and training, agrees that performance appraisal often is a functionless formality. "Just watch the amount of policing the human-resources people do. The more memos you see that say things like, 'You must complete and return these forms to personnel by the 15th,' the more likely it is that the system is run for personnel purposes and is meaningless to the line managers. Fortunately, these systems frequently break down under the weight of the paper they generate."

3. *Ratings systems don't produce objective measures of performance.* Sally Coltrin, a professor at the University of North Florida in Jacksonville, catalogued the psychometric problems—i.e., rating errors—that plague performance appraisal forms for ASPA's committee. The five most common are:

● *Central tendency*: Managers tend to rate everyone about the same or, at least, they avoid extreme ratings. People tend to do this when they rate *anything*.

● *Leniency*: Managers shun low ratings to avoid conflict or because they believe that low ratings reflect badly on the rater.

● *Halo*: Raters pay too much attention to one factor, allowing a high rating in one area to influence ratings in others.

● *Recency*: Raters focus on the most recent examples of behavior rather than considering performance across time.

● *Constancy*: Some managers rate their subordinates in rank-order rather than on an individual basis and adjust scores to match the rank-ordering.

While some rating methods have been proven to be less susceptible to rating errors than others, no system is immune. Unfortunately, as many researchers have pointed out, raters typically resist more time-consuming, but psychometrically superior, techniques and opt for those that are seriously flawed by errors.

Other problems unearthed by various researchers include:

● Racial bias: White supervisors tend to rate white subordinates higher than black supervisors rate white subordinates. Black supervisors rate blacks higher than whites rate blacks. In addition, white supervisors tend to give white employees more diverse ratings than they give black employees.

● Length of service and the "compliancy" of the person being rated can affect ratings significantly.

● Previous review ratings influence current reviews, whether the previous review was done by the current supervisor or a former one.

● Supervisors "guess" when they aren't sure or don't have a lot of experience with a given employee's behavior.

● A rating form with fewer than four or more than 10 categories produces inconsistent ratings. (One recent study found organizations using rating forms with as few as three and as many as 19 categories. The average was 10.)

● When scales are used to assign ratings, high and low ratings tend to be consistent, but mid-range ratings are inconsistent. That is, very good and very poor performers will be scored accordingly by several different raters, but employees between those extremes will be scored inconsistently. Failure to produce reliable ratings for employees who range from slightly above to slightly below average becomes a problem when pay or promotional opportunities are tied to such distinctions—as they often are.

● Self-evaluations suffer from most of the same problems as do supervisor/subordinate ratings.

● Appraisal systems that are based on specific performance objectives and agreed-upon goals (MBO-based systems) are as open to unfairness as other systems. A common problem is that forces beyond the performer's control can conspire to thwart the achievement of goals. A strike, an economic slump or a price increase could adversely affect a salesperson's ratings without reflecting on the person's effort in the least.

Interestingly, the accuracy of ratings has been shown to depend as much, if not more, on the training of the raters as on the work that went into making a clear, usable scale. The literature reveals that intensive rater training on how to systematically observe and record representative work behaviors can go a long way toward eliminating technical and interpersonal problems of performance appraisals. One study, conducted by industrial psychologist Walter Bormann, indicated that as little as five minutes of explanation and graphic presentation significantly reduces the most stubborn of all errors—the halo effect.

De Vries, along with many of the cognitive researchers Rice interviewed, argues that rating forms and procedures are really a trivial part of the assessment problem despite the years of research that have gone into them. His contention, one with which PDI's Davis agrees, is that the focus on paper and processes—how the evaluation forms should be designed, how the information should be collected and presented, how the meeting should be conducted and so forth—is misplaced effort.

This is not to say that procedural improvements can't help alleviate certain deficiencies in the performance appraisal process. An elaborate behaviorally anchored rating scale (BARS), for example, with specific descriptors of good, average and poor performance for several aspects of the job is a far cry from a simple ranking system whereby supervisors stack up their employees on the basis of a single overall rating. Not only does a system like a BARS help reduce the subjectivity of the ratings with its behaviorally based criteria, but it also provides more useful information about employees' strengths and weaknesses. The catch is that such systems require extensive analyses of individual jobs—an expensive and time-consuming proposition. And many jobs, especially at the management level, have proven very difficult to break down and quantify according to specific, measurable criteria.

According to De Vries, however, the *degree* to which such systems have been shown to increase reliability over simpler, more subjective systems is disappointingly slight. In other words, the organization invests a great deal of time, effort and money—perhaps further alienating line managers in the process—in return for an elaborate system that's only a little bit better at distinguishing a "fair" performer from a "satisfactory" performer.

To De Vries, the real issue is simple: "Does management buy it? Does management buy into the need for performance *improvement* and the belief that a performance appraisal system—driven by line management—will help some significant performance problems in the organiza-

tion? If management doesn't own the system, forget it. The game is over."

Why bother?

You may be wondering (hoping?) if this onslaught of bad news is leading up to an excuse to junk your performance appraisal system and be done with the whole bothersome business. Sorry, but even the sternest critics are loath to recommend so radical a remedy.

De Vries in defense of formal appraisal: "We don't exactly overwhelm people with direct feedback about performance. [The Center for Creative Leadership] from time to time asks managers 'How do you find out how you are doing?' We actually had one tell us, 'My boss' secretary told me she overheard my boss tell somebody else I was the best he had.' That's extreme, but. . .people do have to scratch long and hard to find out how they are doing. Anything we can do to avoid that, to make performance information more readily available, has to be better than nothing at all."

PDI's Davis adds a second dimension: expectations. "It's not easy, but if you do it right, you have a mechanism for making sure people know what's expected of them and how they will be measured." And both agree that as long as management and compensation experts operate under the assumption that pay should be linked to performance—that those who perform better will be paid better—then we have to keep on trying to remove the bias from performance appraisal systems.

Patrick Pinto, a professor of industrial relations at the University of Minnesota and a specialist in appraisal systems, brings up another consideration: the law. According to Pinto, an organization without a working, standardized performance appraisal system can run into severe legal ramifications. "The courts have been pretty specific. If an employee challenges a dismissal or missed promotion or disciplinary action, you had better have a performance appraisal system in place."

And, Pinto adds, it had better be a system that uses standardized forms and procedures, is based on a clear and relevant job analysis, and is covered by training for the people doing the rating. "In other words, the courts

want proof that due process has been adhered to in your personnel procedures."

Pinto cites the case of Zia vs. Brito Co., in which a federal court made it abundantly clear that an organization is *not* at liberty to fire or lay off on the basis of "subjective and non-reviewable standards." The court's ruling also reconfirmed earlier adverse-impact decisions that require the rater of the affected employees to be trained to do the rating and to have sufficient exposure to the employees' behavior to assess performance accurately.

So now what?

Our story so far: One, performance appraisal systems are far from perfect.

Two, the challenge of improving them appears to have little to do with the remedies traditionally offered for ailing systems, i.e., newer and "better" rating forms that offer newer and "better" rating criteria.

But, three, despite all that, people want and need feedback about how well they're doing their jobs. (Some studies *do* support the idea that performance appraisal interviews that give "real" performance-related feedback *do* affect performance positively.)

Four, there are significant legal reasons why an organization should maintain a formal performance appraisal system regardless of its imperfections.

What to do? Opinions vary, but advice from these critics is mostly organizational rather than psychometric ("design a better form") in nature. De Vries insists that the only meaningful performance appraisal systems will be "owned, driven and designed by line management [as opposed to staff-driven], and focused on line management's objectives and purposes." His view is that staffers—personnel people in particular—see the world differently, have a different pace and prefer a more reflective, analytical style than line managers. The systems that personnel people design for line managers reflect those biases.

At the same time, De Vries believes staffers have an important supporting role. "Line managers expect professional help from staff people—once they themselves have sorted out the issues." De Vries suggests several critical roles for the staff specialist:

● Ensure that the appraisal system

meets minimum legal guidelines. "Don't be afraid of this responsibility," he cautions. "It isn't like the testing cases. The court cases [involving performance appraisal] have been based on flagrant, not subtle, abuses."

• Ensure that the assessment process and its forms meet at least basic standards of reliability and validity. Again, fine distinctions may be a problem, but at minimum, De Vries says, your system should "reliably tell you who high, middle-of-the-pack and low performers are. The goal is to be able to discriminate between mediocre and good performance so you can treat these groups differently."

• Ensure that the process is carried out as prescribed, that procedures are followed, and that the aggregate ratings don't seem biased, skewed or unrepresentative of actual job performance.

Davis offers these additional suggestions:

• Get commitment from the top people. Senior executives must be willing to participate in the performance appraisal process along with every other manager.

• Tie the system to the "normal business cycle." Setting performance objectives and doing year-end appraisals should fit into the organization's normal planning cycle.

• If you intend to tie pay to performance, make sure the system is perceived that way. "People wrestle with being fair, but it may be more important to work on the *perception* that pay and performance are linked."

• Be sure that the system balances results and behavior—that both are assessed or appraised.

• See that appraisals are con-

'WELL, HERE'S ANOTHER FINE MESS, STANLEY'

BY RON ZEMKE

Wonderful! For 30 years we've dutifully swallowed the experts' claims that a well-tuned performance appraisal system produces everything from renewed organizational vigor to clear sinuses. Now the experts aren't so sure.

So here we are. On one side, the law implies and, in some cases, insists that personnel decisions be based on a sound, documented performance appraisal system. On the other side, long-suffering customers (managers—the reviewers) and consumers (employees—the reviewees) want to know just where the debate over this particular sacred cow leaves them.

Now what, fellow advice-givers? We could do worse than turn to the musings of one Thomas H. Patten, Jr., an industrial relations professor at Michigan State University. In a low-key, practical 1982 book called *A Manager's Guide to Performance Appraisal* (The Free Press, New York City), Patten distilled the literature and research on performance appraisal into a series of simple dictums for those charged with making an organization's system work as well as possible. For that is what the issue really boils down to: Making the best of imperfect systems.

Though Patten's preference is for a management-by-objectives-type approach to performance appraisal, his guideposts are helpful whether your system is based on MBO, BARS or the cross-your-fingers-and-hope method. Here's a condensed version of his points:

1. Measure or appraise performance as behavior; forget about personality traits.

2. Critique the work done, not the potential for work yet to be done.

3. Keep the system simple and the paperwork minimal.

4. Separate systems oriented toward employee compensation from systems oriented toward employee development—at least initially.

5. Once a system has been decided upon, apply it for several years; don't tinker with it annually.

6. Forget about applying performance appraisal to unionized employees once they have seniority.

7. Do not rely on formal performance appraisals alone to communicate about performance; day-to-day contacts must do the bulk of the job.

8. Review performance formally at least once a year. Write down the appraisal, but limit it to one side of an $8\frac{1}{2} \times 11$ sheet of paper.

9. Require the human resources department to audit, oversee and spot-check the appraisals after the fact, but also stipulate that appraisals should be kept on file for no more than two years.

10. Train managers to carry out their performance appraisal responsibility. Never just hand an appraisal package to managers and hope they'll make it all work. They won't.

11. Accept the fact that some managers will never become adept at performance appraisal. They see it as playing God—and they don't want to play.

12. Recognize that some employees couldn't care less what others think about them. A constructive appraisal requires that the participants have sufficient self-awareness and insight to profit from the experience.

13. Realize that the real experts on employees' performance are the employees and their bosses—*not* Freud, McGregor, Maslow, the government or the human resources department.

14. In mature organizations, tie pay to performance appraisal.

15. Recognize that top managers who operate by the panic button, constantly shifting attention from one problem to another, cannot provide the stability required for an effective appraisal system.

16. Be sure managers are aware of the evolving legal principles about performance appraisals and that they know how to base their evaluations and actions on defensible, objective data.

Is that everything you'll ever need to know about performance appraisal? No. In fact, even Patten's original list of key principles is 45 items long. The point is that while the search for the ultimate appraisal system continues, you do need the tools and guidance to do at least an adequate job of assessing performance and giving employees meaningful feedback.

Reprinted from TRAINING, December 1985

ducted at the lowest level possible. If a "one-level-up" review will work, do it.

● Remember that both the law and the research suggest that managers need training to make any system work—even one they helped design.

Finally, when it comes to forms, follow the KISS principle: Keep It Short and Sweet (or was that Simple, Stupid?). In either case, there is no excuse for a 27-page performance appraisal form. Stick to objectives to be achieved and assessments of those achievements; a scaled rating of a few key performance factors; an area where managers and employee can discuss strengths, weaknesses and developmental needs; an overall rating of some sort; and a sign-off where supervisors and subordinates can acknowledge that they discussed the content.

Despite all the ingenuity invested in 30-plus years of research and application, performance appraisal remains one of management's toughest and least satisfying tasks. All the same, it's still hard to find an expert (we certainly couldn't) willing to go on record stating that the agony isn't necessary for the organization and the employee if both are to grow and prosper.

Since the bottom line in this recent disenchantment with the process amounts to, "Performance appraisal doesn't work very well but we have to do it anyway," and since that line has a familiar ring dating back a lot longer than a few years, a question arises: Is the real paper tiger in this picture performance appraisal or the recent disenchantment with it?

One has to suspect that at least some of the criticism leveled against appraisal systems has its basis in simple frustration. Perhaps it demonstrates once again our endless aggravation at the fact that there are no magic bullets, no simple, sure-fire steps for solving the human performance problems in organizations. There is no perfect system—even after 30 years.

Reprinted from TRAINING, December 1985

THE HIDDEN AGENDA OF PERFORMANCE APPRAISALS

Companies train managers to do accurate, 'objective' performance appraisals. But is accuracy their main concern? In a lot of cases, no

BY BEVERLY GEBER

If anyone remains out there who hasn't yet knuckled under, come now and do so. Admit the futility of hunting for some complex, magic formula. Confess that it is pointless to dream of a pure and perfect performance appraisal system. Repent, oh ye who cling like barnacles to the notion that you can design subjectivity out of appraisals, that you can teach managers to suppress their biases and use your system in exactly the way you intend it to be used. There is, in short, no way to design appraisals that ensure perfect objectivity.

This is by no means a new argument, and some of you are sniffing in bored disgust, feeling archly superior to others of you whose eyebrows just stuck to the ceiling. The debate over performance appraisals has continued, in fits and starts, for much of this century. No less a light than Douglas McGregor, writing in the *Harvard Business Review* in 1957, criticized the then-popular performance appraisal systems and proposed a management-by-objectives approach that would allow each employee to set objectives for a set time period, and then do a self-appraisal with the manager at the end of the period.

Yet even McGregor added a cautionary note: "I have deliberately slighted the many problems of judgment involved in administering promotions and salaries. These are by no means minor, and this approach will not automatically solve them."

It's a mournful fact of HRD life that no matter how well-designed the appraisal system, no matter how painstakingly it's described in a training course, no matter how often you role play the methods managers need to use, when you turn those managers loose in the real world...they fudge the ratings.

It's enough to drive you crazy. Here you've spent enormous energy searching for the best of all possible systems and adapting it to your organization. You've defined precisely what needs to be measured—whether achievements, behavior, effort, attitude or some combination. You've set up a system with checks and balances to make sure managers measure the right things. You've worked out all the bugs and wheedled the support of top management and put managers through a training course that teaches the system and emphasizes how crucial it is to the organization that they do it exactly this way.

"Most of us in this [training] field understand that there is a technology to doing it and we want it as pure as possible," says David DeVries, executive vice president of the Center for Creative Leadership (CCL) in Greensboro, NC.

Yet managers fudge the ratings. And when you come down to it, it's not that they haven't been trained to do the proper things and to strive for accuracy above all else in performance appraisal. Sometimes, it's that they just plain refuse to play according to the system's rules. What's more, they have some logical-sounding reasons for taking your perfect instrument and using it as one more discretionary management tool.

That's assuming, of course, they'll reveal their hidden agendas at all. If the primary thrust of performance appraisal at your organization is accuracy, a manager may not be exactly forthcoming with the news that he inflated a rating to temporarily buoy a worker who lost his wife and family in a car crash and may be understandably distracted at work these days. Or perhaps she'd rather not admit to a natural human aversion to confronting a brilliant but volatile employee over his tendency to be a few days late in finishing projects. After all, she might reason, is the minor inconvenience of missed deadlines worth alienating someone so crucial to the department's performance? In trade-offs like those, accuracy loses.

Dismayed trainers who see ratings distorted for these reasons argue that managers are choosing short-term comfort and convenience over long-term, nightmarish consequences for the organization. Employees who receive inflated ratings, they argue, are being groomed to become tomorrow's deadwood. And it's bad for the morale of superior performers if poor performers receive ratings nearly equal to their own.

Rationales

But still they do it. Why? Any good facilitator with a flip chart and a roomful of candid managers would be able to create a lengthy list in no time. Clinton Longenecker, associate professor of management at the University of Toledo, used another kind of research method. He conducted 90-minute, semistructured interviews with 60 upper-level executives from large organizations who had experience in conducting performance appraisals.

All of them admitted to employing some subjectivity in the appraisal process. In his findings, Longenecker did not report a reason unless it was mentioned by at least 72 percent of the sample. Some reasons why bosses inflate appraisals:

- To make sure the boss' own subordinates get as much as possible of an unusually small pool of money for merit increases.
- Empathy for someone whose work is suffering because of temporary personal problems.
- To avoid airing the department's dirty laundry, especially if the appraisals will be reviewed by others.
- To avoid creating a permanent record of poor performance that will hound the employee in the future.
- To avoid a confrontation with certain hard-to-manage employees.
- To encourage an employee whose performance was marginal during the first part of the rating period, but improved greatly during the latter part of the period.
- Deviously, to promote a disliked employee up and out of the boss' department.

The reasons to deflate appraisals are not as numerous, Longenecker says, and deflation does not occur as frequently as inflation. He suggests that managers fear the consequences of deflating appraisals more than those of inflating them. Some rationales he found:

- To scare better performance out of an employee.
- To subdue a defiant employee.
- To encourage a problem employee to quit.
- To create a record to justify a planned firing.

With the possible exception of that last reason—which may owe its life to recent lawsuits—the reasons all seem to be based on some pretty basic human traits: sympathy, loyalty, concern, deviousness and an urge for power. Rating accuracy is much less important to managers than the ability to use a tool like performance appraisal to motivate their employees.

"The performance appraisal literature says that accuracy should be the primary goal of the rater," says Longenecker. "From the point of view of the managers, [the main consideration] is how effectively they can use it."

This raises the question of whether trainers and management theorists pursue a chimera in their quest for the perfect appraisal system that will eliminate subjectivity. Longenecker argues that no system is immune to

it, although training and post-appraisal reviews can lessen the effects.

Maurice Cayer, manager of human resource research and strategy for J.C. Penney Company Inc., puts it neatly: "I think appraisal is always subjective. To criticize it for being subjective is to criticize a snowflake for being cold."

Being human, managers carry the baggage of their values to their appraisal duties. One manager may value and reward the ability to come up with brilliant ideas and to implement them. Another rater may cherish the kind of employee who is able to nurture strong relationships with clients.

A strongly articulated value system that comes down from top management may help to even out some of the wide fluctuations. But even within a carefully designed system that emphasizes accomplishments or observable behaviors, two different managers could come to different conclusions in rating the same employee's performance, Cayer says. "People are very imperfect in processing information. It's not a right or wrong kind of thing. It's just a difference in the way people look at things."

Those are largely unconscious kinds of biases, Cayer says. As he points out (and as Longenecker's list shows), managers have other sorts of reasons for avoiding the bald truth in performance appraisal—reasons of which they are quite aware. Even trainers who understand the pitfalls of performance appraisal and teach the process to others fall victim. Cayer, for instance.

He had a part-time computer jockey working for him. During the few days this employee worked each week, he would report to work in clothing that was "unprofessional" by the company's standards. "It festered in me," Cayer says, "because I knew that others would make judgments about me as a manager for not confronting this guy. I let it go because I knew he would give me a hard time, and he could make a case for his opinion."

But Cayer knew that he had good reasons for asking the part-timer to conform. Other employees, for instance, might start to ask if they could wear more comfortable clothing to work. Eventually he confronted the man, who was predictably upset but

complied with Cayer's request.

What's so bad about feeling good?

So subjectivity creeps into performance appraisals. Just how threatening is that?

Even among those who are quickest to advance the idea that in the real world, managers sometimes play fast and loose with the truth, there is no argument that they ought to be allowed to twist performance appraisals according to whim.

The CCL's DeVries says that HRD people have to recognize that managers know their people best and understand better than trainers when rules can be profitably broken. But trainers should be concentrating on planing down the sharp edges and knocking out the most egregious errors.

For instance, DeVries says, suppose a manager clings to the idea that men are inherently more capable and intelligent than women. Over time, that kind of bias should show up in a pattern of consistently above-average ratings for men and consistently below-average ratings for women. That gives you evidence of an egregious error.

Or take a situation in which two managers have strikingly different approaches to rating their subordinates. The company uses a standard five-category rating system (terrific, commendable, satisfactory, fair and poor—or words to that effect). Manager A believes that all his subordinates are superstars. If those same employees worked for Manager B, they'd have to perform miracles to get an above-average rating. If those patterns go unchecked, and the low-rated employees in Manager B's department figure it out, morale could plummet.

When these kinds of patterns surface, the offending manager should be confronted with the documented evidence. This is the time for a little friendly persuasion, preferably by the manager's boss.

In other cases, ratings inflation seems to hit the whole organization. It feeds on itself when managers see one another rating their people highly—each manager thinks (with reason) that she risks low morale or even mutiny if her employees discover their salary increases are proportionately lower than those of other people in the company.

In those cases, review boards and a little creative number-crunching can come in handy. At J.C. Penney, for instance, Cayer and his colleagues examined the ratings of the company's top managers and found that 75 percent of the executives received the top two ratings of a five-category scale. The ratings seemed extreme to Cayer. So he analyzed the company against its major competitors by using a variety of common financial indicators. It fell into the bottom quartile compared with the competition. And its executives are getting outstanding performance ratings? Cayer presented his results to the CEO, who presented them to top managers. "That makes a very poignant message," Cayer says.

Statistics were used less dramatically at Research-Cottrell, an environmental engineering company in Somerville, NJ. Michael Smith, the firm's human resource manager, discovered that 80 percent of the employees were rated in the top two slots of a five-category rating system. Smith shied away from a forced distribution system, considering it too arbitrary and potentially unfair, so he assembled the statistics and confronted managers.

"When you have ratings inflation and a limited budget, you end up giving average raises to people who have high ratings," he says. That's antithetical to the notion of merit pay increases.

And that's potentially the most damaging, long-term effect of managers' tendency to inflate ratings. Evelyn Rogers, director of people development and information for Young & Rubicam Inc., the New York City advertising agency, believes that subjectivity is bad for everyone involved—employee, manager and organization. "The employee doesn't know how to improve. They don't know what they did well on and poorly on. The company loses in terms of productivity. And the manager loses because often he walks away frustrated," she says.

Many experts say that subjectivity can be controlled if managers can only be persuaded to coach and monitor their subordinates continually and provide timely feedback to them. The annual or semiannual performance appraisal, they argue, should be just one part of a broader performance management system, in which

employees get feedback at numerous intervals throughout the year.

According to this reasoning, if managers are evaluating performance as they go along, the correct rating will seem the only logical choice at the end. It is the communication between manager and subordinate that makes it work.

At Los Alamos National Laboratory in Los Alamos, NM, training specialist Rodney Brown has devised a system that requires the supervisor to describe upcoming jobs for the employee in the coming year. Meanwhile, the employee has completed a work sheet describing what she considers her main accomplishments in the preceding year. Then the two have an informal, off-the-record discussion of the two work sheets. The supervisor writes an essay-style performance appraisal that culminates in one of two ratings: meets job requirements or does not meet job requirements. He gives it back to the employee, who has a chance to comment on it. Then the actual performance appraisal meeting takes place. The appraisals are all checked by the next highest level in the hierarchy.

Brown believes it is the informal meeting, combined with other informal meetings during the year that take place when job assignments change, that helps the supervisor and employee agree on how well the employee performed. "It's still going to be subjective, there's no way around it. But it won't be *as* subjective."

Confrontational training

In most cases, the methods mentioned so far do help control extreme cases of subjectivity. But what about the subtle kinds that Longenecker discovered in his research? Is there any preventative way to get at the causes of inflation or deflation? And should we even want to? Those questions lead, naturally, to training.

One of the most interesting findings from Longenecker's study is that all the executives said their performance appraisal training courses did not directly address the specific reasons that executives might inflate or deflate ratings.

Longenecker thinks that's a mistake. If those things are not addressed in training, managers feel like surreptitious cheats when they inflate or deflate ratings. That's another source of

stress to them during a process that is inherently stressful. And if trainers aren't dealing with those issues directly, they aren't addressing all the important dynamics of performance appraisal, he argues. His preferred approach during some of the training courses he gives is to confront the subjectivity issue directly.

He breaks managers into small groups and asks them to list things that prevent them from doing a good job in performance appraisals. Then he brings them together and asks them point-blank if accuracy is their primary concern in doing appraisals. Inevitably, the question triggers many of the same kinds of responses that Longenecker discovered during his study.

"It's a ticklish thing [for managers] to discuss," he says. "They know that a lot of things hang in the balance in the appraisal process. Nobody likes to admit that they inflate ratings and play games with the process."

And what's the point of such soul-baring? Cayer says it's hard to attack subjectivity unless you first can get managers to admit they do it. Once they've done that, a candid discussion might bring managers to some consensus on when it may be justified to fudge ratings (the employee whose family died in the car crash) and when distortion may be merely the easy way out for the manager. "Now we have their private subjective value systems out on the table so that at the end of it, there may be more uniformity than before," Cayer says.

Managers sometimes need to understand that the assumptions that lead to their distortions may be false. It may not be demotivating, for instance, for a manager to tell an employee that her performance is merely average, but that he's certain she has what it takes to improve. "It's the building of realistic hope that separates the good managers from the bad managers," Cayer says.

Jerks aside, most people dislike rendering negative judgments on others. Cayer says that whenever he comes to the part of his training sessions in which he discusses how to gently deliver bad news, he gets wide eyes and perked ears. But back in the real world, it's a safe bet that some managers will ignore Cayer's advice and continue to avoid unpleasantness—especially if they can convince themselves they're doing the right thing.

"Underneath it all is a certain set of beliefs like 'I need to get along with my people,' or 'I need to be loved'—which is not part of the role of the manager," Cayer says. "People can overcome these things, but it takes conscious effort. It takes interventions like training and pressure from their supervisors."

Role playing and behavior modeling are other ways to supplement the case-study method of confronting subjectivity. And don't forget to make sure that examples of "real-world" modeling match what you're teaching, cautions Longenecker. In other words, if top executives like those at J.C. Penney are inflating ratings for the senior managers in the company, it's no surprise that the attitude filters downward.

To accommodate all this, Cayer suggests that training should be drawn out over a long period of time—perhaps six to eight weeks, with a half-day of instruction each week, along with homework assignments. With the luxury of time, trainers won't feel obliged to cover only the mechanics of performance appraisal, with just a hasty warning about the evils of subjectivity.

"The training [most trainers] do on performance appraisal focuses on the form or the system and [they] seldom have enough time to address these issues," says DeVries. "[They] work quickly through the form and the process. The conversation stays fairly abstract and [they] don't have the kind of exercises that would get at these things."

Tim Iorio, corporate manager of human resources for SSOE Inc., an architectural design company in Toledo, OH, says his company spends more time on performance appraisals than any other management development course. He delivers a performance appraisal refresher course that brings all managers together each year to discuss specific cases that have caused problems in the past. No names are mentioned, since the sessions are for learning, not chastisement.

For instance, the managers will discuss the implications of a situation in which a technical employee—brilliant in his work, but with horrible people skills—gets a high rating from his supervisor. His brutalized co-workers somehow find out and suddenly there's an outcry that Iorio calls a "volcano effect." In addressing these situations, managers are encouraged to discuss what the boss might be thinking as she administers the appraisal and how she could have done things differently to head off problems.

"I think a lot of firms get caught up in the forms and the documenting and they forget the human element," Iorio says. "It's easy to work with the forms and format. The hard thing is the human beings involved—their upbringing and their value systems."

Reprinted from TRAINING, June 1988

PERFORMANCE MANAGEMENT: NOT JUST AN ANNUAL APPRAISAL

If you think performance appraisal is something managers should be doing year-round you're confusing it with something else

BY KATHLEEN GUINN

"Performance appraisal is not an annual event. For best results, it should be a series of events throughout the year. Effective appraisal is an ongoing activity that should be part of every manager's routine."

How many times have managers been offered that line of pat advice? It's, oh, so familiar . . . and, oh, so confusing—if not downright misleading—to people who are struggling to conduct effective performance appraisals.

Asking managers to make performance appraisal part of their daily routine is asking the impossible. Formidable tasks such as analyzing past performance, assigning ratings, completing appraisal forms and discussing salary increases cannot be done on an "ongoing" basis.

Performance appraisal is not an unimportant or easy management task. But trying to make it a continuous activity only increases confusion and exaggerates its difficulty. Performance appraisal is, and should be, a once-a-year event. It is *performance management*, a different thing altogether, that is and should be a year-round activity.

This is where the alert reader perhaps accuses me of setting up a straw man. People who talk about making performance appraisal an ongoing activity aren't suggesting that evaluation sheets be filled out and ratings assigned and salary discussed every day, you object. And you're right; they aren't suggesting that at all. But by speaking of performance appraisal and performance management as if they're the same process, we cloud an important distinction. And we make two difficult tasks that much more difficult.

The alleged objective of performance appraisal is to produce informed, motivated employees who are committed to improving the effectiveness of their performance—in short, to improving their productivity. Yet there is no proven link between performance appraisal and increased productivity. There is, however, a strong correlation between performance management and increased productivity. Ironically, performance appraisal research clearly establishes that correlation.

Ineffective objectives

The reason we conduct performance appraisals in the first place is that we believe (or claim to believe) that they will accomplish two things:

• Help employees understand the quality of their current performance and identify what they must do to im-

prove it. Obviously, this objective implies changing employees' behavior.

• Motivate employees to improve their performance. Again, clearly the implication is behavior change.

Now consider these objectives against what we know about achieving behavioral changes. To be effective in changing behavior, performance feedback must occur as soon as possible after the employee displays the behavior you wish to change. Rapping a puppy on the nose for soiling the rug three months after the event will not make the puppy stop soiling the rug, much less affect its understanding or motivation.

Does this mean that because a formal appraisal occurs months after the actual performance, we have to redefine it to make it something it is not? No. It simply means that a performance-appraisal system is not designed to provide immediate feedback on performance; performance management is.

The difference between the two is analogous to two different but equally important activities in the world of business and finance: financial management and the annual audit. The annual audit benefits managers responsible for the organization's financial performance by providing a "snapshot" of its financial situation that can be studied, analyzed and evaluated. Managers use the event to identify trends in financial performance, build on strengths, develop strategies, solve problems and establish goals. All of these things result in a healthier, stronger organization.

However, the audit itself is not part of the daily process of managing the organization's financial performance. No one would propose that to be effective, the annual audit should be "something that goes on all year. . .a day-in and day-out activity."

Similarly, performance appraisal is only one step in an effective performance-management process. Just like the annual audit, the annual performance appraisal provides a "snapshot" that allows study, analysis and evaluation. Managers use the event to identify trends in performance, build on strengths, develop strategies, solve problems and establish goals. All of these activities are aimed at strengthening employee performance and, consequently, the organization's performance.

Thus, the primary objective of performance appraisal, positioned as a single step in a performance management system, is to provide a data base for planning and targeting changes in future performance. Focusing on this objective also alleviates many of the complaints managers and employees voice about annual performance appraisals (see accompanying story).

The performance management approach

Since performance management occurs on a year-round basis, it can help employees understand the nature and quality of their recent performance, identify what they must do to improve and motivate them to improve. Effective performance management has three basic components: planning, managing and appraising performance.

1 *Performance planning* is the process of identifying the desired performance and gaining employees' commitment to perform to those expectations.

Corporate performance is generally described in terms of results: short- and long-term profits, dividends, return on assets and return on investment. Similarly, performance planning focuses on individual results: *what* an individual achieves and, perhaps just as importantly, *how* these results are achieved.

Appraisal forms often recognize the importance of the "how" aspect by addressing areas such as cooperation, initiative and leadership. But managers need to be trained to identify and assess those intangible qualities. Managers also must be able to gain employees' commitment to using desirable behaviors by relating the use of the behaviors to the attainment of specific results: tying the "how" to the "what" during the performance planning phase. Only then

---

CURING THE APPRAISAL BLUES

BY KATHLEEN GUINN

Performance appraisal systems that are forced into doing double duty as performance management systems are bound to create difficulties for bosses, employees and organizations. By approaching performance appraisal as simply a step in the performance-management approach, however, you can eliminate or at least minimize many of these common problems.

● *Appraisals are perceived as confrontations.* If the objective of performance appraisal is to plan for the next cycle, there is nothing to "confront." Blame for past performance becomes irrelevant. The manager directs the discussion from the perspective of "Here's what was. Now how do we reach our goals for this year?" Focusing on the future helps to minimize defensiveness; it's unnecessary to "defend" what has yet to happen.

Because performance management includes handling poor performance when it occurs, there is no need to reopen lengthy discussions during the appraisal itself. The unacceptable behavior was identified and dealt with; now it is only a part of the data base under consideration. Eliminating the confrontational nature of the performance appraisal creates less anxiety and, thus, more opportunity for collaborating on future actions.

● *Managers must act as judges of individual worth.* While it would be ideal to take ratings out of performance appraisals, that's unlikely to happen as long as they are used to justify salary decisions. Indeed, many progressive companies are tying salary and performance even closer together through pay-for-performance systems. These systems, however, do not *require* "ratings" of performance. They do require clearly established performance goals or objectives, an equally essential part of a performance-management approach.

Nonetheless, when the objective of performance appraisal is to provide a data base for *planning* future performance, ratings are more easily tied to past performance, not the employee's personal worth. In other words, the focus on planning helps the manager aim feedback at the behavior and the accomplishments, instead of at the person.

● *Performance appraisals often are conducted without clear objectives in mind.* When managers stop to think why they are doing these appraisals, they come up with vague and confusing reasons—"to create understanding," "to motivate the employee to do better," or even "because I have to." With the performance-management approach, the appraisal is conducted with a single, clearly established objective: to review past performance to provide a data base for planning future performance.

● *The appraisal focuses on filling out the form.* Forms become less important when the objective is to provide a data base for future plans. Since performance management builds a working relationship between the manager and subordinate, the appraisal form becomes simply a convenient job aid for the manager, rather than the structural force for the performance-appraisal discussion.

● *Performance data is seldom gathered in advance.* Performance management helps the boss and subordinate gather data in smaller, more convenient units throughout the year. Sources for tracking results and frequency of review are established when the performance expectations are identified. Review of performance on a monthly or quarterly basis is easier, quicker and usually more accurate because the information is current.

Interim reviews are filed for future reference prior to the yearly performance appraisal. This eliminates the last-minute rush—or more accurately, the desperate attempt—to find data to support general impressions. Because data are readily available, both parties are less likely to drift into subjective general impressions or statements that inevitably provoke emotional reactions.

● *Clear-cut action plans are not established.* When the objective of the appraisal is to plan future performance, it is virtually impossible to walk out of the discussion without an action plan. Clear, specific goals are established for the upcoming performance cycle.

Reprinted from TRAINING, June 1988

can the manager justify subsequent feedback, coaching and appraisal.

Performance planning that clearly identifies the expected results, as well as the behaviors and skills the individual is expected to demonstrate, provides a specific action plan aimed at a clear target. A planning strategy that solicits the active participation of subordinates in the process will help build commitment and minimize conflict in subsequent appraisal discussions.

2 *Performance managing* is the daily process of working toward the performance expectations established in the planning phase. To-gether, manager and employee review the employee's performance on a periodic basis. If it's on track or exceeding expectations, the manager provides positive reinforcement to keep performance at a high level (see Figure 1). If performance is lacking, the manager coaches the employee on improving trouble spots. This involves developing strategies *with* the employee to determine appropriate action plans.

Coaching on a timely basis eliminates the often unpleasant—and unproductive—"postmortem" aspects of performance appraisal. Problems are handled when action can be taken, also eliminating the "gotcha" element of the appraisal interview. When the manager's role becomes one of coach rather than judge, boss and subordinate can work together to achieve the individual's performance goals, which are, after all, the unit's goals and, ultimately, the organization's goals.

Managers who periodically track and review performance let employees know where they stand; performance-appraisal discussions hold no surprises. Instead, boss and subordinate discuss performance when it actually occurs—the ideal time to affect behavior. The year-end performance review becomes a summary with little or no new information, and dis-

APPRAISING PERFORMANCE APPRAISALS

Performance appraisal is one of those necessary evils of corporate life. In some form or another, the annual or semiannual performance review has been around for much of this century, but nobody has ever been able to turn it into an exact science. For that reason, there's still a lot of discussion and research done on the topic.

Here's more. Last fall, ODT Associates, a consulting firm based in Amherst, MA, polled about 1,900 clients and would-be clients who stopped by the firm's booths at various training conferences. About 176 usable responses were returned, giving the survey a response rate of 9 percent.

The survey turned up a few findings worth pondering. When respondents were given 18 common complaints about performance appraisal systems and were asked to cite the ones that applied to their own systems, the two they named most frequently were that some supervisors (meaning bosses in general) don't know how to give appraisals and that the rating levels on the scale are sometimes interpreted differently by different supervisors. Nearly three of four respondents mentioned those two complaints.

The other three most popular complaints, in descending order of fre-quency, were: 1) Supervisors sometimes avoid being specific on the forms. 2) Information revealed in the appraisal is sometimes a surprise to the person being appraised. 3) Sometimes ratings are inconsistent with actual performance.

Most of the respondents (78 percent) reported that performance appraisals are done annually. The rest of the respondents said they are done more than once a year. Most often (42 percent), the appraisals are done to coincide with hiring anniversaries. One of three respondents said their companies did all appraisals at the same time.

Does the frequency with which an organization conducts appraisals have any effect on the types of complaints it hears from employees? The only statistically significant finding from this survey, the researchers say, was that organizations that do appraisals more than once a year tend to report a larger number of complaints that the process is too complicated. However, those same organizations also had fewer than the average number of complaints that ratings come as a surprise to employees, that the rating levels were interpreted differently by different supervisors and that supervisors avoid being specific on the forms.

Forty-four percent of the respondents said their organizations deliver mandatory in-house training on how to conduct performance appraisals. Three of 10 make the training voluntary while about one of four compa-nies have no in-house training.

In most cases, complaints were more numerous in companies whose training was voluntary or non-existent than in those that mandated training. But the survey found no connection between the length of the training offered and the frequency of complaints; in other words, more training did not mean fewer complaints. The researchers note, however, that they did not poll respondents on the content or process of the training.

Finally, respondents were asked to rank order a list of common objectives of the appraisal system according to their companies' standards (that is, What does the company say it wants to accomplish with its appraisal system?). Then they were asked to rank the same list according to the priorities they believed supervisors actually followed in conducting appraisals.

The companies' most common intended objectives? "Performance" and "measurement" (as in maintaining and measuring employees' performance) shared top honors. Following those two, in descending order, were communication, compensation, employee development, promotion and manpower planning.

And the supervisors' real priorities? In descending order of importance, the respondents selected compensation, measurement, performance, communication, development, promotion and manpower planning.

Reprinted from TRAINING, June 1988

cussion focuses on planning for the future performance cycle.

3 *Performance appraisal*, the final step in the performance-management process, provides the opportunity to step back from day-to-day activities, assess performance trends and plan for the future. Because periodic performance reviews have essentially eliminated any surprises, both boss and employee can anticipate the nature of the discussion and prepare for the meeting accordingly. Career development, a natural outgrowth of this discussion, helps build the employee's commitment and loyalty to the organization, increasing motivation and productivity as well.

The performance appraisal is both the beginning and the end point of performance management. The analysis of past performance provides the basis for planning next year's expectations; at the same time, it "closes the loop" of the current cycle. Employees know what is expected of them and what they need to do to achieve results in the next performance period. The organization knows what results it can expect from employees and what resources are needed to help them achieve those results.

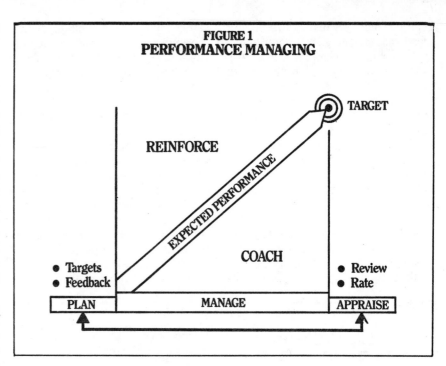

FIGURE 1
PERFORMANCE MANAGING

Reprinted from TRAINING, August 1987

WHY NO ONE LIKES YOUR PERFORMANCE APPRAISAL SYSTEM

Maybe it's just the nature of the beast. Then again, maybe popularity is beside the point

BY ALAN G. MOMEYER

In survey after survey, managers overwhelmingly report dissatisfaction with their companies' performance appraisal systems. Typical complaints charge that the systems are a waste of time at best, and destructive to the boss-employee relationship at worst. After the balloon show that accompanies the kickoff of a new performance appraisal program, it promptly becomes "that form we have to send to the personnel department once a year."

Is the problem inherent in the concept itself or are we doing something wrong? I'd like to suggest that it's some of both, and offer some guidelines for effective performance appraisal.

Inherent problems

● Performance appraisal sessions almost never go smoothly. Honest differences exist between people as to what was expected, and why it was or wasn't achieved. But this is only bad if the expectations are for unanimity of opinion and cosmetic appeal.

Most organizations function on a somewhat static level, harmony and civility being highly valued norms. The appraisal interview, on the other hand, works best when people are willing to violate the norms and confront real issues. This naturally results in some upset, but the success of your performance appraisal program is determined by its impact, not its popularity. The subordinate who learns of room for improvement may not enjoy the session, but may improve. The supervisor who learns that he's not providing clear directions won't like what he hears, but may change his approach.

● Performance appraisal requires the exercise of authority over others. Many supervisors are uncomfortable with that. The frequently heard lament that doing performance appraisals is like "playing God" is an overstatement that should tell us something about just how anxious they are.

Attempts to ease this anxiety and make supervisors feel "comfortable" are mostly futile. Despite our rhetoric about it being a "scientific" process, performance appraisal decisions are basically subjective. They rely a great deal on perceptions. Furthermore, despite all of managements' disavowals, the most influential factor in a performance appraisal is the employee's attitude. The happy, friendly, cooperative employee will be rated more favorably than his quiet, colorless, sullen counterpart who produces an identical amount of identically satisfactory work. At some level, most supervisors are aware of this, and feel guilty; employees are aware of it, and the ones whose ratings suffer because of it feel resentment.

But none of this means that performance appraisal decisions are unfair, or even inaccurate. The organization has a right to reward any work behavior it thinks desirable, and entrusts the supervisor to make the call. The decision can have a significant impact on the employee's work life, future with the company and (perhaps) self-image. With these at stake, supervisors *ought* to be anxious.

● The word appraisal derives from the Latin word for price, or value. Employees trade work for pay, and management decides whether the deal is a fair one, whether the organization is getting its money's worth. Performance ratings and salary decisions are therefore intertwined. Even when management attempts a sleight-of-hand, as in the much-ballyhooed practice of making the salary decision at a different time of year from the performance-rating decision, few people are comforted—or fooled.

As long as we link pay and performance, there will be tension. Furthermore, pay will be in the driver's seat and performance issues will be hitching a ride. Employees who get the raise they want will be delighted with their appraisal; those who don't, won't. Nor will they benefit greatly by an in-depth discussion of their accomplishments and deficiencies, since the pay decision tells them everything they really need to know about the value the company places on them and their work.

Suggestions

What are we doing wrong? Lots of things. Here are some of the less obvious ones:

● Most companies have performance rating categories that range from "outstanding" to "unsatisfactory." In the middle is one called something like "satisfactory" or "meets expectations" or "average." This is the level that most people perform at most of the time. Our compensation systems demand that the great majority of employees be rated in this category. However, since more than 90% of all people say they are "above average" when asked to assess their own performance, it should come as no surprise that they feel damned with faint praise when rated "average." As for supervisors, the "satisfactory" rating places them in the awkward position of praising employees all year long (as we urge them to do), then failing to follow through when and where it counts.

Let's stop trying to bend human nature. If the average person has an "above average" self-image, then labeling him "average" is pejorative. If he has any pride, he won't like coming to his next performance appraisal meeting. Call your middle performance category something that compliments a person for having achieved it, like "excellent," or "very good." This, too, may smack of sleight-of-hand, but in one organization, it doubled the number of employees whom managers were willing to project (for budget purposes) as performing at the middle level.

● We play the "job standards" game with employees at performance appraisal time, insisting that their rating be determined according to "specific, measurable and quantifiable outputs." The litany of measurement devices—time per transaction, weekly quantity, quality as measured by rejects, etc.—work fine for measuring the output of machines, but not at all, in many cases, for the performance of our people.

In the world of business, we do not just pay employees for "what" but also for "how." Attitude and personal qualities, particularly in service industries, are at least as important as the "what." Our neat and nifty, 10-words-or-less, specific and measurable standards will never adequately express the *feeling* we try to create.

We want our employees to do their jobs willingly and well. This requires that they be knowledgeable, skilled and personable. We can only communicate accurate expectations, train employees accordingly and trust that they have the good judgment, maturity and intelligence to perform well. Contrived measurement devices that relate only obliquely to the behavior we desire do not advance the purpose of creating a human environment which encourages that behavior.

● Many performance appraisal programs encourage phony participation. Managers typically ask employees to present appraisals of their own performance. Managers then respond with the "correct" appraisal. Any variance between the two versions leaves the employee feeling conned or sandbagged.

People want to know how they're doing. They want the opinion of their supervisor, the person with the most influence on their professional lives. They want this viewpoint, subjectivity and all. They don't want a make-believe negotiation session.

This does not mean the appraisal meeting should be an entirely one-way communication. There are many valid areas for participation—personal goals, career goals, plans for achieving those goals, obstacles to performance, assistance needed, etc. But in the actual appraisal of how the employee has performed, the supervisor's viewpoint is the one that counts.

● Professionals in the human resources field search for a perfect performance appraisal form the way Sir Galahad searched for the Holy Grail. At conferences, the traffic in forms has reached a gridlock condition. In response to his request for forms from colleagues in other companies, one personnel manager received in the mail a copy of his own organization's form, with a new logo.

The notion that somehow a perfect form will create a perfect performance appraisal system is comforting but misguided. In fact, the quality of a program has almost nothing to do with the form it uses. A good performance appraisal hinges on straight talk between supervisor and employee on what was expected, how well the job was done and what will be expected in the future. If your organization is healthy enough to encourage the exchange of honest opinions, the form won't matter an awful lot.

Each organization may determine why its performance appraisal system is not popular. Many of the reasons are inherent; others, we can and should do something about. Although it is worthwhile to try to improve our systems, it's time we realized that measuring their worth by their popularity is a tactical blunder. Performance appraisal should be presented as what it is: a time-consuming, difficult, discomforting, but exceedingly valuable management tool.

Reprinted from TRAINING, October 1986

HOW TO CONDUCT A REAL PERFORMANCE AUDIT

You may know what you mean by a 'performance audit,'
but do you know what your CEO means?

BY WILLIAM J. ROTHWELL

Performance audit' is a term that means different things to different people. To some, it is synonymous with performance analysis, the step in instructional design that identifies discrepancies between the performance you're getting from someone and the performance you want. To others, it connotes a form of needs assessment that considers the context of the job, the person doing the job, job actions, job results and feedback on results.

The traditional performance audit, as trainers see it, focuses either on instructional outcomes alone or on outcomes within a work environment.

On the other hand, accountants and some management consultants, who are familiar with financial and compliance audits, think of the performance audit in quite a different way. They see it as an extension of more traditional auditing that deals wih broad issues of organizational efficiency and effectiveness. The focus is not on *instructional* outcomes or *individual* competence, but on *organizational* outcomes or on overall *organizational* competence and productivity.

Trainers can learn some important lessons about performance auditing from people outside the field of human resources development. And once they understand this type of audit, HRD professionals will be able to draw their own conclusions about its value and potential application in the training environment.

What is it?

The performance audit is a *comprehensive* examination of an organization or of any activity, conducted by an *independent analyst* reporting to an *interested third party*, that assesses *how well results match intentions* or *how well resource utilization matches results*.

There are two types of performance audits: 1) the management audit, which examines the use of resources and thus addresses *efficiency*, and 2) the program audit, which examines results and thus addresses *effectiveness*.

Performance audits are comprehensive in scope. They recognize an organization's relationship to its environment as well as the relationships among its parts. In short, they accept the assumptions of open-systems theory.

To be credible, audits must be conducted by people who are removed from possible rewards or retributions. For this reason, organization-wide performance audits usually are conducted by independent analysts. And the analysts report to people *other than* those who stand to gain or lose directly by the audit's findings: to third parties such as stockholders or the corporate board in the private sector, or to the legislative branch in the public sector. Audits of a single function such as personnel or marketing may be reported to the organization's chief executive, but are conducted by an external consultant.

Management audits compare the use of resources—land, labor, capital or time—to norms such as organizational policies or procedures, industry averages, common business practice or academic research findings. They emphasize the relationship between the organization's *inputs* and *outputs*. They compare present *conditions* (What is?) to desirable *criteria* (What should be?).

Program audits compare achievements to stated goals, objectives or intentions. They emphasize the relationship between the organization's stated purpose or mission and its achievements in several arenas: financial (return on investment, profit), social (contributions to social justice), economical (market share), geographical (impact on the surrounding community), technical (innovations affecting the industry) and strategic (long-term).

Any form of research that compares a norm to an existing condition or is conducted to improve existing conditions and induce change resembles a performance audit (see Parallels to the Performance Audit for some examples).

PARALLELS TO THE PERFORMANCE AUDIT

• Evaluation research, which compares an existing program to the features of a desired one.

• Action research—the basis of organization development—which compares existing conditions to the goals of the client or change agent.

• Critical research—an outgrowth of Marxist change theory—which identifies key aspects of an ideology (i.e., a value system) and uses inconsistencies between beliefs and practices to induce change.

• Job analysis, which compares an employee's duties and responsibilities to predetermined norms.

• Performance analysis, which compares employee performance to predefined standards.

Reprinted from TRAINING, June 1984

Finally, a key point: Performance audits assume a rational approach to organizational change. That is, their entire justification is based on the belief that decision makers will choose what is best for the organization if only the facts are sound. They do not assume that internal politics or interpersonal relationships will greatly influence decisions.

Conducting the performance audit

Though not all writers on the subject agree on the steps or sequence of steps in conducting a performance audit, most would include the 12 points outlined in Figure 1.

Step 1. Every audit begins with a directive: Somebody in authority *requests* the audit to explore a special issue. In other words, an audit grows out of the stated needs of decision makers or those who monitor the decision makers. The directive clearly defines the type of audit and the issues to be examined.

Step 2. The directive establishes the audit's objectives. The auditors must translate those objectives into an action plan—tasks to be completed and deadlines to be met during the audit project. At this point, the plan is tentative and subject to change as more information is gathered.

Step 3. Selection of the audit staff is a crucial step. The people chosen for the project must know something about the issue to be explored and the audit methods to be used to explore it. Suppose, for example, that the directive requires auditors to answer

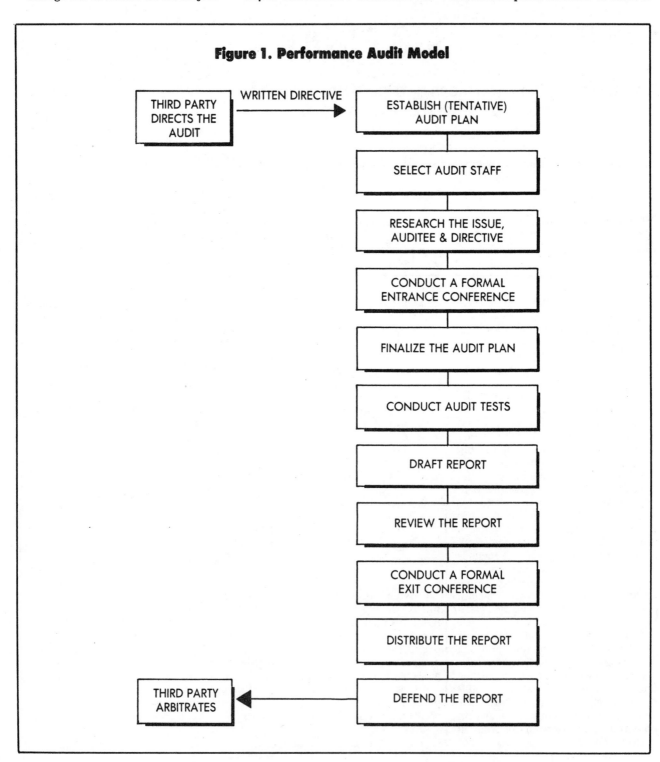

Figure 1. Performance Audit Model

THIRD PARTY DIRECTS THE AUDIT

WRITTEN DIRECTIVE

ESTABLISH (TENTATIVE) AUDIT PLAN

SELECT AUDIT STAFF

RESEARCH THE ISSUE, AUDITEE & DIRECTIVE

CONDUCT A FORMAL ENTRANCE CONFERENCE

FINALIZE THE AUDIT PLAN

CONDUCT AUDIT TESTS

DRAFT REPORT

REVIEW THE REPORT

CONDUCT A FORMAL EXIT CONFERENCE

DISTRIBUTE THE REPORT

THIRD PARTY ARBITRATES

DEFEND THE REPORT

the question: "Is excessive turnover hampering the efficiency of Factory X?" The audit objectives must specify *how the question will be answered* and what is meant by terms such as "excessive," "turnover" and "efficiency." The staff must be competent in examining turnover and in using the methods selected for doing so.

Step 4. The auditors need to research the project thoroughly. They must understand what prompted the audit to be sure their findings will be useful to those who wanted the issue examined in the first place. At the same time, they must research the issue itself. In a turnover study, for

---

Never invest in a full-scale audit to address simple issues or decisions that require immediate attention.

---

instance, they may want to locate reliable figures on national, local or industry turnover, and collect academic studies or other material on the subject. Finally, auditors must learn about the "auditee," the entity to be subjected to the audit. What is its history, structure, general reputation and purpose? Do these circumstances have any special bearing on the issues to be examined?

Step 5. The formal entrance conference is the first direct contact between auditors and auditees. If an entire organization is under audit, the conference is held with the top-management team. If only a part of the organization is to be audited, the conference is held only with the managers and supervisors in that section. The meeting's purpose is to make sure everybody understands the directive and the audit's objectives. At the same time, it gives auditors a chance to hear reactions from the people they'll be auditing and to gather more information on the issues.

Step 6. The auditors reformulate the objectives from the information gathered during background research and the entrance conference. The final plan spells out *what* will be examined, *how* it will be examined (see Performance Audit Tests) and *when* it will be examined. To ensure the plan's validity, auditors occasionally will ask

their colleagues to review it before implementation.

Step 7. Audit tests typically are conducted in the field. Auditors gather information on the "condition" of the auditee or on conditions affected by the auditee. When there is a significant gap between some criterion (What should be?) and the condition (What is?), auditors write a *finding* that stipulates cause, effect, criteria, condition and significance. They also may write a recommendation for dealing with the problem.

The types of tests selected by the auditors depend upon the issue under examination. Most quantitative and qualitative research methods—varying from linear programming to surveys—may be used. In a study of turnover, for example, statistical methods could reveal significant differences between rates in one company facility and others.

Step 8. The auditors draft a report that provides background information on the auditee and the issues. The report also presents important findings and recommendations for improvement. Each finding is supported by documentation that could stand up to rigorous scrutiny by third-party experts commissioned by the auditee.

Documentation is to the auditor what evidence is to a lawyer. Most auditors record any information they collect on work papers. Supervisors, the arbiters of quality control, check

the work papers for completeness and accuracy. Audit reports are written directly from work papers, and all facts are checked and rechecked.

Step 9. The draft report is given to the auditee for review. At this point the auditee may respond to the findings in writing, suggesting corrections, additions or modifications. Auditors can weigh these remarks and accept or reject them. Either way, however, auditee responses are included in the final draft report.

Step 10. The auditors meet with the key decision makers in the organization for an exit conference. Its purpose is to go over the final report, including any changes made as a result of the auditee's review. The exit conference presents an opportunity to make any last-minute changes or to discuss the implications of any part of the report.

Step 11. The final report is distributed to the auditee and to the third party that initiated the audit. The report is self-explanatory; it answers the questions found in the original directive.

Step 12. Auditors, auditee and third party meet to examine the issues, findings and recommendations in the report. The auditors function as plaintiffs, the auditees as defendants, and the third party as judge and jury. Based on the outcome of this meeting, the third party can a) reject the auditor's report, b) accept parts of the report or c) accept the entire report,

---

PERFORMANCE AUDIT TESTS

A performance audit test is any comparison between a normative criterion (What should be?) and the condition of the auditee (What is?). Auditors assume that all is well until the facts show otherwise; they do not try to second-guess management actions or decisions without extremely good reasons. Hence, two matters are of crucial concern: first, the *selection of criteria* that are authoritative, credible and convincing; second, the *selection of appropriate measurement methods* for assessing condition against criteria. Some examples include:

CRITERIA (What should be?)	MEASUREMENT METHODS (How can condition be compared to criteria?)	
• Information collected by government agencies	• Survey research	• Accounting techniques
• Information collected by industry or associations	• Cost/benefit analysis	• Queuing theory
• Information collected by academic researchers	• Linear programming	• Flowcharts
• Legal information	• Systems analysis	• Many others

Reprinted from TRAINING, June 1984

direct the auditee to change methods accordingly and establish some means to monitor those changes.

Clearly, the performance audit stresses the notion that management is *accountable* to others.

Depending on the issues to be ex-

Trainers too often tackle performance issues by the seat of their pants.

---

plored, such audits can require massive amounts of time, money and effort. They should never be initiated for addressing relatively simple issues or decisions that require immediate attention.

How trainers can use the performance audit

Performance auditors make some fundamental assumptions and use techniques that can be valuable to HRD specialists in their own performance-auditing activities.

Auditors usually limit their efforts strictly to projects at which they are *directed*. The reason? A directive implies that an issue genuinely matters to someone whose opinion counts. In other words, it implies powerful support for the audit. If auditors indiscriminately initiated their own efforts, they would be perceived as self-serving and run the risk that their findings and recommendations would be ignored.

Auditors follow rigorous standards, document their findings and submit their documentation for review by others—but they allow a third party to direct any action based on their results. They want to preserve the integrity of their work and, more important, their credibility.

Auditors may examine *any* facet of an organization's activities. Their playing field is not restricted to financial or instructional matters or even to individuals in a work environment. Hence, they are relatively free to take on issues of strategic planning or organizational culture traditionally ignored by accountants and trainers.

The trainer's role in many organizations is evolving beyond the simple providing of instruction related to specific tasks—evolving toward a broader role of engineering human performance. If that trend widens the focus of attention to include not only individual competence but *organizational* competence, it is a good sign.

But trainers too often tackle performance issues by the seat of their pants. The predictable result is that a (nominal) performance-based approach to training will be tried, will fail miserably, and will stunt the evolution of this healthy trend.

Trainers can learn valuable lessons from people who approach the performance audit differently. By doing some learning as well as training, they can improve their own techniques and the outcomes of their audits.

Reprinted from TRAINING, June 1984

MORE ON THE PERFORMANCE AUDIT

Gilbert, Thomas F., *Human Competence: Engineering Worthy Performance*. (McGraw-Hill, New York, 1978).

Herbert, L., *Auditing the Performance of Management*. (Lifetime Learning, Belmont, CA, 1979).

Rummler, Geary, "The Performance Audit" (*Training and Development Handbook*, R.L. Craig, ed., 2nd ed., McGraw-Hill, New York, NY, 1976).

"Operational and program auditing: Introduction." A training course complete with videotape and trainee workbooks geared to novices. (CSG, 1979, Lexington, KY).

Standards for Audit of Governmental Organizations, Programs, Activities and Functions (The Comptroller General of the United States, Washington, DC).

A PERFORMANCE PLANNING PRIMER

How do supervisors get results? By getting
performance from the people they supervise

BY RICHARD H. MAGEE, MARY FINN
MAGEE AND MELINDA MAGEE DAVIES

The paramount responsibility of every supervisor is to get results. Supervisors get results by managing material and human resources. Of the two, only the human variety—people—can grow and develop. A key to every supervisor's success is his or her ability to plan the performance of subordinates so that growth and development do, indeed, occur.

This is not an easy task. Planning for performance—designing a detailed action plan—takes thought, analysis and imagination. Planning focuses on results. It directs movement toward specific goals. Goals, in turn, give meaning to tasks.

Planning subordinates' performance can be rendered especially difficult by two fundamental obstacles. First, it is surprisingly common for supervisors to have only a vague idea of what it is their employees actually do. Research shows that often there is little agreement or understanding between supervisors and subordinates when each is asked to describe the subordinate's tasks and responsibilities. Supervisors can neither plan performance nor control it until both parties agree on the purpose of the subordinate's job and the activities it involves.

Secondly, bosses and employees view the employee's job from their own perspectives. Supervisors look at their subordinates' jobs from the outside and employees look at them from the inside. Bosses are likely to take adequate job performance for granted. And a boss is especially sensitive to deficiencies in performance that create problems for him. Subordinates, on the other hand, know the challenges they have overcome and the barriers they have surmounted. They tend to be less likely to blame themselves for poor performance and more likely to attribute it to factors beyond their control. Thus, attempts at performance planning often cast boss and subordinate as adversaries. Differences are highlighted and understanding is thwarted rather than promoted.

Performance planning is most successful when both the supervisor and the subordinate are involved in the process. Each must know precisely what the other has in mind. They need to have mutual goals, expectations and understanding in order for growth and development to occur. To accomplish any of this, most bosses and subordinates need some sort of framework—a performance-planning system. We recommend one comprised of three steps: develop a "performance contract"; negotiate a performance-planning worksheet; and appraise job performance.

The performance contract

The performance contract is the bedrock of the system, the essential planning tool. It is a written agreement between the supervisor and subordinate.

The contract consists of four components: the expectations and obligations of both parties; the relationship and interaction between the two; the results to be achieved; and a framework for subordinate decision-making which also can serve as an outline for performance evaluation.

The essence of any contract is that there is something in it for each party, and both parties agree to do what it specifies. In a performance contract, the boss is expected to provide resources, guidance and support. The subordinate is expected to get results. The contract is, however, a living document. It is amenable to change as conditions change. For example, critical shifts in business or operating strategies will require adjustments to the document.

Subordinate's Responsibilities: Subordinates are expected to produce results. Specifically, they are to meet objectives in three key performance areas.

• *Operations*—efficiency and effectiveness in delivering services and/or products.

• *Staff management*—supervision and development of their own subordinates.

• *Personal development*—increasing their own management and/or technical competence.

Each of these performance areas has to be broken down into a series of appropriate subtopics. For example, "operations" for a plant manager might include such areas as manufacturing, quality control, production control, inventory control, warehousing, shipping and receiving. Items under "staff management" might include training, performance appraisal and EEO. "Personal development" might mean attending workshops, giving presentations and tackling special projects.

Supervisor's Responsibilities: Supervisors are expected to help subordinates achieve results. Their contract commitment covers six critical areas.

• *Culture*—supervisors must make sure that employees understand the organization's philosophy and culture, "culture" referring to shared beliefs, practices and values.

Understanding culture provides a frame of reference and a code of ethics; it suggests acceptable and unacceptable behavior. As some popular management books have been pointing out lately, rules and regulations formalize culture, but other valuable information is unwritten, yet equally important.

• *Goals and standards*—goals give focus and direction. They add challenge and motivation to human endeavor. They ensure that everyone works toward the same end. Supervisors are responsible for seeing that goals are set, but subordinates need to be involved in the process. Their contribution will add to the substance of the goals and to their willingness to accept them.

Goals are useless without standards—the yardsticks that measure job performance. Standards add specificity to goals. They can be expressed in terms of time, cost, quantity and quality. For instance, "train personnel to use computers" is a goal, but it's not specific enough. It needs standards to give it real meaning: "to have 50% of the production-control staff trained and using personal computers with 90% accuracy, by July 1, at a training cost not to exceed $10,000." Both boss and subordinate need the feedback that standards provide.

• *Responsibility and authority*—the supervisor must make sure the subordinate understands not only what his (the subordinate's) responsibilities are, but also what his authority is. Together, boss and subordinate must define the power the subordinate has to make decisions, to solve problems and to meet opportunities. They must nail down areas where the subordinate is independent and areas where constraints apply.

• *Resources*—the boss must provide the subordinate with appropriate resources: funds, facilities, equip-

---

FIGURE 2
TASK PLANNING WORKSHEET

Objective	Tasks	Due Date
1.1	determine subjects to be taught by supervisors	1/30
	select supervisor instructors	2/15
	train supervisors	4/1
	conduct pilot programs	5/1
1.2	identify subjects	3/1
	engage outside consultants for program development	5/1
	conduct pilot programs	8/1
	modify program (if necessary); add to roster of training activities	11/1
2.1	prepare program outline; check it out with prospective "clients"	2/1
	develop the program	4/1
	conduct pilot programs	5/1
	modify program (if necessary); add to roster of training activities	6/1
2.2	etc.	

FIGURE 1
PERFORMANCE PLANNING WORKSHEET

Position: Training Director
Unit Mission Statement: To be a growing, profitable retailer of groceries and related consumer goods and services.
Position Mission Statement: To enhance the effectiveness and efficiency of the unit by strengthening the management and technical skills of employees through a variety of staff training and development activities.

RESULTS AREAS	OBJECTIVES AND STANDARDS
1. Program presentation	1.1 to have unit supervisors serve as part-time instructors in 30% of the workshops during the second half of the year
	1.2 to have 20% of technical training presented in programmed-learning format by Dec. 31; not to exceed $15,000 budget
	1.3 to achieve a "good" to "excellent" rating of programs by trainees 90% of the time
2. Program development	2.1 to develop a two-day report writing program by June 1
	2.2 to develop a two-day performance appraisal workshop by September 1
3. Needs analysis	3.1 to update, by questionnaire and interviews, the priority of unit training needs by March 15
4. Program evaluation	4.1 to develop a system of evaluation that measures the impact of training on actual job performance; to test the system with one management and one technical program during the third quarter
5. Personal development	5.1 to prepare a career plan and review it with boss by February 15
	5.2 to join local chapter of the American Society for Training and Development immediately
	5.3 to attend the University of Wisconsin's Staff Training Workshop in April
6. Promotion	6.1 to publish two articles about training this year in the company news magazine

ment, systems and, if the subordinate is a supervisor, people.

• *Rewards*—bosses and subordinates must agree on appropriate rewards. Discussing rewards for performance in negotiating a contract is a healthy way to explore candidly what the subordinate needs in terms of economic and psychological pay. Economic considerations are usually easy to identify; psychological considerations are more difficult. The supervisor must understand the relative worth to the subordinate of such motivators as money, power, independence, recognition, achievement, growth, acceptance and security— and how these incentives can be made a part of the "compensation package."

• *Clarity*—first, the performance contract itself must be clear, precise and measurable. Second, subordinates must understand where and how they fit into the organization. They must understand their impact on it. They must understand the channels of communication and the organization's formal and informal chain of command.

In developing the performance contract, the boss and the subordinate are forging another, more subtle agreement—a psychological understanding. It embraces the assumptions and expectations the individuals hold about each other. This psychological understanding also may need to be spelled out to some degree. But whether explicitly or implicitly, both parties must understand three things: how conflicts between them will be resolved; the balance of power in their relationship (what role the supervisor will play in the subordinate's bailiwick); and how trust will be established and strengthened between them—what values and skills are important, etc.

The worksheet

The performance contract and the psychological understanding lay the foundation for effective performance planning. The next step is to determine more specifically the employee's responsibilities. This is done by filling out a performance-planning worksheet. The supervisor and the subordinate, working independently of each other, complete the worksheet for the subordinate's job. Figure 1 shows an example.

The first step in completing the performance-planning worksheet is to develop a *mission statement* for the unit or department managed by the boss: Why does the unit exist? What is its purpose? The statement must be in harmony with the mission statements of other units in the company and with the corporate mission statement.

Step two is to prepare a *"position mission statement"* or results-oriented job description: What is the basic purpose of the subordinate's job? The statement should be concise, definitive and supportive of the unit mission statement.

Step three is to identify and list in priority order the *"key results areas"*—the major components of the job. These are critical output areas that focus on results, rather than activities, and on objectives, rather than tasks. Most jobs have between six and 10 results areas. Achieving objectives in these areas should lead to achieving the mission of the job. Results areas spring from the three performance areas discussed earlier: operations, staff management and personal development.

The fourth step is to set *objectives and standards* in results areas. Objectives state specific performance targets and focus on new and challenging expectations. They cause the

---

NO EXCUSES WITH SMART PERFORMANCE STANDARDS

One of the toughest parts of designing a performance appraisal system is coming up with objective standards for measuring people's work.

If you're going to conduct formal performance appraisals (and who isn't these days?), you've got to have some reliable yardsticks. The ones you use must be fair to both employee and employer, should provoke as little argument and interpretation as possible and must be balanced across all groups of employees. Short of calling in a federal mediator, how do you design such standards?

One widely accepted way to evaluate your standards is to make sure they're smart—better make that SMART. The letters stand for Specific, Measurable, Attainable, Results-oriented and Time-related. The idea isn't new, but it's usually workable. And, according to John Reddish and George Bickley, SMART is a great way to measure the progress of employees toward just about any goal.

Reddish, a West Chester, PA, management consultant, and Bickley, president of Glenn Industries, Inc., a real estate company, define SMARTly designed performance standards as:

Specific—that is, not defined in vague, global terms, but in precise language that leaves no doubt as to

what's expected. They illustrate with an analogy about a man with two cars, two sons and two gallons of antifreeze. The father tells each son to put a gallon of antifreeze in one of the cars. One son puts it in the radiator, the other stows it in the trunk. Both are right, because the message wasn't clear enough.

Measurable—in quantifiable terms that are meaningful, but that leave no doubt about when a performance goal has been achieved. For example, you wouldn't measure sales performance by number of calls made or sales courses attended; you'd look at the revenue the salesperson generated.

Attainable—in that employees should be able to reach the measurable standard at least half the time. If a standard is unrealistic, people will feel they're being set up for failure.

Results-oriented—to ensure that you're measuring output, and not the process of achieving it. Hours spent on the job, paperwork shuffled, courses logged—all become meaningless if they produce no results.

Time-related—to the extent that the results expected have a time frame. Every job standard should have a maximum time line, and only results achieved within it should count.

Standards such as these, Reddish and Bickley say, put the responsibility for performance in any job on the person doing the job, and make it difficult for marginal performers to maintain excuses such as, "You really can't measure my job."

Reprinted from TRAINING, April 1986

subordinate to "stretch," to improve on past performance or to develop new skills. They are the end to which effort is directed. They lead to meeting the missions of the job, the unit and the company.

Standards enable job performance to be measured against objectives. As noted earlier, they clarify expectations and quantify results. They are the core of an effective feedback and control system.

The final step is to complete a *task-planning worksheet.* Each key result is the product of tasks (activities, duties, projects) done in a particular order. As shown in Figure 2, the task-planning worksheet links tasks to objectives and results areas.

The master worksheet

Up to this point, the employee and the supervisor have been working separately, each completing a worksheet on the subordinate's job. Now they come together for the most critical discussion they may have all year. The purpose of this meeting is to negotiate the "Master Performance-Planning Worksheet." Through compromise, collaboration, discussion and probably some conflict, boss and subordinate reach an agreement on what the employee's job really is. Together, they complete the subordinate's final worksheet—one to which both parties are willing to commit. This becomes a performance contract—and a blueprint for the future.

Drawing up a master performance-planning worksheet is neither easy nor quick. It demands careful thought from both boss and subordinate. However, monitoring performance becomes easier within its framework. Clarity of standards and expectations makes communication easier and more productive. But, as with any contract, its success will depend largely upon mutual trust and confidence.

Performance appraisal

The final step in the performance-planning system is the appraisal. Performance appraisals are neither easy to give nor to receive. Managers tend to view them as time-consuming, difficult and bureaucratic. Employees may see them as one-sided, critical analyses of their job performance or, worse, of their personality and character.

But when supervisor and subordinate work together ahead of time to plan for performance, the appraisal that follows almost certainly will be less capricious and subjective. It becomes a logical third step in the planning process. It concentrates on strengthening job performance and on developing the subordinate.

The performance-appraisal interview is, in essence, a review of the past. Boss and subordinate look at the objectives they negotiated months before. The flavor of this review does not smack of "report-card time" but rather of a problem-solving discussion. Were objectives met? Why or why not? What should have been done differently? The subordinate's activities, decisions and behavior are discussed only as they have had an impact on results.

This review of the past leads to a game plan for the future and the performance-planning cycle begins anew.

Reprinted from TRAINING, May 1985

THINKING ABOUT PERFORMANCE

Exceptional bosses expect—and get—the most from their employees. How do they do it?

BY KENNETH R. JUNKINS
AND JOHN O'MEARA

Your people are getting their work done. The work is accurate, complete and on time. Results are up, complaints are down, quality is better than ever and you're not looking too bad yourself.

Every manager's dream? Maybe. But some managers make it a reality. They work within the same constraints and face the same problems as less-effective managers, but they come up with ways to improve results. They create a working environment where employees thrive, success is the order of the day and people genuinely enjoy what they do.

Perhaps you have worked for one of these exceptional managers. Remember? The one who believed in you and consistently brought out the best in you? The one who was open and honest with you? The one who supported you, perhaps, when no one else would? Most of us have had the good fortune to have worked for someone like this at some point in our careers. What is it that these managers do differently that separates them from the rest of the herd?

Typically, exceptional bosses do very few things differently from "average" bosses. In fact, the ho-hum manager often does 90% to 95% of the same things the exceptional manager does. It's that 5% to 10% that makes the difference.

One characteristic that makes the difference is that the best managers are not satisfied with the status quo. They constantly search for ways to improve. The way they *think* about performance helps them see opportunities for improvement.

They are keenly aware of "performance gaps"—the difference between where their people are now and where they can be. These managers see performance in terms that are simple, clear and precise. They have four criteria for performance. They think of it as observable, measurable, results-oriented and positive.

Performance is observable

Performance can be seen, heard and in most cases touched. You can see someone installing equipment, hear someone talking to customers and touch an automobile as it progresses along an assembly line.

Performance is not attitudes, feelings or thoughts. One test for the language of performance: When I describe performance, will *all* my people get the same picture in their minds? Will they all agree on what I am describing?

Donna, an exceptional manager, speaks of performance in precise, objective terms. Her subordinates know exactly what she means when she talks with them about how they do their jobs. Which of the following statements would Donna be likely to use to describe performance?

1. John's attitude has really deteriorated lately.
2. Marco has called in sick three times more often this quarter than last.
3. Steve has brought in four new accounts this week—more than anyone else in the region.
4. Mary has fallen behind by 30% in entering purchase orders.
5. Jim doesn't like his new assignment at all.
6. Karen must think this company is managed by idiots.
7. Barbara really seems to enjoy her work on the committee.

If you chose numbers 2, 3 and 4, you chose well. Exceptional managers ask themselves questions such as:

• What tells me that John has a bad attitude?
• What evidence do I have that Jim doesn't like his new assignment?
• How do I know that Karen is critical of management?

Performance is measurable

Generally, if performance is observable it is also measurable, i.e., it can be counted or quantified in some way and compared to past performance levels. Some managers measure activities, items or outputs that have little or no impact on bottom-line results. Or they use such complex measurements that the system gets in the way of collecting information of any value.

Jack, on the other hand, prefers simple measurement methods; they may not be statistically perfect but they do the job. His highest priority is profitability. When he speaks to Joe about profitability, however, Jack may never use the word. Instead, he might discuss the number of times Joe calls ahead to confirm customer appointments before going out. Calling ahead saves the company time and money, and is more meaningful to Joe than a vague term like profitability. It gives Joe a simple way to determine how well he is doing.

When exceptional managers measure performance, they also use rate (speed, quantity), accuracy (absence of errors), completeness (thoroughness) and timeliness (meets deadlines). Each of these is directly related to the others. For instance, the fact that someone works quickly is irrelevant if the work is full of errors. Completeness has little value if it takes someone six months to finish a job that should take just two days. When a subordinate excels in all four of these measurement areas, that's "quality" performance.

Specific, accurate wording can improve performance levels by making it easier for people to relate a manager's comments to their actual performance.

Vague: "Your work has fallen off lately."

Specific: "Your order-processing rate is down by 15% compared to last month."

Vague: "Your work is really accurate."

Specific: "You made 50% fewer errors this week. Our goal is to get all 25 entries correct, but that's an outstanding improvement!"

Vague: "You just don't seem to care about doing quality work anymore."

Specific: "Your sales report for March had seven inaccurate figures out of 30 for the number of referral sales."

Think about the words you use when you discuss performance with your people. Do you zero in on specifics?

Performance is results-oriented

Managers who "think perform-ance" differentiate between the process of work and the results of work. One way to tell whether a manager is process-oriented or results-oriented is to listen to employees when the boss comes around. If you hear, "Look busy, the boss is coming," you are probably dealing with a process manager. This manager likes people moving and doing things—it's a reassuring sight. Exceptional managers, while aware of activity, always place more value on what is accomplished than on appearances.

A process-oriented manager uses language that focuses on activities—Sharon types fast, Chris talks on the phone, Ron is never in the office—whereas a results-oriented manager talks in terms of accomplishments—reports completed, orders taken, customers visited.

If your people are working on a lot of projects and you see a lot of activity, but results are not what you'd expect, ask yourself: "Am I focusing on results or processes?" and "Am I focusing on the right activities to obtain the results I want?"

Performance is positive

Bob looks at people in terms of what they can do well and how they can contribute to the organization. Yes, he considers complaints, errors and missed deadlines, but he *focuses* on what his people do well. Bob realizes, as do all exceptional managers, that it is more effective to build on the positive than to punish the negative.

There may be just one or two "correct" ways to perform a task, but there are limitless ways to screw it up. While punishment has its place, such as in dangerous situations, it does not necessarily bring about the desired result. Suppose an employee's rude behavior is causing a lot of customer complaints. A two-day suspension without pay may get him to stop being rude, but the complaints may continue or even increase if he begins to miss appointments or do shoddy work. His negative behaviors have simply been redirected rather than improved.

Exceptional managers focus on the positive performance they want from their people more than on the behavior they want to eliminate. They determine where the highest payoff is in a situation, as well as the lowest risk of undesirable reaction. They think in terms of increasing customer satisfaction, meeting deadlines, improving accuracy, saving time and ensuring promptness, not in terms of customer complaints, missed deadlines, errors, wasted time and tardiness.

Some managers do think about performance differently. As a result, they tend to be more effective at identifying opportunities to close performance gaps. They have a system, whether they realize it or not, of logical steps to bring about improvements.

Reprinted from TRAINING, August 1985

PERFORMANCE-APPRAISAL TRAINING: OBSTACLES AND OPPORTUNITIES

Organizations and individuals create roadblocks to effective performance-appraisal training—but savvy trainers can build strategies to overcome them

BY DENNIS C. KINLAW

Before you can design and deliver training that enables managers and supervisors to use your organization's performance-appraisal system to everyone's best advantage, you've got some formidable obstacles to overcome.

The fact is, the people who have to do the appraising often receive *no* training in performance appraisal. It is not uncommon for new managers and supervisors to give their first serious thought to the whole idea the same day that their appraisals on subordinates are due.

Even when they do receive performance-appraisal training, the instruction often focuses solely on information *about* the appraisal system and its legal ramifications. The major purpose of such training is to teach them how to stay out of trouble and how to avoid grievances. The upshot? They receive no skill training at all.

Managers and supervisors may make little connection between their formal appraisal system and the ongoing practices of good management. They do not see the formal process of appraisal as a complement to the routine and informal processes of work planning, work review and feedback. Formal appraisal is viewed as an administrative burden that has little to do with the *real* work of getting the job done.

Managers and supervisors rarely possess the skills needed to develop useful standards of performance. If they are able to write measurable standards, the standards are trite. When they try to develop standards that are complex and representative of the real work of the job, they are unable to make the standards measurable.

Chances are they also lack the skills to structure and conduct an effective appraisal interview. They probably don't know exactly what outcomes they hope to achieve in their interviews; they typically have no experience in helping subordinates prepare for interviews; and they often have only the vaguest notion of how to use nonjudgmental communication or to avoid unproductive conflict.

The need for performance-appraisal training for managers and supervisors (to say nothing of employees) is profound and persistent. It is a type of training that represents a genuine opportunity to help organizations maintain and enhance performance and productivity. But to take advantage of this opportunity, you must be able to overcome obstacles created by both the organization and the people who will receive the training.

Obstacles from the organization

The organization does not, of course, set out to create obstacles to performance-appraisal training. Organizations don't intend to engage in any self-defeating activity—such as punishing creativity and awarding conformity—but they do. Here are some of the obstacles that organizations place in the path of useful performance-appraisal training.

● The training program often is introduced with an administrative bias. Sponsors of the training may limit their objectives to teaching managers and supervisors how to complete the appraisal form, convincing them of the importance of getting the forms in on time and showing them how to avoid a few pitfalls.

This kind of bias ignores the most important goals of the training: Participants should learn the planning and communication skills needed to use the organization's appraisal system effectively, and they should develop a commitment to the process as a useful management tool. Premature and misplaced emphasis on completing the appraisal form creates a basic understanding of performance appraisal which has little to do with sound management practices. Such an emphasis can only serve to underscore what managers already believe—performance appraisal is a burden to be endured, not a tool to be used.

● The appraisal system itself can be a major obstacle. Some systems have so many design flaws that if managers were trained to use them as written, the results would be disastrous. These systems "work" only *because* people improvise end runs around them.

All systems have some weaknesses. All systems are the result of various compromises. They usually are created by several different groups (management, personnel, a collective-bargaining unit, etc.) and travel a circuitous route from conception to publication. To avoid serious training obstacles, at least four characteristics must be present in the system: The result is a genuine appraisal, not a list of the worker's personality traits; measurable performance standards are used; supervisors and subordinates use a mutual planning process; and regular performance reviews are required.

● The organization may direct most appraisal training (when it does any at all) to first- and second-level supervisors. Omitting middle and senior managers from the training is likely to create dissonance between what one group is taught to do and what that group sees its superiors doing. This dissonance will be resolved in the bosses' favor and, as a result, the appraisal training will be discredited in the eyes of lower-level managers.

Most managers who receive performance-appraisal training have been in the roles of both appraiser and appraisee. Their experiences can create a number of obstacles.

● Managers and supervisors do not enjoy the task of appraisal. Most would like to avoid the whole process—especially when appraisal requires a one-on-one interview with a subordinate. Many managers feel uncomfortable giving any negative feedback at all. Others must balance their desire to be fair against their desire to avoid the paper hassle that could result from rating a subordinate very high or very low.

Given this general attitude toward appraisal, you can expect many participants in performance-appraisal training to show up with a heartfelt desire to avoid the whole subject. They may not overtly resist the training, but they will participate reluctantly.

• Trainees may come into the training session feeling frustrated and angry. I remember asking a group of supervisors in a federal agency at the beginning of a training session to identify the positive results they had experienced over the past year in using their appraisal system. They could not—or would not—identify a single one.

Managers and supervisors may feel that they are being forced to play a game. They may have given up trying to rate their subordinates honestly because their ratings are dictated by a higher authority in order to meet some predetermined distribution curve. Also, they may know that the appraisals have little to do with personnel actions such as promotions, selection for transfer and merit pay.

No wonder managers and supervisors feel that, as one trainee put it, "any time spent on performance appraisal is too much time." This attitude obviously creates resistance to performance-appraisal training that can be very difficult to overcome.

• Participants may be highly skeptical of the value of performance appraisal as a useful management tool. Many have little or no experience or understanding of how performance appraisal can help maintain and improve performance. They don't see that it has much connection with the way they manage and the way other people in the organization manage.

We shall overcome

Some of these obstacles are formidable indeed. But several strategies can help you overcome them. The key is the way in which performance-appraisal training is planned, structured and delivered.

• *Plan the training with managers.* It is always sound practice to ask managers to participate in planning any management-training program. In the case of performance-appraisal training, it is essential.

Managers themselves are the best source of information about how to focus the program on what they need in order to make the best use of the organization's system. You have to be sure that administrative issues are presented in proper context and with appropriate emphasis, that flaws in the system are minimized and that your training design places the appraisal system within the larger framework of managing performance. Managers want to make appraisal a practical tool; work with them to ensure that this practical concern dominates the training.

• *Use experienced and senior managers as trainers.* This technique emphasizes the fact that performance appraisal is a significant management responsibility. Participants are encouraged to take a cooperative, problem-solving approach to appraisal and to find ways to make the system as useful as possible. Using managers as trainers reduces the adversarial role between the organization (personified in the trainer) and the managers being trained. It becomes easier for participants to put aside their anger, to stop playing "Ain't it awful?" and to be receptive to the positive aspects of appraisal.

To take full advantage of the impact experienced managers can have on the training, use panels of managers in addition to the manager who serves as primary instructor. The panel should respond to any and all questions from the participants; but their role is to share their experience, not to provide pat answers.

• *Train managers in family groups.* By training managers with their subordinate managers and employees, you link the hierarchical layers and greatly increase the likelihood of developing a set of common and consistent appraisal practices throughout the organization. A highly participative approach will reduce the dissonance that can result from appraisal training, increase the desire to find a meaningful use of the system, and clarify what expectations each layer of management has of the layer above and the layer below. The mutual search for a meaningful use of the system also reduces the participants' tendency to view appraisal as a painful process.

• *Balance the content in appraisal training.* Content should, of course, be derived from the training objectives. Plan your objectives in the following sequence:

1. Ensure that participants understand and value performance appraisal as a tool for maintaining and improving their performance and that of their subordinates.

2. Develop the skills for writing performance objectives and measurable standards.

3. Provide information about the organization's system with helpful hints for making it work.

4. Develop the skills for structuring and conducting an appraisal interview to maximize positive results.

• *Space the delivery of training.* By training managers in family groups and spacing the training sessions over several weeks, you can tie the content to on-the-job activities. This reinforces learning and increases the probability that the learning will be applied.

These objectives provide an outline for a four-module program. Between each module the family work groups can meet and engage in activities that reinforce their learning. For example, they can write and critique performance standards, identify additional ways to use the system, discuss problems related to the appraisal interview and ways to prepare themselves and their employees for interviews.

Performance-appraisal training is an extraordinary opportunity to respond to real management needs and help an organization maintain and improve performance. At the same time, if you conduct it without taking into account the obstacles that surround it, you can make a bad situation worse. A carefully thought-out training strategy will improve your odds on turning opportunity into reality.

Reprinted from TRAINING, January 1984

HOW TO DESIGN AN OBJECTIVE PERFORMANCE-EVALUATION SYSTEM

If you believe meaningful evaluations must be based on measurable standards related to things employees really do, your system probably needs work

BY R.C. RICHARDS

per·form (pər-fôrm) v.-formed, -forming, -forms. **1.** to begin and carry through to completion; do: perform an appendectomy. **2.** to take action in accordance with the requirements of; fulfill (a promise or duty, for example).
American Heritage Dictionary

As the dictionary suggests, the word *perform* is an action verb. To observe someone perform we must know what people *do*—what actions they must take to fulfill our job requirements. Traditional performance-evaluation systems have focused most on how we *feel* about how people perform, not on what people do.

When we focus on how we feel people are doing in their jobs, our evaluations of them are subjective. Subjective evaluations create problems both for those doing the evaluating and those being evaluated. Subjective evaluations create disagreements, disappointments and damaging results.

For example, the term *leadership* tends to be a "garbage" word. It refers to a number of behaviors and meanings which rarely are carefully defined. When we hear the term leadership, we should ask questions such as: "How would I know a leader if one walked into my office?" "What do leaders *do*?" and most of all, "What specific things do I want my people to do when I ask them to 'improve their leader-

ship skills?'"

The terms or rating factors we observe in traditional performance reviews are not bad in and of themselves; it's the way they're used that creates the problem.

Typically, performance reviews focus on factors such as quantity of work, quality of work, communications, leadership, creativity, initiative, personal appearance, dependability, interpersonal relations, professional knowledge, decision-making, delegation, attendance, housekeeping, and so on, ad infinitum.

The question is, how can we measure an employee's performance in these areas?

That question often is complicated by attempts to produce generic performance-review reporting forms which are designed to serve too many purposes (i.e., justification for salaries, promotion, discipline or termination). Rarely are they designed as a tool for supervisors and employees to clarify

job responsibilities, set performance standards, review performance in relation to standards, and to coach or manage for improved performance.

Most forms list broad statements or "constructs" of performance. They do not encourage or require supervisors to observe employees as unique individuals performing unique tasks. To measure performance realistically, objectively and productively, we must base our reviews on job content rather than job constructs. Further, we need objective standards of performance to measure that job content.

Content vs. constructs

Constructs are broad, often self-evident terms which describe a general task, activity or requirement. An example might be "communication skills." Few of us would argue the need for skills in communication for most employees. Our problem is how to define the garbage term in light of our job requirements. Do we want our employee(s) to:

- Write memos?
- Write letters?
- Conduct interviews?
- Deliver public speeches?
- Present proposals?
- Describe features, advantages and benefits of our product or service?
- Resolve face-to-face conflicts?
- Handle customer complaints?
- Write job descriptions?
- Describe and define job standards?
- Manage meetings to consensus?
- Present ideas to top management?

Unless we specify the behavior we want in the context of job-content requirements, we find ourselves hard put to measure someone's performance under the generic construct of "communications." We must determine the sort of communicating the job requires the employee to do.

Some organizations attempt to aid supervisors by providing rating scales that are anchored to descriptions of performance. In most cases, the raters and ratees are left on their own to define the meanings of these performance factors. There would be

Initiative: Resourceful in taking necessary or appropriate action on own responsibility.				
UNSATISFACTORY	**POOR**	**SATISFACTORY**	**GOOD**	**EXCELLENT**
Often waits unnecessarily for direction.	A routine worker; usually waits to be told what to do, requiring constant direction.	Does regular work without waiting for directions. Follows directions with little follow-up.	Resourceful; alert to opportunities for improvement of work. Volunteers suggestions.	Seeks and gets added tasks for self; highly self-reliant. Assumes responsibility.

Figure 1. *Good, but not enough.*

nothing wrong with that approach *if* supervisors made those definitions specific and objective.

Some organizations make an effort to describe the intent of the words. Others attempt to provide examples of satisfactory or unsatisfactory performance along a scale. An example might look like the one shown in Figure 1.

While the scale in Figure 1 is better than those that offer no anchors (rating descriptions) at all, it still lacks something. Unless we tie performance to job responsibilities, standards or specific examples of behavior, we could still argue over the ratings: They're *subjective* and *unmeasurable*.

Responsibilities and standards

Job responsibilities are detailed listings of tasks or activities we expect in the performance of a job—not unlike a list of specifications we might provide an architect before he designs a house, or the "specs" we place on engineering drawings and ask vendors to adhere to when supplying equipment.

Performance standards are the measures we place on job responsibilities to let employees know how well they are doing in the performance of their tasks or activities. They might be compared to quality standards for products or services. Most often they describe minimum, average and outstanding performance against a scale of behavior or quantitative factors.

Figure 2 shows how we might identify job responsibilities. Notice that some of the responsibilities listed might be job *constructs* for many bartenders. We must ensure that we validate these responsibilities in terms of the job content *we* expect or require of the bartender we supervise. The real meaning of the words in Figure 2 may differ from bar to bar or even from shift to shift. Therefore, job responsibilities must be defined and tailored for each and every job.

JOB: BARTENDER	
Job Responsibilities	
Mix Drinks	
Cost Control	
Inventory Control	
Housekeeping	
Safety	
Law Enforcement	
Supervision	
Customer Relations	
Etc.	

Figure 2. *What does the job involve?*

JOB: BARTENDER	
Job Responsibilities	**Indicators**
Mix Drinks Etc.	Complaints Returns Measurements Used (Recipe) Brands Used Appearance Time No. of Drinks Per Bottle Etc.

Figure 3. *What are the guideposts?*

JOB: BARTENDER				
Job Responsibilities	**Indicators**	**Standards**		
		Minimum	**Satisfactory**	**Outstanding**
Mix Drinks	Complaints	4/Week	2/Week	0

Figure 4. *What are our standards?*

Figure 3 takes us through an intermediate process we may find useful (for learning purposes) to arrive at job standards. It guides us toward finding measures for job responsibilities by identifying "indicators of performance."

Notice that at the outset, we list all possible ways to measure a job responsibility. These indicators of performance probably will need to be reviewed with care to select those which can be controlled by the bartender, those that are important to us as a business and those that are measurable.

Figure 4 takes us to the step of setting performance standards. We need to decide what we can expect in terms of outstanding performance, what is satisfactory and what is the minimum level of performance we can tolerate. This is a subjective determination, yes; but once it is made, performance can be measured objectively against the standard. (Note: Standards should be set based on what we require or need in the performance of a job. They should *not* be based on our estimate of a person's ability to do the job.)

When we set performance standards that way, we can become effective managers of a genuinely productive performance-review process.

Review and evaluation

When measuring performance, we want to look for ways to make the evaluation process as productive and painless as possible for all concerned. To do this, we need some goals. We want: objective evaluations; rater/ratee satisfaction; no surprises; measurable standards of performance; forward-looking planning; an ongoing process; and a system that will become part of the management lifestyle.

Let's examine each of these goals further.

Objective Evaluations: To be objective, we must have material evidence of behavior that has been observed in relation to some measurable performance standard. Employees' acceptance of objective evaluations depends heavily on the face validity of our observations about how they perform. When the person being rated agrees with our observations and how they relate to an accepted performance standard, we have face validity. Without that agreement, the rater is placed in a defensive posture, having to rationalize or justify the assessment.

Rater/ratee Satisfaction: When supervisors and employees can come away from an appraisal process comfortable that past performance has been assessed fairly, and when both are clear about what needs to be done to improve performance in the future, we generally have rater/ratee satisfaction. In order to achieve that level of satisfaction, we first must be sure we're working with realistic and achievable performance standards. Then, we must handle the appraisal in a "coaching" manner that is meant to be timely, constructive and useful—helping employees become as much as they want to, or are able to, become.

No Surprises: Whether formal or informal, performance reviews are productive and painless when supervisors and employees know what is expected in terms of performance and when both agree on how well the employee is performing. If we manage our planning, review and evaluation processes well, employees and supervisors know how they are doing at all times. This obviously helps avoid fear, distrust and lack of openness.

Measurable Standards of Performance: A familiar argument holds that not all things can be measured or judged according to set standards of performance. My inclination is to respond by asking the familiar question about whether we would know if those things were done at all and how much we really need them. In any case, our aim should be to identify exactly what we want our employees to do (job responsibilities) and work hard to set standards so we know how well they do their jobs. This goal is the backbone of the whole process. Without measurable standards of performance, we set ourselves up for hardship and end with a performance-review process that is virtually worthless. We have chaos.

Forward-looking Planning: Traditional performance reviews focus on past behavior—mostly on what went wrong. Instead, most of the effort should be spent on what's to be done in the future. What can we make right? Looking backward rarely is constructive and is devoted, in essence, to tearing employees down rather than building them up. The past cannot be recovered or repaired. What counts is what's happening now (in terms of performance) and what we want in the future. Those are things we can control and upon which we can take positive, productive action. I would argue that building employees for future performance is the primary legitimate role for performance reviews.

Ongoing Process: Science tells us that little, if anything, remains static in this universe. People change, conditions change, technology changes, the needs of the organization change—and they all change constantly. That's why performance evaluation should be thought of as a process, not a program. Programs imply a beginning and an end. And in the world of business, especially, we tend to look at programs as if they involve a set formula, ritual or routine.

Processes change and adapt. A performance-evaluation process must be monitored, assessed and revised on an ongoing basis to remain useful.

The traditional performance review makes the entire effort static: Often it amounts to an annual or semiannual ritual of justifying ratings and reporting nonspecific, untimely and unproductive data. When the ordeal is finished, an enormous sense of relief is shared by supervisors and employees alike.

Without feedback, we do not get

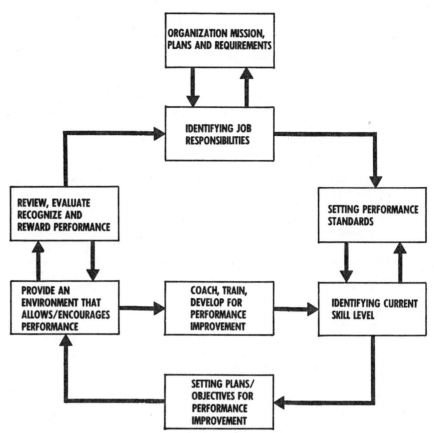

Figure 5: The performance review/evaluation process, AKA—"PREP."

results. Feedback must be continuous, timely and meant to produce the results both supervisors and employees want. Supervisors commonly report that they don't have time to make performance review an ongoing process and still get the job done. But surely this raises a basic question: What else should supervisors do? Managed properly, the performance-evaluation process gets the most important and productive things done—which leads us to the next goal.

A Part of the Management Lifestyle: Most changes die in organizations because they lack the management support that systems need to allow their growth. If the performance-review/evaluation process is to be a worthwhile investment, it must become a part of the management lifestyle—the way to do business. Short of that, we can expect failure. Systems don't run on momentum, they run on vitality. Management provides that vitality when it perceives the planning, review and evaluation process as a key part of the organization's function.

PREP

If we subscribe to the goals described so far, we must begin to place into context the ongoing process

that is to become a part of our management lifestyle. Figure 5 shows a diagram of the performance-review/evaluation process (PREP, for short) that helps us see the whole in relation to its parts. The arrows imply motion or movement from one task to another; it is not meant to be a static display. We should expect action at one or more phases at all times.

What's going on in the various boxes shown in Figure 5?

Organization Mission, Plans and Requirements: Our prime concern for improved performance should be how we affect those needs of the organization that pertain to bottom-line results. To achieve this we need to review what business we're in and why, our short- and long-range objectives, and the skills required to obtain the results we want. These clues help us define what we want our employees to do when we ask them to be "productive."

Identifying Job Responsibilities: The point of a detailed listing of tasks, results or outputs is to provide the specifics that "job descriptions" overlook or leave out. Their express purpose is to clarify what we want our employees to do, relieving them (and us) of guesswork about "what the boss expects." If we don't know what we want our people to do, how can we evaluate the way they do it?

Setting Performance Standards: By letting employees know what minimum, average and outstanding performance look like, we allow them to monitor and adjust their own performance. When we know how we're doing at all times, we should be able to avoid surprise in formal or informal performance reviews.

Identifying Current Skill Level: Before we can go further in the PREP process, we must assess current skills and/or behaviors as they relate to our job responsibilities and the performance standards. If we are getting the results we want from our employees, we need to let them know that and encourage them to maintain their efforts. If there is a shortfall, they need to know that, too. If we want to improve performance from level X to level Z, employees need to know what X is and what Z looks like.

Setting Plans and Objectives for Performance Improvement: Once we know where performance needs improvement and we are clear about how much improvement is needed, we can plan how we are to get the improved performance we want. Setting objectives and formulating plans to achieve them is the best way anyone seems to know of for doing this.

Provide an Environment that Allows and Encourages Performance: A commonly overlooked yet vital phase of the PREP process is that of providing the supportive climate and resources employees need to improve their performance. We have to look for barriers. We have to avoid interfering with or interrupting employees so they can get on with the job. We have to provide adequate tools or resources to allow them to perform. In any case, our job as supervisors must involve working hard to ensure that our employees' efforts to perform are successful.

Coach, Train, Develop for Performance Improvement: In addition to providing a supportive climate, we may need to coach, train or provide developmental opportunities to help employees acquire the skills and behaviors they need to improve performance. Supervisors should know they cannot abdicate this task to someone else. Nor can they ignore it—if they want results.

Notice that at this point in the PREP flowchart a loop is created between "identifying current skill level, setting plans/objectives for performance improvement, providing an environment that allows/encourages performance" and "coaching, training and developing for performance im-provement." This loop of activities continues as an ongoing process until formal performance reviews are held.

Review, Evaluate, Recognize and Reward: From time to time, employees and supervisors need to summarize and document performance. This is done to recognize the employee's growth and contribution to the organization, analyze areas where performance can be improved, and look for changes that might require a revised job-responsibility list. Performance that goes unrewarded is likely to suffer. It's important, then, to provide periodic rewards.

The PREP process should be growth-oriented, it should be flexible, and it should provide for the needs of both employees and the organization. The bottom line is that a process, no matter how well conceived, is only as good as the people who use it. If management's motives are clearly aimed at improved performance for individual and organizational growth, and if the process is applied faithfully both in spirit and in action, a measurable return on investment is virtually guaranteed. It's up to us to know the process well and to develop the skills needed to make it work.

Reprinted from TRAINING, March 1984

IS YOUR PERFORMANCE-APPRAISAL PROCESS READY TO GO TO COURT?

While you're busy evaluating your employees' performance, a judge may be busy evaluating yours

BY BOB RICHARDS

Management theorist Peter Drucker raised eyebrows at a convention a few years ago with the statement, "We will develop little that is new by way of methods or techniques for managing between now and the end of the century. [But] we *will* be held accountable for what we already know how to do."

In the area of systems that organizations use to review and evaluate the performance of their employees, score one for Peter Drucker. If we're talking fundamental approaches instead of jargon, packaging, bells and whistles, then indeed, very little is genuinely new. But over the past few decades, U.S. courts have become increasingly willing to address issues of equity, fairness and discrimination in employee relations: Our evaluation systems are being held accountable.

Whenever an employee's performance is reviewed or evaluated, we are making discriminations. The courts have upheld such discriminations as long as they have been judged valid—that is, fair and equitable.

The question is, can you defend *your* discriminations as fair and equitable? Can you validate the process by which you decided to promote one employee but not another? When giving one person a 6% raise and another 8% under a merit-pay or pay-for-performance policy, can you provide "valid" evidence of 2% difference in performance? If some employees are selected for special attention, such as a fast-track career plan or an advanced training program, when others are not, can you validate that decision?

Validity

The driving legislation requiring validity in discrimination among employees is rooted in the Civil Rights Act of 1964, the Equal Employment Opportunity Act of 1972, and Executive Orders 11246 (1965) and 1135 (1967). But the validity issue really is being defined elsewhere. The prime sources for validation are the Equal Employment Opportunity Commission, the Equal Employment Opportunity Coordinating Council, the United States Code and, of course, the court cases that test our laws and guidelines. In general, the agreed-upon standards are those prepared by the American Psychological Association, last published in 1974 and currently under revision.

What are the criteria? As with any tricky legal question, prudence suggests that you check with a qualified attorney (one with expertise in this area) if you think you have cause to worry. But as rules of thumb, recent court rulings suggest that performance appraisals should meet these criteria:

☐ **Performance ratings must be job-related.** Specifically, the rating must demonstrate its relatedness to the particular job being rated rather than to generalized factors ("appearance," "leadership," etc.) that may or may not have a significant bearing on *this* job. In other words, each job must be measured based on its unique characteristics, which means it is less likely than you probably think that factors or dimensions used to measure one job may be used on another. If job measures must be unique and in context, the implication is that a careful and documented job analysis is needed before you create your rating factors and performance measurements.

☐ **The people who conduct the evaluations must be able to observe the behavior they are rating.** This implies that performance-evaluation processes should be based on factors or dimensions which reflect observable behaviors. The measure of an individual's performance must be based on what we want him to *do*. We must have performance standards and we must observe what this person does as measured against those standards.

☐ **Measurements may not be based upon "constructs," or upon vague or subjective factors.** Without behavioral descriptions or behavioral anchors, factors such as "initiative," "interpersonal communication skills," "leadership," or even "quality of work" and so on may not meet the validity test.

☐ **Rater bias toward race, sex, religion, schooling, past work experience, physical appearance or handicaps must be avoided.** When we make discriminations, they must be based upon valid job requirements which are evaluated against measurable standards of performance by raters who have been trained to observe and report behavior. Raters may need to be trained to avoid terms such as "good," "better," "poor," "weak," and "strong," since such terms most often represent value judgments without valid measures (i.e., how good is "good"?). Raters must report what employees *do* or do *not* do.

☐ **Collection and retention of performance data must protect the employee's right to privacy.** If data is to be collected and stored, it must serve a mutual need (a need of the employee, the supervisor, the company) and the employee must consent to its use and/or disclosure. The rater is responsible for the accuracy, relevance and security of the data. When disclosing data to others (with employee consent), the rater is responsible for making that disclosure personally, as any other source is considered hearsay and is not valid.

Legal exposure

I have observed performance review and evaluation systems in organizations large and small throughout North America, and in my admittedly nonlegal opinion, very few are ready to go to court. Their exposure lies mainly in these areas:

1. Generic design of forms for collecting and keeping performance data. A majority of the forms in use today list rating factors which are not validated from job to job as specific job requirements. To meet the "job-content" validity test, each job could conceivably require a unique list of rating factors or dimensions (unless, of course, you have a lot of duplication of effort going on).

2. Rating factors are not objectively measurable in terms of observable behavior. General statements of employee performance, unsupported by performance standards, are commonplace. Few organizations do any meaningful analysis of individual jobs prior to defining performance requirements and measurements for them. Evidence of rating factors that objectively measure observed behavior against job requirements and standards is lacking in most cases.

3. Multiple use of ratings creates measurement bias. In more than 90% of the performance-evaluation processes I've observed, ratings are used to justify salary recommendations or termination decisions, to select talent for career development or promotion, and for feedback to improve performance. Supervisors consciously or unconsciously reflect on these multiple uses when making judgments on an employee's performance. Such rater bias can undermine a system's validity.

4. Employees are not trained in the use of the performance-evaluation process in a way that ensures valid collection of data and protection of privacy rights. A working knowledge of the legal issues surrounding the performance-review process is rare, not only among supervisors who conduct the evaluations, but among the training- and personnel-department people who should be *informing* the supervisors. Furthermore, few employees understand the process and their rights and obligations related to it.

5. Supervisors are rarely trained to collect and report behavior in an objective, constructive, timely and useful manner. If a judge asks about steps you have taken to ensure that your supervisors are qualified to rate somebody's performance, what will you be able to say?

6. Documentation is too widely distributed, is not properly secured, and is disclosed by someone other than the rater. Traditionally, performance-evaluation forms are routed through a lot of hands before being filed. Too many people see these documents without the employee's consent, without a clear need to know and without any apparent fiduciary/caretaker rights. Few raters maintain security over the documentation (you often find the information in personnel files rather than supervisors' files). And the rating information is commonly disclosed by people in the personnel department because that's where the documents are kept.

Implications

When confronted with these issues, managers often want to back away from the performance-review process altogether: Who wants to think about being sued? This is not a viable alternative, of course, because evaluating employee performance is a management responsibility. The question really is, how can people in training, personnel and supervisory roles become more professional at doing their jobs?

A basic problem often is the willingness of supervisors to abdicate their management responsibilities to the personnel folks or the human resources development (HRD) department. That problem is compounded by the willingness of HRD types to assume tasks that go beyond a staff (advise and consent) role. This role confusion encourages HRD people to design "universal" performance-review systems which attempt to satisfy the needs of all supervisors and employees—an exercise in futility. It also encourages supervisors to avoid acquiring the skills needed to manage an evaluation process in a productive and legal manner: They give up their right and duty to manage.

Legal performance-evaluation methods require managers to analyze the jobs they supervise, define job requirements and performance standards, conduct reviews of performance, evaluate employees based on measurements that relate to observed behavior, document the data collected, maintain the documents securely and, when required, disclose the documentation personally.

Personnel professionals are responsible for knowing how the organization's system stacks up against the laws, agency guidelines and precedent-setting court cases.

Trainers are responsible for understanding—and teaching managers—the skills needed to conduct job analyses, define job responsibilities, set performance standards, observe and report behavior, and document the results.

And somebody had better be responsible for auditing the process to ensure compliance with legal guidelines and organizational policy.

A prime implication of all this is the need for training that will ensure that those involved in the performance-review game know what to do and how to do it. The cost of not training may well be many times the cost of a training program aimed at avoiding unnecessary legal exposure. More important, the productivity gains from a well-run process can net a healthy return on investment. Those threatening legal guidelines, in fact, can force managers to become more professional in their jobs and foster the conditions that allow employees to become more productive, because they know what's expected of them in terms of performance—in terms of actual behavior and concrete accomplishments.

There is not much question of the need for some type of performance-evaluation process. The benefits of review and evaluation are historic. Without feedback and recognition, performance will deteriorate, and that's a fact. The concern is that given the need, can your efforts face the performance test that others place on *you*? Is your process ready to go to court? Experience suggests that the answer probably is no.

Reprinted from TRAINING, August 1984

ON-THE-JOB PERFORMANCE OBJECTIVES

The most a training course can promise is
'can do,' not 'will do.'
Trainers who assume that learning equals
job performance had better not offer
any money-back guarantees

BY FRANK O. HOFFMAN

It happened again just the other day. A client inquiring about one of my standard supervisory training courses asked, "What are the learning objectives? How will supervisors' performance improve? What results will we get for our money?" All this before we had probed the problems to be solved, considered whether training might be part of the solution or identified the specific training activities which might help.

Two things are wrong with these questions: They are premature, and they confuse *learning* with *performance* and *results*. Although many trainers and human resources development (HRD) professionals have rightfully become dedicated to the idea of behavioral learning objectives, they forget that the most a course can guarantee is "can do," not "will do."

Expecting a course to offer you on-the-job performance improvements and payoff results as learning objectives shows naive faith in a simplistic equation:

Learning = job performance = results

Wouldn't that be nice? Unfortunately, once a trainee leaves the learning situation—no matter how solidly the learning has been implanted—many other factors influence whether or not on-the-job behavior will reflect that learning. And even if it does, results are often influenced by circumstances totally outside the realm of learning

or job performance. Thus, a more accurate model is:

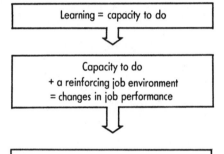

Learning = capacity to do

Capacity to do
+ a reinforcing job environment
= changes in job performance

Changes in job performance
+ relevance to real needs
+ favorable outside conditions
= results/payoff

At best, a training course can provide only the first block of the model; the factors in the second and third blocks are beyond its scope. Learning objectives properly relate only to behavioral changes occurring within the confines of the course.

To guarantee performance or results, the course must become a training *program* that integrates all the factors necessary for the learning-performance-results process to occur. If all the factors are addressed, a training program can have objectives which extend beyond learning to the application of that learning and to the effects of that application. This involves several different types of objectives.

Learning objectives

Since Robert Mager first popularized the concept of behavioral learning ob-

jectives, much has been written about the need to spell out the behavioral changes which will occur if the targeted learning has been produced.

However, the changes in behavior that prove learning has been attained must occur *within* the training situation, not on the job *after* the training is over. Since the behavior you want to change occurs on the job, your natural tendency may be to state learning objectives in terms of job performance and results. This is where Mager and other proponents of behavioral objectives get misinterpreted. Typical learning objectives *misstated* in on-the-job terms are:

• "Using the Chi-analysis technique taught in the course, participants will correctly identify 98% of any improper loan forms submitted to them during the normal workweek."

• "Salespeople will use at least three of the five appropriate closing techniques in every sales call which goes beyond Stage 2."

Obviously, if the loan officers spot the improper forms and the salespeople apply the techniques, learning took place. But did the learning necessarily result from the course? Perhaps the behaviors are being demanded or taught by new influences in the job environment. If so, you could perpetuate a course which teaches nothing simply because its targeted behaviors are occurring on the job.

Worse yet, suppose the loan officers fail to spot the required percentage of improper forms. Does that mean they did not learn how to do so while they were in the training course? If on-the-job influences inhibit the application of learning, you could easily assume the course is at fault for not teaching. If so, you'll mistakenly modify or eliminate the course, rather than working on the job environment—an approach that can be likened to amputating the wrong leg.

Learning should be demonstrated while the training is going on, uncontaminated by outside factors which can give false signals as to whether or not it occurred. This way, you can still do something about it if the objectives are not being met. But keep in mind that when your training department offers a course, the most it can guarantee to produce is *learning*, not on-the-job change.

OTJ performance objectives

Job-performance objectives are not well understood. In the literature, they are rarely differentiated from end-of-course objectives. The technology for establishing and writing them is not at all advanced, probably because neither trainers nor managers have grasped whose responsibility they are.

If a course demonstrates that the students have learned, whose job is it to assure they apply their newly acquired knowledge? The same individual who is responsible for making sure employees know what they need to know in order to do their jobs properly. Obviously, their boss.

Bosses, not trainers or trainees, are accountable for developing and writing on-the-job performance objectives—and ensuring that their employees attain them. Therefore, it is also the boss who should see to it that employees use the targeted learning produced by a course.

As the technology of on-the-job performance objectives matures, it may take three different forms:
• Participant-initiated objectives for behaviors the trainee intends to apply.
• Boss-initiated objectives for trainee behaviors the boss intends to ensure.
• Boss-initiated objectives for activities the *boss* will perform to promote the application of learning by trainees.

From the trainee

Participant-initiated job-performance objectives are somewhat like standard MBO objectives, except that they describe activities as well as results. Remember, on-the-job performance objectives aim at changing *behavior*, therefore the behavior itself should be brought into focus. Rewritten from this perspective, the sample learning objectives would be:
• "I intend to apply the six-step checklist for troubleshooting on at least 90% of the problems I am assigned to diagnose. My goal is to catch 50% of the problems on the first pass."
• "I will apply at least three of the five closing techniques in each sales call which goes beyond Stage 2. My target is to increase the closings of such calls by at least 10% during the first six months and by 15% for the next six months."

To whom the trainee submits these objectives is a critical factor. Trainers who don't understand that line managers are accountable for the *application* of learning often encourage trainees to establish performance commitments with them (the trainers).

This posture assumes that trainees are totally in command of their job performance and that all they need is a sense of commitment: If they want to perform, they will. In the workaday world, however, output pressures, priorities, peer pressures, customer pressures and boss pressures can

easily drive out new behaviors.

Therefore, participant-initiated job-performance objectives should be a matter of commitment between trainees and their bosses. The trainer should stay out of it. The trainer's role in this process is to help participants understand *how* to meet their objectives, and to help bosses understand their responsibility for ensuring that the objectives are met.

From the boss

Boss-initiated objectives for the performance of trainees define what the boss would like to see the trainee doing on the job after the course is completed. Boss objectives might be phrased like this:
• "Salespeople will review the appropriate product descriptions and complete the Advantages Checklist prior to each sales call."
• Prior to setting up the job, foremen will review set-up plans with employees on at least 70% of the work orders.

Again, note that these are objectives for *behavior*, not just the effects of that behavior.

There is nothing magical about having both participant-initiated and boss-initiated performance objectives. These examples merely demonstrate that they can take either form. The ideal process would allow the boss and participant to develop objectives together.

Boss' responsibilities

Objectives initiated by bosses for their own activities should be aimed at creating a job environment that reinforces the newly learned behavior. Simply setting learning objectives or job-performance objectives is not going to change the pressures that caused employees to give low priority to quality, cost control, accurate record keeping or whatever in the first place. Without that crucial change in the job environment, performance probably will revert to the old patterns within a month or so after the training course ends.

Someone has to ensure a job environment that reinforces, rather than extinguishes, the targeted behavior—and that someone is the boss. Bosses must commit themselves to activities *they* will perform to assure that the desired on-the-job behavior will occur.

These objectives include reinforcing changed behavior and removing or reducing conflicting pressures in the job environment. Some sample boss-activity objectives:
• "Once a week I will spot-check at

least one salesperson's Advantages Checklists to see if they jibe with the product manual, and to be sure there is one for each sales call made."
• "I will relax output quotas by 5% for the next two months, so that employees can focus on practicing the quality-building skills taught in Course B."

The beauty of boss-activity objectives is that it doesn't take very many of them to work wonders. The boss doesn't need to develop an exhaustive list—just one or two commitments to action that will reinforce the training and one or two acknowledgements that conflicting counter-pressures will be dealt with.

Do we need 'em?

If you have any doubts that job-performance objectives are necessary, look at the effect learning objectives have had on the technology of course design and instruction. The same phenomenon will happen with job-performance objectives once the concept becomes well understood. No longer will trainers be forced into the untenable position of trying to guarantee that learning alone will produce the desired on-the-job behavior. No longer will we waste time and effort blundering down the false trails created by the notion that on-the-job behavior necesssarily proves or disproves that the intended learning took place in the classroom. If our purpose is to change job performance, we must focus on factors outside the classroom that control performance.

We will come to realize that any trainer who asks a course to produce on-the-job behavior change, without addressing boss objectives, is uninformed. Consultants who promote training courses on the basis of improved performance and results, without describing how they will influence job-environment factors under the control of bosses, will be recognized as charlatans.

The concept of on-the-job behavioral objectives—and especially of boss-initiated objectives—is in its infancy. I believe the next major frontier of training technology lies here. The concepts and techniques involved in things such as front-end analysis, criterion-referenced instruction, documented learning, behavior modeling, multi-image presentation, and computer-assisted instruction already are well advanced, but they don't solve the problem of on-the-job application. If you want to make a contribution to the training profession, experiment with job-performance objectives.

Reprinted from TRAINING, September 1983

NINE WAYS TO UPGRADE PERFORMANCE DISCUSSIONS

You can improve the way you train your clients by improving the way you conduct appraisals with your own staff

BY GEOFF BELLMAN

As human resources development (HRD) professionals, we fulfill an important responsibility in helping the larger organization systematically grow its people. One of the best places to learn about that growth is with the staffs of our own departments. Performance discussions are basic formal vehicles in the growth process. By developing new approaches to discussing work performance with our own people, we strengthen our departments—and that strength can be passed on to our client organizations.

A performance discussion between two HRD professionals— a manager and an employee— contains some special opportunities. We have responsibilities organization-wide that line managers do not share. We build and support performance planning, appraisal and development systems which allow people to grow individually and work more effectively. But HRD managers and their staffs should look to their own performance discussions as an opportunity, often unrealized, to learn and apply the same skills they are trying to build in their clients. This suggests there are alternatives that go beyond what many HRD managers are doing now. Here are nine action areas you might try within your own department and then pass on to others.

1 A performance discussion without objectives is not a performance discussion.

Objectives are basic to all that follows. Whether you call them standards, goals, projects, strategies, tactics or action plans, somehow you and the people working for you need to develop a mutual understanding of and commitment to a common direction. It is this direction and your progress toward it that performance discussions center on.

If you have never held performance discussions with your HRD staffers before, you may get by without clearly defined objectives the first time. You will find it difficult to hold a second session if objectives have not been set in the interim. By objectives, I mean the specific, tangible, measurable, achievable, understandable, challenging, results-oriented creatures the Georges Odiorne and Morrissey talk about. Nothing less will do. HRD has many intangibles and subjective aspects to it. "We can't quantify what we do," many of us claim. "Our results can't be measured objectively. We can't determine our impact." I could muster support for each of these statements— and I know the difficulty of measuring what we do makes it even *more* important to set objectives.

There's an interesting by-product in this. Writing objectives gives you and your staff the opportunity to *manage by objectives*. And managing HRD by objectives aligns you more closely with the line managers you serve. You take on a business perspective more like their own, and by doing that gain a greater appreciation of the problems and opportunities they face day to day in running their organizations.

2 Once a year won't work.

A frequent rediscovery of mine in meeting with line managers regarding performance discussions is that they are thinking in quite different terms than I am. They are thinking, "Once a year it's company policy that we *have* to have performance discussions." Their statement certainly doesn't drip with enthusiasm. On the other hand, I'm thinking, "You need to average *three or four* performance discussions per year with your people to allow the process to work."

The difference between one discussion a year and four discussions a year is not just three; it is different systems. An HRD manager holding one discussion a year with each employee in the department will likely load that meeting to the breaking point with thoughts on performance, career development, merit increase and promotion, training, life planning...even throw in a little personal counseling, just to show how understanding a manager can be. And we're only considering the manager's perspective, without reviewing the load the HRD staffer brings. Though the case may be exaggerated, it's clear that one discussion a year can't handle all the important things that need to be done. With our HRD perspective, we should be especially aware of that, since most of the purposes of regular meetings between manager and staff professional relate to human resources development.

Hold more than one discussion a year and your problems with performance discussions will begin to disappear— or at least change. With constructive intentions and our present skills, most of us can improve on the effectiveness of our performance discussions simply by having them more often. Certainly good discussion skills training could help many of us. But holding four discussions a year rather than one would help even more.

3 Don't guess who needs a performance discussion.

Guessing is exactly what you'll be doing much of the time if you, as manager, are always the one who determines when a performance discussion will be held. Ask your HRD professionals to set up performance discussions with you whenever they want one— and say you'll do the same. Require a few days' notice, so both of you can prepare. Expect that they know better than you do when they need to have a performance discussion with you.

On this basis, in one year as a manager I held as few as two discussions with one employee and as many as eight with another. While I didn't need to talk to the latter eight times, it was clear he needed to talk with me that frequently. As a manager, be available when you're needed, as well as when you're scheduled. Asking employees to take the responsibility for the timing of performance discussions encourages them to initiate a meeting around something important to them. They will be less likely to blame you for discussions not held or poorly timed.

4 You can train half the people half the time...

This point relates as much to our responsibility in developing skills in others as it does to our duties as HRD staff managers. When it comes to building performance discussion skills, most of us train managers and

---

DESIGNING AND USING EFFECTIVE PERFORMANCE APPRAISAL FORMS

BY ANDREA E. HAWKINS

Performance appraisal is a key function of supervision and is integral to the realization of organizational goals. The performance appraisal form is one tool which assists in implementing the process. It can contribute to effective appraisals, but it cannot overcome bad attitudes, lack of communication, or poor supervisory practices. Unfortunately, there is a tendency among managers to focus on the form. If you now have an inadequate system—or no system at all— for evaluating employee performance, avoid the trap of developing a *form*, distributing copies to all supervisors, and calling that a system. Generally, the most serious problems with performance appraisal are not with the forms but with the people who use them.

If you need one, however, here are seven steps to take in designing an effective performance appraisal form.

1. **Clearly define the objectives** for the form within the total performance appraisal process.

2. **Involve staff** from several responsibility levels and different functional areas of the company.

3. **Develop performance evaluation criteria.** These should provide a basis for identifying and recording four types of specific information:
- How well individual employees are performing their assigned tasks.
- What changes, if any, need to be made (through training, transfer or improved supervision) to improve each employee's ability to meet performance expectations.

- How well the company's performance goals are being met.
- What changes, if any, are needed in the human resources utilization program to improve the company's ability to meet its performance goals.

One way is to first identify standards of expected performance which are common to all positions, then add more specific elements by broad classification categories. Even better, consider having sections on the form which require supervisors to list performance standards for each position. This may seem ambitious and time consuming, but it may also contribute to more meaningful evaluations.

4. **Determine types of questions** to include on the form which will elicit the desired information:
- Questions requiring short answers on the employee's functional performance (accuracy and volume of specific tasks, dependability, use of the company's resources, communication skills, adaptability to program changes, willingness to accept direction and correction, ability to suggest more cost-effective procedures).
- Questions focusing on performance objectives for the period of time before the next formal appraisal, or before the first established checkpoint for follow-up.
- Questions which identify skills to be acquired or developed to improve performance in currently assigned tasks, learn to use new techniques for performing currently assigned tasks, or develop new skills for a newly assigned task.
- Questions to identify an individual's long-term development or promotion goals.

5. **Provide room to list** specific follow-up actions, target completion dates and progress checkpoints.

6. **Include a section** for review and response by the employee whose performance is being appraised. Also include space for review by the next level of supervision and/or the personnel officer.

7. **Develop a layout** or format which is functional, easy to understand and use, attractive and economical.

There are some obvious pitfalls to avoid in developing performance appraisal forms. Trait rating lists which simply require checking a box are like popularity contests; they give no clues to improvement, which is one of the most important goals of performance appraisal. Closed questions which cue expected or desirable answers are merely rituals and do not contribute to improving communication between employee and supervisor. Personality characteristics which do not relate directly to job performance usually increase the employee's emotional response to the whole process, while rigid evaluation criteria imposed on all positions— with no regard for differing job requirements— have little credibility with employees. Finally, failure to include space for noting agreed upon follow-up provides no record against which progress can be measured.

Once you have a workable form, it's sometimes a good idea to obtain reactions and solicit additional suggestions for design from a larger group of staff and supervisors. And you should never hesitate to revise the form if necessary. In addition, all employees should have an opportunity to become familiar with it long before an appraisal takes place. (New employees could receive a copy of the form and a description of its use during orientation.) Avoid surprises about the form's content, use and significance. It is *not* to be employed as a supervisor's secret weapon.

Reprinted from TRAINING, February 1981

supervisors and feel that we are serving our organizations very well. By comparison to many other organizations, we may indeed have an enlightened approach— but we've only trained half the people involved. If we are contributing to more effective performance discussions only by building supervisor skills, all we are really doing is augmenting the supervisor's already considerable power base by adding competence and confidence to authority and position.

It takes two people to hold an effective performance discussion; most of us are training only one of them. Look at it from the HRD staff perspective: What training have your own employees had in readying themselves for a performance discussion? The focus of such a meeting is usually the performance of the *employee*. What are we doing to help that individual prepare for the discussion, present opinions and recommendations constructively, or listen nondefensively to what his or her supervisor has to say?

5 Move responsibility to the employee.

Consider the following situations, and decide who has major responsibility for each of them— the HRD manager or the employee:
- deciding employee objectives
- defining performance criteria
- determining discussion agendas
- appraising the employee *first*
- outlining future
- critiquing performance discussions

I am in favor of moving most of the responsibility for each of the above over to the employee. The employee initiates/acts; the manager reviews. Because of the field we are in, we should be searching out ways to treat our people as adults and questioning the ways we presently treat them as children.

Expecting employees to act in the above areas builds their skills in self-appraisal— an important asset to have in our line of work, since so often we work alone.

6 Have a prediscussion meeting.

A lot of the anxiety about performance discussions results from not knowing what's going to happen. How should you start? How do you put the employee at ease? What should you talk about? What should you cover first— more effective or less effective performance? Many of these questions can be anticipated in a prediscussion meeting where both you and your staff member have a chance to talk about what should happen in the

performance discussion itself.

Get together a few days ahead of time to briefly discuss the agenda of the meeting and what aspects of performance you each want to focus on. Talk about how you can create an atmosphere in which you both can be yourselves, acting naturally and comfortably. Make certain you both know what you need to do before the discussion and then do it. Some preparation will be necessary; you may even want to exchange some written information in advance. When the time for the performance discussion comes, if either you or your employee has not completed the preparation you agreed to beforehand, don't hold the meeting. Instead, reschedule it for another time when you know you will both be ready.

7 Focus on growth.

Performance discussions are designed to allow the HRD manager and staff professional to review past performance and set goals for future performance. The "learning" aspects of the discussion are especially important, considering our HRD responsibilities. A discussion focusing on professional growth will work better

than one restricted to the boss' managerial judgment. A discussion encouraging mutual problem solving will be more effective than one dominated by evaluation.

As a footnote to our discussion of objectives, you can emphasize development by formally including it in the objective-setting process. Ask each employee "What will you learn by completing this objective?" Review their written answers as you review each of their objectives.

8 Have performance discussions about your performance discussions.

As a manager— especially an HRD manager—you are interested in what you can do to make your critical managerial activities more effective. Since one of those critical activities is the performance discussion, find out what makes your session work or not work. A short while after a meeting, ask the individual staff member for some constructive feedback on how it went— what worked well, what could have worked better. If you've just completed a number of discussions within your staff, have them meet as a group and talk about what makes performance discussions in HRD ef-

---

EIGHT WAYS TO ENSURE FAIR AND ACCURATE PERFORMANCE APPRAISAL

There's really only one commandment in performance appraisal: Thou Shalt Be Fair and Accurate. If it seems easier said than done (it is), here are guidelines from Beverly L. Kaye and Shelley Krantz, Sherman Oaks, CA-based consultants and authors of *Win-Win Performance Appraisal: A Guide for Managers and Employees.*

- Use factual and first-hand information—oral and written. Verify data and beware of assessments from people with axes to grind (pro and con). Discount hearsay and rumors. Get the whole story.
- If you have counseled the person whose performance you are evaluating, don't let personal confidences interfere with your judgment of job performance. Don't let a worker's personal problems and isolated personality conflicts creep into the appraisal.

- Inaccuracy hurts. Put your true thoughts into the written report. Be specific, but also be aware that there are many ways to say that someone is performing "poorly" while providing helpful hints for improvement and bolstering self-confidence.
- Let your oral and written performance appraisals tell the same story. You must be consistent.
- Equal treatment is an essential issue legally and morally. Use one set of standards for all workers.
- Do not disclose data to anyone without the written consent of the affected worker. It's the law.
- Be prepared to change your written evaluation at the time of the interview if you find it is inaccurate or poorly aimed. Performance appraisal documents live for many years, but they are not sacred. If you can't change the original document, attach a corrective memo that summarizes the new appraisal's orientation.
- Don't blindly accept previous assessments. They could be intentionally wounding or poorly written (vague, unclear) and therefore unfair or inaccurate. Check in person with the originator of any questionable performance appraisal document.

Reprinted from TRAINING, February 1983

fective or ineffective. Learn from the feedback you receive. Demonstrate that, as a manager, you are still learning how you can perform your role better (reinforcing the fact that you expect your staff to do the same).

Because of your HRD responsibilities, you can also use what you learn about performance discussions in dealing with your clients. Your experiences with real discussions, and the critiquing of them, will give you insight into what your organizational clients face as they try to do the same thing with their employees. You can also use your knowledge to improve the training you offer or to review the appraisal system you use, since you will be better able to judge how practical they are for managers.

9 Seek discussions of your own performance.

How many times as a manager have you wondered how you are doing? When was the last time your boss had a performance discussion with you? How effective was it? What could you do to get the quantity and quality of performance discussions you would prefer? Have you ever taken the initiative in asking your boss for one?

While those questions may stimulate some thought— and possible action— in relation to your boss, there is another source of firsthand information on your managerial performance readily available: your staff. If you asked them to critique your performance, what would you hear? How would it fit with what you know about yourself? What could you learn from them that might make you a more effective manager? Are their opinions on your managerial performance important to you?

This vice versa point is to encourage you to consider all the alternatives. It is less prescriptive than it is exploratory. You must decide what you want to do. And do it.

Reprinted from TRAINING, February 1981

GOAL SETTING IS THE FIRST STEP IN ANY PERFORMANCE PROGRAM

Before you shop the incentive catalogs, make sure you have clearly defined your objectives, say Latham and Locke

BY RON ZEMKE

Two of the brightest, toughest researchers in the area of goals, goal setting, performance feedback and performance incentives are Gary P. Latham and Edwin A. Locke. Both have done extensive, pioneering work in the problems of employee motivation and extensive experimentation with the way real-world managers can positively affect employee productivity. In a review paper written for the Autumn 1979 issue of *Organizational Dynamics,* this expert duo concludes that goal setting, independent of any other management system, technique or motivational scheme, is the most effective motivational tool available to managers today.

Their conclusion, based on 14 years of research, is bound to stir considerable controversy. The idea of assigning employees a specific amount of work to be accomplished— a specific task, a quota, a performance standard, an objective, or a deadline— is not new. The task concept, along with time-and-motion study and incentive pay, was the cornerstone of scientific management, founded by Frederick W. Taylor more than 70 years ago. He used his system to increase the productivity of blue-collar workers. About 20 years ago the idea of goal setting reappeared under a new name, management by objectives, but this technique was designed for managers.

Recently, advocates of incentive systems, participative decision making, job enlargement, job enrichment,

behavior modification and organizational dynamics have been basking in the "how-to-motivate-'em" spotlight. But Latham and Locke insist that a close look at the studies conducted by proponents of these various approaches reveals that it is actually through the specification of goals that these other systems affect motivation. Latham and Locke hasten to add that incentives, both internal and external, tangible and intangible, *do* affect movement toward the goal set. They are convinced, however, that the "simple" act of goal setting has its own very powerful motivating effect.

Latham and Locke have culled their applied work on goal setting and concluded that there are seven things we know for sure about goal setting and productivity.

1. Specific, challenging goals lead to better performance than do easy or vague goals, such as "do your best."

2. Feedback (on goal-directed performance) motivates higher performance only when it leads to the setting of higher goals.

3. Goal feedback does provide the worker with a sense of achievement, recognition and accomplishment.

4. Both assigned and participatively set goals lead to substantial improvements in performance. Participation is important only to the extent that it leads to the setting of difficult goals.

• Employees in participative goal-setting groups insist on setting very high goals, regardless of whether or not they have previously performed at that level.

• Employees in assigned-goal groups do best when their supervisor is highly supportive— that is, when he or she doesn't criticize employees for failure to attain goals, lowers goals to an attainable level after failure, and gradually raises goals until employees are achieving at a level to be commensurate with their "potential."

• Employees in both participative and assigned-goals groups report feelings of accomplishment and achievement.

• When goal difficulty is held constant, there's no difference in performance between participative goal setting and assigned-goal groups. Both groups, however, perform better than no-goal and vague-goal groups.

5. Competition—setting one group against another—affects productivity only in the sense that it leads to the acceptance of, and commitment to, the goal. In short, a competitive climate does not directly motivate performance, but it *does* lead to goal acceptance, which, in turn, leads to a conscious striving to meet the goal.

6. Setting a specific production goal, combined with supervisory presence to ensure goal commitment, will increase productivity significantly.

7. When asked to identify conditions leading to *high* and *low* productivity, employees tend to name as *most* important:

High	Low
goal pursuit	goal blockage
large amount of work	small amount of work
deadline or schedule	no deadline
smooth work routine	interrupted work routine

When asked to name the agents behind high and low productivity, employees named *themselves, immediate supervisor* and the *organization* (resources) as being most important to both high and low productivity.

With such clear results, one can't help wondering why goal setting is not emphasized and utilized in a more systematic fashion. According to Latham and Locke:

The concept of goal setting is a very simple one. Interestingly, however, we have gotten two contradictory types of reaction when the idea was introduced to managers. Some claimed it was so simple and self-evident that everyone, including themselves, already used it. This, we have found, is not true. Time after time we have gotten the following response from subordinates after goal setting was introduced: "This is the first time I knew what my supervisor expected of me on this job." Conversely, other managers have argued that the idea would not work, precisely *because* it is so simple (implying that something more radical and complex was needed). Again, results proved them wrong.

Latham and Locke emphasize that even though goal setting is conceptually simple and empirically useful, careful planning and forethought are important to success in any given application. Their research and experience have led them to suggest three critical elements to a successful goal-setting effort.

Defining realistic objectives

The most successful and motivating goals have two main characteristics:
- The goal should be as specific as possible and, whenever possible, should contain a time limit for accomplishment.
- The goal should be challenging, yet reachable. If accepted, difficult goals lead to better performance than do easy goals.

In contrast, if the goals are perceived as unreachable, employees will not accept them. Nor will employees get a sense of achievement from pursuing goals that are never attained. Employees with low self-confidence or ability should be given more easily attainable goals than those with high self-confidence and ability.

Obtaining goal commitment

If goal setting is to work, then the manager must ensure that subordinates will accept, and remain committed to, the goals. Simple instruction, backed by positive support and an absence of threats or intimidation, was enough to ensure goal acceptance in most of their studies. Subordinates must perceive the goals as fair and reasonable, and they must trust man-agement. If they perceive the goals as no more than a means of exploitation, they will probably reject them. Whether goals are assigned or set participatively, support of the immediate superior is critical. A supportive manager or supervisor does not use goals to threaten subordinates but, rather, to clarify what is expected of them. His or her role is that of a helper and goal facilitator.

When employees resist assigned goals, they generally do so for one of two reasons. First, they may think they are incapable of reaching the goal because they lack confidence, ability, knowledge and the like. Second, they may not see any personal benefit— either in terms of personal pride or in terms of external rewards like money, promotion, recognition— in reaching assigned goals.

Providing support

Employees must be given adequate resources— money, equipment, time, help, training—as well as freedom to utilize them in attaining goals, and company policies must not work to block goal attainment. A second level of support here is precise feedback. Employees need to know exactly how close they are to their goals so they can appropriately adjust their effort.

Latham and Locke point out that, while their research shows that feedback isn't a sufficient condition to improve performance, it is necessary nonetheless. That is, feedback *alone* won't improve performance, but without feedback as *one element* of a performance system, performance can't improve.

Latham amd Locke conclude the report on their 14 years of laboratory and real-world research on goal setting this way:

We believe that goal setting is a simple, straightforward, and highly effective technique for motivating employee performance. It is a basic technique, a method on which most other methods depend for their motivational effectiveness. The currently popular technique of behavior modification, for example, is mainly goal setting plus feedback, dressed up in academic terminology.

However, goal setting is no panacea. It will not compensate for underpayment of employees or for poor management. Used incorrectly, goal setting may cause rather than solve problems. If, for example, the goals set are unfair, arbitrary, or unreachable, dissatisfaction and poor performance may result. If difficult goals are set without proper quality controls, quantity may be achieved at the expense of quality. If pressure for immediate results is exerted without regard to how they are attained, short-term improvement may occur at the expense of long-run profits. That is, such pressure often triggers the use of expedient and ultimately costly methods— such as dishonesty, high-pressure tactics, postponing of maintenance expenses, and so on— to attain immediate results. Furthermore, performance goals are more easily set in some areas than in others. It's all too easy, for example, to concentrate on setting readily measured production goals and ignore employee development goals. Like any other management tool, goal setting works only when combined with good managerial judgment.

Our conclusion is that if you really want to understand how goal setting can affect productivity, you *must* read Latham and Locke. Nobody has done more in this area or explained it better.

Reprinted from TRAINING, July 1980

THE 'ROOTS' OF PERFORMANCE MANAGEMENT

Management psychologist Tom Connellan puts into useful perspective the modest beginnings of one of today's hottest training and development technologies—application of performance feedback and positive reinforcement to performance problems

New technologies don't just happen. Henry Ford didn't wander out to the barn one idle weekend and, for want of anything better to do, build the Model T. The computer wasn't an accident. Nor was the theory of relativity a fluke insight gained from misreading a laundry ticket. Yes, serendipity does exist, but the development of new technologies generally is more closely related to gardening than to divine revelation. A tiny organic seed of an idea, planted in the right kind of soil and given, the right amounts of sunshine and rain, slowly grows and flowers.

In the training and development field–if you'll excuse an overextended metaphor–the development process is sometimes obscured by the smoke and thunder created by those who plant and cultivate. And that's too bad, for the "true stories" behind most of our new technologies are as fascinating– and humanizing– as any fiction could ever be. Therefore, we offer you a quick but intriguing look at the "roots" of one of today's hot technologies– performance management, or the application of performance feedback and positive reinforcement to performance problems.

Early in the 1950s, a number of psychologists, systems designers, psychocybernetics enthusiasts, and human factors engineers began speculating— sometimes together, sometimes separately— on the development of better, more precise and, at the same time, more humane techniques for designing work and work systems. Out of these efforts came a number of creations that are, today, taken for granted. Man-

agement by objectives, systems psychology, instructional technology, computer-aided instruction, and performance management are among the most visible.

One of the hotbeds of this developmental activity was the University of Michigan's Bureau of Industrial Relations, Graduate School of Business Administration. The list of Michigan alumni reads like a T&D "Name Droppers Bible." Odiorne, Rummler, Markle, Yaney, Brethower, Schrader, Geis, Connellan and Herrick simply start the roster.

Question: How could one institution spawn so many high-impact people?

Answer: We didn't know, but we kept asking, and recently we had the good fortune to get our answer during a chat with one of those alumni–Dr. Thomas Connellan, president, The Management Group Inc., Ann Arbor, MI.

TRAINING: Tom, we ostensibly got together to discuss your new book,* but would it be okay if we asked you to reminisce a little about your experiences as part of the "Michigan Group"? Would you share a little of your "roots" with us?

CONNELLAN: Love to. Where would you like to start?

TRAINING: How about with the first person singular: How did you get involved with the Bureau of Industrial Relations?

CONNELLAN: The way I first

*How to Improve Human Performance, New York: Harper & Row, 1977, $10.95.

started working for the Center for Programmed Learning, which was part of the bureau, was pretty typical of how things work around George Odiorne, who was the director of the bureau then. A friend of mine worked as a typist at the center, which was just an old converted house at the time. One day I went over to pick up a term paper she was typing for me, and, as I walked in the door, somebody shouted "You're it!" I said, "I'm what?" They said, "You're the one they sent over from part-time employment." I said, "No, but I'm absolutely broke, so if you need something done that I can do, I'm your man." With that, they put me in the basement, where I stuffed envelopes for one of the center's workshops. One of Geary Rummler's workshops, as a matter of fact.

Anyway, I was such a good envelope stuffer, they made me chief envelope stuffer. Then I became chief "notebook-puter-togetherer." Then I became a program coordinator. I would give the "Welcome to Michigan, here is your notebook, here are your lunch tickets, have a good time" speech at the start of the workshops.

Finally, when I got my MBA, Al Schrader made me a job offer—$6,600. Most MBAs were starting at a minimum of 10 grand at the time. Al's recruiting talk was straight to the point: "You won't make much money, but you'll learn a lot." He was right on both counts.

TRAINING: You say your story is "typical" of how people become associated with the center?

CONNELLAN: Very typical. That's how George Odiorne works. He finds people in strange places, sees something in them and convinces them they can learn to walk on water. If memory serves me, Tom Roberts was making pizzas in a Dominicks, B.G.— before George; Clark Caskey was director of an industrial management club in Grand Rapids; Al Schrader was whiling away the hours riding around campus on a motorcycle; and Geary Rummler was converting Spanish courses to programmed instruction at the Institute for Behavioral Research and Programmed Instruction.

George enjoys doing that—looking you in the eye and giving you the old "You can do it" speech. Typically, you say, "Oh no, I can't." He says, "Yes, you can." You say, "Really?" He says, "Yes. Here's the opportunity. Go do it." You believe it, so you come through. That makes sense when you realize what an entrepreneur George is. He started the whole Bureau of Industrial Relations with practically no staff and a $25,000 budget. That was in about 1958. By 1968 the bureau was bringing the university about a million dollars a year in revenue. George isn't there anymore, but Al Schrader heads up what is now called the division of management education, an operation bigger than the management education efforts at either Harvard or Stanford. All from a little converted house in 1958.

The first management-by-objectives workshop I ever taught was also typical of "back then." I was sitting in the back of the room for the umpteenth time, watching George teach. Suddenly, George announces that he has an appointment across town, but Tom Connellan will be the instructor for the remainder of the day. I got up—stunned—told two MBO-related jokes I had heard George tell, they laughed. I relaxed and the whole thing came off as if it had been rehearsed.

TRAINING: How, dare we ask, did that lead to an expertise in performance management?

CONNELLAN: When I went to work for George, I decided to take advantage of the university association and pursue a doctorate. That's not important, except that I was continually looking around for a good thesis—we all were—and asking "why" a lot.

Anyway, I was uncomfortable with the fact that I would go out and teach an MBO seminar for an organization, do a good job and get lots of strokes, but often, when I went back to see the fruits of my labor, nothing was happening in the client organization. The program I'd introduced had never gotten off the ground. The programmed instruction people were finding the same thing. People would leave the workshop and write dandy P.I. stuff that tested out beautifully, but still there was little or no noticeable behavior change in the organization.

So we began looking at systems models, all of which basically said the same thing: you have objectives, you have resources, you have processing activities, you have outputs, and there is a feedback loop. I sort of centered on that feedback loop idea. If you don't have feedback, it's like a rocket with no control. Same thing happens with people; without feedback, they get off in the wrong directions. When I started looking seriously at a total systems model, it was inevitable that I would get more deeply involved in behavior change technology.

TRAINING: So that sort of thinking led to a change in what was being taught and studied at the Center for Programmed Learning?

CONNELLAN: That probing into the "why training programs don't always take" question led to two more courses for the center—a "Training Systems Workshop" and something called "The Management of Behavior Change,"

probably the first performance management course for business and industry ever taught.

TRAINING: Didn't the students from those workshops produce some pretty impressive results?

CONNELLAN: Absolutely. There were many outstanding graduates of those courses, but I remember three in particular: Dan Grady at Michigan Bell, Ed Feeney at Emery Air Freight, and Howard McPherson at Jacobsen Manufacturing. Dan has applied the techniques in a number of performance areas, including some fairly innovative implementations within the areas of absenteeism control and attendance. Ed Feeney used the techniques at Emery Air Freight to improve container utilization and phone answering. Both Dan and Ed were participants in a workshop that Geary Rummler led while he and I were both at the University of Michigan. I think it's fair to say that both of them learned well from Geary and did good jobs of applying those techniques. Howard, on the other hand, was a client of mine and participated in an in-company workshop I ran for Jacobsen Manufacturing. He ended up saving a little over a million dollars a year in the area of quality control by using performance feedback and reinforcement.

TRAINING: It sounds as if most of the developmental work went on in the mid Sixties. Why is the performance management, systems approach, feedback/reinforcement, whatever-you-want-to-call-it model just catching on?

CONNELLAN: For a couple of reasons. First, it wasn't until recently that people saw that performance management is what management is all about. The systematic process of specifying the results you want, identifying the behaviors required to get those results and doing those things necessary to get those behaviors is fairly recent management thinking.

A second factor has to do with the term "behavioral sciences." In the Thirties, behavioral sciences became a synonym for what Daniel Bell calls "Cow Sociology": Contented cows give more milk and contented workers make more widgets.

We are just learning how to position what we do so that it won't be confused with that "Cow Sociology," the be-nice-to-people concept of behavioral sciences.

In fact, we're really learning to avoid being identified with the behavioral science school and image by talking about a performance management technology. We're pushing bottom-line results and playing down the human relations aspects.

There never was anything very scientific about the soft behavioral sciences in the first place. But that movement co-opted the behavioral sciences term, so we've learned to stay away from it. When I talk to management people, I simply explain that performance management is like every other technology. It has four distinguishing elements: the ability to identify variables that control performance, the ability to predict what will happen if the variables are changed, some techniques for actually changing the variables and, finally, the ability to repeat or replicate the process—to repeat the experiment, so to speak. When we tell the story that way and show results other people have achieved, then people listen. And that's what leads you to suggest that performance management, behavioral technology, whatever you call it is being rediscovered.

TRAINING: So your advice to anyone who is trying to influence an organization using the general feedback/reinforcement model would be to stay with pragmatics and forget the psychobabble?

CONNELLAN: Exactly. Look, in the "old days," which really weren't that long ago, we taught a lot of pigeon-rat psychology in behavior management courses. Not because we loved pigeons and rats, but because we didn't have that many people—normal people in the day-to-day workplace—examples. Tell a sales manager, "Here are some tools to help you better control the behavior of your salespeople"—things like getting reports in on time, making cold calls—and he listens and understands. But if you talk about controlling and manipulating employee behavior or the ramifications of the social environment, the typical sales manager shies away. That doesn't mean that there aren't a lot of socio-technical problems to be discussed and resolved, but I don't think the organizational context is the right forum. The job of the manager is to manage, not to resolve sociological and political issues.

TRAINING: During our discussion, you've never used the term behavior modification. Why not?

CONNELLAN: Performance management sounds good; behavior modification sounds bad. In fact, the two overlap but only to a limited extent. When you mention b'mod, you end up discussing manipulation and how many angels can dance on the head of a pin.

TRAINING: How *would* you answer the manipulation-of-people charge?

CONNELLAN: If forced to, I guess I'd start this way: Isn't it interesting that if I say I do a good job of delegating, I'm applauded for being a good manager. If I refer to the same accomplishment as a good job of behavior change, I'm accused of manipulation. It fascinates me that manipulate is such an automatically negative and pejorative word. Webster's first definition of the word is simply "to do by hand." The second is "to manage or utilize skillfully." The Third is "to change by unfair means to serve one's purpose." If you accuse someone of being a manipulator, and by that mean "one who gives a helping hand" or "one who manages skillfully," I'll gladly plead guilty.

TRAINING: You became interested in feedback and positive reinforcement technology when you noticed that the same training program sometimes made an impact and sometimes was a bust. Your solution was to look at the work environment and study what people were rewarded and punished for and how that affected the behavior they learned to exhibit in the training program. Question: You now train people to consciously control the reinforcement and feedback in their environment. How do you go about ensuring that your PF/PR training actually *takes,* that it doesn't suffer the whimsical fate of those early MBO programs you mentioned?

CONNELLAN: Let me answer that with three words. First, involvement. Second, commitment. Third, follow-up.

Sending the first- and second-line management groups to a management program but leaving the third, fourth, and fifth levels of the management team at home automatically decreases the probability that something good will happen when the first and second level managers return to the job. But that's the real world: It's tough to get senior and middle management involved for the amount of time required.

An alternative that the trainer can easily use is the minimum-involvement follow-on system. I have had good luck with this three-step follow-on system. First, I tell my trainees that the first thing they must do when they return to the workplace is to meet with their supervisors. At that meeting, they will be expected to review what they learned and present a plan for applying what they learned in the program. In effect, they make performance contracts with their supervisors. During that first meeting, a second meeting, to review progress on the plan, is scheduled.

The second part of the follow-on plan is a very detailed letter to the trainee's supervisor. This letter specifies— in detail— the supervisor's role in maximizing the trainee's transfer of his or her new skills to the job environment— what to expect during the trainee's first day, first week, and first month back on the job.

PERFORMANCE APPRAISALS: EFFECTS FIRST, CAUSES SECOND

Performance appraisals, like taxes, have become a necessary evil in many organizations; they add little except irritation, headaches and paperwork. They come around once a year—twice in progressive companies that really enjoy the pain—and seem to do everything except what they were designed to do: measure personal improvement and contribute to organizational improvement.

Graham Johns, internal auditing manager for the East Kentucky Power Cooperative in Winchester, KY, has been perplexed by the performance appraisal process more than once. He is particularly nonplussed by the discrepancy between what he has seen and a dictionary definition of the word "performance," which is simply "something accomplished." Why do performance appraisals examine everything except performance? he wonders.

Johns' perception is that most appraisal forms differ very little from one another and almost all of them miss the point. They discuss the character traits of the employee being appraised but barely address the issue of what the person actually accomplished. For example, most forms include sections on human relations or communication. What if the person you are appraising is a meter reader for the gas company? Shouldn't the appraisal focus primarily on the numbers of meters read and the accuracy of the readings? Isn't that the main point of the job?

Students of the long-running controversy over performance appraisals will recognize this argument as belonging to the behaviorist or management-by-objectives (MBO) school of thought. But Johns parts company with the hard-line behavioral point of view by refusing to argue that character traits should play no role at all in appraisals.

The problem, as Johns sees it, is simply one of misplaced priorities. Most performance appraisals put the cart before the horse by concentrating on possible *causes* of behavior while skimming over the observable *effects.* He concedes that qualities like innovativeness, timeliness and goal orientation indeed may underlie good performance. But ratings of these traits do not measure the effects produced or results achieved by performing work. You can't have a meaningful discussion about the psychological or attitudinal reasons for an individual's good or bad performance until you have established whether, in fact, the performance has been good or bad. When character-based appraisals ignore or breeze past the matter of concrete accomplishments, they're a waste of time.

Johns' prescription for the problem borrows heavily from classic MBO. If you're going to talk real performance in performance appraisal sessions, employees must know beforehand what is expected of them. They must have clearly defined areas of responsibility and concrete goals.

That means quantitative goals, Johns says. Don't bother with statements like, "I'd like to see you communicate better with your coworkers." Try something like, "Let's aim for a 7.5 percent increase in revenue next year." If they do it, great. If they don't, *then* it might be time to discuss the whys and wherefores—including character traits. The point is, the underlying reasons for bad performance can only be examined after bad performance has been established.

If you want to improve performance, measure performance, Johns concludes. Better still, he says, "If we provide employees the tools to monitor their own performance, they can get almost instant feedback. Positive or negative trends will confirm improved performance or signal areas to take corrective action." Nothing motivates people like knowing where they stand.

Reprinted from TRAINING, March 1990

The third step is feedback from the trainee on how well the supervisor fulfilled his or her support role.

Now, you have to be careful that this system isn't perceived as a "gottcha." Everyone involved should know that a follow-on system will be required and that it will demand some time and effort of those people who sent the supervisor to tbe training program in the first place.

TRAINING: In other words, management involvement, in the form of follow-up and expectation setting, should be planned and included in the training design.

CONNELLAN: Management people know that new ideas and new projects require care and feeding. We simply need to remind them that the same applies to new ways of managing people.

Reprinted from TRAINING, November 1978

HUMAN COMPETENCE: ENGINEERING *WORTHY* PERFORMANCE

Some trainers spend so much time changing, measuring and promoting a behavior that they forget to question the worth of the accomplishments at which that behavior (or behavior change) are aimed. Tom Gilbert puts us back on track—which is why his new book is so valuable

BY RON ZEMKE

George S. Odiorne, writing in the *Journal of Behavior Management,* suggests that Gilbert's book, *Human Competence: Engineering Worthy Performance* (McGraw-Hill Book Company: New York, 1978), will be cited and emulated for some time to come. Dr. Odiorne may have understated the case. Gilbert's book certainly is one of the most original, perceptive and useful HRD books of the 70s.

To those unfamiliar with Thomas F. Gilbert, we assure you that he is a seasoned veteran, not a newcomer with a magic solution. In 1962 Dr. Gilbert founded *The Journal of Mathematics,* probably the first publication devoted exclusively to instructional design technology. Though it lasted only four issues, it is still cited and referenced. In 1967 Gilbert founded the Praxis Corporation, one of the earliest and most successful instructional technology and performance management corporations. Through Praxis, Gilbert and his partner Dr. Geary Rummler, have encountered every variety of performance problem this book addresses. *Human Competence,* however, is neither a condensation nor a rehash of Praxis course material. It is, instead, the product of 20 years of caring about people and performance and three years of dedicated writing and thinking. So much for author credibility.

Gilbert calls *Human Competence* "a book of theory; but [one from which] practical-minded readers need not turn away." He suggests that the book has four objectives:

- "to define human competence in a precise and unambiguous way..."
- to suggest "...a method for measuring competence with considerable precision."
- to provide "...a model for engineering human competence— for finding out why it's lacking and what to do about it."
- and, finally, "...to translate theoretical principles...into step-by-step procedures...."

He admirably meets all four objectives.

Gilbert's beginning assumption is that human competence is neither psychology, philosophy, economics, education or sociology. Nor is it an absolute. Human competence to Gilbert "is a function of worthy performance (W) which is a function of the ratio of valuable accomplishments (A) to costly behavior (B)." This pseudo mathematical approach to defining competence may put you off at first. But don't let it. Gilbert simply is making the point that the true value of competence is derived from accomplishment, not from behavior.

Most of us in the training field spend so much time and effort testing, ranking, predicting, changing, measuring and promoting behavior, that we forget to question the worth of the accomplishments that behavior and/or behavior change are aimed at. Gilbert suggests the value of his viewpoint by analogy. "It [his definition of competence] tells us that great accomplishments are not worthy if the cost in human behavior is also very great. In my opinion, the Egyptian pyramids stand as silent monuments to worthless achievement, although the subcult of knowledge would have us honor them. A really worthy, though less honored, achievement of the early Arabs was the alphabet, a labor-saving device of incalculable worth." His mission with this definition of competence is simply to "warn us against confusing the cow (behavior) with the crop (accomplishment)."

To measure competence, Gilbert has invented the P.I.P.—Potential for Improving Performance. It's a ratio of exemplary performance to average performance. The concept of an Exemplar is not the same as Aristotle's Ideal but rather that of the best of a particular performance. If, for example, the best teller at Big City Bank correctly handles 60 transactions an hour, but the average of all tellers is 30 transactions an hour, the Potential for Improved Performance among Big City Bank tellers is 2.0. It doesn't necessarily matter that the best Little Town Bank teller handles only 40 an hour or that the average transaction rate for tellers at Cross Town Bank is 50 transactions per hour. What matters, is that at Big City Bank, the P.I.P. is 2.0. Exemplary performance, says Gilbert, is the most sustained worthy performance we can reasonably expect to attain in a given situation. Clearly, Gilbert wants us to put an engineer's, not a scientist's, eye to the matter of measuring performance and expressing competence. Build the bridge to cross the river in front of you, Gilbert might suggest. Don't worry about an ideal bridge because the river isn't ideal either.

Gilbert builds his system of specifying, measuring and engineering worthy performance on four "leisurely theorems." The first is his definition of competence, the second— what he calls the measurement theorem— is his definition and explanation of the P.I.P. His third is that, "for any given accomplishment, a deficiency in performance always has as its immediate cause a deficiency in a behavior repertory, or in the environment that supports the repertory, or in both. But its ultimate cause will be found in a deficiency of the management system." If you recognize a similarity to the behavior modification dictum that "the performer is always right," you get an A+. But if you immediately assume that Gilbert is pushing a behaviorist psychology dressed up in engineering gray, you have a surprise coming.

It is just at this point that Gilbert

seriously challenges the B-Mod Squad. Says Gilbert: "The practitioners of behavior modification hold as their subject matter behavior itself....But the subject matter of performance engineering is not behavior....Behavior modification theories have simply avoided the central questions of value that any engineering discipline must begin with....I cannot live with his [Skinner's] work." Gilbert concludes that behavior modification and the operant theory of learning and performance are simply too limiting and narrow to build an entire engineering discipline on; other arts and sciences have too much to contribute to the solution of practical problems.

The fourth and final leisurely theorem is that "We can view human accomplishments at several levels of generality, and the values we assign to these accomplishments at each level will be derived from the level just above them." Here Gilbert tackles the matter of differences in perceived value of an accomplishment. He takes us down this potentially tenuous and ponderous track of differences in viewpoints and values with a delightful story from his youth in which he recounts an argument over the competence of Robert E. Lee among six of his southern relatives.

A warning: Our account of *Human Competence* may be leading you to conclude that this is a heavy, dry, egg-headed book. It is none of these. Gilbert does have a penchant for using pseudo mathematical formulas to specify his theorems and corollaries. And occasionally he makes up tongue-tangling words such as teleonomics and metachronic. But neither of these seriously detracts from the power of his arguments— made in simple English— and the clarity and fun of the "real life" examples he shares with us. Far from being boring, *Human Competence* is one of the most provocative, instructive— and yet simply delightful— HRD books we have encountered in years.

Reprinted from TRAINING, November 1978

MEASURING POTENTIAL FOR PERFORMANCE IMPROVEMENT

This nifty system helps you tell how competent your people already are, and helps determine opportunity for improvement

BY THOMAS F. GILBERT

When we make judgments about the competence of human conduct, we often confuse behavior with performance. Behavior is a necessary and integral part of performance, but to equate the two is like confusing a sale with the seller. Naturally, we cannot have one without the other. But the sale is a unitary transaction, with properties all of its own; and we can know a great deal about it even though we know little—perhaps nothing at all—about the seller.

In performance, behavior is a means, and its consequence is the end. And we seldom have any reason to try to modify other people's behavior in complete isolation of consequences. About the only reason would be to study it. By viewing behavior in convenient isolation we can learn many things about it, ranging from measures of visual acuity to useful information about the perseveration of habits. But those things *by themselves* tell us very little about performance.

Nor do we have much reason to modify people's performance in isolation from its context. Is the performance of killing legal and moral—or is it a heinous crime? We cannot tell this merely by observing the whole performance transaction. We can measure the frequency or accuracy of striking the target; we can measure how many bullets were used. We can even correlate these measures with our measures of behavior. But none of these measures will tell us whether the performance is valuable, legal, or moral.

No sensible person tries to modify other people's behavior just because it is there, or their performance just because it can be done. When we set about to engineer performance, we should view it in a context of value. We should not train someone to do something unless we place a value on the consequence—unless we see that consequence as a valuable *accomplishment (A)*. So, the kind of performance we want to engineer is *valuable performance,* which can be expressed in shorthand as

$$P = B \rightarrow A$$

Now we have limited our definition of performance to valuable performance. If, for example, we can change the way a hunter handles his gun so that he can hit the rabbits we value, we have engineered valuable performance.

Worthy performance

But is the performance worth it?

Suppose that we really do value the rabbits we have taught the hunter to kill. But the hunter requires an expensive rifle, charges us heavily for his services, and uses a lot of ammunition. Although we may value his accomplishment, we will not find the performance worthy because his behavior costs us too much. Our engineering, then, is a failure. So, what we really want to engineer is not just valuable performance, but *worthy performance*—in which the value of the accomplishment exceeds the cost of the behavior.

All engineering begins with the simple economic purpose of creating valuable results at a cost that makes those results worth it. Worth, then, is the net we have when we subtract the costs from the values: $W = V - C$. Or, we can express worth in another way: as the ratio of value to cost:

$$\text{Worth} = \frac{\text{Value}}{\text{Cost}}$$

Which says only that worth gets greater as value increases and cost decreases.

When we set out to engineer human performance, it is axiomatic that we place value on accomplishments but that the behavior costs us something. We may value the rabbit; but we must pay for the hunter's work, knowledge, and incentives, as well as for his gun and ammunition. We value the crop but pay for the plow and the plowman.

Roughly speaking, *competent* people are those who can create valuable results without using excessively costly behavior.

Behavior vs. accomplishment

Nothing better illustrates the importance of distinguishing behavior and accomplishment than a study of the ways in which we can measure performance. When we think of measuring performance, we usually think of tests. And psychologists have certainly provided us with enough of those. By the traditional view, the way to assess performance is to administer tests of apparent job or school relevance (e.g., mathematics, spatial relations, mechanical aptitude), and then to establish a cut-off score for the selection of employees or the advancement of students.

This traditional view is mistaken in two ways. First, traditional tests, at their best, are only crude statistical instruments, usually poorly correlated with the economic realities of performance. For example, personality tests for salespeople have been cor-

49

related with such supervisory ratings as "interpersonal effectiveness" and "ability to conduct an interview," but never, to my knowledge, with the quality of sales prospecting. Very often those things so easily assumed to be correlatives of actual performance simply are not. As a matter of fact, the best salesperson (by dollar volume) I have ever seen never smiled and had a fish-like handshake; and a leading medical photographer I once knew is color-blind, one-eyed, and severely astigmatic in the one "good" eye.

Second, tests are unfair in that the people who score poorly on them have far more potential for successful job and school performance than we have been able to tap. A test score rates people low on the *assumed* correlatives of the job or school requirements; but it does not identify precisely what must be developed in them for us to make good their potential. Tests are usually too indirect; we need to go more directly to performance. And that is what psychological testing has helped prevent us from doing. That is also why psychological test batteries have been so half-heartedly accepted in industry. They have been better accepted in the schools, but only because the schools have been so little concerned with the worldly use of human performance.

Assessment of human performance has teetered on a dilemma. Here are its horns:

1. We all know that there are great individual differences among people (the statistical "science" of psychological testing is grounded in this assumption).

2. But we know equally well that people are pretty much alike (or there could be no science of human beings, biological or psychological).

Now, I believe both of these propositions, and so does everyone else I have ever talked to about them. But their contradiction is clear and surely needs a resolution. The system of performance analysis described here has emerged from a resolution of this dilemma— from realizing how both of these commanding, yet seemingly contradictory, beliefs about differences in human performance can be true but not contradictory.

Measuring human competence

I believe wholeheartedly: Any kind of performance can be measured—reliably and with considerable precision. We can measure the performance of poets, managers, teachers, physicians, lawyers, research scientists, psychotherapists, composers, and politicians— not just that of production workers and athletes. The belief that the more complex forms of performance are not subject to measurement and quantification arises simply from ignorance about how to do it. Once you get the knack, performance that you once thought unmeasurable will usually be not nearly so difficult to measure as, say, the radiation of Martian soil or the fertility of farm land. I hope to convince you of this here.

But performance alone is not what I have set out to measure, because per-

---

The engineer's model for worthy performance has an important message for trainers: Competent people create valuable results without using excessively costly behavior.

---

formance alone is not competence. Competence is a social concept, a comparative judgment about the worth of performance. In order to convert measures of performance into measures of competence, we require a social standard. Once we find that standard, competence will be as easy to measure as performance.

We get the competence of any one person, institution, or culture only by comparing the very best instance of that performance with what is typical. Mark Spitz, the Olympic swimmer, was (at his best) only about 20% faster than the average high school swim-contest entrant, which means that the average high school entrant is exceptionally competent. Mark Spitz, of course, was a perfectly competent swimmer, because he was the exemplar. I call this measure of competence, the ratio of the exemplar's performance to typical performance, the PIP (*potential for improving performance*); and it doubly serves us. First, it tells us how much competence we already have; second, it tells us how much potential we have for improvement.

I define *exemplary* performance as the worth of the historically best instance of the performance. And notice that we need not accept mediocrity as a standard. For example, if a greenhorn's acre yields $1,000 in grain at a cost of $500, the typical worth index (W_t) is 2. If the best green thumb yields $2,000 in value at a cost of $250, the exemplary worth index (W_{ex}) is 8. Then the greenhorn's PIP is 4, meaning that the greenhorn has the potential for doing four times as well. (Dollars are convenient units, but the PIP is by no means restricted to them.)

Human competence, then, is further defined by the Second Leisurely Theorem (or the Measurement Theorem), which states: *Typical competence is inversely proportional to the potential for improving performance (the PIP), which is the ratio of exemplary performance to typical performance. The ratio, to be meaningful, must be stated for an identifiable accomplishment, because there is no "general quality of competence." In shorthand, this theorem states that:*

$$PIP = \frac{W_{ex}}{W_t}$$

There is also an interesting corollary: *The lower the PIP of any person or group, the more competitive that person or group is.* Now, the word *competitive* is a delight to some people; to others, it signals unpleasant things. But that is because the cult of behavior has us confuse certain behavioral properties, such as greed, aggression, determination, and the expenditure of energy, with competing. All I mean by competing is performing with comparative competence.

PIP characteristics

You will note that the PIP is a measure of opportunity, the very stuff human capital is made of. The PIP does not assign feeble limitations to people as the IQ does, but takes the humane *and* practical view that poor performers usually have great potential. Also, our measurement theorem does not posit competence mystically inside people's heads, but places it in performance. People are not competent; performance is. People have opportunities, which the PIP can express with precision and validity.

Indeed, the PIP can be measured as precisely and as accurately as we choose. Competence may vary from time to time, but our methods of measuring it need not. I have devised practical methods of measuring the PIP, and they need not be validated against criterion measures, because the PIP, when properly used, *is* the performance criterion. And, naturally, when applied in the world of work, the PIP yields accurate measures of the economic potential for improving performance.

The PIP is principally a conceptual tool, which gives us a basis for comparing potential opportunities to improve performance. In general, the smaller the PIP, the less possibility there is to improve performance and the more difficult it is to reduce the PIP to 1.0. It is easier to reduce a PIP from, say, 4.0 to 1.5 than it is to shrink a PIP of 1.2 to 1.1. This rule is no longer true, however, if two circumstances hold. One is if we have full knowledge of why the exemplar is a superior performer, and we also have *full* control over those variables—that is, when we can give typical performers the training, information, tools, or motivation they require to emulate the exemplar. The second circumstance is even more important: when we can improve on the exemplar. Thus, the PIP is a "dynamic" measure, because new exemplary standards can always be set.

But here is something more to be considered. Even if we gave all performers the information, knowledge, tools, and so on, of the exemplar, some variance in performance would remain—someone would still manage to shine as the best performer. In a "perfectly" competitive world, where we have arranged for everyone to have everything necessary in order to emulate the exemplar, such inherent characteristics as quickness, strength, "intelligence," and ambition will give some people a slight edge. In athletics, that slight edge is the critical distinction, but in the world of work or in the world of schools it would usually be of no special economic significance at all. It is, I believe, virtually impossible to reduce PIPs to 1.0, simply because someone will always discover a better way of doing it, have some natural superiority, or possess an unusual degree of motive to excel.

What I am saying is that, in general, the more incompetent a person or a group of people are, the easier it is to improve their performance. This contradicts the way we often think. But that is because we rarely think as performance engineers. Left to "nature"— to uncontrolled and unplanned events— exemplary performers are likely to improve themselves, setting new standards of exemplary performance. But as a situation becomes more "unmanaged," PIPs will grow—with the result that management has more potential for realizing them. Although large PIPs may discourage the uninitiated, they

are a welcome opportunity to performance engineers.

The size of the PIP, of course, only indicates potential for improving performance—not how economically valuable that potential is. To put an economic value on a change in a PIP, we must translate it into what I call "stakes." (Stakes are the money value of realizing the PIP.) A PIP of 4.0 in the speed at which janitors clean a building, say, does not translate into as much economic potential as a PIP of 1.5 in the speed of the production line. Later, I shall discuss the relatively

---

Any kind of performance can be measured reliably and with considerable precision—even that of poets and managers.

---

simple techniques of translating PIPs into stakes; meanwhile, it is important to see the use of the PIP as a conceptual measure, pointing us in the direction of engineering opportunity.

A case in point

A case history, based on real events, illustrates how the use of the PIP can be a solid clue of great economic importance to a performance engineer faced with a really unfamiliar performance system. In this case, we shall see a performance engineer, Frank Roby, face an unfamiliar situation and find opportunities to improve it greatly— opportunities of the kind that experienced management misses every day.

The manufacturing vice president of Surfside Seasonings, Inc., Willis Angel, is dissatisfied with the performance of his plants. He is determined to find some way to improve that performance, and he assigns three groups of people to conduct independent studies to tell him which programs he should invest in. Two of these groups are the corporate training and organizational development departments of Surfside. The third group is a consulting firm specializing in management development. When Angel reads the three reports, he can hardly believe that the studies were independent because their recommendations are so similar. All three reports finger the first-line supervisors

of the work force in the processing area as the culprits most responsible for the poor showing in the plants. The once stable, but aging, hourly workers have been largely replaced by young women from the ghetto. All three reports agree that the old first-line supervisors simply don't know how to manage the new breed. A training program in new styles of supervision, and in human relations, will be required; and the management consulting firm offers to develop one for $78,000. For a $400 million business, this does not seem too large an investment in good supervision.

Angel, of course, is impressed by the substantial agreement of the three studies he has commissioned. And the arguments have a certain face validity: The culture of the work force has changed, and there is no doubting that. But the $78,000 training-development cost for an operation that has been losing money gives Angel trouble. He can't quite make up his mind, and he decides to get another opinion. He has heard of a consultant named Frank Roby, a man with a mixed reputation. Some say that Roby is completely without professional qualifications and imply that he is a charlatan. Others insist that although his methods are truly unorthodox, Roby gets results. The word *results* sounds sweet to Angel, so he hires Roby at $750 a day.

Because of Roby's reputation, Angel decides to watch him work. Roby shows up one morning and makes the mandatory tour of a manufacturing plant, seemingly without noticing a thing. He then spends the rest of the day talking with the corporate accountant, the plant production manager, and the chief quality-control inspector. To Angel's surprise, Roby appears in his office at 5:00 p.m. saying that he is ready to deliver his report and suggests that they conclude the study in the nearest bar over Vidalia Specials, a mixture of orange juice and sour mash bourbon.

While Angel begins his adaptation to this curious blend, he asks Roby if he has ever been in a manufacturing plant like Surfside's. "Not exactly," Roby replies, "but I once helped some folks in a chewing gum factory."

So much for Roby's credentials. Angel begins the audition with deep suspicion, but after an hour Roby has completely convinced him that the best way for Surfside Seasoning to waste its time and money is to train first-line supervisors; and that, indeed, the company has an extraordinarily competent corps of foremen in the processing areas. (Mind you, Roby never so much as interviewed a supervisor.) Besides, Roby tells Angel exactly where he thinks the problem is, why it is there, and what can be done about it. He is so convincing that the next morning Angel seeks authorization to spend the $150,000 that Roby said would be required for the program.

Only 18 months later, Angel has sufficient data to prove that the adoption of Roby's program is netting the company a return of several million dollars a year in greatly increased labor productivity, decreased waste, lower employee turnover, and fewer grievances. And Angel finds himself taking all the credit—not that he's that kind of guy. But how could he ever convince anyone that a man could walk into a seasonings plant for the first time and after a day tell you how to turn the plant around—and against all the advice of seasoned professionals?

We can look at just a sample of the data that Roby studied to reach his conclusions: Table 1 shows some production data for three* representative supervisory groups at Surfside Seasonings. (Of course, Roby didn't depend on these data alone, but they contributed far more than anything else to his remarkable conclusions.) In examining these data, Roby could see at once that the potential for improving the performance of the

TABLE 1 COMPARATIVE MANUFACTURING PRODUCTIVITY					
Supervisor A		Supervisor B		Supervisor C	
Employee no.	Hrly. prod.	Employee no.	Hrly. prod.	Employee no.	Hrly. prod.
1	163	11	194	21	172
2	149	12	138	22	137
3	118	13	137	23	136
4	108	14	131	24	135
5	106	15	110	25	127
6	93	16	89	26	100
7	60	17	61	27	56
8	57	18	49	28	52
9	42	19	48	29	41
10	30	20	41	30	28
Average	92.6	Average	99.8	Average	98.4

hourly employees was considerable, but that the differences among supervisors was small. Even though Supervisor B had the best supervisory performance in the company, getting other supervisors to perform as he does would not improve matters greatly. If the situation were reversed and there were large differences among the supervisors, his conclusions would have been quite different.

The average production is 96.93, and the best employee produces 194 units; so the employee PIP (assuming that costs and quality are the constants) is

$$\text{Employee PIP} = \frac{194}{96.9} = 2.00$$

This employee PIP shows that the average hourly employee has the potential for doubling productivity. But the supervisory PIP is negligible— unusually low, in fact. Roby looked at these variances and then noticed that the job the employees had to do was to operate complex low-tolerance equipment. A lot of learning is required to master it. He also heard people say that it simply took a lot of experience to get maximum production. And he learned that the hourly employees got no formal training— mostly because production managers didn't think that formal training was as good as on-the-job experience. He considered this nonsense, of course, and he advised Angel that $150,000 invested in proper training in the theory and troubleshooting of the equipment could get any new employee producing at about 150 units an hour, reducing the employee PIP to less than 1.3. Roby proved to be right— and the most important information he had was the PIP measures. Management had hidden the data in its books, but not in the form of Table 1.

*In the real case, there were 32 groups. Three are chosen here to simplify the argument.

Frank Roby is a real person, and this is an almost true story. It is true in every important respect except for the time it took— Roby has never met anyone as open minded as Willis Angel; it usually takes weeks or months to build up sufficient appearance of credibility for his advice to be taken seriously. Roby has no magic, no mysterious capacity for insight. Indeed, his methods are so simple that when people watch his behavior, they cannot help but be unimpressed. Roby has learned to observe measures of competence and to make sense of them. Those simple measures can be powerful instruments in our pursuit of competence if we can set aside our behavioral biases long enough to see how they can be used.

Whose performance can be measured?

The Roby example deals with relatively simple performance that can be measured quite easily— in units of production. You might argue, however, that much of the world of human performance is not so simple; and you might reasonably question whether other kinds of performance can be measured to yield neat units like the PIP. At least consider my proposition that any kind of performance can be measured.

Oh, the thrill when we first broke through what seemed to be the dense underbrush of John Donne's poetry. But if Donne was a competent poet, how can one measure that competence? Is there any way to say precisely that Donne is 2.3 times the poet that Herrick is, or 3.0 times Lowell? The obvious answer comes much too easily: There is no way to quantify beauty or spiritual power.

The problem is not *whether* we can measure Donne's performance, but what it is we expect from poetry— what we consider a valuable poetic contribution. Measuring noncreative competence seems to be easier than measuring the competence of creative artists— but only because people can more easily come to an agreement about what is expected of noncreative performance. Anyone's performance can be measured in many different ways, and those measures become measures of competence whenever we can agree on what it is about the accomplishments that we value. It should be sufficient to say that we can measure any kind of performance. And to argue that performance is too difficult to measure is, it seems to me, the luxury view of things. If most people did not live in poverty and abject servitude, this view would be easier to accept. Indeed, in that distant day (should it arrive) when all people have broken the bonds of ignorance and need, and we sit sipping mint juleps on some warm veranda, poetry itself may become the currency of the land, and all the absurd numbers will be safely confined to the computers. But until that time I for one must believe that it is possible to measure performance and competence, even John Donne's, and to make those measures mean something. It may not always be easy, but the stakes are reasonably high. Indeed, if we cannot measure competence, there is very little reason to talk about it at all.

The widespread feeling that many of the important characteristics of human conduct resist measurement is a result, I believe, of the familiar confusion between behavior and performance. There are at least two reasons why behavior is often difficult to measure satisfactorily: much of it is covert and not easily observed; and it is often hard to specify exactly what behavior is required for exemplary performance, because two exemplars may behave in considerably different ways.

If I were to build a scale of poetic competence, be assured that I would not start by observing the *behavior* of poets. Donne's poems speak for themselves— clearly to a few, not too clearly for most. No end of analysis of his behavior would add one scintilla to a proper assessment of his performance. Besides, as I have said, Donne's behavior is no longer available. And behavior is not competence any more than an eight-cylinder engine is a Sunday drive in the country. Once we lock that concept firmly in mind, it becomes much easier to measure human competence.

Reprinted from TRAINING, December 1978

PERFORMANCE IS THE PURPOSE

Join the growing number of organizations that realize training alone is almost never an appropriate cure

BY GEARY A. RUMMLER

Most organizations are missing an opportunity to increase the contribution of their training functions tenfold. To realize this opportunity, top management must change its expectation and perception of the training function. Actually, this change in expectation and the resultant improvement in the contribution of the training function already has taken place in a number of major organizations.

To oversimplify a bit, you must view the training function not as a keeper of the corporate "schoolhouse" but as a "performance improver." This means changing the mission of the training function from "Number of employees trained" or "training programs produced" to "organization performance improved." Naturally, this will lead to a difference in how management (and the personnel function to which training usually reports directly) evaluates the training function.

Under the current mission of "employees trained," evaluation of the training function is some variant of "heads trained per training budget dollar." This, of course, emphasizes the volume of training conducted, not the value. Under the proposed mission of "organization performance improved," the evaluation will necessarily have to be a variant of "bottom-line contribution per training-budget dollar." This will correctly emphasize the worth of the training, not the amount.

Obviously, such a change in mission and evaluation of the training function will produce changes in how the training function operates.

But the changes aren't going to be nearly as great as you might fear; many training professionals have been moving in this direction for the past five years. Much of the "technology" required for such a change (i.e., analysis of performance problems, measurement of impact on organization performance) already has been developed and adopted.

The key to the change is getting top management to:

1. Expect—even demand—something different and better from training; to view the training director as a business person who must show a return, not as the "dean" of the corporate schoolhouse, somehow exempt from evaluation because of the "high purpose" of his or her operation.

2. Let the training function operate in order to accomplish this new mission.

I know many training people who have been "bottom-line oriented" for years, but who have been limited in what they could do because of insufficient technology and strategies. However, it is now technologically possible in most cases. For you to comprehend the potential of your training group, you must understand something about this technology, which is generally known as *performance analysis*. The purpose of performance analysis is to view organization performance as a function of the individual *and* the job environment; any modification of performance has to deal with *both* parts. In other words, the human performer is only one of the following five components in a performance system: the job *situation*, or occasion to perform; the *performer;* the *response* (action or decision) that is to occur; the *consequence* of that behavior to the performer; the *feedback* to the performer on the consequences of the behavior.

Schematically, the relationship of the five components can be seen in Figure 1.

In any job, there is a *situation* or occasion where a particular *performer* is expected to make a particular *response* or take some action which results in some *consequence* to the performer. That consequence may be considered positive, negative, or of little value by the performer. Finally, information on that consequence is *fed back* to the performer.

It is imperative to understand that poor performance (i.e., failure to see the desired response) may result from a breakdown in *any* of the five components of this performance system. For example:

The job situation—perhaps it isn't clear that the situation merits the desired action;

2. The performer—perhaps he doesn't know how to perform or is physically or mentally incapable;

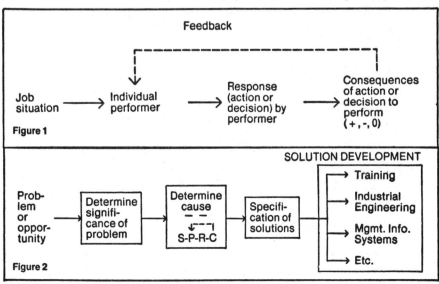

Feedback

Job situation → Individual performer → Response (action or decision) by performer → Consequences of action or decision to perform (+, -, 0)

Figure 1

SOLUTION DEVELOPMENT

Problem or opportunity → Determine significance of problem → Determine cause S-P-R-C → Specification of solutions → Training / Industrial Engineering / Mgmt. Info. Systems / Etc.

Figure 2

3. The response—perhaps the performer doesn't know he is supposed to make the response or doesn't know how, or it is physically impossible to make it, or the performer lacks the necessary tools or support;

4. The consequence—perhaps the consequence is punishing or nonexistent;

5. The feedback—the performer receives no information about his response—whether it was adequate or inadequate, and if inadequate, how to improve it.

Using the "performance system," let's examine a typical request for training.

The marketing function of a bank has launched a major "sales" campaign in which the branch bank tellers will sell additional bank services, with particular emphasis on personal loans. After six months the campaign seems to have fizzled: The tellers aren't selling. Management concludes that the tellers don't know *how* to sell other bank services, so the training department is directed to retrain or conduct refresher training. In terms of the performance system, management has concluded that the desired action—selling—is not forthcoming because of some failure in the performer component, i.e., tellers don't know *how* to perform. In fact, the breakdown was in the consequence component.

First, there were immediate negative consequences to the tellers for errors in handling money, failure to balance at the end of the day, and taking bad checks. This, coupled with long lines, kept the tellers' mind on the essentials of their job. Second, there was no support from branch management for the personal-loan emphasis. The positive consequences for the branch manager (attracting attention downtown) were for building up a sizeable loan portfolio—which could be done quicker and cheaper by making a $1 million loan to a small corporation; it takes a lot of $3,000 personal loans (and considerable expense per loan) to equal $1 million.

Given these two sets of consequences, 30 weeks of training in "selling services" would have negligible effect on personal loans as long as the *balance* of consequences itself was unchanged.

Had this particular training department utilized the principles of performance analysis, they would have:

1. Questioned the extent of the "problem" reported by management to determine the value of solving the problem.

2. Determined the precise cause or causes of the performance discrepancy, using a framework such as the performance system.

3. Corrected the cause or recommended the necessary corrections, should they be beyond their capability or organization charter.

Based on 10 years' experience with performance analysis, we can predict that: Training is *infrequently* an appropriate solution; training alone is almost never an appropriate solution: the cause of performance problems is almost always a combination of "faulty" components in the performance system.

A number of training organizations are aware of performance analysis and capable of applying it. However, the organization realities they face are usually: low tolerance for analysis ("You people aren't the R&D Department, you know"), and less tolerance for suggesting alternative solutions to training based on the analysis ("Are you the training department or not? I want training").

The result: The frustration of developing training to solve what is essentially a non-training "problem."

An organization shortcoming

In addition to the problems faced by training, the performance system points up a shortcoming in the organization of most institutions. In short, they are not organized to solve problems. An organization can't really deal with a "problem" until it is classified in *terms of some solution*, be it a *training, communications, wage-and-salary, labor-relations* or *engineering* problem.

Once classified, the problem can be referred to the appropriate department (or solution pigeonhole) for action. Frequently, the recipient department is reluctant to claim the problem, saying "we can have some impact, but this won't solve the problem." The result is a program which produces only marginal results. Why? Because the other faulty components in the per-

formance system have gone undiagnosed and unattended.

The concept of the performance system suggests the need to analyze all performance problems thoroughly, to diagnose *all causes* and, to put together comprehensive solution strategies. This, in turn, suggests two organizational needs. The first one is for some organizational entity—function or department—to be responsible for an accurate, objective analysis of organization performance problems and the specifications for correcting them. The general process followed by such a function might look like that diagrammed in Figure 2.

I call this process (and would be inclined to call the function) *performance engineering*, as it goes beyond training or any other single "solution."

The second organizational need suggested by the performance system is that of preparing managers to diagnose or troubleshoot human-performance problems in order to enhance the communication between managers and the "performance engineering" function.

As noted earlier, a number of major organizations are moving toward some form of performance engineering or performance oriented training. Their efforts have assumed a continuum of forms like those diagrammed in Figure 3.

If you, as management, want more from your training function, shift the focus from training programs to improved organization performance. Ultimately, the training function should become the foundation for the performance-engineering department. The people in training are philosophically oriented toward improving human performance and, in many cases, already possess the required basic analysis skills.

Unquestionably, the most critical change required to improve training begins when you *demand improved performance* for your training dollar. Only then can the training people do the professional job of performance analysis that is required.

Reprinted from TRAINING, October 1977

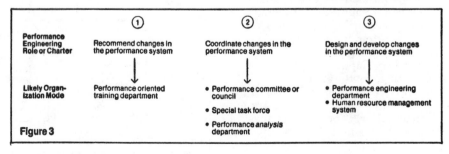

Performance Engineering Role or Charter	① Recommend changes in the performance system	② Coordinate changes in the performance system	③ Design and develop changes in the performance system
	↓	↓	↓
Likely Organization Mode	Performance oriented training department	• Performance committee or council • Special task force • Performance *analysis* department	• Performance engineering department • Human resource management system

Figure 3

EMPOWERMENT: HELPING PEOPLE TAKE CHARGE

Think Murphy's Law will kick in if you empower employees? Think again

BY RON ZEMKE

Stew Leonard is the founder of Stew Leonard's Dairy in Norwalk, CT, the world's largest dairy store and, according to the *Guinness Book of World Records,* the world's most profitable retail store of any kind (100,000 square feet of store and 1986 gross revenue of $100 million). He tells this story about one of his employees.

At about 6 o'clock one evening, Leonard's son Tom found a note in one of the suggestion boxes in the Danbury, CT, store. It had been written only half an hour earlier. "I'm upset," the note read. "I made a special stop on my way home from work to buy chicken breasts for dinner, but you're sold out and now I'll eat a TV dinner instead."

As Tom was reading the note, Leonard continues, "Les Slater, our Norwalk manager who lives in Danbury, stopped by on his way home to say hello. Just then, the big white Perdue chicken truck backed into the loading dock to make a delivery. Five minutes later, Les was in his car taking a little detour. You can imagine the smile on the customer's face when he answered the door at 6:20 p.m. and found Les with a complimentary two-pound package of fresh Perdue chicken breasts!"

To Stew Leonard, the moral is simply that customer service is an every time, not a sometimes, thing. Everyone from janitor to store manager to founding father and sons is expected to go the extra mile to deliver. To the rest of the world, it seems an improbable tale at best—if true, a modern miracle. It's the kind of story you hear today when the talk turns to "excellence." It's also the kind of story that causes seasoned managers to shake their heads and mutter, "Yeah, but my people could never. . . . "

To a growing legion of management scientists and human resources development professionals, that story is just one more example of what can happen in an organization when employees are *empowered* to work on behalf of the customers—when they are turned loose with the proper training and motivation and told to "get out there and do what has to be done," for the customer, for productivity, for quality, for whatever.

To empower, according to Webster's, means both to authorize—as in, "the president is empowered to veto legislation"—and to enable, as in, "a good education empowers one to succeed." In an HRD context, the idea usually is to empower employees to achieve the organization's goals rather than strictly personal ones.

James Barkesdale, chief operating office of Federal Express Corp., was asked at a recent Penn State seminar how Federal Express managers had so quickly authorized the middle-of-the-night airlift that took special equipment from California to Texas so drillers could execute the internationally televised rescue of baby Jessica McClure from an abandoned well. Barkesdale's answer: No management authorization was required. "The operator who answered the call in our regional center just said yes and started the ball rolling."

An incredulous listener asked how that could be. "Look," Barkesdale explained, "my job is to see to it that we hire, train and pay people to make that kind of decision right there on the front line. If that person calls me at home in the middle of the night to OK spending $7,500 on a thing that important, I've failed as a manager."

That's empowerment. Much as we all love this kind of talk, however, the admonition to "go forth and empower your employees," whether to serve customers or to create better products, is as frustrating as it is compelling.

Here's a different kind of empowerment story from a trainer at a bank. "We really hammered our management: 'Let the line employees make check-cashing decisions we traditionally reserve for branch management. You'll see. They can do it! And it will free up the branch managers for other things.' Well, it backfired. The tellers got together and wrote these rules for check cashing that would have made the president show three forms of ID to deposit his paycheck. So much for 'Just turn 'em loose to serve the customer.' We learned quickly that there is much more to it than saying, 'Go do it.' "

Managers with a healthy respect for Murphy's Law will be both exhilarated and awed by the prospect of vesting substantial responsibility in the hands of the people nearest the problems to be solved. Nonetheless, the pressure for improved productivity in goods and services, accentuated by the thinning of middle management ranks, is leading more and more people to ask, "How can we get more responsibility down to the line, where it belongs?"

In *The Change Masters* (Simon & Schuster, 1983), Harvard Business School professor Rosabeth Moss Kanter argues that three basic "power tools" must be in place before employees can "reach outside of and beyond the authority of position to develop ideas for change." These power tools are *information* (data, technical knowledge, political intelligence, expertise); *resources* (funds, materials, space, time); and *support* (endorsement, backing, approval, legitimacy).

And there's more, Kanter says. If employees are to take grass-roots responsibility for creativity, productivity, quality and responsiveness to customers—the promised outcomes of a workplace of empowered people—each individual must believe that there are "opportunities" to perform in an empowered way. Each must have a high degree of self-esteem. Each must accept "ownership" or responsibility for the job to be done, feel part of a team and believe he is involved in something of importance or purpose.

In his new book *Thriving On Chaos* (Knopf, 1987), Tom Peters says the goal of empowerment is to increase the organization's flexibility: ". . .give the sales and service people wide latitude to act as 'the company' when they are in the field or on the phone, and especially when they are confronting a problem. . . . [involve] all personnel at all levels in all functions in virtually everything." He offers two "guiding premises," five "supports," and three "inhibitors" of empowerment.

The guiding premises: involve everyone in everything and use self-managed teams. The five supports: listen/celebrate/recognize; spend time lavishly on recruiting; train and retrain; provide incentive pay for everyone; and provide an employment guarantee. How to get rid of the inhibitors: simplify/reduce structure; reconceive the middle manager's role; and eliminate bureaucratic rules and humiliating conditions.

Not to be outdone by his former collaborator, Robert H. Waterman Jr., coauthor of *In Search of Excellence*, also takes up the question of empowerment in his new book, *The Renewal Factor* (Bantam, 1987). The goal, he says, is to have "people down the line implementing imaginative programs for renewal." To reach that goal, management must have unswerving faith in the principle that "the person doing the job knows far better than anyone else the best way of doing the job and therefore is the one best fitted to improve it."

To his credit, Waterman notes that these concepts have been around since Juran and Deming were teenagers. The question is, as always, how do you make it work? He argues that the key to creating an empowered work force is to develop a style of management he calls directed autonomy: "People in every nook and cranny of the organization [are] empowered—encouraged in fact—to do things their way. Suggestions are actively sought. But this all takes place within a context of direction. People know what the boundaries are; they know where they should act on their own and where not. The boss knows that his or her job is to establish those boundaries, and then truly get out of the way."

Waterman leans on a metaphor from higher mathematics to describe the process of "gaining control by giving up control" that is at the heart of directed autonomy. "[Many mathematical problems] have a host of feasible solutions contained inside a set of boundaries. . . . Business problems are like that. Lots of reasonable, good answers. The manager's job is to establish the boundaries around a fairly broad space. The individual's responsibility is to find the best way of doing things within that space . . . . The heart of the solution-space idea is that within the boundaries there is no 'optimum' answer, other than what employees suggest. If what people come up with fits within the solution space and they like it, that is about as close to optimum as you can get. In fact, that is the test of the optimum."

Regardless of who is talking about empowerment, the concept boils down to an effort to make it possible and worthwhile for employees to be committed, concerned and involved. The potential "tools" vary from creating a philosophical viewpoint to designing specific operational procedures. But it always seems to begin with a commitment to the effort itself. As Peter Block, author of *The Empowered Manager* (Jossey-Bass, 1987), puts it, empowering yourself or others begins with "an act of faith. . . . We commit ourselves to operate in a way that we believe in because it is what we have to do. Other people's experience may act as signposts for us, but we take the trip alone."

Reprinted from TRAINING, January 1988

ZAPP!

Excerpts from a new book about the human 'lightning of empowerment' in which the lightning is entirely literal

"Once upon a time, in a magic land called America, there lived a normal guy named Ralph Rosco.

"Ralph worked in Department N of the Normal Co. in Normalburg, USA. For years, Normal had been a leading manufacturer of normalators, those amazing devices that are so fundamental to society as we know it.

"As you might expect, just about everything was normal at Normal, including the understanding of who was normally supposed to do what: Managers did the thinking. Supervisors did the talking. And employees did the doing."

Thus begins Zapp! The Human Lightning of Empowerment. *The authors are* **William C. Byham,** *president of Development Dimensions International (DDI) of Pittsburgh, a training and consulting firm, and* **Jeff Cox,** *a free-lance writer. Why a fable? For one thing, Byham says, though a lot has been written about empowerment over the past few years, "few managers really understand what it is and even fewer know how to do it." Fables can explain things in ways that standard "managementese" can't.*

Zapp! *is essentially a detective story—an exercise in discovery learning. Empowerment appears as a mysterious force. The characters try to figure out what it is and how to make it work—first for Department N and finally for the entire Normal Co.*

Some background leading up to the excerpts presented here:

Stealing time from his normal job duties, Ralph Rosco invents the Ralpholator, a device that plunges him and Department N's supervisor, Joe Schmo, into the 12th Dimension. From that perspective, the Normal Co. appears as a gloomy medieval castle. What little light there is emanates from people—except that in Department N, the people are zombies and mummies; their radiance is practically nil. Managers are brutal trolls. The biggest, meanest troll is barely recognizable as Joe Schmo's boss, Mary Ellen Krabofski, also known as upper management. Ralph and Joe realize that what they're seeing is the way people actually feel—about themselves, their jobs and one another.

The situation is equally bleak everywhere they wander. But finally Ralph and Joe stumble upon a section of the Normal castle where things are decidedly abnormal. The light is much brighter. A knight in armor fights a dragon. Some other people—all quite human—build a hot-air balloon to cross a bottomless chasm and get to a diamond-encrusted mountain. In the center of all this activity is a woman wearing a wizard hat. Bolts of lightning shoot from her fingertips into the people around her, renewing them and giving them strength. These Zapps are clearly the source of their extraordinary energy.

Ralph and Joe return abruptly to the normal world and discover that they are in Department Z. The wizard is revealed as supervisor Lucy Storm. She offers them a tour. The work in Department Z strikes them as even duller than their own work in Department N, but the employees seem charged up and intensely interested in it. . .

Joe Schmo started to wonder. How come he ran a department where people only cared about quitting time while Lucy Storm ran a department where people really cared about making things better and better?

How come he kept getting yelled at by his boss for not being good enough while she, even with a lean staff, could deliver great performance?

How come?

What was it down there in Department Z that had made those people so turned on about their work? What was Lucy Storm doing that he was not?

Surely it had something to do with the lightning Zapping between the people. What was that lightning? What made it work?

Of course, the easy thing to do would have been to go to Lucy Storm, talk to her directly and openly, and try to learn from her.

Nah! Joe Schmo entertained that possibility for only the briefest of split seconds. That would have violated Joe Schmo's Three Ironclad Rules:

1. Never ask for help.
2. Never let it seem you can't handle everything on your own.
3. And never ever talk to anyone about anything important unless you have no other choice.

Besides, if he could do this on his own, he might be able to grab all the credit for it. So Joe Schmo decided he would figure this out by himself. The first thing he did was give the lightning a name. He called it Zapp: a force that energizes people.

Now, how could he generate Zapp in Department N? The problem was you couldn't see Zapp, but it was there. Kind of like excitement—and enthusiasm. Then he remembered that in Department Z everybody seemed enthusiastic.

"Aha!" said Joe Schmo. "She must give them pep talks."

The next day, Joe called everyone together and tried giving them a pep talk.

But nothing much happened. A

few people were enthusiastic for about five minutes, then everybody went back to being the way they had been before.

Joe did some more thinking. "Hmmm. Lucy seemed like she was nice to everybody," he thought. "So I'll try being a nice guy for a while."

But that didn't do much either. Most people were nice in return, but nobody did a better job or was more committed to their work as a result.

"Well, no more Mr. Nice Guy," thought Joe Schmo. "If being nice didn't make lightning, I'll be Mr. Mean!"

But being Mr. Mean was no more effective than being Mr. Nice Guy, and sometimes it made things worse. People would jump when Joe appeared, just to slack off when he turned his back. Tensions ran high. Quality plummeted. Union grievances soared.

Not only that, but after Joe did some checking around, he learned it was extremely rare for Lucy Storm ever to raise her voice to anyone. Yet her people applied themselves to their work, got things done on time and accepted responsibility.

What could he try next?

Then Joe said, "Hey, I'll bet Zapp is nothing more than one of those quality-circle programs!"

He looked into it and indeed Department Z did have a quality-circle program. But then so did Department Q and Department B and Department K—and Joe knew they performed no better than his own Department N.

Years ago, even Department N had had its own quality circle. But it had been a big disappointment and, like most of those programs, had soon faded away.

So quality circles were not the same as Zapp.

"I know! Money! Money always talks!" thought Joe. "Those people in Storm's department must get some kind of special bonuses or incentives."

But he did some checking around and learned that Department Z abided by Normal's normal pay plans, which of course meant no special incentives.

He also found that a few departments had tried bonuses and incentives, but had gotten mixed results. The extra money was always welcomed by those getting it, but often did not do very much except increase costs.

By now, Joe was out of guesses. So he went to Normal's company library, and on one of the dusty shelves he came across a book that mentioned something called "participative management."

It said:

Whatever Happened To Participative Management?

Participative management stems from the idea of involving employees in the decision-making process. The basic idea has been around for a long time, but it's had its ups and downs in terms of popularity.

One of the big problems is that hardly anybody understood what it really meant. In the '50s, managers thought it meant being friendly to employees. In the '60s, it meant being sensitive to the needs and motivations of people. In the '70s, it meant asking employees for help. In the '80s, it meant having lots of group meetings.

Using it, different managers would get different results. One manager would call a meeting and try to get people involved—and it would work. Another manager would do the same thing and nothing would happen.

The very name "participative management" seemed to imply that it was something management did (which in turn seemed to limit the degree to which employees would or could participate). Actually, "employee involvement" is a term that goes hand in hand with participative management, and the two terms might almost be used interchangeably.

While participative management has not been a failure, confusion over what it is (and is not) has prevented widespread success.

Could Department Z be using participative management? Joe didn't know. He was too confused.

Then Joe read something about job-enrichment programs, quality-of-work-life programs and various other kinds of programs. But Department Z didn't even have any of those.

Maybe it had to do with the way the company was organized.

The entire Normal Co. had gone through a reorganization last year that had removed some layers of middle management. The top managers had called it "flattening the organization" in the company newspaper and it was supposed to be a good thing.

Joe wasn't so sure. Right after the flattening, *he* had nearly been flattened by the weight of new responsibilities dropped on him. It seemed to Joe that if there were good things about a flattened organization, only Department Z seemed to know about them.

Then he remembered the group of people sitting around the table in Department Z—the team!

"That's it!" said Joe. "Work teams!"

But no, lots of other departments had tried putting people into work teams. Department Z still had something they did not.

And then Joe thought about things like suggestion systems, more training, better communications, a closer labor-management relationship, job security and lots of others.

Nearly all the ideas he considered were, he had to admit, very good ones. In every case, if Department Z had them, they worked. But if other Normal departments had them they didn't seem to matter much. Results were usually mixed, short-lived, disappointing, counterproductive, confusing or insignificant.

Now what did that mean?

"That Department Z has the key to making all these other new ideas and programs work, something we're still missing," Joe concluded.

"That must be the lightning," said Joe. "Whatever that Zapp is, it's got to be powerful stuff."

But at this point, Joe saw he was still no closer to understanding what Zapp was. He knew he needed help. He decided to violate Ironclad Rule No. 1.

So one day, near quitting time, he went to see Ralph Rosco.

The very next day, Ralph reassembled the Ralpholator, fired it up and vanished into the 12th Dimension.

He started wandering around. Everything and everybody in Department N was about the same as that first morning—dim and gloomy, with all the charm of a minimum-security prison.

In the midst of this was Joe Schmo,

dressed that day (to the eyes of those in the 12th Dimension) in a cowboy hat, boots and spurs, and toting six-guns, ready to blast anyone who got in his way.

Ralph was about to mosey on over to Department Z when he saw something he had not noticed on his first visit.

Ralph watched as Joe walked up to Marty, who was still wrapped in mummy tape. Soon after Joe started talking, there was a flash of—well, it was not lightning.

Instead of a flash of light, there was a flash of night.

Kind of like blinking your eyes.

And there was a sound.

It did not go Zapp!

It went "Ssssapp."

To Ralph, it kind of sounded like a balloon deflating. After the Sapp happened, Ralph watched Marty get a couple more turns of mummy tape around him, making the light left inside him a shade dimmer.

Then Ralph noticed Becky trying to say something to Joe, and Joe walking away, not paying any attention to her.

Sapp. And Becky became even more zombie-like.

Next, Ralph heard Joe tell Phyllis how to do a job she had often done before without bothering to listen to how she thought it should be done.

Sapp. And a fresh new sandbag appeared on the growing fortifications around her desk.

He saw Joe rush over to someone who was having a problem and immediately pull him off the job and start solving the problem himself.

Sapp.

But it wasn't just what Joe was doing. Ralph heard some people telling other people not to work so hard— that it was "bad for all of us."

Sapp.

He heard one worker telling some others, "That's not our problem. Let the bosses worry about it."

Sapp.

What was going on here, Ralph wondered. These were just routine, everyday, normal occurrences—nothing that most people would notice.

But when these things happened, people got dimmer and slower instead of brighter and faster. Sometimes, a few new stones would appear on the maze of walls crisscrossing the department, or a new chain would wrap itself around someone's arm or

leg, or some other constraint would form.

Whatever was happening, it was keeping people divided and confined, draining their energy or damming it up so it couldn't be used.

And Joe Schmo was a big part of it. He went through the day Sapping people left and right.

"He's like a black hole, absorbing energy from everyone who works for him," thought Ralph.

These things were not just in Department N. Ralph wandered through the Normal Co. and saw Sapp happening lots of places and lots of ways.

By the end of the day, throughout most of Normal, the majority of people were dull and de-energized. When the light from the opening doors streaked in at quitting time, everybody bolted for it, glad that the day was over.

Ralph watched them go, rushing for the fix of energy they needed from home and family and the things they did after work. He wandered back through the fog toward Department N. When he got there, he saw Joe was in trouble.

It was Joe Schmo alone in the midst of an enormous cloud of flashing night. He was beaten and bruised, cowboy hat lost, standing his ground as jaws and claws came out of the fog from all directions. He had been bravely firing away with his six-guns at this many-faced thing. Though his bullets had wounded some of the monsters, there were many more than he could shoot at, and his guns were now empty.

What was this thing confronting Joe? Ralph stood and watched him fight his losing battle. And then Ralph had a gut hunch what it was.

It was everything Joe had Sapped from everyone else. What Joe had taken away, had not shared, was now beating him. What was it?

It was Responsibility. It was Authority. It was Identity. It was Energy. It was Power. . . .

Some say it came from Engineering, that it was the creation of Bob, a junior-grade designer whose mind was numbed by the spell of an evil wizard from another galaxy.

Some say it came from the Executive Suite, where it had been sleeping for several years under a vice president's desk—hibernating until awak-

ened by the fanfare accompanying a management proclamation of a new corporate policy.

And some say it had been in Operations all along, small and cute at first, but growing, slinking about by night, gorging itself on memos, reports and other combustibles.

Wherever it came from, it was a big mother dragon. And it stalked the Normal halls in the 12th Dimension looking for places to lay eggs.

Ralph saw it one day. He was taking a reading with his newly developed Zappometer (pronounced "Zapp-aw'-met-er"), which measures Sapp-Zapp ratios and lightning levels.

Department N had become a much brighter place. In the past week, Ralph had observed a 1-2 ratio in Sapp-Zapp frequency as well as an improvement of 14 bolts in the department's average Zapp charge.

Ralph watched Joe Schmo walking through Department N. Joe still had his cowboy hat and spurs, but he seldom reached for his six-guns anymore. As he said and did enZapping things—maintaining each person's self-esteem, listening to each person and responding with empathy—little forks of lightning flashed between him and the others.

Things had improved, but the lightning still did not reach very far or last very long. When Joe was not around, people quickly got dull. Their glow would fade, like red-hot steel cooling down and turning gray. Unlike in Department Z, the Zapp did not interconnect them and the charge of energy never reached the threshold to become self-sustaining.

As Ralph was considering this, he felt a tremor in the floor. Then, from around the corner, came the purple, scaly snout of the dragon.

Like all industrial dragons, this one was invisible to the normal world, but its effects were quite real. A swipe of its talons, and data in the Normal computer would be randomly trashed. One switch of its tail, and a critical machine would break down. Wherever this dragon breathed, fires broke out—a thousand parts would arrive late and a third of them would be defective.

The dragon squeezed its wings through the main door of Department N, took a deep breath and— whoosh—a long stream of red and orange arched across the department, igniting one of the normalators, which burst into a tower of flames.

Joe Schmo, who had been in the middle of responding with empathy to something Dan had said, immediately broke off in midsentence and rushed to the fire, his cowboy hat bending and twisting as he hurried until it became a white fireman's helmet.

Marty, who was closest to the conflagration, had already grabbed a 12th Dimension fire hose and was about to turn on the water, but Joe Schmo got there and wrestled it away from him.

Sapp. And Marty's Zapp charge, such as it was, got grounded out.

"Stand aside!" said Joe. "Everybody out of the way!"

Joe stood there figuring out how to turn on the hose while the flames rose higher.

Meanwhile, the dragon wandered down the aisle, flicked its long, forked tongue—and the data disk in Mrs. Estello's word processor went up in smoke.

Of course, Mrs. Estello had no idea what to do. Her job was just to type, wasn't it? So she got up and took the smoking disk down the aisle to Joe Schmo, who, of course, was too busy wielding the fire hose to listen to her.

Sapp. So Mrs. Estello left the smoking data disk in Joe's office and went out for a break.

And the dragon roared again. More red and orange streaked through the air, and another fire erupted on the far side of the department. Then the dragon whipped its tail around to spread the flames.

Now three or four little fires were beginning to burn, and Joe was too busy fighting the first fire to notice them. Actually, he was too busy enjoying the fight. It was fun being a fireman. In fact, he was not about to hand his hose or fireman's helmet over to anybody. Why should he? Wasn't this his job?

He just about had the first fire doused when he saw the smoke from the others. All of a sudden, fire fighting wasn't so much fun. He tried rushing back and forth between them, spraying one, then the next. But as soon as he turned his back, the fires burned up and up and out of control.

Ralph watched, waiting for someone to help Joe, but no one did. Joe Schmo may have been giving them little Zapps now and then, but who

were they to face invisible dragons and raging fires? Against those, they were still just a bunch of Sapped zombies.

All but oblivious to Joe's heroics, they kept doing what they normally did, or just stood around and basked in the heat while Joe ran from fire to fire and Mrs. Estello, back from her break, tagged along with her charred data disk, waiting for him to tell her what to do.

And the dragon grinned.

When Ralph came back to the normal world, they got together in Ralph's work area. Joe came in as sweaty and tired as a fireman could be—and more than a little impatient and frustrated.

"Ralph, this Zapp stuff isn't working," he complained. "I've got five normalators out there that won't pass inspection. Paperwork is backed up because Mrs. Estello doesn't have enough Zapp to figure out what's wrong with her word processor disk. And I'm too busy solving all the problems around here to Zapp anyone!"

But Ralph, after some talking, persuaded Joe to come have a look at what the dragon was doing.

By then, having had its fun, the dragon had deposited a few eggs to hatch sometime later, incubated by the heat of smoldering fires, and wandered on.

Its trail was easy to follow. In department after department, the supervisors and managers were the ones fighting the fires, figuring out the problems, straightening out the dragon's mayhem. . . .

Then, from down the corridor, came the sirens. It was the executive fire truck, gleefully driven by Mary Ellen Krabofski herself, trollish as ever, her fire-engine red fingernails curled around the steering wheel.

Riding the truck with her was the entire executive volunteer fire brigade. "Fire Expert," it said in bold gold letters on each of their slickers.

Mary Ellen brought the fire truck screeching to a halt and hopped out. The first thing she did was run over and take the fire hose out of a department manager's hands.

"Gimme that," she said.

Sapp.

And what did the expert fire fighters do? First they ran around the truck half a dozen times, chasing everybody away.

Sapp. Sapp. Sapp.

Then they grabbed the buckets and started splashing water.

From down the hall where the fire truck had come, there now came a clatter of hooves. Yes, it was a knight in shining armor on a white horse.

The knight rode up to Mary Ellen.

"Hi, I'm Hugh Galahad, Mother Dragon Specialist," he said.

"About time you got here," she said.

"Wow, looks like you've got a big one," said the knight.

"We know that," said Mary Ellen, gesturing with the fire hose in hand. "Now go slay it or I'll rust your armor."

Without even pausing to ask anyone where the dragon might be, the knight dropped his visor, lowered the point of his lance, and charged into the smoke. Unfortunately, his visibility limited by the tiny slits in the visor, the knight galloped right past the dragon and speared two of the workers.

And the dragon slipped out the fire escape. It headed for the executive floor, figuring to spit some sparks under the carpets while no one was around.

Ralph and Joe followed at a discreet distance.

Of course, Department Z was not exempt from visitations by the monsters and calamities of business. Eventually the mother dragon came down the hall toward Department Z, as invisible to Lucy Storm as it was to anyone in the normal world.

Joe and Ralph arrived just after the dragon had entered Department Z. As elsewhere, it huffed and puffed and breathed fire right into the middle of things.

But Lucy did not try to solve the problem of the dragon on her own. She did not put on armor and fight the dragon, or put on a fire helmet and fight the fire.

At the first whiff of smoke, she went to the person nearest the fire hose and, lightning bolt forming in her hand, said, "We have a problem. I'd like your help. . . ."

Zapp! And that person picked up the fire hose and figured out how to fight the fire.

Lucy pulled some others together into a group and said, "We have a big problem and I'd like all of your help. . . ."

Zapp! Zapp! Zapp!

Those people then started talking among themselves about what to do, while Lucy went back to check on the fire. By the time she returned, they had an action plan worked out.

At a nod from Lucy, some of them put on fire helmets. Then Lucy got them some fire extinguishers and they went to work on the new fires the dragon was starting.

The rest of the group put on armor and went to chase the dragon. Unlike many previous dragons, this one was too big for them to slay or tame on their own, but they did succeed in harassing it into leaving. (And it did not take so very long, because dragons, as you know, prefer dark and foggy places to lay their eggs, and there was too much energy and light in Department Z for it to linger long or lay many eggs.)

Meanwhile, Lucy had gone around to every other person in Department Z and said, "We're trying to solve a problem and I'd like your help. . . . "

Zapp! And each of the people had filled in here and there for the others so that the regular work got done.

After it was gone, it was clear that the dragon had not Sapped the department. With an abundance of Zapp, it had been a lot like fighting fire with fire. In fact, the Zapp now glowed even brighter than before; people were charged up by having met the challenge.

Watching it all, Joe realized that Zapp did work. He simply did not yet have enough of it in his department and he was not yet using it fully.

Just as he and Ralph were about to leave, Hugh Galahad charged into the department. Lucy Storm had to hurry over and grab the reins before he carelessly speared one of her workers.

"Whoa!" she said. "Can I help you with something?"

Joe Schmo's Notebook

The first three steps to Zapp:
- Maintain people's self-esteem.
- Listen and respond with empathy.
- Ask for help in solving problems.

They lead to the soul of Zapp:
- Offer help without taking responsibility.

One afternoon on his way home, Joe finally admitted something to himself he really didn't want to.

He was finding it harder, not easier, to keep people Zapped as time went on.

He was using everything he already knew, but he could not get the kind of quantum improvement in involvement and performance he had been getting before. Zapp as he would, he even found the overall lightning level falling off just a little. And he knew it even without Ralph telling him the exact measurements.

"Well, maybe we've reached the limits," Joe thought. "Maybe this is as good as it gets."

About a week later, Ralph came into Joe Schmo's office with a copy of the *The Normal News,* the company newspaper, and said, "Hey, Joe, have you seen this?"

On the front page was a story that read:

Department Z Paves Way To Rewarding New Business For Normal

Normal Vice President Mary Ellen Krabofski congratulated Department Z's Lucy Storm and a group of employees who call themselves the "Diamond Team" for developing what is expected to be a profitable new business for the Normal Co.

"Fire up that machine of yours and let's go find out what they're doing," said Joe.

When they got to Department Z, everything at first looked about the same as always. Lucy was walking around in her wizard hat and the usual miraculous things were going on. Then Ralph started getting a very strong reading on his Zappometer.

"Look at this, Joe. Department Z is running at 100 bolts an hour!" said Ralph. "The best we've ever done is 75."

"How could that be?" asked Joe Schmo. "We were the same just a little while ago."

"What can I say?" said Ralph. "The Zappometer does not lie."

Then Ralph saw that new, strange kind of lightning he noticed the day Lucy Storm had bumped into him. It came from a group working on the far side of the bottomless chasm.

Joe and Ralph moved closer to the new lightning, and as they did, the Zappometer went off the scale.

But they didn't need an instrument to tell them they were seeing something different from the usual Zapp they were accustomed to seeing.

Because this was a wheel of lightning.

There was the Diamond Team working on their gem-encrusted mountain. The hot-air balloon they had first used to get across the chasm hung limply from a rocky ledge, discarded on the other side and swaying in the 12th Dimension breeze. The team now had built a bridge across the chasm.

This wheel of Zapp ran round and round between them, both directions at once, and back and forth over the diameter of the group as they worked.

The kind of Zapp that Ralph and Joe had been used to seeing in the 12th Dimension was mostly the simple, linear kind. That is, it sparked from the person in charge to the person working for the person in charge—Joe to Ralph or from Joe to Mrs. Estello. It did not go round and round, from one person to the next to the next, and back and forth through the group.

But this Zapp did.

"So what is it?" Joe Schmo asked.

"Gee, I don't know," said Ralph. "It must be because of the work team we read about in *The Normal News.*"

"What could be enZapping about a work team?" Joe Schmo wondered. "They've been tried before."

"What I want to know," said Ralph, "is what's making it happen? Lucy is way over there. She's not around to do the Zapping."

And that was the other very unusual thing about this type of Zapp. It seemed to have no single source, but instead was generated by the group itself.

Joe Schmo watched the wheel of Zapp and knew there was more to Zapp than was yet known. Could Zapping people in teams be the next step?

It couldn't be too hard to set up some teams, Joe reasoned. That night, he went over the list of employees in Department N and divided them into teams. The next day, he came to work and told everybody which teams they were on. Then he asked Ralph to monitor what happened.

A few days later, Ralph came in to announce that the Zapp count had risen. It was now up to 76 bolts per hour instead of 75.

"Is that all?" said Joe Schmo. "OK, Ralph, I'd like your help finding out what's wrong with our teams."

After some investigating, Ralph determined that the teams were not really teams. The Zapp still flowed from Joe Schmo to each individual, rather than around and among the people in the group.

"You might be calling them teams," said Ralph, "but the people in them have no more sense of involvement than if they were just a bunch of men and women working next to each other. They're teams in name only."

"Then how come the teams in De-partment Z are enZapping and ours are not?" Joe wondered out loud.

The phone rang.

"Because ours aren't your normal work teams," said Lucy Storm when Joe Schmo answered the call. "Our teams are Zapped. . . . "

Reprinted from TRAINING, April 1989

HOW TO MANAGE WILD DUCKS

They're the independent, innovative people you often find in R&D. What makes them tick? And how do you get them to fly in formation?

BY BEVERLY GEBER

Credit Thomas J. Watson Jr. with the term. The former chairman of IBM Corp. liked to tell a little parable about wild ducks. Normally, he said, ducks fly south for the winter. But one autumn, a duck lover fed them lavishly as they stopped to rest along the way. The ducks lingered and he kept doling out food. Seduced by the comfort and security of being fed three square meals a day without the necessity of foraging in brush, the ducks didn't bother to fly south. Years passed. Some of the ducks grew so fat and langorous they could barely fly. No longer were they magnificent wild ducks. They were kept pets.

The lesson? You can tame wild ducks but you can't make tamed ducks wild again. Watson thought the story had special meaning for IBM, a company that flourished on the strength of its technological innovations. Watson knew that technological breakthroughs came most often from the company's "wild ducks": those quirky, individualistic, highly intelligent employees who ignore bureaucratic procedures, shun set schedules and resist attempts to make them more "efficient." In a corporate environment in which the de facto uniform was a dark blue suit and white shirt, Watson felt it was imperative that the company create and maintain an atmosphere in which wild ducks could thrive.

That's the challenge that faces organizations today, whether they are technological giants like IBM or wee companies that produce $1.99 widgets. Wild ducks can nest in just about any department in just about any kind of organization. They might be scientists, advertising copywriters, engineers or newspaper reporters. But no matter where you find them, the management problem remains the same: How do you refrain from taming those wild ducks yet still keep them flying in formation?

Many companies these days refer to this challenge as "managing innovation." They want the most innovation in the least amount of time from their most creative people. The philosophy of managing innovation is applied most frequently to research and development functions because the technical professionals—scientists and engineers—who work in R&D are considered the most likely candidates to be corporate wild ducks. The principles are strongly rooted in empowerment; you hear the term "self-management" quite often. Managing innovation means to create an environment that contains minimal constraints on creative freedom, but enough control to get results as quickly as possible.

Apple Computer CEO John Sculley described some of the elements of his recipe for nurturing creativity in an essay in his book *Odyssey: Pepsi to Apple*. For one thing, he says, you must allow—even celebrate—intelligent failure. Tell people which way to go but don't give them specific goals. Provide them with a warm, comfortable environment. Be generous with rewards and recognition. Make them accountable for results, but release them from rigid schedules. Finally, he says, organizations must encourage "contrarian" thinking. "There should be a level of tension between discipline and anarchy," he wrote. "I would worry if there weren't always a little bit of anarchy in the organization."

Examine Sculley's list and you might presume he was giving advice for managing any employee. Human resources development (HRD) practitioners could surely recite most of the list in their sleep. Is the management of wild ducks really any different from managing the rest of the aviary?

Bernard Rosenbaum, president of MOHR Development Inc., a consulting firm in Stamford, CT, believes there are significant differences. His company observed and interviewed more than 300 managers of technical employees at 19 high-technology companies over three years. Technical professionals are people whose needs for autonomy and for achievement are among the strongest in the occupational world, Rosenbaum says. Moreover, they are among the most likely groups of employees to resist organizational goals.

People who actually manage technical professionals often believe that doing so is much different from managing others. "Technical professionals are more self-directed," says Scott Beth, manager of project management training for Hewlett-Packard in Palo Alto, CA. "The motivation of the technical professional is different from [that of] someone who is involved in a more operational environment."

Who are these guys?

There are many species of wild ducks. You'll find them in professions such as engineering, pharmacy, architecture and all types of science. They're the people who design the innards of mainframe computers as well as the software that runs on personal computers. They figure out ways to make televisions with clearer pictures, car engines that produce more power with less mass, buildings that are beautiful but functional, or drugs that cure diseases. You probably have one for a neighbor.

In his book, *Clash of Cultures: Managers and Professionals,* Joseph A. Raelin suggests that "wild ducks" (or his more conservative term, "technical professionals") usually have a hard time nestling into an organization. It's almost inevitable that they will clash with management. The main reason is that technical professionals and professional managers tend to have vastly different backgrounds and orientations to their work.

Professionals, particularly those in the sciences, have spent years in school learning a professional discipline and becoming committed to its principles. They have overcome all manner of hurdles to enter an elite club. They are experts. It's vastly more important to them to be respected by their professional peers than to be admired by people in other departments in the organization. They are often loyal to their profession first and to the organization second. More than most other kinds of employees, they are wedded to their careers.

Managers lack a similar devotion to some firmly grounded set of professional principles. Witness all the management fads that come and go. Management is an art, not a science, and few practitioners can be considered "experts" in management. Consequently, managers are primarily committed to the success of the organization. Seldom do they have divided loyalties; it's hard for a manager to understand why a technical professional might have trouble supporting some goal or policy that the manager sees as good for the organization.

Stanley Gryskiewicz, director of the innovation and creativity group for the Center for Creative Leadership (CCL) in Greensboro, NC, believes that clashes can arise between managers and technical professionals partly because managers are geared to the present and science is oriented to the future. Scientists in basic research take a series of small, unhurried, incremental steps as they advance toward an indistinct goal. It's a process that can be maddening to managers concerned about more immediate concerns, such as quarterly profits.

In some companies, the clash isn't a severe problem, because most employees are technical professionals and most managers used to be. The culture of those organizations holds technical professionals in particularly high esteem. Dow Chemical, for instance, believes so strongly that R&D should propel the company that it promotes to top management only homegrown managers with technical backgrounds. That minimizes the chance that top management will kill projects that don't produce instant results.

At 15-year-old Microsoft in Redmond, WA, the culture created by founder William Gates III is aggressively pro-technology and mildly anti-management. Gates, a computer programmer himself, has nurtured a certain attitude. "Career managers aren't really the most happy people

---

Corporate 'wild ducks': those quirky, individualistic, highly intelligent employees who ignore bureaucracy, shun set schedules and resist efficiency.

---

around here," says John Prumatico, director of training and personnel administration. "Our development staff *is* the company. Everybody else supports that effort." Of Microsoft's 5,000 employees, about half are technical professionals.

All organizations try to manage potential clashes by doing all they can to get those professionals to understand the company's goals and what the organization is up against in the marketplace.

Rosenbaum believes it's necessary to broaden the technical professional's perspective. Give them the big picture and update it frequently. Get them to understand that R&D can't take place in a vacuum. He recalls one instance in which an engineer in a semiconductor manufacturing company was making a change to a part. "I finally realized that what was going to be done would cost $100,000 but the value to the customer was remote," Rosenbaum says. "The engineer was being elegant in his design, but it was overengi-neered. The engineer's goals were not the same as the organization's goals."

Don't imagine that all technical professionals have the tunnel vision of that engineer, who was more concerned with scientific perfection than organizational goals. Not all wild ducks are alike. Raelin argues that technical professionals are scattered along a spectrum. On one end are "cosmopolitans," the true wild ducks. These are people who would rather advance their professional reputations and scientific knowledge than advance within the company. They insist on deciding what they'll work on, and at what pace. Cosmopolitans get so much intrinsic satisfaction from the work they do that they would likely stay on the job even if the company cut their salaries. They can't imagine moving into another line of work. You'll frequently find these kinds of ducks in organizations that do basic research.

On the other end of the spectrum are what Raelin calls "locals." These are technical professionals whose bond to their profession is weaker. Their goals are more closely aligned to those of the company. Often their ambition is to win a promotion into management, rather than winning recognition from fellow professionals. These people most often settle into applied R&D operations that are geared specifically to producing a product.

Rosenbaum speculates that technical professionals probably start out with a tendency to be independent—maybe even a bit antisocial. "You're dealing with a population that is more comfortable with things than with people," he says. Schooling does nothing to temper that tendency. In the sciences, students learn to devise and conduct experiments on their own. They are coached by faculty advisers, but largely, research is a lonely activity; seldom does a university ask its students to form collaborative teams to conduct research.

Hitting home runs

Technical professionals arrive at companies with strong desires for autonomy and personal achievement. It's true that other types of employees like autonomy, too, but they don't demand it with quite the same tone of entitlement as does the technical professional. He's spent a great deal of time expanding his technical capabilities and he wants managers to stand back—way back—and let him use his skills.

The challenge for companies is to provide an environment that caters to those needs without tipping the balance into anarchy. In 1987, the Center for Creative Leadership tried to find out what kinds of things contributed to high creativity in R&D. The CCL's Gryskiewicz and Teresa Amabile conducted lengthy interviews with 120 R&D scientists in three large organizations. The scientists were asked to tell two stories, one illustrating a work event involving high creativity, and one illustrating low creativity. Gryskiewicz and Amabile analyzed the stories and found two broad sets of factors that could be stimulants or barriers to creativity. One set involved environmental factors, the other focused on personal characteristics of the scientists themselves. Environmental factors were mentioned much more frequently than personal qualities in both the high creativity and low creativity events.

High creativity events were stimulated by environmental factors such as sufficient resources and time, recognition and challenge. But the most commonly cited catalyst was freedom. Some scientists described that freedom as the ability to decide what they would work on. Others described autonomy as the ability to decide how they would achieve a goal that someone else set. Generally, they described autonomy as a sense of control over their work and ideas, and a freedom from constraints.

Autonomy is probably the most critical issue companies will address as they decide how to manage their technical professionals. Organizations are forever treading the fine line between stifling them and coaxing them to produce results as efficiently as possible. How much control can you exert and still expect wild ducks to fly?

The optimum degree of control is often a function of how wild the ducks are, the culture of the organization and the type of industry it's in. But generally, says Raelin, the best way to "control" technical professionals is to control the ends and not the means. All but the most independent of ducks will concede that it's the organization's prerogative to decide strategy. Top management should sketch broad outlines of what should be researched and what kinds of things should ultimately spring from that research.

But smart executives will always ask their technical professionals for advice in setting those goals. Then, when the goals are set, technical professionals will feel they had a hand in shaping them. Operational control, meaning the decision on how to reach a goal, should rest with the technical professionals themselves.

Johnson & Johnson subscribes to that theory, but allows individual technical managers to decide how much control to exert along the way, says Don Jones, director of R&D planning and administration for J&J Consumer Products Inc., in Skillman, NJ.

Cosmopolitans get so much intrinsic satisfaction from the work they do that they would likely stay on the job even if the company cut their salaries.

Usually, it works fine. J&J researchers know that the company is tightly focused on developing consumer products, not on basic research. They expect tighter control. Jones admits that on the few occasions when J&J has hired experienced university professors, who were used to following their noses in research, "the adjustment was not easy." It's much less sexy for researchers to develop a better Band-Aid than it is to invent an exotic new adhesive. J&J prefers to hire R&D professionals from other companies or to hire college graduates with bachelors' degrees and then develop them.

Even companies that develop fairly specific marketing objectives try to give their technical professionals as much leeway as possible in achieving them. Union Carbide Industrial Gases Inc., in Tarrytown, NY, wanted to increase the market for the gas argon. Management desired a large-scale application for the gas, says Frank Death, director of technology for the Linde Division of Union Carbide, but

didn't specify what kind of product should be developed. With that goal in mind, researchers came up with a process that is now one of the most commonly used ways to make high-alloy metals, such as stainless steel.

That kind of direction is fine if the researchers are pining to develop a new process that uses argon. But what if their passions lie in some kind of research that is marginally different? What if they have a wild idea for some new product or process tangential to the company's main business?

Some companies try to accommodate them by allowing a modest amount of discretionary time to work on things that interest them. That's one of the hallmarks of 3M Corp., which ranks second in innovativeness only to Merck Corp. in *Fortune* magazine's 1990 poll of America's most admired companies. 3M ranked third, behind Merck and Phillip Morris, in its ability to attract, develop and keep talented people—so apparently the St. Paul, MN-based company is doing something right. For the past four years, 3M has introduced about 200 new products annually. It spends 6.5 percent of its sales revenues on R&D, twice the average of U.S. companies, according to *Fortune*.

One of the ways 3M tries to blend autonomy with control is to allow its technical professionals to spend up to 15 percent of their time researching things that don't fit into the company's grand research plan—yet. That's how the now-ubiquitous Post-It note was invented.

Dean Ostlie, manager of technical management development, says it isn't always easy or possible to allow each professional that extra time, but "it's imperative [to do it] if you want to continue to keep the new ideas and the growth going." One reason 3M allows such latitude is that it's an excellent way to reach a corporate goal: No less than 25 percent of a division's annual sales must come from products developed in the previous five years.

3M, like many other companies with strong R&D functions, provides a pool of seed money for promising projects unrelated to its current crop of products. 3M's Genesis program will provide up to $50,000 annually to researchers who haven't been able to win funding from their business units. People who win those grants are afforded a great deal of operational freedom.

While it's necessary to have at least a few proven researchers squirreled off in a corner doing basic research, it's often impossible to give all—or even most—technical professionals discretionary time for nondirected research. The marketplace is so competitive, companies have become so lean, and product development cycles are so fast these days that companies simply can't spare the technical professional's time. At Genentech, the South San Francisco company that is a leader in the biotechnology field, the goal is to give researchers as much latitude as possible. The reality is that technical professionals usually find their discretionary time limited to Sunday afternoons, says Larry Setren, vice president of human resources.

When the company was first launched, the field was so new and so open that scientists felt free to follow their instincts in deciding what to research. In the early days, Setren says, there were lots of breakthroughs. But now all the "easy" discoveries in biotechnology have been made. The company has had to become much more focused on producing what the market wants.

One HRD director of a respected pharmaceutical company says it would be lovely to allow technical professionals to spend 15 percent of their time on self-directed research; but it also would be a hopeless luxury. "The scientists have all they can do just to produce what the company needs to survive in the next five to 10 years," he says.

Sterile buildings and dress codes

It may be impossible to give wild ducks abundant free time for discretionary research, but there are other ways to feed their needs. The CCL's study found that besides autonomy, technical professionals also crave encouragement and recognition.

Encouragement, according to Gryskiewicz and Amabile, means that an organization is open to new ideas and actively encourages them. A trademark of companies with good R&D departments is their insistence upon procedures such as peer review, in which projects are critiqued by knowledgeable professionals in the organization. As it happens, peer review also is one of the best ways to keep some control of a project without making the technical professional feel stifled.

Hewlett-Packard holds "code walkthroughs," in which programmers get together to go over a block of computer code to see if they can find ways to improve it. "The technical leader may not have the expertise or the time to review all the work," says Beth.

An organization's willingness to encourage technical professionals shows up starkly in its attitude toward failure. The best companies celebrate intelligent failure. Rosenbaum recommends that organizations announce the fact that the project didn't achieve its ends, but also explain how the research advanced knowledge on the

---

It's much less sexy for researchers to develop a better band-aid than it is to invent some exotic new adhesive.

---

topic.

"The last thing you want to do is to say, 'Well, that's too bad. Here's the next project,'" says Robert E. Bacon, manager of technical intelligence at the Eastman Kodak research labs in Rochester, NY.

One of the most important things organizations can do is to shower technical professionals with recognition. They thrive on it. Scientists, in particular, are accustomed to a professional climate in which they earn respect for published research results. Acclaim from outside peers is extremely important to them, says Rosenbaum. Whenever possible, organizations should allow scientists to publish the results of their work.

Sometimes, researchers make stunning discoveries but can't tell the world because the information is proprietary. Some of the bigger companies take pains to honor technical professionals inside the organization in much the same way they would be recognized outside. Each year, Dow Chemical holds an "Inventors Day" in which it fetes the researchers who developed

patents for the company in the previous year. And each of the company's research sites sponsors an annual juried technical symposium that is closed to the public.

Top achievers at 3M can be nominated by their peers to the Circle of Technical Excellence, an award to honor exceptional achievement during the previous year. And the Carlton Society is the ultimate recognition for 3M technical professionals. It's a corporate "hall of fame" for people who have made significant contributions to the company during their careers.

At IBM, where R&D's two goals are to be famous for science and feed the business goals of the company, top achievers are called fellows and are honored by a five-year grant to pursue whatever research strikes their fancy. There are about 50 fellows, who are chosen through a rigorous process and approved by the chairman of the board. "When you talk about recognition and accomplishment, that's the pinnacle," says Donna Granate, director of personnel for IBM's research division.

There are other ways that organizations can create environments that contribute to innovation. Genentech, which spends about 40 percent of its revenue on R&D, tries to recruit the most brilliant people it can find, because it knows that technical professionals want to work with the best researchers in the business. It doesn't hurt that the company exists to find cures for diseases; researchers often find that a powerful intrinsic motivator.

3M insists on keeping its business units small and decentralized, since large units begin to create the kind of bureaucracy that can curb autonomy. Some companies flatten hierarchies to a pancake or spin off subsidiaries as soon as they grow to a certain size. And for organizations that want to confer the same kind of compensation and prestige on exceptional technical professionals that they do on managers, dual career ladders are a must.

Organizations also must provide the resources that technical professionals need. More than half of the researchers who described highly creative events to the CCL researchers mentioned the fact that they had sufficient resources. This doesn't always mean an unlimited research budget. Researchers love to work in companies that maintain technical resource centers that rival university libraries.

Technical professionals also want to use the best equipment available. Dow Chemical considers itself the industry leader in the use of robotics in the lab, says Jack Hipple, laboratory director of applied engineering research and process development. Not only do researchers appreciate working with state-of-the-art equipment, but it makes their time more productive.

Technical professionals also can be sensitive to the kinds of facilities in which they are housed and the schedules they are expected to keep. Are they in sterile-looking buildings with administrators who get fussy when they tack things to the walls? Are they expected to meet dress codes and come to work every day?

Microsoft tries hard to keep things from becoming that rigid. It has no dress code and it expects researchers to work the hours that suit them. The company deliberately designed its offices to be the antithesis of the usual corporate head office. "We don't have a corporate headquarters. We have a corporate campus," says Prumatico. "We have individual offices and meeting rooms and eating areas designed in such a way that it looks like a fairly modern college campus."

Genentech's corporate headquarters has a similar look. Once a week, everybody gets together for a "ho-ho," a Friday afternoon beer bust that has been a tradition since the company was founded. The parties often have themes—one had a Latin theme, with a Carmen Miranda look-alike contest—and are seen as ways to blow off steam and let employees mingle with people in other divisions.

No more Einsteins

Dual career ladders, decentralization, awards and corporate campuses are fine as far as they go. But it isn't enough to structure an organization to encourage innovation. You also must have supervisors who do a good job of managing wild ducks and their work. This is one of the areas in which organizations face particular challenges, especially because of the way the technical professional's job has changed in the past few years.

Technical professionals are no longer latter-day Einsteins, off in secluded corners concocting unfathomable things alone. "The era of the individual contributor making a significant difference in a technological

organization is quickly coming to an end," says Rosenbaum. "Practically all of them operate in a matrix or project-management type of team structure."

Cross-functional teams are, naturally, more prevalent in applied R&D than in basic research. Not only does the team structure help speed up development cycles, it's another way to give an organization an air of smallness. Hewlett-Packard may have sites that employ thousands, but it tries to have its people work in small, close-knit teams often numbering no more than 15. The self-managed team is so

---

Scientists, in particular, are accustomed to a professional climate in which they earn respect for published research results.

---

much a part of the way R&D departments are organized these days that some large organizations hesitate to hire brilliant loners because they won't fit in.

"When I hire technical professionals, they must have the teamwork skills," says Hewlett-Packard's Beth. "We're moving away from the time when one project equals one product. Now we're moving to the time when several projects make up a product. A balance of technical expertise and teamwork skills is desired."

The CCL's Gryskiewicz says he sees a clear trend toward hiring technical professionals who are capable of working in teams or capable of learning how. That's not to say that all companies are adamant about it. Brilliant loners can still find work in some organizations that place a premium on pure research. Organizations simply find ways to accommodate them, through mentors or supervisors who exist mainly to buffer them from the rest of the organization.

Organizations spend a considerable amount of time these days putting their

technical professionals and supervisors through teamwork training. In the past, technical professionals never really needed to know such niceties as how to be assertive but not judgmental in a meeting, or how to give constructive feedback. The CCL offers a popular simulation for scientists and engineers that forces five or six team members to work through a compressed project from idea to implementation.

Besides teamwork training, organizations are also providing a great deal of training for supervisors of those technical wizards. "Managing innovation" is what they invariably call it. Setren says each Genentech technical manager will go through a course this year that teaches the principles of how to supervise technical professionals. In large part, the courses examine the things that motivate technical professionals—autonomy, challenge, a fascinating project, recognition from peers and so on.

During its study of technical leaders, MOHR Development Corp. distilled what it considered to be the best practices for supervising technical professionals. The best technical leaders, MOHR says, are coaches who listen, ask, facilitate, integrate and provide administrative support. They run interference with the organization and shelter the professional from red tape. They orchestrate professional development and expand individual productivity through teamwork. Finally, they allow self-management.

One might think that supervisors of technical professionals who were once technical professionals themselves would have a natural feel for all this. But technical supervisors sometimes overcontrol the work. Their expertise is still so rooted in the technical work that they want to butt into the details of the research, directing the technical professional down avenues of research he doesn't want to pursue. The technical leader could be motivated partly by a fear of becoming professionally obsolete; primarily though, the technical professional just doesn't know how to execute the softer skills of management.

The best way to supervise technical professionals, says Rosenbaum, is loosely. The emphasis should be on leading, not managing. The technical leader communicates the goals of the organization in as much detail as possible and gets the technical professional to set goals and rough timetables that correspond to the larger goals. Then, says Rosenbaum, the best technical leaders let the researchers self-manage their way to the result, either in groups or alone.

Progress reviews are necessary, of course, but the number of them depends on the project. "We can afford a lot of people playing around for a year," says Hipple. "When [projects] require more resources, then ideas are scrutinized a bit stronger to see whether there has been sufficient progress. But the trick is not to overmanage early on."

If possible, technical leaders should allow professionals to choose their own projects. That's important, because the single most frequently mentioned personal characteristic of researchers involved in highly creative events is intrinsic motivation, according to the CCL study. The scientists who described highly creative events reported an overwhelming interest in the work itself.

The CCL's Gryskiewicz says there are ways to allow that kind of freedom but still gently direct the researcher. He likens the exercise to a mountain climber leading an expedition who assembles some of the best climbers in the world. He might point out 10 different mountains they could climb and ask them which ones they wanted to climb. Or, Gryskiewicz says, the leader could point out the 10 mountains, then say, "I'm going for the second one. Who wants to come with me?" Using either method would give the technical professional some opportunity to work on something that excites her.

Genentech tries to coax its professionals into projects by holding symposia at which budding new projects are described. The company hopes that intrigued scientists will get together and form a project team. "You can't tell scientists, 'You will turn this into a project.'" Setren says. "You show it to scientists and they will get passionate about it or not."

Passionate is probably an apt adjective to describe technical professionals. They can be some of the most productive and innovative people in the organization, if they're treated right. Wild ducks are essential to most organizations. But remember the warning from IBM's Watson: Don't tame them.

Reprinted from TRAINING, May 1990

TWO WAYS TO THE TOP?

Parallel career paths allow both managers and technical specialists to climb the organizational ladder. Nice idea, but what goes on in the real world?

BY DALE FEUER

J im is a physicist. He works for a major research-and-development company on the East Coast. Having reached the top level as a technical specialist in his organization after only four years with the company. Jim realized that the only way to get ahead now is to take a management job. It would mean a promotion, a bigger office and a fatter paycheck, but it would also mean giving up what he likes best about his work.

"I enjoy working in the lab and being in close touch with scientific developments," he says. "I even like the hands-on, mechanical part of the job. I know of a few top managers who maintain their own labs with technicians supporting them, but I don't know how often they actually get in there themselves."

Professional organizations such as the American Physical Society or the Institute of Electrical Electronic Engineers offer people like Jim alternative sources of recognition and reward. Jim can join, present papers, run for office and generally improve his stature in the scientific community. But that won't change the fact that he makes about half as much money as a full-time manager in his company or that his career as a specialist has virtually plateaued.

The career development supervisor at the company where Jim works explains the dilemma facing technical professionals who want to remain "individual contributors" instead of going into management. "People wonder what's wrong with you if you don't get promoted in a certain amount of time. Saying, 'Look, I don't want it,' takes a degree of chutzpah."

But what's even more difficult for Jim to reconcile at this stage in his career is the major shift in values that a move into management would demand.

The conflict between "scientific" and "economic" values is aptly described by Raymond Hill, an associate professor of behavioral science at the University of Michigan: "In management, the pressure is for short-term results and profitability. In the world of science, freedom and long-term pursuits are paramount. Scientists are not as concerned about economic efficiency. Most people go one way or the other."

Judy Baker, director of human resources at Cray Research, the Minneapolis-based manufacturer of supercomputers, contends that the transition from individual contributor to manager is more difficult than the reverse. "It is difficult to change from an internal, personal perspective. Management doesn't seem like real work until you find out what it is."

"Most professional individual contributors have more of a personal-development orientation," says Sam Campbell, a former "fellow" (well-paid, senior-level nonmanagement specialist) at Honeywell Corp. "They think about honing their skills toward mastering a craft. Managers are more concerned with vertical growth; they think about advancing in their careers."

"Technical specialists are interested in doing what they do better," Hill echoes. "They care deeply about autonomy, and they don't like intrusions." And if it's two things that managers must tolerate, it's working with others and the countless distractions that go along with supervision.

The dual ladder system

"Often, technical experts make atrocious managers," says Jim Lenarz, a Minneapolis human-resource consultant who has helped several companies select and develop technical managers. "They are so task-oriented that they don't handle management responsibility well." Similarly, super salespeople frequently falter when promoted into management ranks, because they lack interest and/or ability in budgeting, coaching, recruiting and other management roles. The same principle applies in the case of star accountants, lawyers and trainers; excellence in a functional specialty does not a great manager make.

Nevertheless, these are people who make valuable contributions in their areas of expertise, people who might very well leave their companies for better career opportunities elsewhere. Jim Metts, vice president of human resources at H. B. Fuller Co., a multinational chemical manufacturing company, says that good chemists were leaving the company because managers were the only ones who were financially motivated to excel. "Our technical workers concluded that in order to get ahead, they had to get out of the lab. And that caused a brain drain on our most critical resource."

In an attempt to retain valuable contributors and to promote technical and professional excellence, a number of organizations have set up separate-but-equal career ladders for nonmanagement employees so that grade levels, pay ranges, recognition and rewards for these people correspond to positions in the management hierarchy.

Some companies, like IBM and Control Data Corp., have had parallel career ladders for years. Others, like H. B. Fuller, have only recently put them in place. Pressure to thin management ranks, stimulate technical innovation in an increasingly competitive marketplace and appease a work force that demands more intrinsic rewards from work than ever before have combined to create widespread interest in the parallel-career-ladder concept.

How well does the idea of separate-but-equal career paths translate into practice? Here is a sampling of organizations that have some kind of formal, alternative career path for their nonmanagement employees. As you'll see, the rules, conditions and reasons for implementing parallel systems vary all over the map.

IBM CORP.

An organization decidedly driven by technological expertise, this corporate giant has had a dual ladder system for its engineers, programmers and scientists for more than 30 years. Of 400,000 employees worldwide, about 100,000 are technical professionals. "We encourage people to pursue the nonmanagement ladder," says George Howie, director of technical professional programs. "There are some who clearly belong there."

At IBM, all employees must advance through three levels before they even arrive at the fork in the career path. At that fourth platform, they must decide whether to start up the management or nonmanagement ladder, each of which has three "reasonably equitable" rungs. "Essentially, we pay people the same at corresponding levels—the ranges are the same," Howie says.

Employees on the technical ladder are promoted if they are performing well in their current jobs *and* if an opening exists at the next level. "Typically, if you're that good, we will find you a job with added responsibilities. In other words, you won't have to wait forever to get a promotion," says Howie.

"If you're truly exceptional," he continues, "you can be promoted to senior technical staff member [the top rung on the nonmanagement ladder]." The line manager nominates the senior staff member for this position; the division president, who may manage up to 20,000 employees, ap-

proves the nomination; and the corporate staff head grants the final approval.

Beyond the top of the technical ladder is a position so exalted that it is as much an award as it is a promotion. Every year, two to five candidates for the role of IBM fellow are considered by a committee of 12 senior technical managers. "Fellows are chosen on the basis of existing and sustained outstanding performance over a period of time," says Howie. "Some people have made it reasonably early in their careers."

Named by the chief executive officer and paid at the executive level, fellows are financed by the company for five full years and given as much autonomy as they desire. "Some take their five years of freedom to pursue a pet project," Howie explains, "while others don't even change their jobs." After the five years are up, IBM fellows are free to request a continuation of their projects, return to management jobs or choose among a number of other options. Whatever they decide, they remain fellows for as long as they stay with the company. Currently, IBM employs 55 fellows in various areas of the company.

In addition to opportunities for advancement, IBM offers technical professionals financial awards for valuable individual contributions. These bonuses range from informal awards of $100 and dinner for two to formal presentations of $25,000. "If someone gets $10,000 or more," says Howie, "we gather everyone in the department together and tell them." This type of recognition is designed to publicize the awards. "We want to know if someone has been overlooked," he adds. "We will check into it, and we'll give it to them if we find that they deserve it."

ITT

At ITT, the parallel ladder system is an option for any of the corporation's numerous operating companies worldwide. To aid the individual organization that wants to introduce a dual ladder, the corporation has issued a generic set of guidelines.

Sarah Armstrong, director of employee compensation, describes the essential requirements of a parallel ladder at ITT. Dual ladders, she says, must be analogous in terms of height, importance to the organization, recognition and rewards. They also must

provide a path for progressive achievement, with "rungs" that represent meaningful distinctions between levels. In order for the parallel ladder system to work, Armstrong asserts, people in the top spots on both ladders must have input into strategic and policy decisions.

"We certainly have taken the parallel ladder system seriously here. But the response has been mixed," says Armstrong. "It has been fully implemented in a couple of businesses overseas, and several domestic operations have implemented plans locally; that means there are lots of variations." On paper, Armstrong explains, it looks as though ITT has a complete and comprehensive parallel career program in all of its companies. But, as might be expected, the company is not as far along in installing the parallel ladders as it is in conceptualizing the master plan.

"Certainly, there are some companies where it's not necessary, and therefore not appropriate. For instance, in some of our smaller, more manufacturing-oriented companies, the need for high-level specialty work is not that great.

"It's not that parallel ladders only exist in high-tech businesses. Some occur in low-tech organizations. For instance, the MIS functions within [ITT's] Sheraton Hotel chain and Hartford Insurance group have dual ladders. In these industries, MIS is about the only technical part of the business—an island of technology."

Where dual ladders do exist, Armstrong says, it helps to have a formal system whereby the individual contributor can influence strategy and be involved in decision-making. At ITT's Advanced Technology Center in Shelton, CT, for example, senior technical leaders sit on the committee that recommends strategy and allocates resources. "First you must figure out what the particular decision-making process is in the company, and then you decide how to incorporate technical people into this process. Maybe it means including senior-level nonmanagers in the general managers' staff meetings."

In addition to the parallel-career-path option, ITT also offers special awards for individual contributors. Employees who want to work on a project that doesn't fit well with their existing job can submit a proposal to a selection committee composed of senior managers. If the proposal is accepted, ITT will fund the project for up to one year, covering the person's salary, requested budget, travel expenses, support resources, etc.

CONTROL DATA CORP.

According to Jim Stathopoulos, vice president of corporate personnel services, Control Data Corp. (CDC) initiated parallel ladders for all job families more than two decades ago because "we needed individual expertise in all areas of the organization. If you cut off employees' opportunities to advance, you truncate their ability to contribute. And they might go to another company where they can do what they want to do."

Although CDC does have separate career paths for nontechnical professionals—lawyers, purchasing personnel, compensation administrators, etc.—"the system works better, in terms of numbers, with technical jobs," says Stathopoulos. "We have 300 to 400 technical professionals in middle management grades and pay ranges who don't have people reporting to them. Joe Mcgregor, general manager of human resources planning, reports that middle managers outnumber "consultants" (the nonmanagement title corresponding to manager) by about two to one.

At CDC, job titles, grading systems and pay ranges vary by department and by job family. Therefore, a consultant in purchasing or a manager of a clerical staff might make less than a senior engineer. Or a newly hired engineer might earn more than a plant foreman. "The ceiling or height of the particular dual ladder is based on a combination of the size of the individual's contribution and the person's market value," Stathopoulos explains. "Technical experts draw bigger salaries these days."

Another complicating factor is that people can switch back and forth between the management and consultant tracks. Stathopoulos himself is leaving his present job as manager of 120 employees to take a consulting position in which he will have only one person reporting to him. "Our dual path isn't a very discrete thing," notes Mcgregor. "In reality, there are alternative paths and a lot of crossover."

ATLANTIC RICHFIELD CO.

In use since 1983, Atlantic Rich-field's Technical Career Program was loosely modeled after IBM's parallel ladder system, according to compensation consultant Jerry Frank. The program features four generic positions—advisor, senior advisor, distinguished advisor and executive advisor—for engineers, scientists, geologists and other research-and-development employees. These non-management rungs correspond to middle-management through executive levels, with individual operating companies supplying the specific qualification criteria and job descriptions for each technical rung. So far, approximately 40 technical employees have made it to one of the four levels on the technical ladder.

Executive advisors "basically get a blank check for doing whatever they want to do," says Frank. "They must have done something extraordinary or have the potential to do so. One research chemist developed a friction-reducing substance that increases the flow through the Alaska pipeline. Now he's working on something to make the refinery process more productive. If he has to take a cruise around the world to think about it, the company would probably let him do that."

People on the technical career ladder are, however, evaluated constantly. "If they are not making the kind of contribution they are expected to make, then they are taken off the technical ladder," says Frank.

H. B. FULLER CO.

Just six months ago, the H. B. Fuller Co. implemented a dual ladder for its technical employees worldwide. "We place a high premium on technical excellence," says Jim Metts. "We felt we weren't doing enough to minimize the roadblocks to technological breakthroughs. We built a new lab and sustained the budget for technical research, but failed to enhance the salaries of our technical experts."

Now, technical specialists can become research, senior or principal fellows—positions that correspond to high-level operating managers—based on their past, present and potential technological contributions.

"For research and development types, we tend to weigh past performance more heavily," Metts says. "That's because results in this area aren't seen so fast."

For the first time in the company's history, technical people are eligible for the bonus plan. While promotions into fellow positions (only two so far) are formally recognized by the company, bonus awards are kept personal and low-key, in contrast with the hoopla surrounding large cash awards at IBM. "We consciously decided not to 'anoint' those who get bonuses. It will change every year, and the same person may not receive it again. Also, the budget for bonuses may be down next year," says Metts.

CRAY RESEARCH INC.

"Like almost anything here," says Judy Baker, "the dual ladder system is somewhat less than formal. It's our policy not to have policy. But the system is practiced; it is real."

The career of the company's founder, Seymour Cray, is, in a sense, the epitome of the dual career path. Baker explains, "He decided he didn't want to manage the company and became the senior technical guy. Ultimately, he chose not to be an employee at all." Although still a director and member of the executive committee, Cray works for the company as an external consultant.

"A senior technical contributor can certainly do as well here as a manager. In fact, recognition and reward are heavily weighted to the technical side. But that's because we're a technologically driven company."

Although Cray Research is still small—3,000 employees worldwide—and has only a 13-year history, movement between management and individual-contributor status has been fairly common, Baker says. "I feel confident that if I didn't want to be director of human resources anymore, I could move into a consulting role. Lateral movement is an accepted practice."

HONEYWELL CORP.

Begun eight years ago as a way of recognizing and rewarding technological achievement, Honeywell's parallel career system, known as the "Fellows Program," recently expanded to include all professional jobs within the company's domestic operations. "As people learn more about how to do their jobs better, they should be rewarded, whether or not they go into management," says David Dotlich, vice president of human resources planning and development.

"Not everyone is born and raised

to be a manager; there are individual differences . . . . There is nothing worse than taking a technical expert, forcing him into management and having a lousy manager as a result. Long-term, as the organization flattens out, the dual ladder system will be critical to our success," Dotlich predicts.

Honeywell has 109 fellows, two of whom are human resource specialists. In addition, the company is currently considering a nominee from the information systems area. Fellows often have salaries, budgets and offices as large as those of senior managers at the division level, but they never make as much as the company's top-level executives. Current considerations with regard to the dual ladder system: Should it go higher on the technical side? Is the total number of fellows unduly restricted?

Culture

Most people who have had experience with parallel ladders will tell you that the success of the system hinges on how compatible the concept is with the organization's culture. Hewlett-Packard, for example, is one high-tech company where the corporate culture does not reinforce the idea of the dual track.

"We really don't have dual paths, but the system is sufficiently flexible that a scientist can earn as much as someone in the first two or three levels of management," says Ray Price, Hewlett-Packard's manager of engineer training. "We don't encourage our technical people to pursue the nonmanagerial path, however, because we want them to be the managers of our company."

HP's manager of executive development, Sandy Mobley, explains why the company doesn't support a dual ladder system: "We're so focused on teamwork here that it would go against our philosophy to reward someone too much for an individual contribution. We feel that at some point, no one person can make as strong a contribution as an individual who can manage a team and lead them to achieving the goals of the company."

Contrast this to the corporate culture at Cray Research, where a premium is placed on diversity and individual perspective. "If we were driven by something other than technology, like marketing, it would be more difficult," says Judy Baker. "But the culture of the organization supports it. The 'Cray style' emphasizes the individual contributor. We believe that people should be free to try

HOW TO TORPEDO A DUAL LADDER SYSTEM

BY DALE FEUER

Many a well-intended dual ladder system has fallen by the wayside. Sometimes, it's because such a system is inappropriate for the organization in the first place, due to the nature of its business, corporate culture or employee population. But even when an organization is an ideal candidate for a dual ladder, several pitfalls still exist.

The number one reason dual ladders fail? They are frequently misused as dumping grounds for incompetent managers. According to ITT's director of employee compensation, Sarah Armstrong, whenever the parallel ladder is introduced, people's first reaction is " 'Oh, this is a wonderful solution for old Charlie,' who's been an engineering manager for 10 weeks or 10 years and who doesn't get along well with people or isn't a good finance man or whatever." Putting old Charlie on the nonmanagement track is the worst thing you can do, says Armstrong. "It completely devalues the ladder."

Another common mistake that undermines the credibility of the dual ladder is to establish career paths that are separate but *not* equal in terms of compensation, recognition or responsibility. In some cases, the company merely gives the impression of advancement opportunities by creating new titles and higher positions on the nonmanagement ladder without offering proportionately larger salaries.

Conversely, outstanding individual contributors may get hefty raises without taking on greater responsibility. "You have to make sure that the size of the contribution is as great for nonmanagers as it is for managers. They have to have the same equity in the company," says Sandy Mobley, manager of executive development at Hewlett-Packard.

In short, there must be meaningful and analogous distinctions between the rungs of the parallel ladders. Unfortunately, says Brigham Young University professor Paul Thompson, "People on the science/technical ladder begin to be paid more on the basis of seniority than on the basis of technological contribution, and that has torpedoed many dual career systems. Managers are measured in terms of short-term goal achievement and return on investment. It's difficult to reward technological contribution, which may take five to 10 years to pay off, with the same degree of certainty."

Personnel consultant Jim Lenarz says that nonmanagement ladder climbers may not get sufficient resources to pursue their projects. "All too often, technical people at high levels don't have the resources that managers at equivalent levels have, especially in terms of support staff and discretionary time. The reality is in many cases that you've still got a boss somewhere who wants your time."

Finally, experts agree that any dual career system is doomed if top management doesn't get behind it all the way. In part, this means setting realistic standards for technological or individual professional achievement. If the criteria for promotion onto the nonmanagement ladder virtually require candidates to walk on water, then the whole setup is a charade. Says Sam Campbell, a recently retired Honeywell fellow (the top-level nonmanagement position in the company): "There are a lot of very talented people in the corporation—masters in their fields—who have never made it into the fellows ranks. That's because there's a lid on it. It costs a lot of money."

Reprinted from TRAINING, February 1986

out new things without leaving the company."

Atlantic Richfield's Frank points out, "You have to recognize that [a dual ladder] means that you're putting people into boxes and paying them to think, whether or not they get immediate results. If you have an MBO [management by objectives] program, a dual ladder might not function. The top guy doesn't always know what he's doing next."

Cultural considerations extend beyond corporate walls to national boundaries. "It's also a cross-cultural issue," says ITT's Armstrong. "We've had an impossible time even discussing [the parallel ladder system] in Germany, where very traditional hierarchical organizational structures prevail. In Spain and Italy, it has been much less of an issue." And in U.S. organizations, she adds, where organizational structures vary from traditional to unorthodox, so does the status afforded management and nonmanagement positions.

A management bias

Some experts argue that because most organizations implicitly value short-term economic success, dual ladder systems are usually biased toward the management side. Consultant Jim Lenarz puts it like this: "In our capitalist system, when a company has a bunch of stock owners looking for short-term gain, a guy with his own lab somewhere doing his own research is not going to pay off.

"My acid test for whether a dual ladder really exists is to look at the numbers on each side. If you have two or three people on the technical side vs. 100 to 150 on the management side, then managers still control the system," he continues.

"The culture in most companies is dominated by economic values," says the University of Michigan's Hill. "Even with dual ladders, technical professionals still feel like a cultural minority."

The people at Hewlett-Packard are quite candid about their management bias. Clearly, technical employees are encouraged to choose careers in management. "And not very subtly, either," says Ray Price. "At HP, you are paid to apply your knowledge in an economic manner, and managers are in a better position to do that."

To have a balanced and effective parallel system, Lenarz says, "you have to have peer involvement, peer control and peer nomination. You've also got to give some decision-making power to the people on the technical ladder."

The problem is that individual contributor types typically don't want to attend lots of meetings and work out strategies for the long-range success of the company, according to Lenarz. In his work with technical specialists at a large Midwestern electronic systems company, Lenarz observed that "the technical people didn't tend to see themselves as corporate citizens. They didn't seem to even understand the big picture or want to take responsibility for identifying leading-edge opportunities."

Peter Krembs, a Minneapolis-based consultant who has worked with Lenarz, concurs. "One of the most difficult aspects of getting technical people to become managers is changing their perspective from an interest in individual achievement to one of exerting influence. For many of them, exerting influence over others is associated with a lot of negative imagery."

Honeywell's Dotlich disagrees about the basic nature of the individual contributor. He says that during the last few years, Honeywell fellows have organized themselves in an attempt to be more effective in influencing strategy. "Empowerment is a big issue for them. Being part of management discussions is often the biggest reward for technical people," he says.

Paul Thompson, a management professor from Brigham Young University who has developed a four-stage model of professional development that applies to managers as well as nonmanagers, also believes that the balance of power between managers and individual contributors is crucial to the success of a dual ladder system. "Nonmanagement professionals often complain that they have the title and the salary, but no involvement in the decision-making process."

Many organizations have failed in their attempts to install dual ladder programs, Thompson says, because "the programs have dichotomized the technical and the managerial roles." Senior-level employees, whether they are managers or nonmanagers, must train and develop others, deal with people on the outside, and influence the direction of important projects and activities. These responsibilities are a function of the skills and experience of people in advanced stages of their careers, not merely exclusive obligations of those in the management ranks.

If dual ladders do create artificial distinctions between the roles and responsibilities of managers and nonmanagers, as Thompson and others suggest, then the argument that they also restrict career choices is the follow-up. In many systems, crossover between the two ladders is not possible once the professional gets to a certain level. Technical managers, for instance, eventually lose touch with the state-of-the-art technical developments in their fields.

"In any specialty, there is probably a 'drop-dead' time," says Cray's Baker. "For instance, an engineer with a design specialty may decide to go into management and then switch back two years later. In five years, that might not be possible. They say the half-life of an engineer's knowledge is two-and-a-half years."

Conversely, Krembs points out, "Technical experts can lock themselves out of management by pursuing the technical ladder unless they are willing to take a huge cut in pay, starting off as new managers. The key is not to develop a system that locks people into tracks, but one that maximizes career options."

Todd White, president of Blessing White, a firm that specializes in career planning and counseling, also believes that career paths tend to limit a person's awareness of the possibilities. "Because of reorganization, change and unanticipated opportunities," he says, "the notion of a career—if you do job 'a', 'b' and 'c', it will lead to job 'd'—has the effect of narrowing people's perspective. All of a sudden job 'l' comes along, and they're not ready for it."

Is it worth it?

Probably the biggest reason that organizations don't initiate parallel ladders is the cost: Installing those other escalators means upgrading the pay ranges for one or more groups of employees. In organizations where managers earn substantially more than senior individual contributors, dual ladders would significantly boost payroll expenses.

On the other hand, when good people leave the company because they have little or no opportunity for advancement, turnover and training costs add up. The process of identifying and selecting new qualified people isn't cheap either. "You can easily spend anywhere from $5,000 to $25,000 on recruiting a technical specialist," Baker asserts. And let's not forget what may be the greatest, albeit immeasurable, cost of not implementing a dual ladder—falling behind in the competitive marketplace because of a lack of innovation and lackluster technical and professional performance.

According to ITT's Armstrong, all organizations should consider two critical questions before implementing a dual ladder system: Do you have enough candidates for the second ladder to justify setting one up? Can the job be graded highly enough through the job description and evaluation process without setting up a parallel career ladder?

Even more basic, she says, is this one: "Are you doing functional work, be it legal, human resource or scientific, that is at such a level of specialty that you need a separate, high-level status and pay scale to reward the individual contributor and entice him to stay?"

IBM is one company for which the last answer is an unmitigated "yes." But IBM's Howie warns that the undertaking is not a trivial one. "If you're going to do it," he advises, "top management must be committed to it. Early on, it takes a lot of reinforcement. But after a while it becomes natural. It's not painless, but if you're willing to take some pain, it can work."

Reprinted from TRAINING, February 1986

BEYOND TEAMWORK

All 'teams' are not created equal. At some companies, workers really do run their own show—sometimes with spectacular results

BY CHRIS LEE

A potential customer approached a Wisconsin food-processing company with an offer to buy large quantities of the company's product on a regular basis. This was an attractive proposition except for one problem: The company couldn't handle the job with its existing production capacity.

Ordinarily, a CEO would consider the pros and cons of stretching production capacity, then bestow a decision on the employees. Instead, the president of this company called a meeting of all the team members—workers, that is—in the plant that would manufacture the product. He gave them every scrap of information about the situation that he possessed. He pointed out that to supply this large customer, the company would have to make a capital investment in new equipment. The workers, at least initially, would have to put in grueling seven-day weeks, although the new business eventually would boost profits and increase everybody's bonuses. He asked them to ponder the benefits and drawbacks to tackling the job. Then he left the decision up to them. After 10 days of deliberations, the teams decided to go ahead and do it.

To anyone familiar with the workings of the decision-making process in the average American company, this probably sounds like a utopian fiction concocted by some impractical dreamer who has never been eyeball-to-eyeball with a real business decision. But there's nothing fictional about it. The incident occurred at Johnsonville Foods in Sheboygan Falls, WI, where it's standard operating procedure to ask employees to take responsibility for the decisions that affect them.

Once a traditional organization with the usual management hierarchy and the usual disaffected employees, Johnsonville has become a low-hierarchy, high-involvement, team-directed operation. Thanks to the conviction of president Ralph Stayer that the people closest to the work must make the decisions that affect that work, Johnsonville has discovered that teamwork pays off. Since 1986, productivity has risen more than 50 percent.

And Johnsonville isn't alone. Accounts of companies that have achieved seemingly miraculous results by instituting a team approach to producing their products or services have begun to trickle into the mainstream business press in the past few years. Those accounts often cite productivity increases in the double digits and equally grand leaps in quality improvement.

A recent report in *Fortune*, for example, credits teamwork for productivity increases of up to 40 percent at a General Mills plant in Lodi, CA. The same story cites a Federal Express team that spotted and solved a billing problem that was costing the company more than $2 million a year. According to *Business Week,* the insurance operation of the Aid Association for Lutherans boosted productivity by 20 percent and reduced case-processing time by as much as 75 percent by using work teams.

Work teams and the potential they hold for producing wondrous results are being billed as the productivity breakthrough of the '90s. There's certainly little doubt that their popularity is on the rise. Companies that have committed to a work-team approach—or their consultants—often label the change they have undergone a "transformation," a "revolution" or the unveiling of a "new paradigm."

This, of course, sounds like hyperbole. Teamwork a "new paradigm"? Please. We've been talking about teams ever since the first sports analogy dribbled from the lips of the first motivational speaker, probably in ancient Egypt. In America we've been "taking proposals back to our teams" for 15 years. We've learned to label endless varieties of training programs "team-building experiences," whether they consist of watching a safety video in the lunchroom or white-water rafting through the Grand Canyon.

But this new breed of work team is a whole different animal. It's called by many names: self-directed, self-managing, high-performance and sociotechnical design are a few of the more common ones.

Sometimes these different labels really do connote important differences. Some organizations consider "self-managing" a misnomer for their work teams, for example, because the companies do retain a management structure. They prefer to describe their teams as "semiself-managing" or "shared management." But whatever you call them, these "new-design" teams have one thing in common: They fundamentally change the way work is organized and performed.

Robert B. Reich, professor of political economy and management at the John F. Kennedy School of Government at Harvard, frames the change in terms of uniquely American cultural myths: the heroism of Horatio Alger vs. that of the team. In "Entrepreneurship Reconsidered: The Team as Hero," an article that appeared in the *Harvard Business Review* in 1987, he wrote: "In this paradigm, entrepreneurship isn't the sole province of the company's founder or its top managers. Rather, it is a capability and attitude that is diffused throughout the company. Experimentation and development go on all the time as the company searches for new ways to capture and build on the knowledge already accumulated by its workers."

Like many revolutionary ideas, this one is simple. Much of it boils down to a belief, like Stayer's, in giving responsibility to the people who do the work. But the implications of that belief are staggering. Putting it into effect is guaranteed to send shock waves throughout an organization—waves that sweep away many time-honored practices.

The real thing

What we're talking about here is not a meager frosting of employee involvement drizzled over an organization, or a training program that emphasizes participative management techniques. "With self-managing teams, you're looking at a work system with the full participation of the people doing the work," says Marvin Weisbord, a partner in Block-Petrella-Weisbord, a consulting firm in Plainfield, NJ.

Certainly employee involvement is nothing new. A 1987 study conducted by the American Productivity & Quality Center found that 80 percent of *Fortune 1,000* companies were using some form of employee involvement. According to one of the study's authors, Edward E. Lawler III, professor of management and director of the Center for Effective Organizations at the University of Southern California, about 30 percent of the companies said they were using teams in some way, usually for a small percentage of their work forces. Half the respondents said they intended to increase their use of work teams.

Self-directed work teams tend to reflect the idiosyncrasies of their companies and the products they produce, so their personalities may vary greatly. In general, however, these teams have several distinguishing characteristics:

• They usually have eight to 15 members who are responsible for producing a well-defined output—either a product or a service.

• Team members learn all the tasks their team must perform, and each person rotates from job to job. As a result, most organizations that adopt work teams implement some sort of pay-for-knowledge compensation system. Many also tie employee compensation directly to the companies' fortunes with gain- or profit-sharing programs.

• As the team matures, it takes over supervisory and support responsibilities such as scheduling, hiring, firing, training, troubleshooting, maintenance, ordering materials, and so on.

• Because the team takes on supervisory, and in some cases, managerial tasks, the number of management layers decreases until the organization takes on a flattened, informal structure.

Still not convinced these work teams are a different breed of cat? Consider one well-worn vehicle for describing teams: the sports analogy. Lake Superior Paper Industries, a paper mill in Duluth, MN, that uses teams, studied the characteristics of five sports while its design team tinkered with the idea of emulating one at the new mill.

The designers finally settled on volleyball as their working analogy because the game requires specialized, but cross-trained team members, who must adapt quickly to the action of the game. "...The action is too fast-paced for the coach (read supervisor) to call all the plays, and the team members have to rotate through all positions. (It was the compulsory rotation that made volleyball the winner. It narrowly edged out basketball.)," reports the American Productivity & Quality Center's newsletter.

A gradual revolution

This team approach causes a major upheaval in the way most companies are accustomed to doing business. Obviously, an autocratic organization with a rigid chain of command has a lot of groundwork to do before creating work teams. But so does a company accustomed to the trappings of participative management.

At Corning Inc., for example, where all the plants are in the process of implementing what the company terms a high-performance work system, employee involvement was already a way of life. "We had suggestion systems, policy meetings, coffee klatches and plant newspapers to get employees involved," says Ed O'Brien, director of education and training.

And when the company launched a total quality system in the early '80s, it dramatically increased the level of employee participation. Even so, the introduction of high-performance teams, which O'Brien calls "the ultimate in terms of participation," required "a lot of time, a lot of training and a hell of a lot of work."

Teams go through several predictable stages, requiring increasing levels of employee involvement, on their journey from traditional to self-management—a journey that can take anywhere from two to 10 years to complete. It helps to visualize these stages as stops along a continuum. At one extreme is the supervisor-controlled work group, in which the boss makes all the decisions; at the other is the self-managed team, in which the team functions autonomously, with little or no supervision.

One example of a company that is pushing toward the true self-managing end of the evolutionary continuum is Semco S/A, a diversified Brazilian manufacturer. In "Managing Without Managers," an article he wrote for the *Harvard Business Review*, Semco's president Ricardo Semler describes a telling incident. When the company needed a bigger plant a few years ago, employees located and inspected three potential sites. Everybody voted and the winner was a site the company's "counselors" (similar to executives) didn't want. "It was an interesting situation," Semler writes, "one that tested our commitment to participatory management.... But we accepted the employees' decision, because we believe that in the long run, letting people participate in the decisions that affect their lives will have a positive effect on employee morale and motivation."

Many of Johnsonville's teams also have reached a high level of autonomy. Teams take responsibility for tasks that formerly belonged to supervisors and middle managers. In fact, the company no longer has traditional supervisors or middle managers, says Johnsonville's Linda Honold, whose title is coach for member development resources. As the teams matured, management and supervisory roles evolved into those of coordinator among plants or coach and resource person for team members. "Essentially the role becomes one of teacher," she explains.

Initially, she says, supervisors were uncomfortable relinquishing authority. "It's a common trouble spot during the transition to teams. What do you do with supervisors?" Gradually, however, Johnsonville phased out supervisory and management roles. At this point, Honold describes the company's structure ("We don't talk about a hierarchy at all," she emphasizes.) as a series of three concentric circles with dotted lines between them. They represent the operating group, which is responsible for strategic direction; the coach group, which consists of those who provide resources (such as training, troubleshooting or coordinating with other plants) to teams; and the team members. Informality is the hallmark of this structure, she says. "A team member can pick up a telephone any time and talk to a member of the operating group."

Development Dimensions International (DDI), a Pittsburgh-based consulting firm, uses a model of the self-directed work team continuum that shows seven steps along the way to full autonomy. According to Lawrence Holpp, DDI's director of quality and team development, the crucial stage—the sticking point for many budding work teams—comes when it's time for the team to take over responsibility from the supervisor for productivity and quality. "They jump back and forth between steps three and four," he says.

Another evolutionary model frames team development in terms of five stages: start-up, state of confusion, leader-centered, tightly-formed and, finally, self-directed. This one comes from *Self-Directed Work Teams: The New American Challenge*, a book written by several authors from Zenger-Miller Inc., a San Jose, CA, consulting company, which will be published in July by Dow-Jones Irwin. The model suggests that rotating leadership, rather than an "informal" leader who takes the place of the supervisor, is one characteristic of a work team that is on its way to becoming self-directed.

The Tempe, AZ, plant of Schreiber Foods Inc., a Green Bay, WI-based cheese processor, has been organized around work teams for five years. According to Judy Robinson, personnel manager for the plant, its production teams recently took that rotating-leader step toward autonomy.

"We used to have one team adviser for each [of four] production teams; now we have one," Robinson says. "We asked the teams how they wanted

to handle the team advisers' duties. They responded by designing a team communicator position that rotates every six weeks."

The team communicator attends three production meetings each week, discusses problems and events that occurred on each shift, handles scheduling and the necessary paperwork—and trains the next team member who will rotate into the position. Essentially, says Robinson, the teams have picked up the administrative pieces of what used to be a management position.

Lawler, author of *High-Involvement Management*, a 1986 book that examines self-managing teams and many of the issues that surround them, is a long-time observer of a variety of employee-involvement techniques. The degree to which a team actually may be considered self-managing is simple to judge, he says. "It's the number and kind of management responsibilities they take on."

The revolt against scientific management

Here's how Corning's O'Brien sums up the rationale for going through the stress and expense of converting to a work-team approach: "Evolutionary changes were no longer adequate. It was not sufficient to keep tweaking our processes to improve production yields by 2 percent a year. The [competitive] environment demanded revolutionary changes."

Weisbord insists that the team movement is a revolution comparable to the one that took place when scientific management swept the industrial world at the turn of the century. Only this revolution is exploding some of the principles of Frederick Taylor's movement.

This new revolution did not suddenly spring to life in the '80s. Its roots go back to the 1940s.

In *Productive Workplaces: Organizing and Managing for Dignity, Meaning and Community*, Weisbord explains why many tenets of scientific management needed undoing: "Taylor worked backward from the obvious task [i.e., creating the product; making a bicycle, for instance]. He reduced discretion at each step, reasoning that scientifically designed jobs would be learned fast and carried out accurately, and would yield more. This led to 'dumber' jobs and a reduction in

required skill at every level of work, including, ironically, managers and specialists. Taylor's system evolved inexorably to deprive *everybody* of a whole view of what was being done."

Enter Eric Trist and London's Tavistock Institute. In the late '40s Trist and his colleagues studied a South Yorkshire coal mine, where changing technology allowed the miners to work in self-regulating teams, sharing jobs and responsibilities. "In marked contrast to most mines, cooperation between task groups was everywhere in evidence; personal commitment was obvious, absenteeism low, accidents infrequent, productivity high," Trist observed.

From that realization was born the concept of sociotechnical systems (STS), an approach to designing work that encompasses both the technical and social aspects of the job. Fundamental to STS is the idea that work is a system, not a series of discrete tasks, and must be treated as such. Those closest to the work must help design jobs, and jobs themselves must be broad enough in scope so that workers don't lose sight of the end result—the product or service. This is the idea that Trist and his colleague Fred Emery labeled "a paradigm shift," that is, a shift away from scientific management's segmentation of work into dull, repetitive jobs.

"The heart of the matter is restructuring the work," says Weisbord. "We're redistributing power, authority and responsibility so that the people closest to the customer, the product, the end result, have power." When work is designed with these principles in mind, he adds, organizational structure becomes flatter because you no longer have any need for many management and support-staff functions.

At Semco, for example, the commitment to self-management has resulted in a corporate structure similar to Johnsonville's. Three concentric circles, representing three management layers, have replaced the traditional hierarchy. Semler describes this idea using the analogy of a hunt for woolly mammoths:

"At Semco, we try to respect the hunter that dominated the first 99.9 percent of the history of our species. If you had to kill a mammoth or do without supper, there was no time to draw up an organization chart, assign tasks or delegate authority. Basically, the person who saw the mammoth from farthest away was the Official Sighter, the one who ran fastest was the Head Runner, whoever threw the most accurate spear was the Grand Marksman, and the person all the others respected most and listened to was the Chief. That's all there was to it. Distributing little charts to produce an appearance of order would have been a waste of time. It still is...."

At the same time, the new paradigm doesn't torpedo scientific management altogether. While Taylorism compartmentalized work into narrow jobs, it also suggested careful measurement of results, points out Ed Musselwhite, executive vice president of research and product development at Zenger-Miller. Unfortunately, "in the United States, what we decided to do was not measure, but to functionalize everything. [The work team approach] says measure, but don't functionalize. Teams demand lots of measurements of their output and lots of feedback. They want to know how they're doing."

Gearing up for teams

Usually the impetus for putting work teams into place is straightforward: Management sees that it must improve quality, productivity or customer service—or begin losing market share to competitors. Without a clear and pressing business reason driving the need, any attempt to convert a company to a team structure is probably doomed, says Holpp. "You can't sell people ideas whose time has not come."

Likewise, the concepts of employee involvement and empowerment had better be part of the organization's vocabulary. Top management must be convinced that the people closest to the work should be responsible for doing the job and deciding how it should be done.

According to Holpp, the first step generally comes when a management steering committee creates a vision statement that articulates the values the company intends to hold. The steering committee also encourages and may even chart the course that work teams will follow on their journey toward self-management. Particularly in large organizations, a common approach is to test that vision by forming work teams in a new plant or location.

These new plants are conceived, designed, built and staffed around the work-team idea. They are often called "greenfield plants," a moniker that harkens back to when the auto industry first began to look at manufacturing locations outside Detroit or similar urban areas.

One of the earliest team-design plants was the General Foods' Gravy Train pet food plant in Topeka, KS. The factory began operating in 1971—nearly two decades ago—and adopted many of the characteristics considered cutting-edge today. Workers went through a rigorous assessment and selection procedure; they were organized into autonomous work teams; they were cross-trained so that they could rotate among jobs; they had a pay-for-knowledge compensation system; team members voted on hiring, firing and other decisions.

Procter & Gamble Co. also began experimenting with work teams in the '70s. Although P&G remained closemouthed about the results of its early experiments, in 1986 *Business Week* reported that the company's teamwork plants were 30 percent to 40 percent more productive than its traditional facilities. Digital Equipment Corp., TRW and Cummins Engine also were among the handful of pioneering organizations.

Like many of these companies, Corning Inc. began to tinker with the work-team concept at just one location. In 1988 its Blacksburg, VA, plant geared up as a new-design facility. Candidates for work at that plant went through an extensive hiring procedure designed to screen for high-caliber employees who had the aptitude to work in a team environment.

It's easier to launch a work-team approach at a greenfield site, says O'Brien. You're starting out with a work force selected for a high-involvement environment. In what he terms a "retrofit"—converting to work teams in an existing plant—"people have to understand why you're doing this. This process is a lot of work. You're asking people to adapt to dramatic change."

He's referring to a change in which a once-familiar work environment suddenly requires new skills, not to mention new behaviors. The magnitude of this change is likely to become clear when line workers—those closest to the job—are asked to participate in designing the work of the team.

"A self-managing team is the result of a design exercise. It's not a prescription that [top management] legislates," says Weisbord. Ideally, he says, design teams should include representatives from staff functions such as human resources, as well as industrial engineers, operators, supervisors and managers. A common mistake is to exclude higher-level managers, assuming that operators won't open up if managers are present. Chances are that each individual will have knowledge that others don't. The cross section of functions is essential to get a clear view of the whole work system. "They educate each other about the work system," says Weisbord.

The designers may extend the "boundaries" of jobs so that in addition to learning to perform the jobs of other team members, the work teams may absorb responsibilities as varied as quality control, parts ordering, shift scheduling, maintenance, safety, training and supervisory duties such as hiring, discipline, performance appraisal, and so on. The goal, Weisbord says, is to produce "whole jobs" that are clearly linked to the end product or service. And they should be "good" jobs, he says. "If there are any crummy jobs at all—if you have any file clerks left—you haven't finished."

Training and more training

Not only must team members learn one another's jobs—a massive cross-training effort in itself—they also must learn how to work as a team. At Corning, employees spend 15 percent to 20 percent of their time in training. That's the equivalent of one day each week.

That investment in training is about par for companies that are serious about work teams, says Corning's O'Brien. "We checked it out. We kept hoping we were different, that there would be shortcuts we could take to get there faster, but we found there weren't."

"This is a training intervention that changes the organization," says Musselwhite, unequivocally. "Without training, you can't make the transition."

To O'Brien's way of thinking, training's crucial role begins in the process of communicating the whys and wherefores to employees. A good starting place, he says, is a course on global competition, designed to help employees—all employees—understand why there is a need for revolutionary change. "Change is hard on people. They're in pain. They'd better believe it's for a damn good reason," he adds.

Next comes a general introduction to the concepts involved in work teams; then courses designed to teach the skills necessary for team members—problem solving, decision making, resolving conflicts, giving feedback and the like. At the same time, he points out, "a tremendous amount of technical training is necessary. Every team member must be able to do every job."

At Schreiber Foods, as at many work-team plants, the teams themselves are responsible for cross-training members in technical skills. Some of that training is the informal, on-the-job variety, explains Robinson; some consists of more formal training on specifics such as quality assurance or personal computer skills. To earn skill-based pay increases, workers are tested to make sure that they have mastered the subject.

The Aid Association for Lutherans (AAL), a fraternal society in Appleton, WI, that operates a large insurance business, is one of the few service organizations that has made the switch to work teams. In two years, nearly half its work force—some 600 employees—have become work-team members. Training played a crucial role in the transition.

In 1985 a new president and CEO, Richard L. Gunderson, decided that AAL needed to cut costs and improve customer service by pushing decision making down into the organization. He replaced 25 of 27 top managers with managers accustomed to working in a participative environment. One of the newcomers was Jerry Laubenstein, vice president of the insurance department, who headed a group of managers and employees that studied ways to reorganize the department.

Once they hit upon the self-directed team approach, Laubenstein and his team studied other organizations that had adopted the system. After visiting another insurance company that was using teams, they began to comprehend the importance of training in making the transition, says Rick Stach, director of human resources development at AAL.

The company the AAL team visited had no soft-skills training designed to help its teams function, Stach says. And those teams were foundering. "Nothing was in place to help them with the management-type tasks they were being asked to perform. We saw a lot of frustration."

Determined that this would not be the case at AAL, representatives from line management and HRD developed a two-year curriculum that began with courses aimed at the individual team member and progressed to training directed at the team. The idea, says Stach, was to help individuals become active, viable team members and then teach them about team dynamics and how to manage them.

Line managers, not trainers, did the instructing while HRD offered support when it was necessary. As a result, Stach says, "an outstanding rapport developed between the line divisions and HRD. There was some resistance on the part of some employees and managers to the amount of training we were suggesting, but over time they began to connect training to the success of their teams."

Technical training at AAL is handled by the team members themselves. Employees learn to master one service area at a time from their coworkers, although some technical training is bolstered by computer-based training programs.

AAL work teams are compensated on a "pay-for-service-provided" basis, Stach explains. "We have 167 services that can be provided. So your base salary is based on the primary service you provide. The team certifies you for other services, if it's in need of that particular skill." Checks and balances are built into the system as well. "Since the team is responsible for its own budget, it is not about to certify a member for something it doesn't need."

Johnsonville Foods takes a different training tack. "Our philosophy is not to train people in team building, but to put people in a situation where they have to develop those skills and provide coaching for them," Honold explains. This approach, which she calls "learn-by-doing," extends well beyond soft-skills training. For example, when a plant needed a new production line, a group of employees—not industrial engineers—designed it. To do so, they had to learn about budgets, capital proposals, costs of refitting and blueprints. An engineer acted as a resource person, she says, but the group did the designing.

How did employees benefit from going through this process? Commitment and learning, says Honold. If engineers had laid out the new line, any problems with it would have sim-

ply been blamed on the engineers. Instead, since the operators themselves had taken responsibility for it, they fixed problems—themselves—immediately.

Johnsonville also uses a pay-for-knowledge compensation system, but there, too, it has added some unique wrinkles. Employees earn bonuses based on the company's performance as well as on knowledge—any knowledge, job-related or not—they have gained in the previous year. This may range from learning a new software system to learning how to turkey shoot, says Honold. That's one of the ways the company demonstrates it's serious about supporting the concept of life-long learning for its employees.

Land mines

The road to self-directing teams is littered with land mines that can surprise the unwary. As a matter of fact, even the wary are liable to find the process uncomfortable, confusing and excruciatingly slow.

Work teams are not the ideal way to organize work for every type of operation. According to Musselwhite, if an organization's product or service requires a significant labor component, it likely would benefit from the work-team approach. The question to consider is whether an increase in human efficiency will generate an increase in productivity, he says. In a continuous-process chemical plant, for example, where two workers with very specialized skills watch over $4 million worth of equipment, improving the productivity of those two enormously is going to have a negligible overall impact.

Most of the early new-design operations were manufacturing facilities, although service businesses are beginning to get into the act as well. "Service businesses are different, but not as different as people would guess," Musselwhite says. If you look at their outputs—a paid insurance claim, a new customer's credit application processed and approved—as products, most service organizations follow a pattern similar to a production flow.

The other factor to consider is the content of individual jobs. If production jobs require only a single rudimentary skill, work teams won't provide any productivity gains. The same thing applies on the other end of the skill spectrum; the team approach could be counterproductive when jobs are highly specialized, says Musselwhite. *Self-Directed Work Teams,* Zenger-Miller's forthcoming book, offers an example: "A Connecticut company producing clothing fasteners found that, given their technology, the most they wanted was better dialogue with workers. The equipment for making buttons, rivets and clasps had not changed for generations, and each unique machine required an artisan to pass on his or her skill to an apprentice, usually a relative. Subtle skills like these, requiring extended observation and practice, don't lend themselves to the cross-training so essential to self-directed teams."

The steering committee that initially studies the feasibility of using work teams in the organization is the group that must defuse as many potential land mines as possible. *Self-Directed Work Teams* recommends that the committee focus on six key questions: "Are the work processes compatible with self-directed work teams? Are employees willing and able to make self-direction work? Can managers master and apply the hands-off leadership style required by self-directed teams? Is the market healthy or promising enough to support improved productivity without reducing the work force? Will the organization's policies and culture support the transition to teams? Will the community support the transition to teams?"

Part of the steering committee's task also is to comb the policies and practices out of the system that are barriers to work teams, says Holpp. Operations accustomed to using seniority to determine who gets the most desirable tasks, for example, have got to let go of that value in order for this to work. Information hoarding is another management "value" that must be flushed. "Self-directed teams are very radical," says Holpp. "They demand resources, training and information from man-

agement."

In his description of his company's participatory management structure in *HBR*, Ricardo Semler notes: "Managers and the status and money they enjoy—in a word, hierarchy—are the single biggest obstacle to participatory management."

And first-level supervisors are one of the prickliest. The reasons are fairly obvious. After all, smoothly functioning work teams will gradually assume most of the supervisor's responsibilities. "[The transition to teams] is probably most threatening to first-level supervisors," O'Brien says. "They have to let go of authority and let the team make decisions for itself. They're wondering if they're even going to have a job when we're done."

"The supervisory role may become an anachronism," Weisbord says, "but that doesn't mean the people aren't needed, especially in a transitional system."

Supervisors often move into advisory and, eventually, coaching roles. "They may become facilitators who work across teams," says Musselwhite. Some become team members; some move into management. If the system is set up so that there's no loss in status, he says, supervisors may become senior technical experts.

And some bail out. According to Musselwhite, the number of supervisors who choose to quit during a transition to work teams varies greatly. About 5 percent turnover among supervisors is common; 50 percent is "the most we've ever observed," he says. The primary variable governing that turnover? Training.

After the transition to work teams, team members probably will continue doing about 60 percent of what they used to do, but the supervisors' jobs change completely, he points out. They must become convinced that their old authoritarian style is no longer useful.

They must learn to coach and counsel rather than order. They must learn to allow teams to go through the sometimes arduous process of group decision making. To do so, they need enormous amounts of training.

For adults only

When managers glance back and see the competition gaining, they have plenty of motivation for trying to reap the benefits that self-directed teams offer. Before jumping in, however, they must be aware that the whole thing is built around a couple of basic concepts: trust and empowerment.

"Empowerment starts with the way work is designed," Weisbord contends. It's pointless to empower workers—to give them authority—without giving them knowledge of the work system, he says. It's also pointless to give them knowledge of the system and fail to empower them.

Semler points out that managing without managers is based on the assumption that employees are trustworthy adults. "Think about that," he wrote in *HBR*. "Outside the factory, workers are men and women who elect governments, serve in the army, lead community projects, raise and educate families, and make decisions every day about the future.... But the moment they walk into the factory, the company transforms them into adolescents." His radical notion: "We hire adults, and then we treat them like adults."

To make work teams work, management must learn to give employees responsibility, just as parents must learn to allow their children to make decisions, says Corning's O'Brien. "When I see high-performance teams working, how enthusiastic they are, how good they are at their jobs, I think, shame on us for not empowering employees years ago."

Reprinted from TRAINING, June 1990

CHAPTER 2

MOTIVATING PERFORMANCE

THE SCIENCE OF WINNING

Wherein we observe coach
Paul "Bear" Bryant build a winning
team—but not the way he said he did

BY THOMAS F. GILBERT
AND MARILYN B. GILBERT

As productivity in American business continues its dogged decline, managers persist in drawing their favorite remedies from athletics. There is much talking of "winning." And the way to win, we hear, it to select the right people for the job, inspire them and provide them with leadership to make sure they give their all ("hard work," it's called). Above all, be a good listener. And, oh yes, don't forget the Hawthorne Effect. You know what that's supposed to be: Show your people you care about them, and they'll work like hell for you.

Really?

We're going to tell you about the late Paul W. Bryant, better known as the "Bear" for once having wrestled one in a carnival. Bear Bryant was the most successful coach in the history of major college football. In his 25 years at the University of Alabama, he won six national championships. His lifetime record of 323 victories is 35 percent higher than that of his modern runner-up, Woody Hayes of Ohio State. Managers wishing to emulate athletic winners will have to grant Bryant a spot at the top of their lists. And indeed, they could well use him as a model—provided they lay aside all their preconceptions about what probably made him a winner.

You see, there is a simple explanation why all those athletic themes that so enrapture managers have no impact whatsoever on their organizations' productivity. Here it is: In order to learn something useful from Bear Bryant, you'd have to *watch* him do his job. It would be virtually useless—even counterproductive—simply to *ask* him about his winning formula, to invite him to make a speech about it, to read some book he might have written in which he explained the secrets of his success.

We knew Bryant in his heyday [while Thomas Gilbert was a professor of psychology at the University of Alabama—Ed.], and we listened to him very carefully. But he also let us observe him closely as he worked at Denny Field with what he called his "good ol' boys." In the process, we learned a great deal about how he kept turning out winning teams year after year.

Before we proceed, though, stop a moment and sympathize with the marketing problem we run into when we try to teach managers about the unglamorous science of productivity. Our message fails to rivet attention. For years we've preached the vital importance of observing exemplary performers instead of just interviewing them (science observes, it does not rely on hearsay), so that we can pass on their key secrets to average performers and make them exemplary, too. We have demonstrated that exemplary performers differ very little from average ones, but that the differences are enormously valuable. And at the risk of sounding pretentious, we say "exemplary" performers rather than "top" performers for a good reason: People may be "tops" because they cheat, work 80 hours a week, butter up the boss or happen to be geniuses. They obviously are not good exemplars for the rest of us.

Our market is falling asleep. But we persist. As eyelids droop, we preach that the most effective tools for making dramatic changes in productivity are:

- Information improvements. ("Tell me what you want me to accomplish and to what standards, then tell me how well I did it.")
- Observation-based training. ("Show us that you have observed the differences between the way exemplary performers and the others do it.")
- Paying for performance. ("Keep the praise and give us a raise.") When it comes to paying for performance, American business practices the amateur, small-town, high-school football method: Bumblers are carried by the top people. Substandard performers get a bonus while exemplars subsidize them. No? Then what do you call it when top performers characteristically accomplish two or more times what the substandard people achieve, yet get paid only about three percent more?

We tell managers that the least effective thing they can do is to spend a lot of time selecting, motivating and showing people that they "care." We remind them that the Hawthorne Effect has been roundly discredited.*

---

*See Thomas F. Gilbert, *Human Competence* (McGraw Hill, New York, 1978), 183-85. Also see H.M. Parsons, "What Happened at Hawthorne?" *Science,* March 1974. Parsons reviewed the original data from the famous studies conducted in the 1920s and '30s at Western Electric's Hawthorne Works in Chicago. Those studies reported that the performance of relay assemblers *always* improved when they were placed in an "experimental group" (and thus felt that management was paying attention to them). Parsons' review showed that the experimental groups' performance actually differed from that of the control groups because people in the experimental groups received continuous feedback and got paid on the basis of performance. Whenever the counting system broke down, the experimental groups were neither informed nor paid differently. On these occasions, the experimental groups performed no better than the control groups.

But by this time, our audience is nodding off. The exemplary performers we cite as models are too drab; they seem to violate the image expected of them. They're often lowly mortals like Viola, an unattractive, poorly educated woman with a lisp and a habit of staring at the ground rather than into her clients' eyes. She just happens to sell three times as much advertising space as the average rep with whom she competes. Then there's Toni, an elderly, working-class woman with a mustache, whose only outstanding virtue seems to be that she sells four times as much fashion merchandise as her betters.

Managers don't want to hear about this. They spend far more time in seminars devoted to listening skills, body language, inspiration, leadership, sensitivity, assertiveness and all that hokum than they ever spend observing exemplary performers—or observing much else, for that matter. Better to come back from some workshop and practice their self-awareness skills on one another.

No, the managers we preach to want to hear those sports analogies. And football is their favorite: "Go out and get the best good ol' boys (updated to 'best ol' boys and gals'), inspire them to fight like hell, give them great leadership and always show them how much you care! That's how Vince Lombardi did it! That's how Bear Bryant did it!"

So, football it shall be. And this much is true: That's pretty much how Bryant and other legendary coaches *said* they did it. But Bryant is going to help us demonstrate that a very low—even negative—correlation exists between what exemplary performers say and the key things they actually do. As it turns out, Bryant serves nicely as an exemplar. He was one of the finest practitioners of the science of productivity that we have ever observed. His "secrets" can be studied, his success can be emulated. One can learn a lot about managing all kinds of things by attending to the Bear.

What we heard—and saw

Bryant had a local TV and radio show in Tuscaloosa, and he was interviewed all the time by the national press. He was frequently heard to say—indeed it was his favorite theme—that the way you create a great football team is to pick out the best good ol' boys and motivate them. He told his audiences how painstakingly he selected his players and how he had so inspired them with the desire to win that they didn't *have* to be as big as those ol' boys at Oklahoma and Nebraska. ("My boys will outquick 'em," he was fond of saying.)

He also talked a lot about the time he spent showing his players how much he cared for them. "I love my boys, and they know it," he said. Listening to him, you got the impression that Bryant knew each of his players intimately and that they came to him constantly for his fatherly counsel. The image was of the Bear with his arm wrapped about a champion's

---

INCENTIVES AND THE BEAR

BY THOMAS F. GILBERT AND MARILYN B. GILBERT

One word, more than any other, echoes through the forlorn halls of American business: motivation. People always invoke it as if they knew what they were talking about. Of course, they typically are using the word to refer vaguely to something they think is going on inside of people.

What is inside of us, our motives, are indeed a part of motivation—but not the part managers have the most power to control. Far less often do managers talk about the other side of motivation: incentives. We like to think our employees fail because they lack an inner drive to succeed, not because we have failed to provide them sufficient incentives.

How did Bear Bryant inspire his players? He knew that his boys came to him already full of motivation and high expectation. He simply let their own performance determine whether their motives continued. He didn't rely on pep talks. More important, he didn't step in and turn them off before they got started.

For years we've been observing people starting new jobs. You know what? Almost all of them start out excited and wanting to perform. But they quickly get turned off. It isn't the work that turns them off so much—not even if the work is comparatively dull. What turns them off is that, unlike Bryant's players, they seldom know what they're supposed to be accomplishing or how well they are doing, and their rewards are rarely based on whether or not they are actually winners. They quickly learn to do what their managers expect them to do: make big public displays of acting and talking as if they just won the Super Bowl. They look extremely busy and they make a lot of "winning" noises. But boy, do they love it when the clock strikes five.

Yes, we know what you're thinking. But assume at your peril that an intrinsic interest in football explains why Bryant's players didn't get turned off as easily as the people who work for your company. Intrinsic interest? Two-thirds of all fourth-grade kids who sign up voluntarily to learn to play woodwind instruments quit within 60 days. The reason? No indication of any likelihood of success.

What Bear Bryant knew that American managers don't is that when it comes to motivation, phony displays of warmth are no substitute for evidence of successful performance. Reprinted from TRAINING, August 1988

huge shoulders, gazing up at the young giant with all the warmth of summer.

He expressed deep concern for the academic progress of his scholar-athletes. The way he drawled on about education could make even a college professor weep. Sometimes his own eyes would tear up as he spoke.

Bryant was not putting us on. Like all the exemplary performers we have observed, he genuinely believed in what he said—most of the time, at least. (At one cocktail party, after he'd had a few bourbons, we suggested that studies of learning in pigeons had turned up some findings that might be useful to him. "Oh, no," he muttered sadly. "My boys are dumber than pigeons.")

But despite his fundamental sincerity, if you tried to build a college

---

**It would
have been useless
simply to ask
Bryant about
his winning formula.**

---

football team based on what you learned from interviews with Bear Bryant, you'd never win a single game. In fact, one reason for his success may have been that many of his opponents—the losers against whom he racked up his winning record—actually accepted all this malarkey at face value. To understand what Bryant was really talking about, you had to look before you listened.

On a number of occasions, Bryant let us come with him to Denny Field. He always seemed to have time for us—partly because he didn't swallow the ubiquitous babble about hard work, and partly because no one else had ever asked to *observe* him up in his tower above the practice field. People stood in line to interview him and hear him repeat the same nonsense *ad nauseum*, but nobody ever went to watch him work.

It's the same way in the business world. Nobody ever asks to observe exemplary performers. If you discount hearsay—all those shabby interviews—their work is the most unnecessarily mysterious process in industry. More than anyone else we've found, exemplary performers love to be observed at work. Alas, they're also happy to *talk* about how they do things—and you take your chances when you listen out of the context of observation.

Eagerly, we accompanied Bryant to his tower, where he quickly proceeded to validate the principle, "Look before you listen." We looked carefully. And from his platform high above Denny Field, Bryant looked too, observing his performers, as we observed him, our performer.

Here are some things we *never* observed. We never saw Bryant with his arm around a player's shoulders, inspiring the youth to high purpose. We never saw him making any displays of "leadership" or "communication." Forget it. About the only thing we saw him communicate was a snarl when an assistant coach or a camera was repeatedly out of position.

It soon became obvious why we couldn't catch Bryant doing any of the things he talked about on the radio. It was because he didn't do them.

What did we see him do? First, we saw him making sure that his boys were well-trained. Extremely well-trained. Nobody else at the University of Alabama got that kind of training, and it is rare in industry for anyone to receive anything close to its quality.

Bryant practiced what we call observation-based training. He had reliable observations of exactly how his exemplary performers did their jobs, and he established that performance as an objective to be reached by players at every position. He had cameras and specialists viewing each position, gathering detailed information. For example, the expert on right defensive guards observed the feet of right defensive guards, which, Bryant assured us, moved in the opposite direction from those of left defensive guards. He didn't want his players watching their own feet, so he had specialists do it for them.

Cameras filled the field. Did Bryant place them there to inspire his boys or to let them see how much he cared? No. He was gathering data.

When a boy consistently moved his feet wrong, Bryant had him on film. To make him feel bad so he'd promise to do better next time? No. A player saw the films only when he was unable to correct his mistakes. Bryant didn't want to confuse his boys with a lot of unnecessary data; he used the films only to distill useful information. He never forgot that his boys were just like he was: dumber than pigeons.

How did he get his players to adjust? He showed them films of exemplary players at their positions. To inspire them? No, to provide them with exact models of what he wanted. They could see, in slow motion, precisely how a great offensive center placed his hands on the ball, how he positioned his feet and hips, and how he moved his knees on particular

---

**Managers talk
about winning so much
that they confuse
a standoff
with a victory.**

---

kinds of plays.

Observation-based training. It's that rarest of practices that capitalizes on the tiny but precious differences between exemplary performers and the rest of us bumblers. Bear Bryant was an exquisite practitioner of it.

Here's something else we saw him do. He provided his players with regular and frequent feedback—just as positive as he could structure it. "I focus on their progress, not their failures," Bryant would say in his usual grumpy tone. Why? Because he was a kindly father figure and loved his boys? No, because he wanted to reinforce progress instead of failure. The worst thing he could have done was to get them concentrating on what they had done wrong, rather than on what they were doing right.

Hardly an hour went by that the assistant coaches weren't showing the boys where and how they stood. But we saw nobody berating them if they did badly or hugging them if they did well. Exemplary managers don't need to engage in this kind of superstitious nonsense. Bryant's coaches treated the players almost exactly as if they were sensible, adult human beings. They told the boys where they stood, how much they were improving and what they could do to improve further. And they left it at that. All the hugging and hollering was saved until after a victory, when the press could see it.

Thus, training, to Bear Bryant, consisted of about 1 percent talk, 20 percent observation of exemplary performers on video, and the remainder doing the job with a lot of feedback and coaching.

Please don't mistake our enthusiasm for the way Bryant used video as a sweeping endorsement of visual media. Just showing people how experts perform on the screen won't help much unless you have identified the *significant* differences between the experts and your trainees. Most video-based training in the business world is oblivious to those tiny but weighty differences. Observation and analysis, not the media we're using, must determine what and how we teach. Sometimes we can convey those vital differences as effectively with a few words on paper as we can with video or computer-based training.

Selection and the scholar-athlete

How did Bryant do his famed recruiting? Far differently than they do in business—although you wouldn't have guessed that from listening to him talk. Instinctively, he knew that fancy behavioral profiles, no matter how many Ph.D.s stood behind them, simply could not predict success with any high degree of accuracy. So Bryant resorted to using performance as his selection principle. He would take on any kid willing to have his brains knocked about. He knew what the science of productivity teaches: The only valid predictor of future performance is past performance. He would not have needed us to trot out Toni and Viola to make the point that these exemplars would never have made it past a so-called "rigorous behavioral and psychologi-

cal screening process" for job candidates.

And what of Bryant's touching commitment to the education his players received within the hallowed halls of Tuscaloosa? "I don't want my boys to be one-sided," he often said.

This commitment was genuine...in a way. While we were Bear-watching, Joe Harless, now a re-

spected figure in the training business, was a student at Alabama—an "A +" psychology student of ours and a fourth-string right guard for Bryant. Harless wanted very much to play on the first string, but life is not kind; Billy Bob, the first-string right guard, was an All-American. So Harless aimed for second string.

As he played for Bryant, Harless

IF THE BEAR HAD USED BUSINESS TRAINING AS A MODEL . . .

BY THOMAS F. GILBERT AND MARILYN B. GILBERT

If Bear Bryant had treated training as his counterparts in business do, he would have consigned it to the School of Education. Then he'd have placed several layers of management between himself and his trainers. He would have left it to these subordinates to reward the trainers for maintaining tight operating budgets while keeping his boys in classrooms for as long as possible and inventing new things to teach them. There would have been courses in assertiveness, body language, motivation, listening and the psychology of winning. Trainers (and training itself) would be evaluated on the basis of attitude surveys and paper-and-pencil tests; nobody would be held accountable for any standards of effective performance on the field. In fact, if Bryant had really done it the way they do in business, he'd have discouraged his trainers from even knowing how well the players performed.

And his teams would have gone winless, even against Columbia University.

Think we're exaggerating? Consider:

● We'd estimate that fewer than 5 percent of the CEOs of the *Fortune 500* companies have ever observed

training in their organizations enough to tell you anything significant about it. Even fewer have ever systematically observed any of their exemplary performers.

● Virtually no manager at any level in any company can tell you what specific effects training has had on job performance.

● Almost all CEOs can tell you, if they rummage around a bit, what training costs them. But most of their estimates would be off by a factor of 10. Virtually no manager in any company can explain the simple but staggeringly large economics of training. This includes most training directors.

● Many organizations use "days in training," or some variant, as their primary measure of training proficiency. Most of the others do the same thing, only less expressly. This encourages trainers to keep people in classrooms (or in front of video or computer screens) as long as possible.

Had we known these things back when we knew Bear Bryant, we don't think we'd have told him. What with reporters and all, he had enough craziness to worry about.

Reprinted from TRAINING, August 1988

IF THE BEAR HAD USED A BUSINESS MODEL TO HANDLE INFORMATION . . .

BY THOMAS F. GILBERT AND MARILYN B. GILBERT

Had Bear Bryant treated information as they do in the business world, he would have turned the whole matter over to the University Computer Department and rewarded them for piling up data in huge drifts. Naturally, they'd have been discouraged from asking him what sort of information he actually needed; they'd have to guess. Billy Bob's English problems and Joe Harless' tutoring potential would have gone unnoticed, hidden away there on page 15,006.

Aside from what they might accidentally glean from those great stacks of unreadable computer printouts, the only things that Bryant, his staff and his players would know about their performance would be what they read in the *Tuscaloosa News*. Nevertheless, the assistant coaches would be required to file annual or semiannual reports (in something laughably called "performance reviews") on each player's attitude, flexibility, cooperativeness, creativity, punctuality, effort, job knowledge, loyalty, interpersonal skills, leadership and growth.

They would, of course, repair to a resort in the Poconos to do this.

Season record: 0-12.

Remarkably few working people in America really know what is expected of them in their jobs. Rare is the employee who is given clear, frequent pictures of how well he is performing or what he might do to improve his performance. Rarer still is the performer who has available to her the finely honed information that would guide her to do excellent work. There is virtually no information available on what exemplary performers uniquely do.

Technology has made it possible for managers to receive haystacks of data, but managers are ill-trained to discover the needles of useful information hiding therein. Nor would they be well-rewarded for doing so. To switch metaphors, managers seem to prefer the cacophony of the jungle to the orderly environs of Denny Field. Perhaps that's why one meaning of the verb "to manage" is "to muddle through."

Reprinted from TRAINING, August 1988

tried to observe him, too. And he finally got in to see the great man for a full 30 seconds. (Bryant didn't really spend a lot of time Hawthorning around with his good ol' boys.) But one day an assistant coach appeared and hollered, "Harless! Coach wants to see you. On the double!"

As Harless tells it, he felt then that the right hand of God had reached out to touch him. The Bear had noted his effort and his growing skills. The Bear was about to make him the second-string right guard. No doubt the Bear would throw his arm over Harless' big shoulders and inspire him to even more dizzying heights. It would be just like the scenarios in those management books he was beginning to read.

"Harless," said Bryant, "Billy Bob is flunking English. From now on, you're his tutor."

Notice how observation helps you understand Bryant's quite genuine concern for the well-rounded education of his boys. Harless' single 30-second view was worth more than 1,000 hours of interviews.

But here is another important lesson. How did Bryant *know* that Billy Bob was flunking English and that Harless was an "A" student? Because he believed in active listening and in managing by walking around? No. Even if the sources of information these practices draw upon were reliable, which they aren't, he would still miss too much. Bryant had a thorough system for filing vital data. He did not rely on hearsay for his information any more than for his training or his recruiting.

Observation

It's no wonder productivity in America is slipping. Until managers start managing the way Bryant did—instead of the way he said he did—they cannot become winners. We estimate that the average season record in industry is one win, one loss and 10 ties. Maybe the so-called "excellent" companies are going 2-1-9. Managers talk about winning so much that they confuse a standoff with a victory. Bryant hated a draw so much that he once gave up a sure tie for the national championship by gambling for a win.

Certainly we should interview the performers we study as well as observe them. In fact, we learned an especially good lesson from Bryant as we were interviewing him *while* observing him. "You sure use a lot of cameras," we noted. "Care to comment?"

Bryant stared down at Denny Field until we thought he hadn't heard the question. Then, thoughtfully, he drawled, "If I were coaching a boxer, every inch would count. If he develops a habit of throwing his left jab an inch too high or an inch too low, he's going to get battered. To prevent that, I'd have to observe him carefully, since he has no way to knowing. It's the same with my team, except that there are 11 of them throwing a left jab all at once. So we have to observe them, inform them and train them. And you can't do this sloppily. The winning coach is the one who does these things extremely well."

"But, Coach," we protested, "what about all that talk of leadership and inspiration being your keys to success?"

"Aw, people like to hear that shit," Bryant replied. "Winning inspires my boys."

Anyone still interested in managing by athletic analogy?

Reprinted from TRAINING, August 1988

ENHANCING SKILLS ACQUISITION THROUGH ACHIEVEMENT MOTIVATION

Helping trainees behave like high achievers
has another payoff: Trainees learn
complex technical skills faster—and better

BY LAWRENCE HOLPP

Skills training, whether it involves complex or routine tasks, can become boring and arduous work both for trainee and trainer. Seldom is all the information you teach in the classroom used on the job, and the excitement and urgency of the actual work environment is rarely present in training seminars.

Some of the reinforcing properties of on-the-job learning can, however, be built into skills training. One way is to base training on a theoretical model that has been shown to produce trainees motivated by a need for high achievement. That need—a powerful psychological drive—causes people to work harder at doing things better.

Research by David C. McClelland and his associates indicates that individuals who have a high need to achieve (n Achievement) approach goal setting, problem solving, planning and organizing— all key management processes— with a degree of creativity and energy significantly greater than that of their peers. Direct training for n Achievement is effective in motivating owners of small businesses, corporate executives and students to behave in a more aggressive, entrepreneurial manner in their work. Can an approach to skills training that uses an achievement-motivation design have a similar effect?

Work in training underwriters to

be better negotiators suggests that it can. Experience also suggests that n Achievement training can help them master, on the job, many complex technical areas with minimum cost to the organization. An n Achievement design can also produce measurable changes in the climate of an organization, resulting in higher morale, lower turnover rates, increased confidence and specific, quantifiable improvements in sales-related activities.

The need for achievement is a drive. Henry Murry, who first named n Achievement, described it in the following way: "To accomplish something difficult. To master, manipulate, or organize physical objects, human beings or ideas. To do this as rapidly and as independently as possible. To excel oneself." (From *Explorations in Personality*, 1938.)

Overall, this drive produces highly efficient, goal-directed people. However, the nature and strength of drives are variable and subject to competing psychological interpretations. To be measurable, a drive must activate behavior— it must cause the individual to operate on the environment, not merely respond when conditions call it forth. An individual who has operant n Achievement characteristics thinks about achievement and structures his life accordingly. The *respondent* individual may show an interest in achievement, but only when prompted from outside. This is a key difference. The

individual high in n Achievement scans the environment for opportunities; the respondent individual waits for opportunity to knock.

We measure this characteristic by qualitative, not merely quantitative, behavior. High n Achievers may or may not contemplate achievement more often than those low in n Achievement, but they will more frequently focus their achievement-related imagery *toward goals*.

McClelland and his colleagues used Murry's Thematic Apperception Test (T.A.T.) to measure the degree to which n Achievement thinking was present in their subjects. By comparing pre-training and post-training T.A.T. scores of latent n Achievement, McClelland showed that it was possible to increase the number of operant verbal responses indicating n Achievement through training his subjects to think and act in more goal-directed ways. This is important because such increases lead directly to better performance on a variety of tasks. Since organizations are interested in performance, not "operant verbal responses," let us focus on the specific behaviors and conditions research has indicated will increase performance.

N Achievement skills training is based on observed behaviors of individuals high in n Achievement. These behaviors show interest in goal setting, responsibility, feedback and activity— all of which indicate that an n-Achievement design is well suited to organizational development.

● **Goal setting:** N Achievers set goals of moderate difficulty that are challenging but attainable. Moderate goals tell the n Achiever more about how he or she is doing than goals that are either too hard or too easy.

● **Responsibility:** Individuals high in n Achievement like to take responsibility for their actions. They gravitate to jobs that allow them maximum control over the means of attaining their goals.

● **Feedback:** N Achievers select goals and milestones which are concrete and readily measurable. Because profit and loss statements tend to fall in this category, business people often show considerable n Achievement.

● **Activity:** N Achievers are very active. They have high energy levels, and they apply their energy to solving business problems, bringing them closer to their goals.

Training designed around these four characteristics will promote frequent goal setting, encourage and reward people to take responsibility for new ideas, provide a mechanism for feedback and create organizational channels so that activity in new areas is encouraged.

In a program to train underwriters, technical material was structured in a series of cases, or practice sessions, followed by role plays. Scripts were not written for the role plays, but careful directions were given. After every practice session, each participant developed a personal plan for the role play, going back to the technical information presented in the practice session to retrieve needed facts and figures. How well a person did this depended, in part, upon his or her level of *n* Achievement.

In order to develop a plan for the role play, an individual must set moderate but challenging goals, devise his or her own way of reaching those goals, assume responsibility for success or failure (saying "the boss told me so" is not allowed), devise a system for obtaining feedback and engage in systematic planning that includes anticipating problems and developing flexibility to accommodate changing situations. The effects of this kind of training are significant. Participants' confidence and energy levels increase, along with sales calls.

Using coaches

In the underwriter training program, line managers were designated coaches, and the responsibility for creating a positive climate was put in their hands. Their jobs were carefully spelled out to include helping employees set goals and get feedback for their efforts, maintaining an organizational climate conducive to testing new ideas at a line level, facilitating the acquisition of vital skills in product areas and cross-training between departments.

To ensure that the coaches (first- or second-level supervisory managers) kept their people on track, they were in turn supervised by a business development manager who reported directly to the branch manager. Overall team success became an element in measuring the coaches' performance, making it worth their while to give feedback and keep things going.

Climate

Changing the climate in an organization to facilitate high achievement is usually an expensive and complex organizational development effort conducted from the top down. When line managers are used as coaches in skills training and given clear authority to keep organizational channels open, their team members gain access to new challenges and oppor-

tunities for growth and experimentation. This produces an organizational climate conducive to *n* Achievement from the bottom up. Not only is the coach responsible for advocating or running interference for team members, he or she is able to get a payoff at appraisal time for doing so.

Cross-training

In any industry, the more people trained to do several different jobs, the more useful they are and the better they are able to represent their organization. This can be accomplished by forming coaching groups across departmental lines. Any skill which is common to most of the members of an organization can be taught interdepartmentally, with cross-training results.

Summary

Strong evidence suggests that organizations that demonstrate a favorable climate to *n* Achievement are more productive, show increases in sales, decreased turnover, lower rates of absenteeism, healthier employees, greater geographic growth— even more suggestions in the suggestion box. By using a training design shown to be effective in getting employees to behave like high achievers, and by creating a climate that will encourage their efforts, the human-resource professional can help carry the motivating influence of the bench, shop or work unit into the classroom and back again.

This system is good for the organization because it minimizes time off for centralized training and because it has many characteristics of on-the-job learning. In the long run, the success of this approach will earn the trainer valuable support within the organization for infusing new and different ideas— which is, after all, the final purpose of education. And the trainee, to paraphrase a very old saying, has been given not a fish, but a fishing rod and a clear map to a well stocked stream.

References

Litwin, G.H. & Stringer, R.A. *Motivation and Organizational Climate.* Boston. Division of Research, Graduate School of Business Administration, Harvard University, 1968.

McClelland, D.C. (1962) "Business Drive and National Achievement," *Harvard Business Review,* 40:July-August, 99-112.

McClelland, D.C. & Winter, D. *Motivating Economic Achievement.* New York, N.Y. The Free Press, 1969.

McClelland, D.C. (Ed.) *Human Motivation.* Morristown, N.J. General Learning Press, 1973.

Reprinted from TRAINING, June 1980

SELF-FULFILLING PROPHECY: BETTER MANAGEMENT BY MAGIC

The lesson is as important to managers
as it is to trainers:
One of the most powerful tools for
influencing the performance of others is
your own expectations

BY LEN SANDLER

In 1911 two researchers with the unlikely names of Stumpt and Pfungst began an investigation of an even more unlikely horse named Clever Hans. The unlikely thing about Hans was that he could add, subtract, multiply, divide, spell and solve problems involving musical harmony.

Any number of animals had been taught to perform such tricks before, but they all had to be cued by their trainers. The really clever thing about Clever Hans was that he could run through his repertoire even when his owner, a German mathematician named Von Osten, was not present. The horse would answer questions for anyone. Von Osten swore he was mystified by the whole thing.

In *Teachers and the Learning Process* (Prentice-Hall, 1971), Robert Strom describes what Stumpt and Pfungst learned:

"Among the first discoveries made was that if the horse could not see the questioner, Hans was not clever at all. Similarly, if the questioner did not himself know the answer to the question, Hans could not answer it either. . . . A forward inclination of the head of the questioner would start Hans tapping, Pfungst observed. . .as the experimenter straightened up, Hans would stop tapping. . .he found that even the raising of his eyebrows was sufficient. Even the dilation of the

questioner's nostrils was a cue for Hans to stop tapping."

In other words, unwittingly, people were giving the horse the correct answers by communicating their expectations to him via physical signals. Hans was able to pick up on those signals—even subtle ones. He was clever only when people expected him to be.

As it is known and taught today in management and education circles, the notion of the self-fulfilling prophecy was conceptualized by Robert Merton, a professor of sociology at Columbia University. In a 1957 work called *Social Theory and Social Structure*, Merton said the phenomenon occurs when "a false definition of the situation evokes a new behavior which makes the original false conception come true."

In other words, once an expectation is set, even if it isn't accurate, we tend to act in ways that are consistent with that expectation. Surprisingly often, the result is that the expectation, as if by magic, comes true.

Magic certainly was involved in the ancient myth from which the idea of the self-fulfilling prophecy takes its other common name. As Ovid told the story in the tenth book of *Metamorphoses*, the sculptor Pygmalion, a prince of Cyprus, sought to create an ivory statue of the ideal woman. The result, which he named Galatea, was so beautiful that Pygmalion fell desperately in love with his own creation.

He prayed to the goddess Venus to bring Galatea to life. Venus granted his prayer, and the couple lived happily ever after.

That's where the name originated, but a better illustration of the "Pygmalion Effect" is George Bernard Shaw's play *Pygmalion*, in which Professor Henry Higgins insists that he can take a Cockney flower girl and, with some rigorous training, pass her off as a duchess. He succeeds. But a key point lies in a comment by the trainee, Eliza Doolittle, to Higgins' friend Pickering:

"You see, really and truly, apart from the things anyone can pick up (the dressing and the proper way of speaking and so on), the difference between a lady and a flower girl is not how she behaves, but how she's treated. I shall always be a flower girl to Professor Higgins, because he always treats me as a flower girl, and always will; but I know I can be a lady to you because you always treat me as a lady, and always will."

It boils down to this: Consciously or not, we tip people off as to what our expectations are. We exhibit thousands of cues, some as subtle as the tilting of heads, the raising of eyebrows or the dilation of nostrils, but most are much more obvious. And people pick up on those cues. The concept of the self-fulfilling prophecy can be summarized in five key principles:

- We form certain expectations of people or events.
- We communicate those expectations with various cues.
- People tend to respond to these cues by adjusting their behavior to match them.
- The result is that the original expectation becomes true.
- This creates a circle of self-fulfilling prophecies.

Does it really work?

A convincing body of behavioral research says it does. In 1971 Robert Rosenthal, a professor of social psychology at Harvard, described an experiment in which he told a group of students that he had developed a strain of super-intelligent rats that could run mazes quickly. He then passed out perfectly normal rats at random, telling half of the students that they had the new "maze-bright" rats and the other half that they got "maze-dull" rats.

The rats believed to be bright improved daily in running the maze—they ran faster and more accurately. The "dull" rats refused to budge from the starting point 29% of the time, while the "bright" rats refused only 11% of the time.

This experiment illustrates the first of a number of corollaries to our five basic principles.

Corollary #1: High expectations lead to higher performance; low expectations lead to lower performance.

Rosenthal concluded that some students unknowingly communicated high expectations to the supposedly bright rats. The other students communicated low expectations to the supposedly dull ones. But this study went a step further. According to Rosenthal, "Those who believed they were working with intelligent animals *liked* them better and found them more pleasant. Such students said they felt more relaxed with the animals, they treated them more gently and were more enthusiastic about the experiment than the students who thought they had dull rats to work with."

Corollary #2: Better performance resulting from high expectations leads us to like someone more; lower performance resulting from low expectations leads us to like someone less.

Rats aren't good enough for you? In another classic experiment, Rosenthal and Lenore Jacobson worked with elementary school children from 18 classrooms. They randomly chose 20% of the children from each room and told the teachers they were "intellectual bloomers." They explained that these children could be expected to show remarkable gains during the year. The experimental children showed average IQ gains of two points in verbal ability, seven points in reasoning and four points in overall IQ. The "intellectual bloomers" really did bloom!

How can this possibly work? In *Pygmalion in the Classroom* (Holt, Rinehart and Winston, 1968), Rosenthal replies:

"To summarize our speculations, we may say that by what she said, by how and when she said it, by her actual facial expressions, postures and perhaps by her touch, the teacher may have communicated to the children of the experimental group that she expected improved intellectual performance. Such communication together with possible changes in teaching techniques may have helped the child learn by changing his self-concept, his expectations of his own behavior, and his motivation, as well as his cognitive style and skills."

There was no difference in the amount of time the teachers spent with the students. Evidently there was a difference in the quality of the interactions.

Expectations, as if by magic, come true.

The teachers also found the "bloomers" to be more appealing, more affectionate and better adjusted. Some students gained in IQ even though they had not been designated as "bloomers," but they were not regarded to be as appealing, affectionate or well-adjusted. Apparently, the bloomers had done what was expected of them and the teachers were comfortable with them. The other students who did well surprised the teachers; they did the unexpected and the teachers were not as comfortable with them. It may be that they were thought of as overstepping their bounds or labeled as troublemakers.

Corollary #3: We tend to be comfortable with people who meet our expectations, whether they're high or low; we tend *not* to be comfortable with people who don't meet our expectations, whether they're high or low.

As for our expectations of what will happen or how someone will behave, we form them in a thousand ways, many preconceived. We all are prejudiced in the literal sense of the word; we "prejudge" either positively or negatively. We like to think we know what's going to happen before it happens, and we don't like to be proven wrong. We want to feel that we can control things. The impulse has given rise to religion, which says we can influence the gods with prayer; magic, which says we can manipulate events with secret powers; and science, which says we can understand the logic behind events and use it to predict similar events.

Corollary #4: Forming expectations is natural and unavoidable.

And the simple truth is that almost all of us behave pretty much according to the way we're treated. If you keep telling a teenager, for example, that he's worthless, has no sense of right or wrong and isn't going to amount to anything, he'll probably respond accordingly. If you keep telling him (sincerely) that he's important to you, that you have every confidence in his judgment as to what's right or wrong and that you're sure he's going to be successful in whatever he decides to do, he'll also tend to respond accordingly. You transmit those expectations to him and he'll begin to reflect the image you've created for him.

Corollary #5: Once formed, expectations about ourselves tend to be self-sustaining.

Exactly how do we communicate the expectations responsible for the Pygmalion Effect? The process works in very similar ways with people as it did with Clever Hans. In *Educational Sociology: A Realistic Approach* (Holt, Rinehart and Winston, 1980), Thomas Good and J. Brophy list a dozen ways in which teachers may behave differently toward students. Figure 1 shows their list.

Does it work at work?

It doesn't take much of a leap to see how Good and Brophy's list of teacher behaviors might apply to managers and subordinates in the business world, let alone to adult education and training. Figure 2 shows some obvious parallels. And research into the impact of self-fulfilling prophecies has not been limited to the classroom.

In one study a group of female applicants for a machine operator position was tested for intelligence and finger dexterity. Their supervisors were told that some of the women (actually chosen at random) had scored high on the tests. The results? The foremen gave more favorable evaluations to those workers whom they had been led to believe had higher test scores. And there's more: The actual production records of these women were substantially better.

Another example is the work of Albert King, a professor of business administration at Kansas State University. King randomly picked some novice welders, mechanics, presser machine operators and assembler trainees, and told their supervisors that these workers showed special potential for their jobs. Trainees from whom supervisors expected better job performance delivered just that. They were rated higher by their peers, scored better on objective tests and had lower absence rates. The average performance rankings for the high-expectation group were substantially higher than for the control group.

One dramatic illustration of the Pygmalion Effect achieved notoriety in the 1960s when it was reported in *Look* magazine as "Sweeney's Miracle." Jim Sweeney taught at Tulane University and was responsible for the biomedical computer center. He insisted that he could teach a janitor named Johnson to become a computer operator. The University required a certain score on an IQ test to qualify a person to become an operator trainee. Johnson failed the test miserably. Sweeney threatened to quit unless the administration allowed him to give Johnson a chance. After much work, Johnson not only became an operator but wound up running the main computer room and being responsible for the training of new operators.

Sweeney's story brings up an important point. The Pygmalion Effect really begins with a belief in your own ability to manage yourself and others. The best managers share this belief.

Warren Bennis, a professor of management at the University of Southern California who has written extensively on the subject of leadership, recently interviewed 90 successful business leaders and their subordinates to determine what traits the leaders had in common. One of the characteristics that came through loud and clear was a positive self-image.

Why are the best managers able to create high performance expectations while weaker managers cannot? For decades theorists have pointed to the manager's self-confidence. In a 1969 *Harvard Business Review* article called "Pygmalion in Management," J. Sterling Livingston, a professor of business administration at Harvard and president of the Sterling Institute, put it like this:

"If he has confidence in his ability to develop and stimulate them to high levels of performance, he will expect much of them and will treat them with confidence that his expectations will be met. But if he has doubts about his ability to stimulate them, he will expect less of them and will treat them with less confidence."

Why is it that subordinates whose managers have low expectations of them tend to produce lower performance? Livingston uses the example of salespeople to make the point:

"Unsuccessful salesmen have great difficulty maintaining their self-image and self-esteem. In response to low managerial expectations, they typically attempt to prevent additional damage to their egos by avoiding situations that might lead to greater failure. They either reduce the number of sales calls they make or avoid trying to 'close' sales when that might result in further painful rejection, or both. Low expectations and damaged egos lead them to behave in a manner that increases the probability of failure, thereby fulfilling their managers' expectations."

Corollary #6: Good managers pro-

FIGURE 1
HOW TEACHERS COMMUNICATE EXPECTATIONS

- Seating low-expectation students far from the teacher and/or seating them in a group.
- Paying less attention to lows in academic situations (smiling less often, maintaining less eye contact, etc.).
- Calling on lows less often to answer questions or to make public demonstrations.
- Waiting less time for lows to answer questions.
- Not staying with lows in failure situations (e.g., providing fewer clues, asking fewer follow-up questions).
- Criticizing lows more frequently than highs for incorrect responses.
- Praising lows less frequently than highs after successful responses.
- Praising lows more frequently than highs for marginal or inadequate responses.
- Providing lows with less accurate and less detailed feedback than highs.
- Failing to provide lows with feedback about their responses as often as highs.
- Demanding less work and effort from lows than from highs.
- Interrupting lows more frequently than highs.

From *Educational Sociology: A Realistic Approach*, T. Good and J. Brophy, Holt, Rinehart and Winston, New York, 1980.

FIGURE 2
HOW MANAGERS COMMUNICATE EXPECTATIONS

- Seating low-expectation employees in low-prestige office areas far from the manager.
- Paying less attention to lows in business situations (smiling less often and maintaining less eye contact). Giving them less information about what's going on in the department.
- Calling on lows less often to work on special projects, state their opinions, or give presentations.
- Waiting less time for lows to state their opinions.
- Not staying with lows in failure situations (i.e., providing less help or giving less advice when subordinates really need it).
- Criticizing lows more frequently than highs for making mistakes.
- Praising lows less frequently than highs after successful efforts.
- Praising lows more frequently than highs for marginal or inadequate efforts.
- Providing lows with less accurate and less detailed feedback on job performance than highs.
- Failing to provide lows with feedback about their job performance as often as highs.
- Demanding less work and effort from lows than from highs.
- Interrupting lows more frequently than highs.

duce employees who perform well and feel good about themselves; bad managers produce employees who perform poorly and feel badly about themselves.

Pygmalion in action

One of the critical tools a manager uses to influence employees is the performance review. Most managers underestimate its importance. Certainly the review is used as a report card, as a means of calculating the size of raises, as a way to introduce areas needing improvement and as a permanent record of what someone has accomplished. Much more importantly, though, reviews influence future performance. They offer a good example of how self-fulfilling prophecies work, for good or ill.

Take the case of a bright, young, aggressive employee. Let's assume she is abrasive, disruptive and disrespectful at times. However, she can also be creative, hard-working and full of enthusiasm. Given proper channeling, she can produce excellent results.

Some managers, required to assign her to a performance category, would call her "excellent." They're impressed by her strengths. Others, focusing on her weaknesses, would call her "poor." Still others, weighing the pluses and minuses, would call her "average."

Even with the scant information you have, you can see that any of these ratings could be justified. But what these managers are doing, probably unknowingly, is helping to determine the young woman's future performance. If she's rated "excellent," what will happen? She'll tend to be even more abrasive, disruptive and disrespectful. She'll also probably be more creative, enthusiastic and hard-working. She will do more of what she believes her manager wants.

What if she's rated "poor?" She'll likely be less abrasive, but she'll also be less creative and enthusiastic.

Suppose she's rated "average?" Depending on what her manager says about the rating and why she got it, she may adjust her behavior slightly.

The variable here is the manager's rating. It is based on the manager's values, prejudices and feelings. Most employees will take the cues and alter their future behavior accordingly.

Corollary #7: Performance ratings don't just summarize the past, they help determine future performance.

Communication

A manager cannot avoid communicating low expectations because the messages are often nonverbal and unintentional. As with observers communicating to Clever Hans and teachers communicating to students, managers nod their heads, prolong or shorten eye contact, express themselves in a certain tone of voice, etc.

Some managers refuse to admit they communicate negative expectations: "I never said anything negative to him. I hardly spoke to him at all." (As if that doesn't send a powerful message.) The key is not what managers say, but the way they behave.

Corollary #8: The best managers have confidence in themselves and in their ability to hire, develop and motivate people; largely because of that self-confidence, they communicate high expectations to others.

A manager increases or decreases initiative by the frequent or infrequent use of praise, criticism, feedback, information, etc. The manager, therefore, plays a highly significant role in the success or failure of an employee.

Robert Rosenthal breaks down the various ways in which teachers com-municate expectations to students into four general categories. The same categories suggest ways by which managers can influence the success of subordinates.

● *Climate.* Managers create a warmer social and emotional mood for high-expectation employees. They smile more, nod their heads approvingly and look into subordinates' eyes more often. They are generally more supportive, friendly, accepting and encouraging.

● *Input.* More assignments and projects are given to high-expectation employees. In addition, these assignments are more challenging and afford higher visibility.

● *Output.* Managers give high-expectation employees more opportunities to speak at meetings, to offer their opinions or to disagree with the manager's opinions. They pay closer attention to their responses, and give them more assistance or encouragement in generating solutions to problems.

● *Feedback.* Managers give more positive reinforcement to high-expectation employees. They praise them more for good work and criticize them less for making mistakes. Consequently, confidence grows.

Like the teacher with the student and the trainer with the trainee, the manager has a profound impact on the success or failure of the subordinate. To quote Livingston once more, "If he is unskilled, he leaves scars on the careers of the young men (and women), cuts deeply into their self-esteem and distorts their image of themselves as human beings. But if he is skillful and has high expectations of his subordinates, their self-confidence will grow, their capabilities will develop and their productivity will be high. More often than he realizes, the manager is Pygmalion."

Reprinted from TRAINING, February 1986

HOW TO TURN EMPLOYEES OFF: A CONVERSATIONAL PRIMER

A backhand tribute to authoritative management, with some insight from an unlikely source

BY DAN DICKINSON

Flip through the pages of any magazine that deals with human resource issues, and you're quite likely to come across an article about "How to Turn Employees On." Apparently either readers or editors or both are convinced that there's no such thing as one too many of these pieces. As Peter Drucker once put it, none too kindly, "There's always a market for cookbooks and for books on how to motivate people, simply because there are so many people unable to do either."

With the proliferation of quality circles, quality of work-life programs and participative management philosophies, however, it's clear that workplace communication skills are improving. Managers are learning how to turn their people on.

But let us not forget the not-too-subtle art of turning employees off. Once a thriving management practice in organizations across American, it appears to be going the way of other antiquated skills and crafts, such as blacksmithing, basket weaving and lighthouse keeping. In the spirit of preserving our link with the past, I tracked down one of the nation's leading experts on alienating employees to solicit his views on this dying art. What does he think about the changing workplace? What does the future hold for a master demotivator like himself?

I found a few surprises in his historical perspective. Maybe you will, too.

I could hear the guy's voice from the back of the bar, booming over the murmur in the lounge like a moose call bellows over a bubbling brook. I smiled, knowing my search was over. There could be no mistaking those tones. Sure enough, hulking at the bar was Bill Battle, "Bruiser" to his friends, my supervisor on my job first 20 years ago.

Bill's eyes caught mine. "Hey, it's the college kid," he roared. "Come on over and have a beer!"

Bill has the kind of physique you'd politely describe as "impressive"; rumor has it that he moonlights as a bouncer at Hell's Angels conventions. As for his demeanor, well, the stress-reduction folks might term it "involved." The point is that when Bill invites you to have a drink, you *have* a drink.

For a while I small-talked, trying to figure out how to get the information I wanted without offending the guy. Bill wasn't making it easy. As I chatted, he just sat there chain-smoking. By way of responding to me, he'd fist-crush an empty Bud and toss it in a can. Clearly, the man was depressed.

"What's eating you, Bill?"

"Ah, things at the company." He snubbed out a cigarette contemptuously. "They're not so good."

"You've been saying that for years."

"And they've been getting worse for years. But now they've reached the pits. Top management just doesn't know how to get results anymore."

Then Bill began to spill the beans. He was here at the hotel for a training course in communication skills, and he'd much rather be back on the job. To say the least, he was mad. "I've been giving people orders for 30 years, and now they say I gotta learn to *communicate*. What do they think I've been doing? Look kid, you worked for me. Did you ever have any doubts about where I was coming from?"

"Never did," I admitted. One thing about Bill, you knew where he was coming from, and where he was going, too. Problem was, you had no desire to get there with him.

I saw my opening. "Look, Bill, you've been at Snodgrass Screw Machine for over 30 years. You've seen management groups come and go. Maybe you could tell me exactly what worked with people and what didn't. And what's going on now that's got you so upset?"

"Sure," he drawled, ordering another round. "Hell, it's about time someone got my side of the story." He took a hefty swig and started talking.

The old school

"You weren't working for the company when old man Snodgrass ran it, but I remember him well. We didn't have a *personnel director* then. Snodgrass did all the hiring and firing. He ran the show.

"I came into the company right out of the service, and I felt right at home. It was just like the army. Management gave orders, we took 'em, and everything was swell. Sure, there were some big-mouths who didn't like the way things were run, but nobody listened to 'em. Those were great years, kid, back in the '50s. Why, the country was booming so fast you could sell just about anything."

"That was when the union came in, wasn't it?"

"Yeah," Bill sighed. "I told Snodgrass he was letting people get out of hand. He was tough, but I guess he wasn't tough enough. Still, I learned a lot from him."

"How did you get along with the union?"

"Well, I thought it was going to be

95

awful, especially when some of the complainers got elected. And at first it *was* awful. We fought all the time, and it seemed like they were always walking out over one thing or another. But I gotta admit, the union had some advantages. Before the union, I had to put up with everybody's complaints. Afterwards, so long as I stuck to the contract, I didn't have to listen to anyone's guff."

"But I guess old Snodgrass couldn't take it?"

"Yeah. He got tired of fighting. Besides, we were losing money. That's when that Chicago conglomerate bought us up."

"Sounds like you weren't too happy about that."

"I wasn't," Bill snorted in disgust. "They sent a bunch of B-school types up to run the place. First thing they did was get all the managers and supervisors together and tell us they were going to move Snodgrass into the 20th century. We were going to have *modern management*. Hell, what year did they think we were operating in, 1850?"

"Probably," I said. They were wrong, of course. Snodgrass was vintage 1930s.

"Well, I told them, 'If it ain't broke, don't fix it.' But they didn't listen to me. They started to fiddle with everything. They hired a personnel director, and she wrote an employee handbook. It was bad enough I had to deal with the union contract, but now the guys on the floor were saying, 'You can't do this and you can't do that, because the handbook says blah, blah, blah.'

"To make things worse, they sent me to supervisory training classes, as if I didn't know how to fire a guy. Finally, they started raising salaries and benefits and generally fixing up the shop. They dumped a bundle on painting, lockers and the rest. Thought they could buy people's loyalty. But they couldn't. You were there then. Were people happy?"

"No," I admitted, "they weren't." If anything, the employees had disliked the Chicago crew even more than old man Snodgrass. And I thought I knew why. While the modern management gang had improved the tangible aspects of the operation—pay, benefits and safety—they'd done nothing to affect the intangibles. People like Bill still gave the orders, ideas were ignored and management was always

right. People rebelled.

"What happened," Bill concluded, "was that we went from a company with poorly paid, grumpy people to one with well-paid, grumpy people, thanks to the miracle of modern management."

"That was when they started getting desperate," I recalled.

"Hell, yes! And with good reason. They'd sold Chicago on a bill of goods that said if they modern-managed the place, they'd see high profits. Instead, losses were bigger than ever. The B-school guys were in trouble. And that's when they made their biggest mistake."

"They started sharing information, right?"

"Right. How dumb can you get? I warned them, but as usual they ignored me. They really believed that if they just went out and leveled with people about the mess they were in, everyone would automatically rally behind them. Dumb."

I remembered the event clearly. The president called the employees into the cafeteria. He tried to open with a joke. It went over like a lead balloon, and things went downhill from there.

Using charts and statistics prepared by the financial officer, he tried to explain where the company stood in the marketplace, why profits had declined and why everyone's help was needed. Nobody bought any of it. Only a few months before, management had dropped thousands on new lockers; now it was telling sob stories. Over the past few years, salaries had been raised—especially management salaries. (Modern management, after all, wasn't cheap.) Now we were broke? At first, people were sullen. Then they started asking questions. The president reacted by getting defensive. Eventually, the employees' skepticism grew into anger, and he beat a hasty retreat.

"It was a disaster," Bruiser said. An uncharacteristic understatement.

"Bill," I asked, "Do you think the employees understood all those charts and graphs?"

"Hell no. I had two years of college and I didn't understand them. How was anyone supposed to understand? They'd never presented anything like that before."

"But one good thing came out of that session," Bill recalled fondly. "It was the end of modern management.

After that, things went back to what they'd been like under Snodgrass. After awhile, the hotshots even agreed to do things my way, at least some of the time."

The new wave

"I'd left the company to go back to school before that," I said. "I heard you were bought out. Who by?"

"HiTech. You know, the Silicon Valley firm. They wanted to diversify."

"Well, Snodgrass is certainly different."

"Tell me about it. When I saw their execs, with their pink shirts, their long hair and their gold granny glasses, I nearly opted for early retirement. And naturally they took the flakiest one of all and made him the general manager. A guy called Giff Peterson. Maybe you've heard of him?"

"You mean the author of *Managing by Zen*?" The book had been on the best-seller list for months.

"The same. We got him before he joined that California consulting firm."

Giff at Snodgrass? The thought was mind-boggling.

"I hated him," Bruiser declared, annihilating another beer can to reinforce the point. "At first."

"At first?"

"As soon as he got there, he started to change things—always a bad sign. He began an annual tennis tournament in town. Stopped production twice a day for exercise. Held monthly beer blasts. He started writing articles in the company newsletter on alternate life-styles. Hell, the guy was turning up on local TV talking about *personal development*. Show me where the company makes money on any of that junk. I was getting madder and madder. But then I started looking around.

"Most of the guys thought that personal development stuff was bunk. So they just did their jobs and went home. And the ones who liked it— hey, they were the clowns who were always bugging me! Now, instead of challenging authority, they were going to meetings, learning yoga and raising funds for the community chest.

"The more I thought about it, the more it reminded me of the old days. Back then we had the bowling league and gave out free turkeys at Thanksgiving. Now we did sit-ups and went to beer blasts. 'Keep 'em busy, keep 'em happy,' old Snodgrass used to say. And that was just what the pink-shirt brigade was doing. It was keeping the grunts content, without really changing anything important. 'Giff, old boy,' I thought, 'you're one smart s.o.b.' "

That rattled me. I had just heard the cracking sounds of one more idol beginning to crumble. "So you're saying Giff is a phony?"

"Not at all," Bill protested. "Of course he believes in that stuff. How else could he get other people to buy it? And I'm not saying he's wrong, either. He even got me into his course on 'Business and Eastern Mysticism.' "

"*You?*"

"Sure. It was pretty good. Say, you ever read the *Bhagavad-Gita*? It's quite a book."

The last straw

I tried to clear my thoughts. Either Bill or the beer was getting to me. "But you said you weren't happy with things at Snodgrass."

"I'm not. Giff Peterson took off to join that consulting outfit. Just in time, too; we were on the edge of

---

MANAGING MOTIVATION

BY DICK PEARSON

With 35 years of management experience behind me, with bits of hundreds of articles and management books stored in my brain, and with a half dozen years of teaching a senior-level management course, I have come to a conclusion. We have made the management of motivation much more complex and academic than it needs to be.

Motivation boils down to four needs that are as basic as Abraham Maslow's physiological needs for survival. All motivation can be directed to one or another of these needs.

● *The Need to Belong.* Work fills a social as well as an economic need. The interaction of the work group should be, and usually is, conducive to our well-being. We may grumble on a dismal Monday morning that we wish we didn't have to go to work, but separated from the group for long periods, most of us grow restless, irritable or depressed.

This need to belong is essential in building a group that works as a team to reach a goal. The Japanese apparently have become quite adept at tapping into this need. Managers who are good motivators will provide a climate in which the group works together as a team and members respect one another's abilities.

● *The Need to Achieve.* Each of us has a need to achieve. We want the chance to complete something, to take responsibility for something, to prove that what we do has worth. If we are denied this sense of achievement in the workplace, we substitute something like creating a showcase flower garden or becoming a gourmet cook.

Managers who give employees the chance to achieve will generally find that they have a more productive work force because they have capitalized on this need.

● *The Need for Recognition.* This is closely tied to the need to achieve. Very early in our adult lives we become aware, although we may try to repress it, that we pass this way but once. We want to be able to leave some mark of our existence. While this need exists in all adults, it intensifies as we grow older.

In the workplace, this need becomes apparent in employees who strive to be individuals rather than just replaceable cogs in a machine. Most of us want to bring some individuality to our jobs, and we usually want personal recognition as well. The wise manager will find ways to praise an employee for her unique contributions to the success of the work group.

If this need goes unmet, the individual concludes that no one cares. The objective can become, "Do just enough to stay out of trouble and keep my job." The employee will concentrate on achieving recognition in the home or the community. This isn't bad, but organizations are much more productive if some of this need is fulfilled on the job.

Even worse, the unsatisfied employee can become a troublemaker. He can become the organizing force behind a group of unhappy workers who create constant turmoil. The situation can become so bad that firing the ringleader only results in another employee filling the gap. Nothing changes until the organization recognizes that there is an issue that must be identified and corrected.

● *The Need for Equity.* The need for equity is perhaps the most driving need of the four. There are a few loners whose need to belong is small. There are competent workers who do their job in a reasonable manner and accept their paychecks as adequate recognition for their achievements. I don't believe there are as many of these "satisfied" workers as most organizations would like to think, but I am willing to concede that there are some.

But all workers have a need for equitable treatment. "Am I being treated fairly compared with you?" is a universal question. It's vital to recognize that the perception of equity is more important than reality. If I think that I am paid less or expected to do more or criticized more often than you for doing a similar job, then I'm likely to become dissatisfied with my job. If I am not treated fairly, the ways I can dream up to be an ineffective performer defy the imagination of management.

Most rational employees recognize that differences in seniority, skill levels and responsibilities make a difference in pay and recognition. But they won't accept differences in pay, treatment or recognition if they think comparable workers are treated differently.

The supervisor or manager responsible for a group must scrupulously avoid the appearance of favoring one person over another. This may be the most difficult challenge for a leader—no human being is totally objective in dealing with another. We all have biases. But since we cannot be totally objective, we must recognize our subjectivities and compensate for them. To be effective leaders, we must treat our employees fairly.

Reprinted from TRAINING, October 1989

bankruptcy. Then HiTech put us on the block. That's when Charlie Smith bought us out. You remember Charlie?"

"The engineer who was pushing Chicago to use his new plating process?" I didn't mention it, but Smith was also the best-liked person at Snodgrass in my time.

"That's the guy. Charlie got ticked off when they wouldn't try his idea, so he started his own company. A real spoiler. Well, he got lucky, because when HiTech bowed out, he was in a position to buy us. It's been downhill ever since."

"That's surprising," I said. "I'd think Charlie would be a pretty good boss. I mean, at least he knows the business."

"I figured he'd be all right, too." Bruiser crushed another empty and knuckleballed it at the trash can, this time swearing in frustration as he missed. "Boy, was I wrong.

"The first thing he did was call everyone together, on company time, no less. And he told them all that he'd bought the firm because he thought it had an 'underutilized resource.' " Bill practically spat the next words out: "It's people! Can you believe that? I mean, we'd lost money for six of the last 10 years, and he told them they were *good*."

"Maybe he was just trying to get them on his side?"

"Naw. We weren't even close to negotiations. He really believed it, and that was scary.

"Then he started going after the managers, signing us up for courses and running training on *people skills*. It was like he was saying we were part of the problem."

I could imagine how Bill had reacted to that. "I'd guess the supervisors were angry?"

"People are funny," Bill sighed. "I figured they'd be up in arms. But most of them seem to be accepting it. Remember Jimmy Durant down in welding? He told me yesterday he's been waiting for this all his life. Can you beat that?

"But the worst thing about it isn't what Charlie's doing to us," he continued. "It's what he's doing to the people on the floor."

"You think the employees are being abused?" It was an unusual complaint coming from Bill, a guy who thought the Japanese commandant was the hero of *The Bridge Over the River Kwai*.

"Damn right. Look, despite its problems, Snodgrass was always a good place to work. Employees could come in, do what they were told, then go home, have a six-pack and forget about it. Not any more.

"It started when Charlie began running programs on economics for everyone in the place. Real basic stuff on profits, quality, productivity, that sort of thing. He said he was only trying to get everyone up to the same level of understanding, but he didn't fool me. What's understanding economics got to do with working for a living? I knew something was up.

"And I was right. After about five or six of his meetings, he started sneaking it in. Company information. Stuff on our bottom line. Figures on market share, our customers, even on how the government operates. He was giving people the kind of information managers get, treating them like there was no difference between us and them."

"But is that so terrible, Bill?"

"You bet it is! As a manager, I'm paid extra to know about those things. But now everyone's worrying about whether the customer is satisfied. Guys go home and think about international trade instead of the World Series. It isn't right!

"But that's not the worst. It was bad enough that Charlie started giving out all that information. Now he's asking people to do something about it. He's got quality circles, safety teams and suggestion boxes. People are coming up with answers on their own. You can hardly get through the plant without someone hitting you with some idea or another. And Charlie has us respond to all of them, even the dumb ones. It's unreal."

Bill threw up his hands in frustration and lapsed into silence. I sat there thinking that I had been wrong all along about Bill Battle. He wasn't the problem at Snodgrass. For 30 years he'd been loyal to his company. He'd done his job. And he had managed people in exactly the way his bosses really wanted him to, despite what they said or why they said it. All of a sudden, after three decades of what, to Bill, had been perfectly transparent mendacity, charlatanism and naïveté, he was faced with something different. What would the poor guy do?

It was getting late. The bar was mostly empty. But I noticed that Bill had attracted a few listeners among the hangers-on. Like me, they apparently wanted to hear him out.

"Look, kid," Bill focused his eyes directly on me. "When the Chicago B-school gang came in, I didn't like it. But it was okay; nothing really changed. Those techies put me off, too, but I could handle it because underneath things were just the same. Now. . . ."

He shrugged, dropped $20 on the bar and stood up.

"I got five more years 'til retirement. Funny, after all this time, they decide to really change the rules on me. Well, I'm not ready for the graveyard yet. I guess if Jimmy Durant can change, I can, too."

Bill slapped me on the arm and headed out of the lounge. He paused at the door.

"But it won't be easy, you know. Just the other day Sally Hawkes came up to me and said that her job was fun. Twenty years on the job, and now it's fun! Can you believe it? I ask you, how are we supposed to get anything done with attitudes like that?"

Reprinted from TRAINING, March 1986

THE HAWTHORNE EFFECT: ORWELL OR BUSCAGLIA?

The act of training people builds their self-esteem and that leads to improved job performance

BY BEVERLY GEBER

Chameleon words are those shifty-eyed little lizards of the language that assume multiple definitions over the years without ever straying too far from their roots. They come about as close as possible to being all things to all people without compromising themselves in the process.

The word "marriage" is a chameleon. (Remember "open marriage"? Remember "till death do us part"?) In the training world, the "Hawthorne Effect" is a chameleon. Ask several trainers and you'll probably get several definitions, most of them legitimate and all of them true to some aspect of the original experiments in Chicago that produced the term.

Jerome Peloquin, for instance, describes it as the rewards you reap when you pay attention to people. Peloquin, president of Performance Control Corp. of Westchester, PA, says that the mere act of showing people that you're concerned about them usually spurs them to better job performance. That's the Hawthorne Effect.

Suppose you've taken a management trainee and given her specialized training in management skills she doesn't now possess. Without saying a word, you've given the trainee the feeling that she is so valuable to the organization that you'll spend time and money to develop her skills. She feels she's on a track to the top, and that motivates her to work harder and better. The motivation is independent of any particular skills or knowledge she may have gained from the training session. That's the Hawthorne Effect at work.

In a way, the Hawthorne Effect can be construed as an enemy of the modern trainer. Carrying the theory to the edges of cynicism, some would say it doesn't make any difference *what* you teach because the Hawthorne Effect will produce the positive outcome you want.

How do you respond to executives who denigrate training and credit the Hawthorne Effect when productivity rises? Peloquin recommends that you say, "So what?" Effective training performs a dual function: It educates people and it strokes them. And there's nothing wrong with using the Hawthorne Effect to reach this other training goal, Peloquin says. In fact, he contends that about 50% of any successful training session can be attributed to the Hawthorne Effect.

Scott Parry, president of Training House, in Princeton, NJ, calls the Hawthorne Effect the "Somebody Upstairs Cares" syndrome. It's not as simplistic as the idea—popular during the human relations craze 10 years ago—that you just have to be nice to workers. It's more than etiquette. When people spend a large portion of their time at work, they must have a sense of belonging, of being part of a team, Parry says. When they do, they produce better. That's the Hawthorne Effect.

Dana Gaines Robinson, president of Pittsburgh, PA-based Partners in Change, says she often hears a different interpretation of the Hawthorne Effect. George Orwell would understand this version; it has a Big Brother ring that's far less benign than other definitions. Robinson says people use it when they talk about workers under the eye of the supervisor.

She'll hear it when she suggests that someone should subtly observe workers on the job to see if they truly apply new procedures they've learned in a training course. Occasionally, managers object, saying that observation isn't a valid test. "Of course they'll do a good job if you're watching them," they tell her. "Isn't that the Hawthorne Effect?"

Well. . .not exactly.

The Hawthorne Studies (or Experiments) were conducted from 1927 to 1932 at the Western Electric Hawthorne Works in Chicago, where Harvard Business School professor Elton Mayo examined productivity and work conditions.

The studies grew out of preliminary experiments at the plant from 1924 to 1927 on the effect of light on productivity. Those experiments showed no clear connection between productivity and the amount of illumination but researchers began to wonder what kind of changes *would* influence output.

Specifically, Mayo wanted to find out what effect fatigue and monotony had on job productivity and how to control them through such variables as rest breaks, work hours, temperature and humidity. In the process, he stumbled upon a principle of human motivation that would help to revolutionize the theory and practice of management.

Mayo took five women from the assembly line, segregated them from the rest of the factory and put them under the eye of a supervisor who was more a friendly observer than disciplinarian. Mayo made frequent changes in their working conditions, always discussing and explaining the changes in advance.

He changed the hours in the workweek, the hours in the workday, the number of rest breaks, the time of the

99

lunch hour. Occasionally, he would return the women to their original, harder working conditions. To his amazement, he discovered a general upward trend in production, completely independent of any of the changes he made.

His findings didn't mesh with the current theory of the worker as motivated solely by self-interest. It didn't make sense that productivity would continue to rise gradually when he cut out breaks and returned the women to longer working hours. Mayo began to look around and realized that the women, exercising a freedom they didn't have on the factory floor, had formed a social atmosphere that also included the observer who tracked their productivity. They talked, they joked, they began to meet socially outside of work.

Mayo had discovered a fundamental concept that seems obvious today: Workplaces are social environments and within them, people are motivated by much more than economic self-interest. He concluded that all aspects of that industrial environment carried social value. When the women were singled out from the rest of the factory workers, it raised their self-esteem. When they were allowed to have a friendly relationship with

---

Mayo stumbled upon an important finding about human involvement.

---

their supervisor, they felt happier at work. When he discussed changes in advance with them, they felt like part of the team. He had secured their co-operation and loyalty; it explained why productivity rose even when he took away their rest breaks.

The power of the social setting and peer group dynamics became even more obvious to Mayo in a later part of the Hawthorne Studies, when he saw the flip side of his original experiments. A group of 14 men who participated in a similar study *restricted* production because they were distrustful of the goals of the project.

The portion of the Hawthorne Studies that dwelt on the positive effects of benign supervision and concern for workers that made them feel like part of a team became known as the Hawthorne Effect; the studies themselves spawned the human relations school of management that is constantly being recycled in new forms today: witness quality circles, participative management, team building, et al.

Incidentally, the Hawthorne Works, the place where history was made, is history now itself. Western Electric closed it in 1983.

Reprinted from TRAINING, November 1986

30 WAYS TO MOTIVATE EMPLOYEES TO PERFORM BETTER

Whether you try them on your own staff or teach them in your next course, perhaps it's time to review this handy list of . . .

BY DEAN R. SPITZER

What motivates people? No question about human behavior is more frequently asked or more perplexing to answer. Yet knowing what motivates another person is basic to establishing and maintaining effective relations with others. It is absolutely fundamental to the practice of management–the art of getting things done through people.

What can several decades and millions of dollars worth of behavioral research tell us about motivation? Plenty, as you might imagine. But many of the researchers' conclusions are contradictory and some of them based on just plain lousy research. To sort through the literature and extract only the gems is the task we put to motivation researcher Dean R. Spitzer, a frequent contributor to TRAINING and currently senior lecturer at the Western Australian Institute of Technology in Perth.

Spitzer presents his personal synthesis of the literature a collection of principles derived from theoretical and applied research on human motivation. At the end of the article, reference notes are provided for each principle so that interested readers might explore the issues in greater depth.

1 **Use appropriate methods of reinforcement.** Reinforcement is the key to human motivation. People behave in anticipation of positive and rewarding consequences. By using reinforcement appropriately, you can significantly increase motivation. Appropriate reinforcement means the following:

• Rewards should always be contingent on performance; if you give rewards when they aren't deserved, they will lose their reinforcing value.

• Don't give too much reinforcement; too much is almost as bad as none at all.

• Reinforcement is personal; what reinforces one person may not reinforce another. Find out what is pleasant for people and use these pleasant consequences as reinforcers.

• Dispense reinforcers as soon as possible after the desired performance occurs. Then the employee will be more likely to associate the reinforcer with the performance.

2 **Eliminate unnecessary threats and punishments.** Threats and punishment have sometimes been considered acceptable motivational tools, but contemporary thinking contradicts this view. Threats and punishment are negative; they encourage avoidance behavior, rather than positive behavior. In addition, the effects of threats and punishment are often unpredictable and imprecise. Threats and punishment are also inconsistent with the other steps presented in this article.

3 **Make sure that accomplishment is adequately recognized.** Most human beings need to be recognized, but individual accomplishment often seems to get lost in larger organizations. People need to feel important, regardless of how modest their position is. Frequently, the focus of recognition in organizations is entirely on the upper echelons.

4 **Provide people with flexibility and choice.** Whenever possible, permit employees to make decisions. Choice and the personal commitment that results are essential to motivation. People who are not given the opportunity to choose for themselves tend to become passive and lethargic.

5 **Provide support when it is needed.** And make sure that employees don't hesitate to make use of it. One key characteristic of the achievement-oriented person is the willingness to use help when it is needed. Employees should be encouraged to ask for support and assistance; otherwise they will become frustrated. Asking for help should never be considered a sign of weakness; it should be considered a sign of strength.

6 **Provide employees with responsibility along with their accountability.** Nothing motivates people as much as being given appropriate responsibility. Appropriate responsibility means responsibility that is neither too high nor too low for the employee. Often employees are held accountable for tasks that are others' responsibility. This is unfair and can lead to frustration. Few people will reject accountability as long as the tasks in question are within their areas of responsibility.

7 **Encourage employees to set their own goals.** At least they should participate actively in the goal-setting process. People tend to know their *own* capabilities and limitations better than anyone else. In addition, personal goal setting results in a commitment to goal accomplishment.

8 **Make sure that employees are aware of how their tasks relate to personal and organizational goals.** Routine work can result in passivity and boredom unless employees are aware of how these routine tasks contribute to their own development and the success of the organization. A few extra minutes of explanation can increase productivity tremendously.

9 **Clarify your expectations and make sure that employees understand them.** We all know what we mean when we say something but often others do not. Unclear expectations can result in a decrease in motivation and, ultimately, frustration. In order to motivate others effectively, you must let them know what you want them to do and how they are expected to do it.

10 **Provide an appropriate mix of extrinsic rewards and intrinsic satisfaction.** Extrinsic rewards are rarely enough to motivate people on an ongoing basis. Employees also need to obtain intrinsic satisfaction from their jobs. Intrinsic satisfaction results from tasks that are interesting, varied, relatively short and challenging. In addition, you should realize that excessive use of extrinsic rewards, such as praise, can overwhelm intrinsic satisfactions. So be careful to provide an appropriate level of extrinsic rewards while permitting employees to experience the personal satisfaction that results from doing an appropriately challenging job well.

11 **Design tasks and environments to be consistent with employee needs.** Because people have different needs, what satisfies one person obviously may not satisfy another. The observant supervisor is aware of the more basic needs of employees, such as affiliation, approval, and achievement. People with different dominant needs require different working conditions. Although it is impossible to totally individualize working conditions, it is possible to give employees the opportunity to satisfy their own needs. For example, employees with a high need for affiliation should be given the opportunity to work with others. Employees with a high need for achievement should be given more task-oriented activities. Good common sense can result in effective work design.

12 **Individualize your supervision.** People also require different supervisory approaches. In order to maximize individual motivation, you must treat people as individuals. Some people need closer supervision than others, and some people don't need much supervision at all. Motivation can be increased through facilitative supervision, providing the minimum amount of supervision that is required by the individual for optimal performance.

13 **Provide immediate and relevant feedback that will help employees improve their performance in the future.** Feedback is most effective when it follows performance. Feedback should be relevant to the task and should provide employees with clues on how they might improve

their performance at the task. Never give negative evaluative feedback without providing informational feedback.

14 **Recognize and help eliminate barriers to individual achievement.** Many poor performers might have all the skills and motivation needed to accomplish a certain task, but they are held back by some barrier or obstacle. If this barrier is not recognized and removed, this individual might remain an underachiever indefinitely. Many people who are labeled "failures" or "incompetents" are simply being hindered by relatively minor obstacles that supervisors haven't recognized. The tragedy is that, after a while, the employee may begin to accept the "failure" label as a fact.

15 **Exhibit confidence in employees.** Confidence usually results in positive performance. The "self-fulfilling prophesy" is one of the most significant features of current thinking in motivation. There is a great deal of research to support the contention that people who are expected to achieve will do so more frequently than others.

16 **Increase the likelihood that employees will experience accomplishment.** The old saw that "nothing succeeds like success" definitely appears to be true. Every employee should be provided with the opportunity to be successful or at least be a significant part of success. All employees who have contributed to a successful project, no matter how small their contribution might appear, should be given credit for the accomplishment.

17 **Exhibit interest in and knowledge of each individual under your supervision.** People need to feel important and personally significant. Take time to get to know each person individually. Learn names of spouses and children; ask about families; find out about leisure activities. This personal concern will pay off in increased productivity. In addition, personal knowledge of employees will provide clues as to what reinforcers can be used effectively in the future.

18 **Encourage individuals to participate in making decisions that affect them.** Nothing tends to inhibit motivation like a feeling of "powerlessness." Employees should be made to understand that they have control over the things that affect them. One of the most reliable research findings in motivational psychology is that

people who have no control over their destiny become passive, viewing the "locus of control" of their lives as external to themselves. Ultimately, this externality can result in learned helplessness.

19 **Establish a climate of trust and open communication.** Motivation is highest in organizations that encourage openness and trust. As previously mentioned, threat is one of the great obstacles to individual motivation, and it must be eliminated. Research on organizational climate and the preference for Theory Y philosophies of management tend to support this point.

20 **Minimize the use of statutory powers.** Rule of law is sometimes needed, but it does not encourage increased motivation. Whenever possible, the threat of law, rules, and consequent punishment should be discouraged. Attempts should be made to manage democratically, encouraging employee input and participation.

21 **Help individuals to see the integrity, significance and relevance of their work in terms of organizational output.** The literature on job design emphasized that employees must be able to see that their tasks are related to the output of the organization or the department. In addition, employees should be encouraged to work on "whole" tasks rather than piecework whenever possible. Significance of work and the consequent intrinsic satisfaction may well be the most important determinants of work motivation.

22 **Listen to and deal effectively with employee complaints.** Often task-irrelevant problems can greatly reduce productivity when they are not dealt with. It is important to handle problems and complaints before they get blown up out of proportion. In addition, people feel more significant when their complaints are taken seriously. Conversely, nothing hurts as much as when others view a personally significant problem as unimportant.

23 **Point out improvements in performance, no matter how small.** This is particularly important when employees are beginning work on new tasks. The need to reinforce frequently during the early stages of learning is well known. In getting employees to improve performance, frequent encouragement can be useful; however, it should be reduced as the employee becomes more confident and proficient.

24 **Demonstrate your own motivation through behavior and attitude.** Nothing turns people off faster than a supervisor who preaches motivation but doesn't practice what he preaches. The motivator must be motivated; this means animated, striving, realistic, energetic and so on. Modeling appropriate behavior and motivation is a very powerful tool indeed.

25 **Criticize behavior, not people.** Negative feedback on performance should never focus on the performer as an individual. A person can do a task poorly and still be a valuable employee. Too many people are inappropriately labeled "dumb," "incompetent," and "unqualified." The self-fulfilling prophesy lives—and drains motivation.

26 **Make sure that effort pays off in results.** Effort is the currency of motivation; this is how people demonstrate it. If effort does not pay off, there will be a tendency to stop trying. A popular principle of human behavior, the "principle of least effort," applies here. People will expend the least effort necessary in order to obtain satisfactory results. This principle indicates that effort is a scarce and valuable commodity. If effort does not result in accomplishment, effort will be withheld, just as money will be withheld if its purchasing power decreases too much. To a very great extent, motivation is the effective management of effort.

27 **Encourage employees to engage in novel and challenging activities.** The literature on intrinsic motivation tends to support the need for both novelty and challenge in order to facilitate feelings of intrinsic satisfaction. Supervisors can provide employees with opportunities to try new things and assign tasks that are increasingly more difficult (but not too difficult).

28 **Anxiety is fundamental to motivation, so don't eliminate it completely.** There is a common misconception that all anxiety is bad. But

---

WILL THE REAL MOTIVATIONAL THEORY PLEASE STAND UP?

Just say "motivation theory," and you'll conjure up a whole gamut of half-baked approaches and pseudo-scientific methods. That's unfortunate, say the authors of a recent book, because there are concrete and practical ways to motivate employees.

Sheila Murphy and Kenneth Carlisle try to sort out the confusion in *Practical Motivation Handbook* (John Wiley & Sons, 1986). They begin by describing a few of their favorites in the category of soft-headed motivational theories:

The Drill Sergeant Approach. Similar to good, old-fashioned, behind-the-woodshed performance conditioning, it relies on a loud voice and gruff manner. Short-term results are fabulous but long-term results? Sorry.

The Pep Rally. This is what happens when a supervisor gets religion in an off-site motivational program, then comes back to enlighten the heathens. After the dust settles. . .no significant difference.

The Nice Guy Approach. If only supervisors are pleasant and empathic, this method promises better performance. It can actually reduce productivity by overemphasizing appearances at the expense of real motivational goals.

The More Training Approach. This one assumes that people don't do their jobs because they don't know how to do them properly. It encourages us to throw training at performance problems in hopes they'll go away. Of course, the problems are usually more complicated than that.

The Pavlovian Approach. The Pavlovian manager rewards small, increasingly correct behavior changes, presuming they will lead to overall improvement. It works adequately when job tasks are simple and discrete, but breaks down in complex situations.

Participative Approach. Typically, a supervisor confers with employees about problems, encouraging them to apply their own solutions. It works well for high-level, creative jobs but is impractical for low-level, simple jobs.

So what are the components of practical motivation? The authors say they combine the best elements of the approaches above and are based on these six assumptions:

● *Motivation must focus narrowly on individual skills.* Start with specific skills you want your employees to acquire, such as handling problems and complaints, remembering names, self-discipline, better grooming and appearance.

● *Employees must understand how to perform correctly.* They may know what you want them to do but not how. Too often the supervisor says "work harder or else," and the employees plunge fearfully into unproductive busywork. This motivates them to work harder all right but not smarter.

● *Employees must be able to solve problems and make decisions.* They have to be treated as adults if it's going to work. The "defiant dictator" ignores this and defines the problem only as he sees it. He plans the rewards he feels are appropriate, administers the improvement program himself and almost always fails to improve performance.

● *Employees must want to perform well.* Motivation may result from external forces, such as a drill sergeant supervisor. But commitment grows out of an individual's personal decision. Supervisors can't force their employees to be committed to good performance. But supervisors can suggest how commitments are made and how they can help a person succeed.

● *Rewards and consequences must be linked directly to performance.* Incentives must be tied to *correct* performance. If they aren't, they can sabotage a motivational program. For instance, it makes little sense to reward typists for producing more if their rush to produce causes more mistakes.

● *Motivation requires patient, persistent follow-up.* It's a mistake to sacrifice follow-up planning in the haste to improve productivity during a crisis. The crackdown may yield immediate improvement but the team spirit is damaged. Follow-up meetings allow supervisors to review with the employees their progress on a certain skill.

Reprinted from TRAINING, December 1987

the truth is that moderate levels of anxiety can increase motivation. That's why some of the best work sometimes gets done under pressure of time. Know your employees and determine the optimal level of anxiety for them. The total elimination of task anxiety can result in lethargy, while high anxiety can result in disorientation.

29 **Don't believe that "liking" is always correlated with positive performance.** Too often, people believe that liking something is a prerequisite for performing it well. But educators know that just because a student likes a course or instructor does not mean that he or she will learn the material well. "Happiness indexes" are not always good measures or predictors of motivation. If a task results in reward and if the results are satisfying, the task itself could be boring and distasteful. In other words, a task can be intrinsically boring, while the consequences are highly motivating.

30 **Be concerned with short-term and long-term motivation.** Sometimes rewards and incentives are so remote in time that their motivating impact is weakened. People should be given short-term, as well as long-term, reinforcement. Conversely, people who receive only short-term reinforcement and incentives tend to fall short of optimal motivation: they lack a long-term perspective on their jobs. Effective motivational programs utilize a complementary set of short-term and long-term incentives and rewards.

I hope that these 30 research-based principles will provide you with insights into the motivational process. Using these principles will undoubtedly make you more effective as a supervisor and a developer of others. Of course, nobody could be expected to

do everything presented in this article, nor would it be wise. There is always the possibility of "motivational overkill." If, however, you can gradually integrate these principles and considerations into your behav-

ior, I can assure you that you, your employees and your trainees will experience greater satisfaction on the job.

Reprinted from TRAINING, March 1980

Reference notes

1. In one of the finest scholarly texts on motivation theory, you will find a superb explanation of behavioral psychology and reinforcement theory; see Bernard Weiner's *Theories of Motivation: From Mechanism to Cognition* (Chicago: Markham Press, 1972). For a view of the wide variety of available reinforcers, see P. Lewinsohn's *Pleasant Events Schedule* (Eugene: University of Oregon, 1976).

2. B.F. Skinner provides one of the most compelling arguments against threat and punishment in *The Technology of Teaching* (New York: Appleton-Century-Crofts, 1968).

3. Perhaps the most important statement on the need for recognition of accomplishment is provided in Abraham Maslow's *Eupsychian Management* (Homewood, Ill.: Richard D. Irwin, 1965).

4. The importance of choice is carefully documented in terms of intrinsic motivation in Edward Deci's *Intrinsic Motivation* (New York: Plenum Press, 1975). In terms of philosophical theory, Paul Ricoeur, a contemporary existentialist, has provided important insights in his *Freedom and Nature* (Evanston, Ill.: Northwestern University Press, 1966).

5. The ability to use "help" constructively is one of the primary characteristics of the person with high achievement motivation. This is discussed at length in the landmark study by David McClelland and his colleagues, *The Achievement Motive* (New York: Appleton-Century-Crofts, 1953).

6. The critical importance of providing concomitant responsibility along with accountability is discussed in many books. For a good treatment of this issue, see *Personal Goals and Work Design*, edited by P. Warr (London: John Wiley, 1976). Also Birney, Burdick, and Teevan discuss the consequences of accountability without responsibility in *Fear of Failure* (New York: Van Nostrand, 1969).

7. The importance of personal goal setting in motivation is established in Richard deCharms' study of achievement and motivation, *Personal Causation* (New York: Academic Press, 1968). deCharms distinguishes between those who work toward their own goals, "origins," and those who passively wait for others to motivate them, "pawns."

8. Edward Deci discusses this in his *Intrinsic Motivation* (see note 4); also P. Warr, *Personal Goals and Work Design* (see note 6).

9. The importance of clear expectations is a common theme in both management and education texts. For some of the research on this issue, consult deCharms' *Personal Causation* (see note 7) or McClelland et al., *The Achievement Motive* (see note 5).

10. Deci discusses the relationship between intrinsic and extrinsic motivation and its possible confounding influences in his *Intrinsic Motivation* (see note 4). Deci cites some fascinating research on how extrinsic rewards can destroy personal (instrinsic) satisfaction at accomplishing certain tasks.

11. For an excellent discussion of the interaction between personal needs and environmental factors, see J.W. Atkinson, *An Introduction to Motivation* (Princeton: Van Nostrand, 1964).

12. See Maslow's discussion of enlightened management styles in *Eupsychian Management* (see note 3).

13. The importance of feedback in motivating behavior change is discussed in detail in Thoresen and Mahoney's *Behavioral Self-Control* (New York: Holt, Rhinehart, and Winston, 1974).

14. Joe Harless has done a great service in providing us with tools for identifying environmental obstacles to human performance. See his *An Ounce of Analysis*, (McLean, Va.: Harless Performance Guild, 1970) and "Motivation and Front-End Analysis" in the *NSPI Journal* (July 1978).

15. An outstanding presentation of the idea of the self-fulfilling prophesy and the power of expectations may be found in deCharms' *Enhancing Motivation* (New York: Halstead Press, 1976). Although much of the research relates to children there is considerable evidence that the principles also apply to adults.

16. Skinner is the most convincing advocate of ensuring successful accomplishment and then reinforcing it. This view is ably presented in *The Technology of Teaching* (see note 2).

17. This point is stressed by Douglas McGregor in *The Human Side of Enterprise* (New York: McGraw-Hill, 1960).

18. For a most complete treatment of "locus of control," see E.J. Phares' *Locus of Control in Personality* (Morristown, N.J.: General Learning Press, 1976).

19. Douglas McGregor developed the concept of Theory X and Theory Y management philosophies in *The Human Side of Enterprise* (see note 17).

20. The importance of participative management is eloquently discussed in Frederick Herzberg's *Work and the Nature of Man* (New York: World Publishing Company, 1966).

21. Saul Gellerman has provided strong evidence for this in *Motivation and Productivity* (New York: American Management Associations, 1963).

22. Maslow treats this point very well in his *Eupsychian Management* (see note 3).

23. The significance of identifying and reinforcing small improvements en route to larger gains is one of the key principles of behavior management. See, for example, Kazdin, *Behavior Modification in Applied Settings* (Homewood, Ill.: Dorsey Press, 1975).

24. The importance of behavior modeling is explicated by J.B. Rotter in *Social Learning and Clinical Psychology* (Englewood Cliffs, N.J.: Prentice-Hall, 1954), a classic work on the subject.

25. This point forms a part of Albert Ellis' philosophy on rational living. It is irrational to generalize task performance to enduring characteristics of people. See Ellis and Harper, *A Guide to Rational Living* (Hollywood, Ca.: Wilshire Press, 1974).

26. Weiner presents an extremely detailed discussion of research on the importance of human effort in motivation in his *Theories of Motivation: From Mechanism to Cognition* (see note 1).

27. Daniel Berlyne has synthesized the research on novelty and challenge in motivation in his article "Motivational Problems Raised by Exploratory and Epistemic Behavior" in *Psychology: A Study of a Science*, vol 5, edited by S. Koch (New York: McGraw-Hill, 1963). This difficult article is the classic in the field.

28. The importance of anxiety in motivation is discussed by E.E. Levitt in *The Psychology of Anxiety* (Indianapolis: Bobbs-Merrill, 1967).

29. For a good treatment of this point, see R. Bootzin, *Behavior Modification and Therapy: An Introduction* (Cambridge, Ma.: Winthrop Press, 1975).

30. Skinner discusses the importance of engineering both short-term and long-term rewards into task situations in *The Technology of Teaching* (see note 2). Most books on behavior management also discuss this important point; see, for example, Kazdin, *Behavior Modification in Applied Settings* (see note 23).

KEEPING EMPLOYEES IN LINE WITHOUT PUNISHMENT

Traditional discipline programs expect employees to become "better" when they are treated progressively worse. Positive Discipline can improve performance and reduce firings

BY RICHARD C. GROTE

Discipline is the dirty word in the HRD vocabulary. With this one exception, all of our approaches and assumptions are positive. We assume that our employees respond best to Theory Y management. In Herzberg's footsteps, we give jobs more room for real achievement, recognition, discretion, and opportunities for growth and learning. We build training programs and design jobs to allow all to become Maslovian self-actualizers.

Most of the time our approaches work. Most employees do want to be treated as adults. They have sufficient self-respect and ability to do a job well and maintain sufficient self-discipline that their supervisor never needs to talk to them about attendance, poor workmanship, violation of safety rules, overstaying breaks and lunch periods, and the host of other potential problems in any organization.

But sometimes, in spite of our positive approaches and assumptions, an employee does not respond. When a problem persists beyond the point of coaching and counseling, the disciplinary process begins.

Traditional discipline methods

Discipline, as it is applied in almost every large organization, means punishment. The employee whose conduct or attendance has strayed beyond acceptable norms is first given an oral warning by his or her supervisor. If that fails to solve the problem and correct the behavior, the employee is then given a written warning. The supervisor writes a formal warning to the employee advising him that his behavior is unacceptable and that future failure to conform to organizational standards will result in more severe disciplinary action.

And severe action does follow should the employee again transgress. He is hauled into the supervisor's office and told that as a result of his misbehavior he is being laid off without pay for several days. Should another incident ever arise, he will be fired. Finally he *is* fired. The percentage of employees who turn around after a disciplinary layoff and become good workers is microscopic. Angry and hostile upon returning, faced with a supervisor who too often is more concerned with "building a case" than in helping the employee perform at an acceptable level, he steps over the line once more and is terminated.

That's the system we use to deal with disciplinary problems. It is called *progressive discipline* and it typically involves that four-step process of an oral warning, a written warning, a disciplinary layoff, and finally termination.

Positive Discipline

STEP ONE: ORAL REMINDER
The supervisor calls the employee into the office, discusses the offense, reminds the employee of the importance of the rule, and expresses confidence that this will be the last time they will need to discuss it.

STEP TWO: WRITTEN REMINDER
The supervisor calls the employee into the office and discusses the offense in a supportive but serious manner. After the meeting, the supervisor writes a memo to the employee which summarizes the conversation and confirms the employee's agreement to improve in the future.

STEP THREE: DECISION-MAKING LEAVE
The supervisor calls the employee into the office, discusses the offense, then advises the employee that he or she is not to come to work the next day but they will be paid. The employee is to spend that day deciding whether to continue working for the organization and follow all the rules or not. And report the decision the following day.

STEP FOUR: TERMINATION
If the employee decides to continue working for the organization, and another disciplinary problem arises, the employee is terminated.

Progressive Discipline

STEP ONE: ORAL WARNING
The supervisor calls the employee into the office, discusses the offense, and warns the employee not to repeat it.

STEP TWO: WRITTEN WARNING
The supervisor writes a warning then calls the employee into the office. The employee is given the notice and they discuss the offense. The employee is warned that any future problems will lead to more severe disciplinary action.

STEP THREE: DISCIPLINARY LAYOFF
The supervisor calls the employee into the office, discusses the offense, then advises the employee that he or she is being laid off without pay for a specific number of days. The supervisor warns that any future problems will result in termination.

STEP FOUR: TERMINATION
The employee is terminated.

THE BENEFITS OF POSITIVE DISCIPLINE

Early problem confrontation
The traditional Progressive Discipline system requires a supervisor to be punitive and judgmental in dealing with employee performance problems. The supervisor is likely to let minor occurrences slip by, since reprimanding an employee is unpleasant for both parties involved. Positive Discipline makes it easy for supervisors to confront problems as soon as they arise, since they do not have to reprimand the employee in order to bring the problem to his or her attention.

Lower cost/less production disruption
The cost of paying an employee to take a day and "think it over" is a visible one, it typically is the only direct cost involved in using the system. Under the Progressive Discipline system the employee is not paid for the three- to five-day suspension. Yet the organization incurs significant hidden costs not only because of production disruption but also by replacing the worker for days missed. In addition, when the suspended employee returns to work, the anger and hostility produced by the suspension frequently leads to reduced output, subtle (and sometimes flagrant) sabotage, and other costly anti-organizational behavior.

Consistency in administration
Reprimanding employees is a distasteful part of the supervisory job. Positive Discipline allows the supervisor to discuss a problem with an employee in a supportive rather than punishing fashion. Since the system is more comfortable for supervisors to use, the chances are greater that it will be used consistently by all supervisors in the organization.

Reduction in grievances
Since the employee has been paid for the day, the likelihood of his grieving the decision (and winning any grievance submitted) is greatly reduced. (In the seven months following the implementation of the system in a union plant, 11 employees were discharged, none of whom grieved the decision.)

Application to many jobs
The traditional Progressive Discipline system is typically used only with hourly and industrial employees since organizations do not consider formal disciplinary programs appropriate for clerical, sales and management employees. But providing an employee with a day off to "think it over" when disciplinary problems become serious is appropriate whatever the nature of the job or organizational level.

Maintenance of non-union status
One of the union's most powerful selling points is its ability to fight for an employee who has been suspended without pay for disciplinary reasons. Paying the employee for the day removes this tool from the union organizer's arsenal.

Improved morale
Employees sent home without pay typically return angry, hostile and eager to spread their bad feelings to others—misery loves company. The employee returning from a paid decision-making-leave day has far less reason to gripe and complain in order to save face.

Enhancement of the company's reputation
The more fairly a company treats its employees, the better its local reputation is likely to be, thus making it easier to attract and retain good employees.

EEO consistency
With the mounting pressures to assure equal employment opportunity, supervisors are frequently hesitant to take clearly justified disciplinary action against minorities and females for fear of becoming involved in an EEO discrimination complaint. Since Positive Discipline removes all forms of punishment, supervisors find it easier to act, whether the employee is a member of a minority group or not.

Increased employee/supervisor contact
Too frequently the supervisor is seen by the employee as only a dispenser of punishment rather than as a coach, counselor, mentor, or some similar positive role. If the supervisor handles discipline in a positive fashion, the number of contacts between the supervisor and employee is likely to increase.

Employees do change
This is probably the biggest benefit of Positive Discipline. The supervisor's expression of confidence in the employee's ability to change makes it more likely that he or she actually will change. Under the traditional system, employees rarely come back from a disciplinary layoff and become a fully acceptable performer. With Positive Discipline, it is common for an employee to return form the decision-making leave with the determination to do a good job from then on.

Progressive discipline is a failure. For decades we have been using this negative system to try to bring about a change in a problem employee's performance. It doesn't work. It makes the assumption that we can generate good performance by punishing unacceptable behavior.

And what do we know about punishment? We do know that punishment—warning, threats, layoff, suspensions—applied with sufficient frequency and severity, can shut down an undesirable behavior on someone's part. We also know that punishment creates anger and hostility and a desire to get even. We know that punishment destroys self-respect and feelings of confidence. And we know that punishment more frequently teaches people to avoid getting caught than to change their ways.

A positive approach

A couple years ago, a manufacturing plant was experiencing severe disciplinary problems. During the first nine months of the year, 58 employees out of a total work force of 210 had been fired for disciplinary reasons. The situation was intolerable and it was obvious that the continued use for the negative *progressive discipline* system would only make matters worse. A positive approach to discipline was mandatory.

A number of years earlier, in an article in the *Harvard Business Review*. Canadian Industrial Psychologist John Huberman had outlined a system he had developed for a small plywood mill. Huberman substituted "reminders" for warnings and replaced the traditional three-day layoff with a procedure which involved sending the employees home for the balance of their shift to decide whether they wanted to follow the rules or not.

Using Huberman's model, a *positive discipline* system was developed for the plant. In a daylong training session all supervisors reviewed the plant's history with the traditional negative approach and were introduced to the *positive discipline* system. Both the trainer and the plant manager stressed the need for change and supervisors practiced the procedures involved in each step. The *positive discipline* system was implemented the following day.

The result? The first nine months of the next year saw the number of disciplinary terminations reduced from 52 to 16.

Removing punishment works

The system worked for several reasons. First, all punishment was removed from the disciplinary system. In the first step, the focus was on reminding the employee of the need for and importance of the rule, rather than the warning that breaking it again would produce more serious consequences. In step two, the written documentation followed the conversation between the supervisor and employee, rather than indicting the employee in advance of the conversation.

The critical change came in step three. Where the traditional *progressive discipline* system calls for the employee to be sent home for a period of three or five days without pay, in *positive discipline,* the supervisors were instructed to say something similar to this:

Harriet, this is the third time we've had to talk about this problem. The last time we talked I sent you a memo confirming the conversation, in which you indicated that you would do a better job from now on. The problem still has not been corrected and the situation is now extremely serious. You need to make a decision about whether you want to keep on working for the company and follow all the rules or not.

I want you to spend tomorrow at home thinking about whether you want to continue to work for the company, follow all the rules, and be a good employee or not. This really is your decision to make, and I want you to make it a serious one. To indicate our hope that you do decide to change and become a good employee, we are going to pay you for the day. You need to know, though, that if you decide to continue working for us and any other problems arise, you will be terminated. I want you to come back to me at the beginning of your shift the day after tomorrow and let me know what your decision is.

The employee then completes his or her normal shift and spends the next day away from work, *with* pay, making that critical decision. Most employees return and advise their supervisor that they have decided to remain with the company and do a good job.

And, in most cases, that decision turns out to be a good one. It's rare in the traditional system for an employee who has been sent home on a three-day, unpaid disciplinary layoff to return to work and develop into a productive member of the organization. Step three is almost invariably followed by step four. With *positive discipline,* it's common for an employee to change and abandon the past problems that have created the situation.

Following the success in achieving a disciplinary turnaround at this plant, the system was subsequently implemented in several others, including a unionized location. Similar results have been achieved; employees terminated for disciplinary reasons have been reduced and fewer employees reached the final stages of the process.

From its initial implementation in a plywood mill about 15 years ago, the system has spread slowly but successfully and now represents an idea whose time has come. The Positive Discipline approach has been successfully implemented in both union and no-union locations, and has been applied outside the initial target group of hourly

---

UNDERSTANDING MOTIVATION AND BEHAVIOR

The problem with most classical models a trainer might use to help managers understand behavior modification is that they're either too complex for simple application or they don't take adequate account of how motivation figures in, according to Russell Doré, manager of training and education for the Fruehauf Corp.

The ideas of Abraham Maslow, B.F. Skinner and Frederick Herzberg all are useful, Doré says, but what's needed is a synthesis of their theories. "Many trainers want a model that helps managers understand behavior prior to its occurrence, not one that depends solely on behavior and its consequences," he says. A clear, simple way of looking at why employees do what they do and how managers can help them do it better would be welcomed with open arms.

Doré feels he has one. He draws its concepts from the heavyweight theorists mentioned above and ties them together in a broad-scope look at motivation, all based on the KISS principle (Keep It Simple, Stupid). It's called the MBRS model, for motivation, behavior, reinforcement and satisfaction. It focuses on the idea that when managers want employees to change their behavior (show up on time, improve their work, pay more attention or whatever), what really needs looking at is how they can be *motivated* to change.

According to Doré, the term "motivation" in this context means little more than desire. Behavior is something that occurs as a result of a desire to do something (get to work on time, do better work). If the desire's not there, chances are it won't get done. This is where reinforcement comes in.

Traditional behavioral theory states that positive reinforcement leads to a behavior's being repeated and negative reinforcement tends to produce the opposite. Positive reinforcers at work might include praise, recognition, promotion, or increased pay or responsibility. The negative side would include criticism, threats, ridicule, demotion or dismissal. So if managers reinforce a desired behavior often enough, they probably can assume it will become a pattern, right?

You'll recall it all from Psych 101 so far. But Doré says it's helpful to look at *how* reinforcement changes people's motivation to do things differently and not just at the specific things it encourages them to do. Enough positive reinforcement will bring about a state of satisfaction (with the job, in this case), making people *want to do better.* Or, if the reinforcement has been negative, they'll be dissatisfied and have no desire to improve.

Satisfaction or its opposite, then, affects the current motivational state, which in turn affects future behavior in a number of areas, not just in the area where the immediate performance problem is occurring. Doré says that at this point in his system of looking at behavior modification, managers will see the turning of the wheel and will have a decision to make: Do they want to create satisfaction among employees, or the opposite?

Reprinted from TRAINING, July 1985

factory workers. Today, the system, with slight variations, is being used effectively with accounting clerks, salesmen, and even management employees.

Discipline is not an industrial or factory problem, it is an organizational one. *Positive discipline* provides a method for bringing problems to an employee's attention (whatever his or her job) in a way that does not undermine the employee's self-respect, but rather reinforces their ability to solve their own problem.

Getting the message across

Even in organizations without a formal disciplinary process, the paid "decision day" can get the message across to the problem employee that immediate improvement is mandatory:

A night nurse whose tardiness record has not changed after several conversations with her supervisor is more likely to realize the severity of the situation if she spends a night away from the hospital thinking about whether she can (and wants to) maintain an acceptable record.

The manager of a retail store, who previously saw termination as the only solution when a good employee started going sour, can use this dramatic gesture to encourage the employee to regain her old momentum.

A once aggressive but now plateaued middle manager, passed over again for a desired promotion, may start to coast and retire on the job. When he's finally fired, it always comes as a shock, no matter how many times his boss may have told him that he isn't making it any more. An involuntary holiday can frequently, get the "shape up or ship out" message across in a way that no counseling session can.

Implementing positive discipline

Implementation of the system, however, does involve more than the simple announcement of a change in procedures. Supervisors are typically not accustomed to dealing with "disciplinary offenders" in a positive way and need coaching in how to approach employees in a supportive and problem solving fashion. Their initial reaction of skepticism, and sometimes outright hostility toward paying a problem employee to take a paid day off to "think it over" must be overcome, both through training and consistent follow-up and maintenance of the system. After years of using punitive techniques to deal with problem performers, supervisors require much coaching and practice before old habits are successfully abandoned.

Follow-up and maintenance are also mandatory. Provisions must be made when employees transfer to other departments or change shifts to make sure that the receiving supervisor is fully up-to-date on any current disciplinary procedures involving that employee.

Concern with the quality of working life is growing as unions, management and the government apply increasing pressure to humanize and enhance the working environment. *Positive discipline* is a significant step in that direction.

Reprinted from TRAINING, October 1977

MOTIVATION THEORIES

Another in TRAINING's continuing series of refresher courses for trainers and managers

Motivation is a catchall word. When a supervisor or manager says, "John isn't motivated," very little is conveyed to the listener about John's behavior. Is John asleep at his desk? Does he come in late and leave early? Is he selling under quota? Or, did he just have an argument with his manager about a new procedure he doesn't want to follow? Simply saying "It's a motivation problem" obviously doesn't convey much information.

The vagueness clouding the word motivation is a result of the various different uses of the term found in writing and research on the subject. Actually there are two distinct approaches to understanding and clarifying the word motivation—the content theory approach and the process theory approach.

Content theories try to specify the energizers of behavior. Maslow was—and Herzberg is—a content-theory person, interested in looking at motive structures. This clinical, personality approach to motivation relies heavily on the concept that people have innate needs which must be satisfied. Filling or satisfying these needs is what prompts people to do things, to be motivated.

The **process theories** are less concerned with why people do what they do and more interested in how the amount and direction of performance can be controlled. Process theories tend to deal less with the internal structure of people than with external forces—the environment surrounding

the performer. There are some strange bedfellows in the process camp. The strict Skinnerian behaviorist on the one hand and the Lewin type, cognitive-theory-oriented individual on the other. Both qualify as process-theory motivation people.

The process theories tend to be quite complex. One of the currently popular process theories is the Porter and Lawler **Expectancy Model of Motivation** shown here in diagrammatic form.

The Porter and Lawler model of motivation is, in some respects, simpler than a number of the drive-expectancy-performance theories of motivation.

Using the content and process theories

The application emphasis of the two

schools is quite different. The content people are interested in **job satisfaction.** Their belief that satisfaction leads to performance has compelled them to study job satisfaction and eventually to develop the concept of **job enrichment.**

Job enrichment is an attempt to change the quality of on-the-job working life. These changes usually take the form of less control, more work authority, more responsibility, direct feedback on performance, and increased task complexity and difficulty. Job enrichment has roughly four objectives: 1) increase job satisfaction, 2) eliminate job alienation, 3) decrease turnover 4) entice people to join the organization.

The application of the process theories has been in quite different directions. Pay, goal setting and leader behavior are among the prime subjects of interest to the process theorists. For example, process advocates currently are giving renewed attention to the study of leadership as a motivation variable. Their view is exemplified by that of Henry P. Sims of Penn State's College of Business Administration. Sims believes that leadership is a process of reinforcement. That is, leaders can be regarded as "managers of reinforcement contingencies" that influence the behavior of subordinates. Leadership, he believes, can be understood and defined by the way the leader acts in response to the performance of the subordinate.

Writing in *Leadership: The Cutting Edge* (a soon-to-be-released Southern Illinois University Press text, edited by J. G. Hunt and L. L. Larson), Sims reviews his and others' research on the leader as a reinforcement agent. Of particular interest is a study Sims did with MBA students at Indiana University. For six months, Sims collected information on the leader behavior of the students' bosses and the on-job

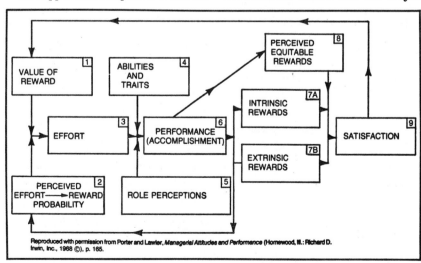

Reproduced with permission from Porter and Lawler, *Managerial Attitudes and Performance* (Homewood, Ill.: Richard D. Irwin, Inc., 1968 ©), p. 165.

performance of the students themselves. Some of the results were predictable, but two were quite surprising.

First, as predicted, Sims found that positive reward behavior on the part of the leader lead to increased performance. Second, punitive or punishment reward behavior did *not* increase performance.

The surprises were:

1. Good performance leads to positive reward behavior. That is, sometimes performance improved and *then* the supervisor began rewarding the performance.

2. Some supervisors automatically "stretched" or "leaned out" the schedule of reinforcement for consistently high performers. That is, they instituted variable ratio reinforcement for consistently high performers.

These results, plus earlier research by Sims and Andrew Szilagyi, which suggests that positive reward behavior can positively effect subordinate satisfaction, move the process-theory approach to motivation much closer to being a practical applied science than many theoretical models and technical research studies would indicate.

The word motivation, with all its fuzziness and multi-meanings, is here to stay—and perhaps perplex us. How one goes about understanding and solving the "John isn't motivated" problems of the world doesn't depend upon a common definition or, for that matter, upon the theory one adheres to. For that you need an understanding of the functional problem, an applications model with a good track record, perseverance, and a little bit o'luck.

Reprinted from TRAINING, January 1978

HOW TO MOTIVATE YOUR TRAINEES

Examined here are several approaches to resolving this perennial problem

BY MARTIN M. BROADWELL

A perennial question most trainers ask is "How do I motivate my trainees?" We haven't solved the problem by a long shot, but we do know some things about getting people motivated. There are several approaches. In this article, we'll look at one of these approaches and, hopefully, we'll shed some light on an age-old question by dressing up the old body in some new-look clothes.

Motivating by "Job Enrichment"

Researcher Frederick Herzberg has suggested that the way to motivate workers is to enrich the job content, not the job environment. He discovered that improving the working conditions doesn't do much in the long run to provide persistent motivation. The things he calls hygiene or maintenance items bother people and they complain about them, but when these things are improved there is little to show in the way of lasting motivation or satisfaction. On the other hand, he found that adding responsibility and recognition and achievement produces more lasting results.

If we transfer these findings to the teaching-learning situation, we'll find that we worry a great deal about the environment, but when we improve it the results are neither very dramatic nor lasting. (For the record, we'll classify things like furniture, temperature, student notebooks, color of the slides, use of the overhead and the lunches as maintenance items; we'll classify the learning experience as "the job itself.") This means we may need to spend more time concerning ourselves with things like the design of the course—what the student is doing, what choices the learner has about the learning activity, the content, the amount of responsibility the learner has for the outcomes (both getting there and measuring the success after arriving) and how much recognition the learner will get in the process. We'll worry less about what the teacher is doing, whether the instructor is using good speech habits, learning on the podium, or using distracting mannerisms. We'll worry less about the impact of different colors on the learners, and worry more about the accountability the learner has for the visuals as they are used.

Design is the key

If we apply the principles of motivation by job enrichment, *design* becomes the key to successful learning. Suddenly, responsibility for learning is shifted to the trainee—not in a harsh, dictatorial manner, but in a meaningful way, with the learner agreeing to the shift. We're saying that the trainee is going to have to be involved in the learning activity in a responsible way. Just putting the group through some involvement exercises—"break into subgroups, take your pencil and paper, make a list, report your findings"—will no longer be perceived as meaningful. On the other hand, if these activities are used to allow the learner to reach a specific goal, one that the learner knows ahead of time and agrees is worth getting to, they will be perceived as meaningful and the exercises will be responsible activities.

"Discovery learning" has meaning under this system because it is the kind of learning that allows the student to be responsible and accountable for the end product. The instructor truly becomes *facilitator* of learning, rather than a *teacher* of learning. The teacher provides a design that allows the trainee to see the end product, that allows the learner in some cases to set the direction, and permits the learner to know where he or she is at any given moment in the process. That's not an easy design, but neither is it an impossible dream. The teacher simply provides enough new information and enough sources of additional information to allow the student to continue down the learning path, discovering things that are of importance.

Changing emphasis

One of the first impacts this approach would have on most organizations is to change the emphasis in their instructor training efforts. To take on the "facilitation" role, instructors will need to find ways to remove themselves from the predominant role, to think less about how they are perceived by the students. That isn't easy. It will require some soul searching to see if their motivation for teaching is to see students able to perform where they couldn't before or if they teach simply to satisfy their egos. It will be difficult for some to maintain their motivation for teaching when they realize that they may be doing their best jobs when the students go home able to perform well on the job, but unable to remember the instructor's name.

Trainers will have to be taught how to deal with the frustration of letting the learner have responsibility, even when the learning activity may not run as smoothly as it would if the teacher were in complete (or near complete) domination. We might liken it to the dominant supervisor who won't give his employees any responsibility for work decisions. He tells the employees what to do and when to do it. They get the work done, but what is often lacking in the employees' motivation is devotion to the job itself. As long as the boss is there and is pressing, the job gets done. When the boss is not around, there is little commitment to the job. But, remember we said the job got done when the boss was there. That may account for why learning still continues to get done when there is a dominant instructor teaching in a very forceful manner. The learning gets done, but there is a lack of motivation.

Changing evaluation processes

If our training evaluation forms ask the students how they liked the furniture, the meals, the housing facilities and the way the instructor conducted the activities, we may be looking at the wrong things. If we get complaints, we change the poor conditions, but we may be tempted to not change the motivation to learn. Our evaluation efforts will need to be more along the lines of what the students *perceive* themselves as having accomplished, and then later on the basis of what they have done differently back on the job. If we're trying to improve the motivation, we'll pay more attention to those items on the evaluation that have to do with the learning process or the learning experience rather than those that have to do with the environment under which the learning took place.

Reprinted from TRAINING, January 1977

HOW PF/PR PAYS OFF FOR HUMAN RESOURCES MANAGERS

"Blue Collar Blues," "White Collar Woes," and employees who have retired—but still have many years to go on-the-job—still are headaches throughout industry, government and health care. In six minutes reading time, this article presents basic PF/PR principles and techniques you'll need to solve these problems in your organization

BY FRED LUTHANS

There is a desperate need for new and more effective approaches to human resources management. The old approaches to managing people have just not worked out. Paying people well, giving them good working conditions and a bundle of fringe benefits has certainly not hurt anything (except for skyrocketing personnel costs) and undoubtedly did some good in the early stages of organization development. But it is clear that these old approaches are not sufficient. New approaches with different theoretical underpinnings need to be explored, developed, and applied. One such approach to human resources management can be called organizational behavior modification, simply O.B. Mod., or performance feedback and positive reinforcement.

The theoretical background

Traditionally, a humanistic approach (e.g., Maslow and McGregor) has dominated the human resources management field. More recently, cognitively based motivational theories (e.g., Vroom's expectancy theory and Adams' equity theory) have become popular in discussions of human resources management. Both the humanistic and the cognitive approaches have value to the understanding of human behavior in organizations but fall short of two other important goals: prediction and control.

Until very recently, the theories and applications from behavioral psychology have been almost totally ignored by human resources management. In particular, reinforcement and operant learning theories (e.g., Thorndike and Skinner) can make valuable contributions to the prediction and control of human behavior in organizations. For example, it is very difficult to predict what behavior will result based solely on the knowledge of an individual's leadership style or the design of his or her job. On the other hand, based on reinforcement theory and the operant paradigm, we can predict that a given behavior, followed by a positive (reinforcing) consequence, will increase in subsequent frequency, while behavior followed by a negative (punishing) consequence will decrease in subsequent frequency. By providing a positive consequence, one can increase behavioral frequency. By providing a negative consequence, one can decrease behavioral frequency.

Catch 23

On paper it may sound simple, but there are two important "catches" to this relatively simple approach to the prediction and control of human behavior. "Catch 23" is that only the *contingent* consequence will have an impact on subsequent behavior. There

are many consequences of employee behaviors in complex organizations. Only the contingent one (the one that is most immediate and given attention to by the individual) will affect subsequent behavior. This explains the fairly common occurrence of a supervisor who observes an employee behaving inappropriately and goes over and "chews him out." On the surface it would appear that the negative consequence (the "chewing out") should lead to a decrease in the inappropriate behavior. What often happens, however, is that the undesirable behavior actually increases instead of decreases. The reason may be that the employee's coworkers are providing a positive competing consequence for the behavior (e.g., "you got the boss's goat that time—nice going"). In this case it is the coworkers' positive consequence and not the supervisor's negative consequence which is contingent and thus has the impact on subsequent behavior.

"Catch 24" is determining which consequences are actually *positive* and which are *negative*. This can only be answered by observing what happens to subsequent behavior. If the behavior increases after a contingent consequence has been applied, then the consequence was positive. If the behavior decreases after a contingent consequence, then it was negative. Yes, the logic is circular, but the procedure works and is therefore of value. Just because the *givee* "thinks" he is giving a contingent reward does not make it so. Only by observing what happens to subsequent behavior can we determine whether the consequence was indeed positive or negative.

Although Catches 23 and 24 complicate things, they certainly do not negate the important role that reinforcement theory and the operant learning paradigm can play in the prediction and control of human behavior in organizations. In fact, based on this type of theoretical background, a new approach to human resource management can be developed and applied.

O.B. Mod. is based on reinforcement theory, the operant learning paradigm, and the principles of behavior modification. It involves both an overall perspective and a specific problem-solving approach. The overall approach involves systematically managing the environment people operate in instead of managing employees per se. As a specific problem-solving approach to behavioral change, Robert Kreitner and I have developed a five-step model to structure and guide the application. The accompanying figure summarizes the model.

Step 1: Identifying the behaviors

As in the first step in any problem-solving approach, the behaviors that are to be changed must be carefully identified. The goal is to select only those behaviors that have a significant impact on performance. Through some type of behavioral audit, the manager/supervisor using O.B. Mod. would attempt to identify the five to 10 percent of the critical behaviors that impact on the 70 to 80 percent of performance. This, of course, is not always easy to accomplish, but traditional job analysis techniques and borrowing from the new techniques that are used to systematically derive critical behaviors for behaviorally anchored rating scales (BARS) in performance appraisal can make this first step easier and more effective. In any event, only observable and measurable behaviors are targeted for change. This gets away from dealing with inner, unobservable states such as needs, moods, feelings, and attitudes.

This first step recognizes that not all behaviors that occur in a given area of an organization directly relate to performance. Technology, training, standards, and ability are examples of other important dimensions of the performance of human resources. However, whereas these latter dimensions have received considerable attention over the years, specific performance-related behaviors have not. By accelerating desirable performance-related behaviors and decelerating the undesirable behaviors that are detracting from performance, significant performance improvements can be realized.

Step 2: Measuring the behaviors

The second step of the model recognizes the need for objective measurement. The frequency of the behavior or behaviors identified in Step 1 are recorded and then transferred to a chart. The behavior is initially measured under existing conditions and is called the baseline period. This baseline is often revealing in and of itself. Sometimes the behavior turns out to be occurring much more frequently than anticipated and sometimes much less. For example, a supervisor may feel that a particular employee is "gone all the time." Upon objective measurement, it is found that the employee in question is absent an average of once a month. Based on this objective data, the supervisor feels he no longer has a

problem. In other cases, the baseline data may indicate a much bigger problem than anticipated.

The method of recording the behaviors will vary with each situation. One caution, however, is that the recorder must be as unobtrusive as possible. Whenever possible, the measurement should be obtained from existing data such as absenteeism records, time sheets, or quality or quantity records. If direct observations are required, the highest ethical standards of full disclosure of what the recorder is doing should always be maintained, but common sense can be

used to diminish as much as possible the impact that the recorder has on the behavioral data being gathered.

Step 3: Conducting a functional analysis

After the critical behaviors have been identified and measured, the next step is to functionally analyze the behavior. This step borrows heavily from the operant paradigm suggested by B.F. Skinner. In particular, this step analyzes and attempts to identify the antecedent cues that precede the behavior and the contingent conse-

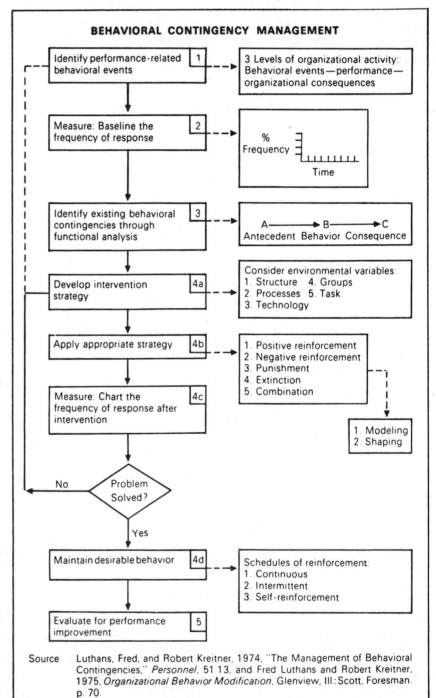

Source: Luthans, Fred, and Robert Kreitner, 1974, "The Management of Behavioral Contingencies," *Personnel*, 51:13, and Fred Luthans and Robert Kreitner, 1975, *Organizational Behavior Modification*, Glenview, Ill.:Scott, Foresman. p. 70.

quences that follow and probably are maintaining the behavior. This step is simply shown in the model as A (antecedent) → B(behavior)→ C(consequence). Understanding the existing antecedent cues (A) and contingent consequences (C) is a necessary prerequisite to developing an intervention strategy in the next step. It is important to recognize that both the A and the C are important to the behavior in question. However, the A does not cause the behavior; it only serves as the occasion for the behavior to be emitted. Behavior is a function of its *consequences* in the operant paradigm, though behavior can be *controlled* by both the A and the C.

An example of controlling behavior through antecedent cues would be to structure the organizational environment so that desirable employee behaviors would more probably be emitted. Even in this case, the positive contingent consequences must occur in the presence of these cues for the behavior to be maintained. The antecedent side of the behavioral contingency is where most of today's organization development techniques (e.g., structural change strategies such as job enrichment or interpersonal process strategies such as team building) are concentrated. Of more direct relevance, however, are contingent consequence strategies for behavioral change.

Step 4: Developing an intervention strategy

The first three steps of the model are preliminary to the intervention—the action step. There are a couple of basic intervention strategies that can be employed: a positive reinforcement strategy to accelerate behaviors and a punishment or extinction strategy to decelerate behaviors. If at all possible, a positive reinforcement strategy is the recommended intervention in O.B. Mod.

As discussed earlier, it may be a problem determining exactly what is a positive reinforcer for a particular individual. Those that come most quickly to mind are money, working conditions, and fringe benefits—the traditional human relations motivators. Upon closer examination, however, it turns out that these are seldom effective as reinforcers because they are administered on a noncontingent basis. Money is usually paid every two weeks or at the end of the month and about the only thing it reinforces is opening a pay envelope or walking up to the pay window. More important to O.B. Mod. are the "natural" reinforcers—those that cur-

rently exist in the work environment and cost nothing to the organization.

The important and very powerful natural reinforcers that can effectively be used in a behavioral change strategy include attention (or recognition) and feedback. Attention contingently applied by the human resource manager can have a very accelerating effect on behaviors. The same is true of feedback. Although management information systems are in most cases supplying an avalanche of job-related data, individual employees still have little feedback on how they are doing. Contingently giving specific feedback, even without accompanying evaluation statements (e.g., "this is good" or "this is bad"), can be very reinforcing for individual or group behaviors.

The use of a punishment strategy is discouraged in the O.B. Mod. approach. The reason is that punishment tends to have many undesirable side effects. For example, punished behavior tends to be only temporarily suppressed, not permanently decreased. Also, punished people just don't like this type of treatment and tend to get very upset and exhibit dysfunctional behaviors. If behavior must be decreased immediately (e.g., an unsafe behavior), then punishment cannot be avoided, but the manager using this strategy must be sure to reinforce the desirable alternative behavior at the first opportunity. It is more appropriate to use an extinction strategy to decelerate behaviors. This is where the manager using O.B. Mod. would simply ignore the undesirable behavior and structure the environment so that there would be no positive reinforcers to maintain the behavior.

The model shows that besides applying an appropriate strategy, there is continued measurement in this step to ensure that the intervention is having its intended impact. The way that the strategy is administered is also important. Initially, a continuous schedule is necessary to get the behavior moving in the desired direction, but then the intermittent schedule is used. The intermittent schedule will tend to strengthen the behavior and permit the manager/supervisor to concentrate on other behaviors and other aspects of the job. The ultimate goal of O.B. Mod. is to have human resources become self-reinforced for performance improvement and goal attainment.

Step 5: Evaluating for performance improvement

The name of the game today in all aspects of management is accountabil-

ity and performance. The final step is to evaluate and ensure that the O.B. Mod. approach is leading to performance improvement. In general, human resource management has been very lax in this regard. If possible, several levels of evaluation should be attempted. First, the reaction of the personnel involved (both those using O.B. Mod. and those having it used on them) should be determined. This can usually be handled by questionnaires and interviews. In addition, an evaluation should be made of the actual behavioral changes that occur on the job. The behavioral frequency charts started in Step 2 can help in this evaluation. In some cases reversals may be attempted (return to baseline conditions and then back to the intervention) to verify that it was the intervention that is causing the change in the behavior and not some other condition in the environment. Most important, however, is the evaluation that is made on overall performance improvement.

We said it before, but we'll say it again: O.B. Mod. has the overriding aim of performance improvement. O.B. Mod. is not intended to be a method of behavioral change for change's sake. Rather, the purpose of the O.B. Mod. approach is to improve objective, "bottom-line" performance.

The O.B. Mod experience

The most widely publicized application of an operant-based approach to human resource management was at Emery Air Freight. Under the direction of Edward Feeney, who was then an Emery vice president, some phenomenal results were reported. Unfortunately, most of the evidence was testimonial rather than the result of accepted research methodology. More recently, Feeney has been applying his approach of feedback and positive reinforcement in a variety of settings through his own consulting firm. There are also a growing number of consulting firms such as Behavioral Systems Inc., based in Atlanta, GA, which are actively implementing comprehensive behavioral change programs. And there also are a number of related, commercially available software items as, TRAINING'S accompanying review section indicates.

The O.B. Mod. model described in this article has been specifically applied to a variety of organizations. The results have been very encouraging so far. In two of the applications (a large- and a medium-sized manufacturing firm), a rigorous three-level evaluation was conducted.

In both cases, the people involved with the O.B. Mod. approach had positive reactions; important job behaviors such as attendance, tardiness, staying at the work station, disruptive complaints, quantity of output, quality of output, following safety regulations, use of idle time, and constructive suggestions were dramatically changed. The supervisors who were trained to use the O.B. Mod. approach brought about significant increases in the overall performance of their departments compared to control groups of supervisors who did not receive the training and were not using the approach.

Other applications of O.B. Mod., especially in nonmanufacturing types of organizational settings, are starting to show up. Some are featured in this issue of TRAINING. All these applications must be systematically evaluated before any broad generalizations can be drawn. O.B. Mod. is by no means a singular answer to solving all human resources management problems. Other approaches and techniques are valuable, valid, and needed. Yet, whether used as an overall perspective (i.e., the job of human resource managers is to manage the contingent environment of employees instead of the employees per se) or as a specific problem solving model for behavioral change leading to performance improvement, O.B. Mod. seems to be an overlooked and potentially very useful approach to more effective human resource management.

Reprinted from TRAINING, December 1976

POWERFUL TOOLS FOR TRAINING, MOTIVATING AND MANAGING BETTER

Use of performance feedback and positive reinforcement principles in the management, training and development of human resources is coming of age. And high time, too

I n the mid-Sixties we training people became rather adept at saying things like: "Management by positive reinforcement is more effective than management by punishment, threat, negative sanction, and coerced compliance." And, "People do a good job when they know what is expected of them, have the time, tools, and training to perform, and receive frequent, meaningful information about how they are doing."

We said these sorts of things, and said them, and said them—mostly to each other at professional meetings, and in journals, and to low-level managers and supervisors in introductory management training courses—but we said them and meant them.

Guess what? Today the concept of management through performance feedback and positive reinforcement is receiving fresh attention. And for good reason. At 3M,* Questor, Ford, United Air Lines, IBM, IT&T, Proctor and Gamble and an increasing number of large, medium, and small organizations, human resources managers are reporting encouraging results. At Milliken and Company, one of the world's largest textile firms, using performance feedback and positive reinforcement "has become a *way of management*, not simply something taught in a training program," Personnel Manager W. Perry Gaines told TRAINING. "Since seeing the results of our first pilot programs in 1972, management has been committed to the behavior management approach."

E. D. Grady, general manager for operator services, Michigan Bell, says, "It has been our experience, over the past 10 years, that when standards are set and feedback provided in a positive manner, performance will reach very high levels—perhaps in the upper 90th percentile, in a very short period of time."

Asked about the bottom line of B.F. Goodrich's Avon Lake, OH chemical plant's positive reinforcement program which includes goal setting and feedback about scheduling, targets, costs and problems, the production manager was enthusiastic: "Our productivity has increased 300 percent over the past five years. Costs are down. We had our best start-up in 1976 and passed our daily production level from last year the second day after we returned from the holidays."

In a survey of 10 organizations known to have experimentally implemented performance feedback/positive reinforcement (PF/PR) technology on a substantial scale, *Organizational Dynamics* found considerable support for the approach. In some cases, as at ACDC Electronics, the entire work force is managed through the systematic use of performance feedback and positive reinforcement. In other organizations, PF/PR is a limited programmatic effort. At Connecticut General Life, for example, PF/PR is being used primarily in an attendance lottery system.

Why the Increased Interest?

The systematic use of PF/PR isn't a new kid on the block. In 1971, *Business Week* carried a fine story on the successful implementation of PF/PR systems at Emery Air Freight.** TRAINING asked Dr. Geary Rummler, managing director of Praxis Corporation, the management consulting company that worked with Emery on its first programs, about the recent surge of interest in PF/PR systems. "You're right," agreed Rummler, "there has been a new interest in behavior management, especially in the last year." Rummler goes on to point out that the general economic conditions of the late Sixties and early Seventies didn't necessitate a precise technology for solving human performance problems.

Most companies were making money in spite of ineffective and counter-effective internal conditions. "After the *Business Week* article," recalls Rummler, "we received more than 50 requests for more information about our services. But when we explained exactly how much work goes into engineering a performance system, all but a couple of the requesters said thanks but no thanks." Moreover, back then admitting to organizational problems was considered socially uncouth." Today, most gross and net figures are so far apart that any promise of help is seriously evaluated.

"We training people did some dumb things back then," adds Rummler. "We flashed our pretty new technology and jargon around a lot but we didn't make many benefit statements. We often left management with the mistaken idea that two notebooks and a one-day seminar would solve all the performance problems. That didn't happen because it couldn't."

Dr. Aubrey Daniels, president of Atlanta-based Behavioral Systems, Inc., credits the rush to a behavior management approach to the technology's dependence on data. To Daniels' way of thinking, "this is the first bona fide results-oriented approach to management. Other approaches have promised, but we have fulfilled, bottom-line expectations. And *that* gets the attention of the guy at the top."

Ed Feeney, who was "Mr. Inside" at Emery Air Freight when that company became the first to go to behavior management in a big way, and who is now president of Feeney Associates, a behavior management consulting firm, attributes the increase in interest to three factors. "First, all of us in the field are better today at producing behavior change than we were—we have a better product. Secondly, we have developed better strategies for implementing and maintaining be-

117

havioral management systems. Last, but not least, we are better at marketing. We have been accumulating success stories and have the data to prove our successes."

It was this proven ability to effect performance in a cost-effective fashion that convinced Douglas Hanson, manufacturing director of the Abrasives Division of 3M to bring behavior management technology to his first-line supervisors. "Our supervisors needed help, and the philosophy and style of this approach was what we wanted our people to learn." The turnkey for Hanson, though, was the demonstrated success. "This wasn't just another training program someone was trying to sell us. The particu-lar consultant we went with had demonstrated success in an industry like ours, was willing to come in and work right on the plant floor with us to make things happen, and was willing to guarantee the bottom line."

It would seem that the time and the technology are right for each other. Organizations are sincerely interested in managing better and increasing human performance effectiveness. And the PF/PR technology has matured.*** Management can see the results others have obtained, intelligently evaluate the efforts that will be required to go with a behavior management program, and calculate reasonable expectations.

*See Jay Beecroft's article, "Behavior Modification Improves Productivity at 3M," *TRAINING*, October 1976.

**See "New Tool: Reinforcement for Good Work," *Business Week*, December 18, 1971.

***We believe the term Performance Feedback and Positive Reinforcement (PF/PR) aptly describes the growing field of technology involved with improving human performance by changing both the way people learn how they're doing on the job and the way people treat each other. The term signifies a debt not only to the clinical psychology of behavior modification but also to cybernetics and information and work systems design.

Used together, the powerful principles behind the two terms are synergistic. They deserve to be stripped from their parentage and considered as a separate union with different concerns and potentials than either or both progenitors.

Reprinted from TRAINING, December 1976

MOTIVATION

A system approach to this most important of employee attributes involves communication and training

BY WILLIAM H. WEISS

A few years ago a research group asked 290 R&D scientists and engineers: "What was the most fruitful learning experience you have had over the past year or two?" The most frequent response (42 percent) was on-the-job problem solving. The responders described it as being assigned "interesting tasks," "broadening projects," and "writing proposals which force me to . . . become current on everything connected with the project."

Not only do workers want to be consulted on decisions that affect their jobs, they also want to make decisions that are important to their company and its business—they want to be involved. In order to be involved, people need to communicate. They wish to speak and they wish to be listened to.

Two-way communication

At the Veterans Administration Hospital in Oteen, NC, an air-conditioning operator went to the chief of the Engineering Division with an idea for changing the controls on the hospital system. The hospital had paid half a million dollars for this system and it had been designed by experts. Yet the chief listened to the operator. A pilot installation of the operator's idea was made and it worked. When all the units were changed, the hospital realized a savings of a quarter of a million dollars over next 10 years.

Two-way communication is essential to good relations between management and employees. The one-way communication of management telling employees just doesn't work. The communicating style most conducive to motivation is the type where face-to-face discussions between employees and their leaders take place.

Most employees welcome better communication with management. The Bailey Meter Co. subsidiary of Babcock & Wilcox Co. in Wickliffe, OH, promised employees that appropriate department heads would answer any complaints, gripes, questions, and suggestions put to them. Over 1000 inquiries were received within six months, and many of the suggestions saved the company money, one resulting in a major corporate policy change. Of most importance to the company, however, was the interest shown by employees in their jobs and their company, interest which management through truthful and sincere response was able to convert to motivation.

Involvement

Employees want to be involved. A problem arises when they do not have the opportunity. Too many organizations make plans and solve problems only at upper levels of management. Unless an individual is in a responsible position, he doesn't have an opportunity to be part of a decision-making team. Overlooked is the fact that if an employee knows that his thinking and opinion were considered in a decision, he is more likely to do better work.

The National Association of Manufacturers in its booklet "Employee Communication for Better Understanding" suggests: "In the course of personal contacts with workers, use every possibility to ask them what they think. Nothing sets up a man in his organization more than having the boss ask his opinion on something."

In order to retain good people in an organization, management must involve them in their work and give them responsibilities. When people feel responsible there is an aura of "we'll get it done." Being permitted to participate makes a big difference in their attitude. The work atmosphere is more pleasant, a sense of camaraderie prevails, and people actually enjoy their work.

There are other pluses, too. Motivated workers are more pleasant and less strained. Since they are not under tension, they do not tire as quickly, thus their work quality and quantity are better.

Commitment

Getting employees committed is a way of getting them involved. Commitment is an emotion related to motivation in that it drives a person to a level of performance higher than that which could be expected from his inherent skill and knowledge. It is analogous to the "will to win" of an athlete which enables him to overcome the superior prowess of a competitor. The "underdog" team wins because its members are determined individuals.

Communication is necessary to an individual who is committed since he needs to "get through" to his superior for approval of what he is doing and for encouragement to reach his goal. A difficulty sometimes exists in that his organization may fail to recognize communication as a requisite for achievement. The company which employs management-by-objectives techniques may be said to be relying on commitment, since the employee who has agreed to work toward specific goals feels committed to attain those goals.

An engineer who must sell his idea and runs into human obstacles along the way must have perseverance and a strong degree of commitment in order to succeed. If he ever feels "the company does not really care what I think," he will be turned off and his commitment lost. Even when he is working on an assignment, if he strongly senses that his plan or design will be rejected, he may not put into his work the best that he is capable of doing.

The problem is that the purpose of the company is to get the work done—communication is only incidental to the objective. Decisions, policy, and requests for action are easily transmitted downward in a company by channels of authority. But the upward flow of ideas and design is different. Every intermediate level of authority is capable of stopping and may stop the flow of information. Thus, management may fail to get feedback from lower levels of the organization because of a communication failure. And always when communication fails, so does motivation.

Training

Training helps to motivate employees because it increases their interest in their jobs. It has been demonstrated time and again that the best way to get a person interested in a new job is to tell him the purpose of his work, how his part contributes to the whole, and the importance of the job.

People interested in their jobs and their company tend to become better workers and to accomplish more. By participating in training sessions, they can learn the skills of the job which enable them to get satisfaction and enjoyment from their work.

Training is efficient and effective only when good communication takes place. A characteristic of successful training techniques is mutual help. Where individuals share

---

TOO LITTLE, TOO LATE?

BY WILLIAM H. WEISS

Although many elements must combine to achieve a high degree of employee motivation, the glue that holds them together is usually communication. Effective two-way communication is difficult to achieve, but managers ignore it at their peril—as the following story illustrates.

A plastic manufacturer decided to build a new plant in southern Illinois. Employees in the home plant first learned of the plan when an engineering firm hired to do the design work came into the plant to study equipment layout and utility requirements. When the engineers reported to the president that employees were asking questions about the new plant, he decided that he should inform his people about his plans. He did this with a short announcement on the company bulletin board. Unfortunately, he was very brief and left many questions unanswered.

The home plant had done fairly well but the employees knew that recent increases in taxes and an argument with the city over utility rates had been troublesome. Rumors began among the employees about the new plant. Many of the workers felt that the home plant would soon be shut down and they would lose their jobs. Some even went so far as to look for other work. In general, there was an uneasiness which affected the employees' morale and output.

When the president finally realized that his people were very much concerned about their jobs, he told them that the new plant would manufacture only one product, demand for which had greatly increased. The home plant would continue to operate without change. While the employees were relieved, most could not understand why the president had not made that news known earlier.

Reprinted from TRAINING, September 1975

---

ideas and thoughts in working on a problem, trainees learn to draw upon the help of others, a practice which is highly developed and used by managers in their work. Group participation also tends to motivate people to learn from others, something which is often diffi-

---

cult to bring about with individual training.

Most management consultants agree that when employees feel they are well informed, their company stands to benefit. The benefits which the company realizes range from greater quantity of work performed to more satisfaction of employees with their working conditions and their pay. Informed employees have better attitudes toward their jobs and their company, and they also have a greater sense of security.

General Electric Company developed a unique way of motivating employees to better understand and realize the importance of their work. The company flew its plant people to a customer site to let them see the products they made in use. A GE official reported, "If any of them had any doubts about the vital importance of the giant powermakers which they help to design and build, this trip dispelled them."

An organization should supplement its formal organizational channels of communication with occasional appeals on company objectives and goals, stressing the ways employees can help attain them. Such downward communication is most effective through the media of the company newspaper and closed-circuit television. The Goodyear Tire & Rubber Company's videotape presentations to its employees in which top officials discuss issues and explain problems facing the company has proved to create much interest and spark participation in efforts to handle the problems.

Participation

People who feel they are part of an organization and making a worthwhile contribution to its success and growth are motivated to good performance. Thus, if people are given the opportunity to participate meaningfully in problem solving and decision making, they will be motivated.

A utility company found that it was having trouble servicing the increasing number of household meters from its growing number of customers. The men in the maintenance and repair shop began to

A TRAINER'S GLOSSARY: BEHAVIOR MODIFICATION

When Benjamin Franklin was a colonel of the Pennsylvania militia, he had a "training" problem. The soldiers weren't attending Sunday services. Rather than lay down the law or chastise the troops, Franklin turned over dispersement of the rum ration to the chaplin. Attendance was no longer a problem. When Franklin's parson began passing out the rum after Sunday services, he was practicing an art referred to variously as **positive reinforcement management, behavioral engineering, operant conditioning, behavior modification, contingency management,** or any of a dozen or so terms meant to describe the process of managing behavior through the systematic use of positive reinforcement.

Parents have always known that a behavior followed by certain consequences (sometimes incorrectly lumped together as "rewards") will continue to be exhibited until it is no longer reinforced. Grandma's law of "work first, then play" is as old as Adam.

What *is* new is the systematic and willful use of a number of "Grandma's laws," old and new, to control many aspects of behavior. The basic premise is that the consequences of a behavior shape the behavior. If the result is aversive, there is less likelihood that the behavior will be repeated; if the results of the behavior are favorable to the behaver, the likelihood of the behavior being repeated is increased. That may seem a complicated way to say good things increase behavior and bad things decrease behavior. But b'mod or operant conditioning isn't that simple. There are five consequences which can possibly follow any behavior. Each has a different effect on the possibility that the behavior will be repeated (see table).

There are some surprises in the table. For example, **punishment** doesn't have a predictable effect on behavior. This invariably is proved by research. Punishment is generally followed by emotional behavior, which neither increases nor decreases the chances that the target behavior will occur again. The only sure way to decrease a behavior is to follow it with an **extinction** procedure, i.e., by doing nothing. It seems so simple. Just pick the behavior you want to see promoted and go promote it. Not that easy. First, what is a reinforcer? Sure, rest for the weary, food for the hungry, activity for the bored, and liquid for the thirsty are all reinforcers, but they are also products of deprivation and we can't fool with **primary needs.**

Fortunately, **secondary reinforcers** are a possibility. When some neutral, non-reinforcing stimulus is repeatedly associated with a primary reinforcer, the formerly neutral stimulus takes on the ability to reinforce. Example: Money is used to purchase things which are primary reinforcers, so money becomes a reinforcer—as long as it still has purchasing power. But even the power of secondary reinforcement is limited, and the guideline for finding usable reinforcing stimuli is often best characterized by the maxim "different strokes for different folks and different ways on different days." Letting the behaver choose his own reinforcer—a process called contracting—is sometimes the only practical solution.

That leads us to a slight procedural problem. To reinforce a behavior, the behavior must occur. In some instances, we can simply wait until the target shows up and then make something "good" happen for the performer. Catch your kids being "good," pass out the positives, and, chances are, they will be "good" again. "Good" in this case defies definition; it's a matter of values and ethics, not technology. This waiting strategy is, alas, useless in many training situations. You can wait forever for your trainee to make his first computer program, but you'll never have anything to reinforce. Instead, you simply will have to reinforce the nearest approximation of the target behavior and then work toward the final target in a stepwise fashion. This is called **shaping**. It is pretty expensive in terms of time to be constantly reinforcing the target behavior. Fortunately, a process called **schedules of reinforcement** helps somewhat. A helpful surprise represented on the table is: A behavior which is only occasionally reinforced *after* it has been shaped into the desired form is more resilient to extinction (going away) than behavior which is reinforced after every occurrence. Don't be fooled, though: The reciprocal cost of getting a desired behavior where none now exists isn't cheap. Reinforcement isn't a something-for-nothing affair. You get when you give. If you stop giving, you eventually stop getting. Remember the story about the two canny rats in the Skinner box? One says to the other, "Look how well I've got this jerk trained. Every time I push the lever he serves up a meal." The only reinforcement system which lasts is the one based on mutual benefit.

Reprinted from TRAINING, June 1976

CONSEQUENCE	CALLED	EFFECT ON POSSIBLE REOCCURRENCE OF TARGET BEHAVIOR
nothing	extinction	decrease in likelihood
something good occurs	positive reinforcement	increase in likelihood
something good withdrawn	punishment	unpredictable
something aversive occurs	punishment	unpredictable
something aversive withdrawn	negative reinforcement	increase

complain about the increased work load, yet the company's budget would not permit providing more room and men in the shop. The shop supervisor asked his men for their ideas on better methods and equipment to enable them to do the increased work without hiring more men.

Among the ideas the men came up with to reduce repair time and floor space were a rotating table for the meters, a rack which permitted complete sandblasting without turning the machine off and a new wrench. By being given the opportunity to participate in problem solving, these men were motivated to come up with ideas that saved the company $150,000 a year.

Job enrichment

Participation can be enhanced by job enrichment. Enriching a job takes advantage of an employee's capabilities and interest in better job performance while also motivating him. Through communication, management can learn about his abilities and goals, thus making it easier to get the participation which satisfies him and helps the company.

The Motorola Company has an answer to the problem of achieving quality output from its operators. Walter Scott, vice president, manufacturing and facilities, says that Motorola plays up the worker's error-free hours. "We'll put a tag on the error-free work station, saying that the operator has done a good job."

Demotivation

When an organization lacks a way or doesn't try to motivate its people, it may be guilty of causing just the reverse—demotivation. Demotivation takes place when a person is made to feel unimportant. It can occur at all job levels including professional people and managers.

Someone is demotivated when he receives inadequate information about his job. The feeling of worthlessness also comes on when a person is not given the opportunity to contribute, when his viewpoints are shunted aside, and when he is ignored.

The shop foreman who is uninterested in and has no respect for his craftsmen is going to have trouble. The quality and quantity of work performed is likely to be low, the accident rate high, and motivation practically nonexistent.

Engineering managers and engineers may feel demotivation when they do not have a strong voice on a design or manufacturing decision although still being expected to perform engineering functions concerning it. They resent engineering decisions being made for them.

Other professional people today also feel frustration in their work. A recent Gallup poll revealed that 70 percent of businessmen and professionals believed "they could produce more each day if they tried." The figure for the total public was 57 percent.

Communication, the lack or inadequacy of it, lies behind demotivation. People want to be informed, to be "in" on things, even when what is going on isn't directly related to their job. Being "in the know" makes a person feel he belongs, that he is important. That feeling is always present in the truly motivated person.

Reprinted from TRAINING, September 1975

WHO KILLED CORPORATE LOYALTY?

Yes, people are less dedicated to companies than they used to be. Does anyone really wonder why?

BY JACK GORDON

Whatever happened to the American worker? Doggone it, the guy used to be a paragon of virtue, a pillar of the Protestant ethic, an honest, hard-working, uncomplaining soul, loyal and obedient to his company, his country and his God—preferably in that order.

Today he—or she—is either a self-absorbed baby boomer or a rapacious yuppie barracuda, a card-carrying, job-hopping member of the Me Generation or the Entitlement Generation or the Maypo Generation or whatever they're calling it this month. (Or calling *them* this month; how many different generations are we talking about anyway?) Doesn't matter. The important thing is that it's nearly impossible to squeeze an ounce of loyalty or an honest day's work out of them, the calculating little weasels.

Well, OK, it's not as if the whole work force has changed. Union workers, for instance, have *always* been a pain in the butt, constantly demanding things like more money and better working conditions.

And if, by "loyal employees," we mean people who wouldn't jump ship at the drop of a hat, we can't really be talking about a change in minimum wage earners either. "Ten cents buys a dishwasher" is a saying you hear in places like Reno, NV. It means that if a hotel needs people to do something like wash dishes, it can lure them away from other hotel kitchens simply by offering 10 cents an hour more than the going rate. Due to the baby bust, service businesses may have to resort to this recruiting tactic more often than they did in the past, but the principle hasn't changed.

No, the real question is, what's gone wrong with professionals and middle managers? Used to be, they'd go to the wall for the company. If you told them to move to Timbuktu, why, they'd pack up and move to Timbuktu. They stuck with a company through thick and thin.

Today, all they want to know is, "What's in it for me?" They're all too busy "networking" and reading the want ads and circulating their résumés to get any work done. They've gotten a whole lot better at interviewing for jobs than they are at doing jobs. Today, if somebody waves a better offer at them, they don't even think twice; it's just, "Adios, amigo." Today, 10 cents buys a middle manager.

Maybe they're changelings or space aliens. It's certainly hard to believe that a lot of these "new workers" are blood descendants of the European immigrants who forged this country's work ethic. You never caught them asking, "What's in it for me?" They weren't the sort of people given to looking out for their own interests.

Absolutely. And this, of course, explains why those immigrants came to the land of opportunity in the first place. Self-interest was the last thing on their minds. They came in search of employers who would ask for their labor and their loyalty as an employer's God-given due. They wanted employers who would offer them nothing in return for that loyalty: no chance to advance, no job security regardless of their performance or tenure, no credible vision of a better life ahead for themselves or their children. These remarkable, selfless people looked all over Europe but they just couldn't find a deal like that anyplace. So they came to America. And waited, selflessly, for the 1980s to arrive.

But seriously, folks...this line of reasoning does get silly pretty quickly, doesn't it? Loyalty to a business enterprise as a character trait that once existed in some psychic realm divorced from self-interest? A Golden Age (alias the 1950s and their afterglow) when loyalty was a one-way street and American workers routinely offered quids without expecting any pro quos? The story ought to be told with a laugh track.

It is certainly possible to score some valid points if you want to talk about the so-called Me Generation. But does anyone seriously believe we *need* a Me Generation to explain any drop in loyalty toward American companies that may have occurred during the past decade?

"Self-interest is the first fundamental of human nature; that doesn't change much," says John Murphy, former director of executive education for GTE Corp. and now a training consultant in Fairfield, CT. What does change, he says, is what people perceive their self-interest to be.

In short, nobody in the 1950s *ever* agreed to move to Timbuktu with the following knowledge: first, that the Timbuktu branch could be "restructured" out of existence at any moment; second, that if the branch did close, the mother company would instantly sever its relations with all employees there, stranding them in Timbuktu with nothing but some pamphlets explaining how to write a résumé.

Who killed corporate loyalty? Murphy proposes that we reframe the question: "What is it that companies want loyalty to?"

Call him Bob. He was a marketing research manager for a division of General Mills Inc. in Minneapolis.

One day in April 1987, Bob looked through an office window and saw some people arguing: the division's general manager, the vice president of personnel, Bob's boss and a few other executives.

"My boss had a piece of paper, and he was gesturing angrily with it," Bob remembers. "Finally the personnel vice president banged his fist on the desk, and that was it. The paper came out of the office and was put into my hands. It explained the conditions of my termination. I'd had no warning at all."

Two years previously, Bob's division had acquired an ice cream plant. Due in part to Bob's efforts ("I liked new-product development," he says), the plant's revenues had grown from $35 million to $100 million. In the '80s, however, that wasn't good enough. The top brass at General Mills was jumpy, worried about the possibility of a takeover attempt. In the executive offices, Bob knew, many scenarios were being developed and plans laid to thwart potential moves by a number of parties rumored to covet the company.

Though the ice cream plant had more than doubled its revenues in two years, its profit margin wasn't as good as that of General Mills' flagship breakfast-cereal business. "In today's environment," Bob says, "any marginal operations that aren't [part of the core business] may be viewed by a takeover artist as suppressing the core profits of the company. He could get cash for selling [the marginal operation], and profit-per-share could be enhanced. Management was scared of anything that could be viewed that way by a Nestlé, a Ralston Purina, a Philip Morris...."

Restructuring had already begun. The layoffs came in waves. Bob was caught in Wave No. 5. His division sold the ice cream plant and Bob was through. He got seven months' salary as severance pay.

Bob was 43 years old. He had worked for General Mills for 19 years. He was still naive enough to be shocked by the discovery that those years counted for nothing.

A second rude awakening was in store when Bob went job hunting. He learned that a résumé showing two decades of loyal service to a company meant no more in the job market than it had to the company that received the service. In fact, Bob says, "Loyalty works *against* you." In interviews with recruiters and prospective employers, he discovered that "being with one company for 19-1/2 years is a sign that you're not aggressive."

Not aggressive? During his tenure with General Mills, Bob says, he had received promotions, he had held seven different positions, and he had played key roles in developing and expanding new businesses, such as the ice cream operation. Somehow, none of that counted as aggressiveness.

Before the '80s, job-hoppers were frowned upon. Now they are heroes. It's the loyalists who are suspect.

So Bob started his own consulting business, handling market-research projects. He says he might take a permanent management job again at some

---

If you told them to move to Timbuktu, why, they'd move to Timbuktu.

---

point. But next time around, Bob will play his cards differently.

"I'm loyal to myself now," he says. "If I go to work for another company, my résumé will always be circulating." And he would not consider an offer in the first place unless it involved a written contract. Why? "Because I do not trust big corporations," says formerly loyal Bob.

"People have *learned* not to be loyal," says George Odiorne of St. Petersburg, FL, consultant, retired college professor and member of the HRD Hall of Fame. "They didn't get the realization on the road to Damascus, they got it on the road to ruin."

During the 1980s, in the manufacturing sector particularly, stories like Bob's played out so often that they became clichés. In 1989 alone, according to *Business Week,* 160,000 U.S. manufacturing jobs evaporated. In 1985 and '86, 600,000 jobs were lost due to cutbacks and restructuring.

And every time the drama unfolds, it unfolds before an audience. The message Bob received has been hammered home again and again, not only to the hundreds of thousands who've gotten the boot, but to the millions who have watched them get it.

It was the lesson of the '80s, one best expressed by AFL-CIO president Lane Kirkland: "Never love a company that can't love you back."

It would be fun to conclude, as the moral of Bob's story, that American corporations are now run by evil people. Top executives certainly have demonstrated an unhesitating willingness to sacrifice the troops on the altar of quarterly profits.

A more likely conclusion would be, however, that companies are run by people who act in their own interests. More precisely, they are run by people who act according to their perception of their interests, which is based on their perception of the world in which they live. (In this, they are much like Bob. He perceived loyalty to General Mills as a pathway to personal success—a way to build a rewarding career, to acquire interesting work, promotions, pay raises, security, college educations for his children, maybe some lakefront property.... His expectations were the same as those that produced loyal employees 30 years ago.)

It's not as if sinister executives everywhere are holding out phony guarantees of lifetime job security. Many companies are perfectly forthright in telling employees that they can no longer promise security. Some foot the bill for consultants to come in and say things like, "The name of the game today is not employment but employability." Some companies even sponsor classes that tell their people how to "pack their own parachutes"—meaning networking, circulating your résumé, etc.

And as for the myopic focus on short-term profits? "I'm not among those who criticize senior managers for short-term thinking," says Vijay Sathe, professor of organizational behavior at Claremont (CA) College's graduate school of business. "If we were in their shoes, we'd probably make the same decisions." Senior managers are not irrational, he says. "They're responding to pressures coming from the markets."

Sathe refers, of course, to Wall Street. Here is William Greider, national editor of *Rolling Stone* magazine, describing the 1980s in his new book *The Trouble With Money:* "[T]he largest companies became captive to finance in new and destabilizing ways.

On one front, managers felt the hot breath of financial adventurers who could assemble staggeringly large packages of debt, buy out the shareholders at a generous price, and profitably cannibalize the corporation. On another front, the fortunes of U.S. export industries now rose and fell capriciously, not based on the quality of their own performance but on the money traders who gambled on currencies in foreign-exchange markets.... Real goods produced by real manufacturers became the tail wagged this way and that by a large, distant dog—the mood swings of financiers and bankers around the globe."

In a January profile of economist Lester Thurow in the *Atlantic Monthly*, writer Charles C. Mann summed it up in a sentence: "As all the world knows by now, American managers have been forced to make the immediate return on investment their first priority, with the price of a share of stock second."

So who takes the blame for the fact that the new reward for 19 years of faithful service is a pink slip, followed by interviews with recruiters who think you're a schmuck? Financial adventurers? Wall Street manipulators? How about global competition and the "creative destruction" for which it is so notorious?

As far as long-term loyalty to a company is concerned, it makes little ultimate difference whether top managers are evil swine or helpless victims of forces beyond their control. When the ax falls on *you,* you'd naturally prefer an executioner who wishes this didn't have to happen, instead of one who cackles with demonic glee and twirls his mustache like Oilcan Harry. But you can't pay the rent with management's regret. No matter how sincere the weeping of a sorrowful CEO upon the occasion of your being canned, his tears won't send your kids to college.

The plain fact is that most organizations can no longer offer convincing arguments that they will remain faithful, in sickness and in health, through the course of a marriage. Therefore, their relationships with employees have started to look more like one-night stands.

The question then becomes, must this necessarily be a bad thing? Apparently, we must redefine what Sathe calls the "psychological contract" between an organization and its employees.

If it no longer makes sense to marry an employer, what does it mean to be loyal to one? When we ask if you are loyal to your company, what is it that we want to know? Do we mean, what's keeping you here aside from a need to eat and a lack of better offers? How attractive would an offer have to be to lure you away? How much energy will you devote to doing a good job instead of just sliding by?

All of those measures no doubt hinge to some degree on the amount of respect and trust that exist between the organization and the employee. That being the case, national opinion polls suggest that if corporations want to talk to workers about loyalty in any form, they had better talk fast.

'They didn't get the realization on the road to Damascus, they got it on the road to ruin.'

• In a 1988 survey of 100,000 working people, Opinion Research Corp. of Princeton, NJ, noted a steep decline in trust and regard for top management. Comparing its figures to those from a 1983 survey, ORC found the 1988 group considerably less likely to feel that their companies were "treating [them] with respect and consideration." That finding is ironic when you consider that from 1983 to 1988, "participation," "communication" and "teamwork" were among the hottest buzzwords in the business world.

ORC's 1988 respondents also had much less respect for the abilities of top executives; that is, fewer employees believe that the people running their companies are competent to do so. The drop in regard for senior executives held true among middle managers, professionals and hourly workers alike.

• Last year, in a telephone survey of 520 workers sponsored by *Time* magazine, 57 percent of the respondents said that companies are less loyal to their employees than they were 10 years ago; 63 percent said employees are less loyal to their companies.

• In *The Cynical Americans: Living*

and Working in an Age of Discontent and Disillusion (Jossey-Bass, 1989), Donald Kanter and Philip Mirvis cite a litany of distressing findings from Harris polls dating back to 1966. Over the past two decades, public confidence in all kinds of institutions has dropped precipitously. Federal, state and local government, organized religion, the press, the medical and legal professions—you name it, fewer people trust it. Watergate, Vietnam, Iran-Contra, Jim and Tammy Bakker, Geraldo Rivera—all have exacted a toll.

But nowhere, the authors say, "has the decline in confidence...been more evident than in people's attitudes about business and its leadership. Confidence in business and business leadership has fallen from approximately a 70 percent level in the late 1960s to about 15 percent today."

Findings like those do not suggest a work force that sees corporate executives as tragic victims of Wall Street piranhas. Look at our friend Bob: He understood perfectly well the financial pressures his company was under, but he still felt raped. Why? Because Bob does not believe that the people who run American corporations resort to layoffs as a painful, desperate, last-ditch measure to save their companies—to keep the enterprise from being cannibalized by financial adventurers. He thinks corporate executives worry about takeovers for one reason only: to protect their own jobs and the "absurd amounts of money they make."

This raises the issue of leadership. Here's where Oilcan Harry *does* make a difference. Was it in order to rescue the enterprise that General Motors executives laid off 30,000 workers a few years ago—and used the savings to award themselves fat bonuses? Was it to rescue the enterprise that those same executives threw huge amounts of GM's money at H. Ross Perot to get him off the board of directors and make him stop calling them names.

Question: From whom does this enterprise need to be rescued? If you're a GM employee, where do you see the cannibals in this picture?

The gap between executive salaries and average worker salaries in the United States has been widening since 1979—and the rift is accelerating. "Chiefs who make 100 times the average Indian's pay are no longer rare," says *Fortune* magazine. In other words, during the very period that executives have "reluctantly" tossed people into unemployment lines by the hundreds of thousands, they themselves have been reaping corporate coin in mind-boggling amounts.

The rationale for paying millions of dollars to a top executive is no secret. It's explained right out loud: If we don't give him spectacular sums of money, a rival company will lure him away. Curiously, when talk turns to the fickleness of today's worker, no-body mentions the obvious corollary: The chief is no more loyal to this organization than anyone else. Ten cents buys a dishwasher? Ten bucks buys a CEO.

The situation becomes downright comical when a company run by a group of multimillion-dollar executives begins to espouse the popular (and convenient) theory that today's employees are not especially motivated by money. The "new worker" would much rather have lots of (free) praise and (inexpensive) motivational pamphlets and (cheap) little heart-shaped lapel pins that tell the world she did a swell job of waiting on a customer. Presumably, the only people left in America for whom money is a primary motivator are CEOs, stock-holders and dishwashers in Reno, NV.

To whom or what shall workers be loyal? To whose standards of honor and self-sacrifice shall they aspire? Has the crew developed a tendency to flee the ship when icebergs loom in-stead of remaining gallantly at their posts? There was a time when it was not laughable to speak of loyalty in that sense. But in those days it was the captain, never the crew, who was expected to go down with the ship. If things go sour today, as Odiorne says, "the very top people have golden para-chutes. They retire to Boca Raton. Everyone else has to look for a job." In other words, if the Ship of Enterprise springs a leak, the one individual aboard who is *not* going down with it is the captain. And everybody knows it.

Whoever or whatever is to blame for the pain wrought by "restructuring," that pain has not been distributed equitably. Says Murphy, "The idea that I should be loyal to you just doesn't play anymore—not after you've been exposed as arrogant, selfish and in-competent."

There is "a vacuum of leadership out there," Murphy adds. But the good news is that when people *do* find lead-ership, they follow. "Yuppies respond to good leadership just like anybody else. Given good leadership, people will still display loyalty to the success and performance of a company—for as long as they're there."

What, then, shall we do? What can the organization expect from its people? "Performance for as long as they're there" pretty much says it all.

"Because of the unpredictability of even the most benign restructuring, managers are less able to guarantee a particular job—or any job at all—no matter what a subordinate's perform-ance level," writes *Harvard Business Review* editor Rosabeth Moss Kanter.

You can't pay the rent with management's regret.

To the degree that this is true, we would appear to have a problem—one that does not boil down merely to the commonplace observation that the corporation can no longer offer "secu-rity" as a reward for good perform-ance. The problem is that employees have less vested interest in the future success of the firm.

Why should people go the extra mile, serve the extra customer, put the extra effort into building a quality product? The traditional answer has been, "Because if Acme Widget grows and prospers, we all will grow and prosper along with it."

But suppose the vast majority of Acme Widget's employees have no reason to believe they will still be around in five or 10 years, regardless of how well they perform. Suppose further that the middle managers and professionals don't even *want* to stick around for more than a few years because they have noticed, along with formerly loyal Bob, that it is damaging to one's career to do so. If they wait too long and *then* get laid off, the job market will treat them like lepers. Question: What difference does it make to these people if, a few years from now, Acme Widget has gone down the tubes?

How does Acme attract talented people? How does it motivate them to perform well? And, not to candy-coat it, how does Acme keep people from leaving as soon as it is convenient for them to go, rather than staying until it becomes convenient for Acme to kick them out?

In a recent essay in the *Harvard Business Review* called "The New Managerial Work," Kanter condensed much popular thinking on the subject of motivation in the present environ-ment into five "tools":

• *Mission:* Try to give people a sense of importance, pride and purpose in their work. This works especially well with technical professionals, Kanter says. They like "to see their work contribute to an excellent final prod-uct."

• *Agenda control:* Give them more control over their own activities. Dele-gate work, delegate decisions, give them time to pursue pet projects. Try to let them choose what to work on next.

• *Share of value creation:* Give people a piece of the action—a share in the profits from a new venture, for instance. She is not talking about companywide profit-sharing plans, but specific incentives for specific achievements: "equity participation in project returns, bonuses pegged to key performance targets," etc. In short, give them money.

• *Learning:* A chance to learn new skills is welcome in today's turbulent environment "because it's oriented toward securing the [employee's] fu-ture.... [A]ccess to training, mentors and challenging projects [can be] more important than pay or benefits." This is because learning can lead to things like bigger pay and benefits down the road.

• *Reputation:* Traditional corporate managers and employees "stayed behind the scenes," Kanter says, but today's professionals "have to make a name for themselves." Help them build reputations, and you motivate them. Do this by creating "stars," recogniz-ing them publicly, giving credit to people for their innovations, plugging them into professional networks, etc.

Notice that none of those induce-ments attempt to link the firm's future to the individual's. Indeed, the last two implicitly assume that the employee's career path will lead out of the firm, rather than up some internal hierarchy.

Some of the five tools are designed primarily with a certain kind of employee in mind: a professional with plenty of attractive options outside the company. This is what people usually mean when they talk about the "new worker."

For example, take "Edward," a 30-year-old software engineer in the Portland, OR, area. In 1986 he was working at Tektronix Inc. when a computer-workstation project in which he was involved got scrubbed. There were layoffs. Edward was asked to stay, but chose not to. "I didn't see a good chance to do interesting work there," he says. "I'm in a position where I get a lot of calls from recruiters, so I started accepting some interviews."

The promise of interesting work (and a substantial pay raise) sent Edward across town to National Semiconductor. A year later, National suddenly canceled the project upon which his group was working. More layoffs. Edward stayed on. A few months later, the entire development center where he worked was closed. Edward was asked to stay long enough to train an engineer from California who would continue to provide customer support for the computer systems the Portland center had developed and that National had sold. He agreed.

Why? Because he needed the job? No. Out of loyalty to National? No. During the first round of layoffs there, Edward's coworkers had discovered they were unemployed when they showed up for work one morning and found that their electronic keys to the building no longer worked. Sudden, brutal "announcements" of this sort, intended to prevent sabotage, are fairly common in the computer industry. But common or not, Edward considered it "tacky," and it left him with no great love for National.

So why did he stay the second time? "Mostly because I liked the guy who'd be doing the support," he says, referring to the California trainee. "Also I liked our customers in the Netherlands who'd need the support. I'd met several of their engineers and felt bad about leaving them out on a limb."

Here is a case where a company's reputation for supporting its products hangs on the tenuous thread of one employee's professional pride and affiliations. Indeed, it hangs partly upon the fact that this employee happened to like some Dutch engineers.

Last year, Edward took his pick of three job offers and returned to Tektronix. He felt his former company was now better managed and was likely to give him interesting work to do. "I'll stay with a company through rough times," he says, "*if* I can gain valuable experience from a technical point of view or *if* I see [that management has] a good plan to turn things around."

I n Edward's story, we see part of the answer to what seems like the $64,000 question—but perhaps isn't. You'd think companies would face a terrible dilemma today: If people's career interests are becoming divorced from the future prospects of any par-

---

If this ship sinks, the one individual who is not going down with it is the captain.

---

ticular firm, how do you get people to work on behalf of the firm's future?

"Oddly, it's not an issue," says Claremont College's Sathe. Along with all the other changes sweeping the working world, he says, we are beginning to see a change in the mind-set that produces quality work. The traditional mind-set was, "I'll do a great job because I'll be with this company for years." This is changing "to a mind-set that says, 'I'll do a great job because I'm a professional.'"

Thus, Edward protects *his* customers in the Netherlands for his own reasons. In doing so, he serves the interests of National Semiconductor.

Performing quality work is in professionals' best interests whether they plan to stay with a company or go, Sathe says. And most of them know it. Right now, "aerospace workers are moving up and down Highway 5" on the West Coast, hiring out their services to whichever manufacturer needs them this month, he says. "Quality has not suffered."

The other piece of the answer is supplied by Murphy. How do you get people to focus on the firm's long-term interests? The only place where

this is an issue worth worrying about is at the top of the corporate pyramid, Murphy says. Only senior executives are in a position to sacrifice a company's future ability to compete by chasing short-term gains. If they're doing so, there isn't much the employees can do to prevent it. If top management *is* trying to build for the future, on the other hand, it doesn't matter if people at lower levels are worried about the next six months or the next 16 years. In the first place, people do what they're rewarded for doing, and top management determines the company's reward structures. In the second place, Murphy says, once you get below the top levels, there is little or no conflict between activities that will make the organization stronger next month and those that will make it stronger next decade.

For instance, what is the long-term issue that concerns you? Continuous quality improvement? "Short-term results lead to long-term results," says Murphy. "People will build momentum by discovering they can succeed at doing small parts of a humongous problem." You begin to achieve a five-year goal by achieving a three-month goal, then another, then another. And you have all sorts of ways to reward people for achieving three-month goals. No conflict.

F or all the attention devoted in recent management literature to "new workers" like Edward, they are, of course, exceptions. Most working people in the United States do not routinely get phone calls from corporate headhunters. They don't spend a lot of time weighing the merits of several attractive job offers. For them, "loyalty" often translates into simple inertia. Job hunting is a painful, punishing experience and few normal people will subject themselves to it as long as they're even moderately happy where they are.

It may be that the world's most underutilized loyalty-building strategy is simply for management to get out of people's way and off their backs. In a lot of companies, management practices and personnel policies (including some humanistic-sounding ones) seem designed to find out how much crap people are willing to take before they finally break down and look for another job.

"Most corporate environments probably violate EPA standards," says

Murphy, expressing the same concept. "You want to say, 'Let's put up an umbrella and ignore the stuff coming down from [management].'"

What about getting people to go the extra mile—to put forth more than the minimum effort required to do their jobs? Employers have a fundamental advantage in this area, if only they have the wit to capitalize upon it. It is simply this: Granting that we have to work for a living, the vast majority of us would rather be good at what we do than lousy at it. It's *more interesting* to do something pridefully and well than to do it poorly.

"Lots of workers do the best job they can regardless of whether they're with the company for three days or three years," Sathe points out.

Employers neutralize this natural advantage, of course, when they give employees reasons to feel used, abused, unappreciated, cheated, lied to, put upon, yanked around, played for suckers, etc.

Companies also can benefit from what we might call ricochet loyalty. People can be fiercely loyal to a particular state, for instance, and will stay with a company in that state even though better career opportunities beckon elsewhere. Dual-career couples also tend to become anchored in one location, even if neither is all that enamored of the region. It's just too big a sacrifice for *somebody* if they leave.

Odiorne suggests that we can look at the whole '80s team-building craze as an attempt—at least in part—to restore lost loyalty. Soldiers demonstrate much more loyalty to their own platoons than to their divisions or battalions. Similarly, workers often will invest more of themselves in the interests of small project teams than they will in the broad interests of the Gigantor Corp. True, there are many reasons why the team concept has gotten hot. But it is more than simple coincidence, says Odiorne, that management fell in love with team building during a period when workers have diminishing reasons to feel any loyalty at all to the Gigantor Corp.

Who killed employee loyalty? "Loyalty as a general instinct is still around," says Odiorne. It simply attaches itself to different objects today.

People will be loyal to a profession, a leader, an industry, a city, a group of peers, an exciting project. All they're refusing to do is love a company that can't love them back.

Reprinted from TRAINING, March 1990

THE NEW EMPLOYMENT CONTRACT

The rules that guided traditional employee-employer relationships no longer apply. What will replace them?

BY CHRIS LEE

Once upon a time the working world was a predictable place. You went to work for a company and were more or less adopted into a stable system. You worked hard, but were well rewarded for your efforts. Because you were loyal to The Company, you earned regular promotions, an increasingly better standard of living and a secure future.

A fairy tale? By today's standards, yes. During the last five years, former bastions of job security—*Fortune 500* companies, banks, utilities—have downsized, restructured and merged themselves into radically different shapes. Managers and professionals who were once almost guaranteed employment, if not regular promotions, have lost their jobs. Meanwhile, the survivors struggle to adapt to a shifting environment.

The result of these changes, according to some observers, has been a rending of the "employment contract" between companies and their employees. To be sure, the traditional expectations shared by employer and employee usually were not formalized by an unbreakable, written document. But there was an implicit agreement about the way the game would be played. The employee provided loyalty, dependability and a fair day's work in exchange for a fair day's pay, a shot at the boss's job and a secure future.

Today, few—if any—companies can assure current or future employees of career stability, advancement or even a job. Employers are reacting with uncertainty, while employees are reacting by suing employers for unjust termination or by quitting and remaining on the job. Social scientists are reacting by decreeing that the problem deserves more study. All the players realize the rules of the game have changed. But no one can be sure what will replace them.

There's been a lot of discussion here about the old and new employment contract—what it was and what it's becoming. In our mpany, we've said, 'If you do a good job, you'll be taken care of.' Now, we find we can't fulfill that contract, that implied understanding that has been ingrained in our culture."

> J.E. Reller
> General Manager, Staffing Technologies
> Control Data Corp.

Control Data Corp., well known for its progressive employee-relations policies, is one of a handful of major corporations that demonstrates its commitment to job security. Although it never *guaranteed* no layoffs, it designed a "rings of defense strategy" in 1980 to protect permanent, full-time employees.

The rings of defense guarantee that before employees lose their jobs, overtime will be eliminated, work subcontracted to outside vendors will be brought inside, supplemental or temporary employees will be laid off, and attrition will be encouraged through hiring restrictions and early retirement.

When the double whammy of the computer slump and increased competition hit CDC, however, the rings of defense collapsed. The trickle of layoffs that began in 1985 rapidly turned into a flood that swept away nearly half the work force by the middle of this year.

Today the slimmed-down company faces a collection of daunting tasks: outplacing employees, reassuring survivors, and rethinking its paternal approach to job security and employee development. "We're trying to help people understand that no one—no company, no government entity—can guarantee employment," says Reller. "High-tech companies like us have been on a rapid growth curve, with multiple opportunities for everyone. Now we're experiencing real trauma trying to adjust to no change—growth has declined, promotions have declined, raises have declined."

CDC is examining its changing employment contract against the backdrop of deeply held principles that emphasize its commitment to employee security and development. "We're in the process of trying to evaluate changes at CDC with these principles in mind," explains Joe McGregor, general manager of human resources planning. "We're working to figure out what will be in the 'new' contract. It's evolving; we're not yet sure ourselves what is going to happen."

Through its strategic planning process, CDC is trying to answer two abiding questions: Where are we now, and where are we going? According to McGregor, thoughts thus far center on a few new realities, including the shift from a growing to a shrinking mode and the switch from a permanent to a temporary, flexible work force. But perhaps the dominant truism for CDC—and every other business—is that stability and predictability have turned into change and uncertainty.

Control Data may be one of the few organizations looking carefully at the changes wrought in the employment contract in the wake of the past few eventful years, but it certainly is not alone in resorting to massive work-force paring. Over the past five years, at least 13 million jobs have been eliminated in the United States, according to a *Forbes* magazine estimate. The Bureau of Labor Statistics puts the toll of lost executive, managerial and administrative jobs over the same period at 500,000.

Like the body counts of a war half a world away, distant news of yet another massive layoff or corporate downsizing has lost its power to stun. But the shock waves resulting from the upheavals in the corporate landscape ripple throughout the work force, creating a cumulative effect that can only be estimated.

The key issue in American industry today is not just downsizing as such, but the effect downsizing has on the consolidation of the company, the decentralization of authority, on managerial systems, and on the morales and performance of the streamlined work force."

Jerome M. Rosow
President
Work in America Institute

A symposium sponsored by the Work in America Institute last spring examined the impact of downsizing and restructuring on American business. In his keynote address, Rosow characterized the massive downsizings of the past few years as "the ripping apart of a social contract" between companies and their employees. Top HR executives at several leading companies explained why they're cutting back their work forces and what they're doing to avoid sacrificing the survivors' morale and commitment.

Prior to the turbulence of the past few years, professionals at General Electric were practically assured of job security, while the company was assured of employee loyalty. "That bond has been broken in the '80s," said Frank Doyle, senior vice president of corporate relations at GE. But he described his company's "delayering" in terms of a new social contract that can benefit both employee and employer.

For the company, Doyle explained, the payoff for breaking that bond is increased flexibility and efficiency in fulfilling its "fundamental economic mission—producing goods and services at the best quality and lowest possible cost. We will perform that mission better if we take steps not only to reshape the management structure, but to extend to employees that same kind of dynamic flexibility we've begun to demonstrate as employers."

What will that flexibility mean to GE employees? According to Doyle, more versatile jobs, the chance to use a broader base of skills and greater participation in decision making.

At AT&T, known for "cradle-to-grave careers," three downsizings in as many years produced a huge culture shock. Hal W. Burlingame, senior vice president of personnel, told the symposium audience that the cutbacks, totaling about one-third of AT&T's work force, followed several other major upheavals: divestiture, deregulation and the revolution in communication technologies. Initially, AT&T stuck to the old rules—even though it was in a whole new ball game.

"The business that built itself into an institution by creating universal service for telephone customers tried to create a universal approach to its people," Burlingame explained. "That mind-set strongly influenced some of our decisions in the early days of downsizing. We began to realize that our concept of fairness and equity, where everyone was treated the same and we had no formal means of differentiating effectively between individuals or skills when we made cuts in the work force, was not always the most fair for the business or its people. Nor was it appropriate in terms of the markets we were addressing.

"As we became more market-focused," he continued, "we realized that we had to devise ways of holding onto the 'critical skills' people—both management and occupational—who would serve us in the future."

In 1986, when the third downsizing took place, AT&T changed its approach. This time, people who were "keepers" were told they had been selected to stay. People who were at risk knew they were at risk. Through it all, AT&T learned to look at human resource management in strategic terms, Burlingame said. "And that is the most effective way to build a new relationship between AT&T and the people who comprise it."

The experiences of these corporate giants raise more questions than they answer about the new employment contract. Having made the decision to shrink your work force, how do you make sure essential employees don't cut and run? Can you expect to engender a sense of loyalty and commitment from employees once you've "broken faith"? What kinds of payoffs will employees value in place of traditional job security?

While companies in the throes of major change struggle to find answers, social scientists have discovered that their corporate soul-searching is justified. Recent studies that track the impact of new workplace realities across organizations have uncovered some alarming trends.

Job satisfaction for middle managers has dropped so precipitously that it is now close to the abysmal levels reported by clerical and hourly workers, proclaims a report from the Center for Management Research in Wellesley, MA. Citing a recent Hay Group/Yankelovich/Clancy Shulman study, this report also points to a decrease in commitment to The Company, diminished career aspirations, and a dwindling sense of job security, particularly among mid-managers and professionals.

These findings echo those of a 1984 Opinion Research Corp. report, "Supervision in the '80s: Trends in Corporate America." ORC, which has been sampling employee attitudes since 1970, uncovered an emerging paradox: While most employees remain highly satisfied with their jobs, their opinions of their companies are steadily declining. ORC found these attitudes hold true across employee classifications: managerial, supervisory, professional, clerical and hourly workers. At the same time, when ORC asked employees if they are committed to their companies' growth and success, at least seven out of 10 said they are.

These seeming contradictions, ORC's report concludes, indicate that employee commitment is out there, but it is not being effectively mobilized. To do so, ORC recommends that organizations:

• Understand employee work values. Management must know what employees value in their jobs in order to tailor rewards to these values.

• Let employees know what the

standards of job performance are.

• Tie performance to rewards and clearly communicate the links between them to employees.

• Provide effective performance evaluations.

• Give supervisors and managers the tools they need to manage—training in communication and appraisal skills, support from management for their actions, authority consistent with their responsibilities and reasons to be committed to the organization.

Our national resource, which is also our national problem is an almost unbelievably large number of educated, motivated and competitive people striving to achieve both traditional and nontraditional kinds of success. Traditionally, they want increasing amounts of responsibility, money, power, status—all the things that come with promotion. Nontraditionally, they also want their work to expand their minds, fulfill their souls and encourage their personal growth—all the things that come from unending challenge. Unfortunately, there aren't all that many such jobs around; and, as the numbers show, it's not going to get much better."

Judith Bardwick
The Plateauing Trap

The "national resource" to which Bardwick refers is, of course, the much-examined baby boom. This bulge in the demographic python has been straining the institutional resources—schools, colleges, hospitals—of this country since the 1950s. Now the squeeze play is on in the workplace. The fact that the boomers' entry into management ranks corresponded with an era of downsizing and decreasing opportunities only exacerbates the impact of both. Clearly, the fact that more people are competing for scarcer promotions demands some changes in the "growth potential" clause of the employment contract.

"Most of the baby boomers have gone as far as they will go in management and will stay in their present jobs another 30 years or so," wrote Peter Drucker in an essay in *The Wall Street Journal* in 1985. In order to create a better match between their career aspirations and reality, he continued, "we will have to redesign managerial and professional jobs so that even able people will still be challenged by the job after five or more years in it. . . . We will have to heap responsibility on people in junior positions. And, above all, we will have to find rewards and recognition other than promotion—more money, bonuses, extra vacations. . .and so on. In the meantime, however, an entire generation has grown up for whom promotion is the only 'real' satisfaction and failure to get one every year or two is equivalent to being a 'loser.' "

How are employers reacting thus far? Some have begun to explore a new direction in career development, one in which the primary responsibility for an individual's career belongs to the individual, not the career development specialist from corporate human resources.

Control Data is just beginning to incorporate this change in emphasis into its orientation program for newly hired employees. It also plans to create a career-management center that will help individuals map out their options—examine their values, update their skills, anticipate career shifts in the future—before they are displaced or simply decide they are misplaced in their current jobs. "Before, we never said, 'Your career is your responsibility,' " says Reller. "Now, our feeling is that 70 percent of the future is the employee's responsibility and maybe 30 percent or less is the company's. We want them to think about that."

Tod White, president of Blessing-White, a consulting company in Princeton, NJ, that specializes in career development, says the old idea of a tidy career path is obsolete, particularly in large companies. "There are fewer rungs [on the career ladder], more qualified and competent 25- to 35-year-olds, and more competition for fewer slots," he says. At the same time, the volume of change—downsizing, restructuring, acquisitions—has increased exponentially. In many organizations, he points out, the people are the same, but all the rules have changed. Increasingly uncertain and anxious employees are asking, "What does all this mean for my career?"

In fact, more employees are more likely to get stuck in jobs they have outgrown. They become dissatisfied, quit their jobs or, perhaps even worse for the organization, quit and remain on the job.

"It's up to the individual to find new kinds of job satisfaction," says White. "The individual has to take the initiative. But it behooves the organization to help employees deal with those concerns. If employees are anxious and confused, the organization is not getting the productivity it needs." He sees the new direction in career development as a partnership between the individual, his or her manager and the organization. Managers play a central role by answering some tough questions about the individual's future in the organization, but it's still incumbent on the individual to *ask* the questions.

Sam Campbell, a principal with Kearney Campbell & Associates, a consulting firm based in Prescott, WI, agrees with White's assessment of shifting career development strategies. "I think there's a really healthy part to this," he says. "In the past, too many people were lulled into complacency about their careers and career planning. Now, they realize they have to think more about their careers. The superior performers always did."

Campbell, who recently retired from Honeywell after more than 20 years in human resources, knows whereof he speaks. He was one of the primary movers behind the company's jobs and relationships studies. (See "The Honeywell Studies: How Managers Learn to Manage," TRAINING, August 1985.) "[Successful managers] told us, 'There are other people just as competent as I am. I just wanted it more.' We called these people self-initiators. Three forces were at work in their careers: self-initiation, boss-initiation and organizational initiation."

Honeywell researchers concluded that an individual's boss needs to act as a mentor, trainer and coach, and the organization needs to sponsor some kind of developmental activities. But according to Campbell, self-initiation was by far the most important factor. "If that didn't happen, none of the rest mattered."

Until fairly recently, the primary unwritten contract in the American workplace offered material well-being and the status of being a breadwinner in exchange for a limited commitment to jobs that were often dull and unrewarding. But it is clear that this kind of contract will not be adequate for a high-discretion/high-expressivism workplace."

Daniel Yankelovich
and Joan Immerwahr
Work in the 21st Century

Expressivism is the term Yankelovich and Immerwahr use to identify the values of what often is called the "new work force." These are the baby boomers who want intangible rewards from their jobs, such as the chance to express themselves and fulfill their potential as individuals. "Those who adhere to the values of expressivism place great emphasis on autonomy and freedom of choice, reacting uneasily to most forms of rigid hierarchy and to lack of involvement with decision making that affects their lives," the authors explain.

In *Work in the 21st Century*, the authors report on research conducted by the Public Agenda Foundation that explored people's "core relationship" to work. The findings lead Yankelovich and Immerwahr to conclude that the philosophy of expressivism is on the rise and that it will continue to increase. "Our survey shows that expressivist jobholders... are much more likely to want freedom about how to do their work, and they are much more concerned with creativity. They are also less concerned with economic security."

A yearning for autonomy, individuality and self-expression. It all sounds as though the values of the "new work force" were custom-designed to match the demands of the new contract being drafted by today's lean and mean workplace.

Other researchers, however, call the idea of the new work force a "myth." Charles Hughes, cofounder of the Center for Values Research Inc. in Dallas, has been collecting data on employee values for 15 years. In his data base of half a million people, he says, "I see very slight changes in values. The data does not support any dramatic change."

Hughes classifies the majority (60 to 70 percent) of the work force into two types: conformist, characterized by the traditional work ethic and loyalty to the organization, and tribalistic, characterized by a desire for security and a preference for paternalistic management.

Where does this leave the idea of the brave new work force? "Oh, the new age is coming," he says, "but slowly, very slowly. Values vary tremendously by location. If you go to a plant in Tuscaloosa, you'll find plenty of people with tribalistic values; go to Bell Labs and you'll find zero. People who are talking about [the new work force] today are not collecting data. They might be talking to managers or vice presidents, but not to workers on the third shift in a factory."

David Jamieson, president of Los Angeles-based Jamieson Consulting Group, has been monitoring the impact of the changing work force on organizations for several years. He thinks the downsizings and restructurings of the last five years have *forced* people to think in new terms. "People look at their working environment and they see that the old trust and loyalty no longer carry any weight. They are reexamining their security needs in light of their value needs."

In Jamieson's view, the members of the new work force do not see themselves as powerless victims in the evolving employer-employee relationship equation. "The employer used to be able to say, 'Here's your salary; your soul is ours.' We're past that now." People know that a company is unlikely to meet their security needs, so the company's ability to meet their "value needs" becomes proportionately more important. Traditionally, employees scrutinized employers in terms of the job, salary and location offers, Jamieson says. Now the employer's offerings of flexible benefits, continuing education, training, child care and other benefits that meet lifestyle needs have become more important trade-offs.

"Employees have become more critical shoppers, and they are shopping for the best 'contract.' " he says. "They have begun to draft the contract in terms of: 'I am leasing my behavior to the organization. What do I want in return?' "

Given economic uncertainties, a growing number of people are finding their smartest career "buy" may be in a small company, where they have the chance to be a bigger fish in a smaller pond, develop a wider range of skills and maintain greater flexibility in career options.

David Birch, author of *Job Creation in America: How Our Smallest Companies Put the Most People to Work* (Free Press, 1987), and a team of researchers at MIT spent seven years mapping out the changing landscape of American business by tracking trends in a data base of 5.6 million companies. He credits small companies (those with fewer than 100 employees) and start-ups with most of the 9 million new jobs created since 1980. This leads him to conclude that small companies are the most vital part of our economy today.

Small companies, although volatile and uncertain by nature, actually offer better odds for job security than large ones, he contends. "The *Fortune 500* have wiped out jobs equivalent to the entire state of Massachusetts since 1980."

We need to erect 'secure bridges' over which workers can safely traverse the path from one job or occupation to the next. A sense of well-being and security, necessary for most workers, would then derive from the knowledge that the bridge is there, rather than from assurances that their jobs are for life. If you know that there is in place a well-defined procedure by which you can move from one job to another without significant sacrifice, you will be just as secure as if granted some form of permanency."

David Birch
Job Creation in America

While Birch thinks individuals need to be responsible for their own careers and security, he argues for a social policy that would establish some sort of middle ground between what he calls "a rampant laissez-faire approach" and a guaranteed job for life. He likens the idea of secure bridges to other types of security already in place in American life: "We offer security at the beginning of a career (guaranteed public education) and at the end (in the form of Social Security) but nothing in the middle. If we are to hold our present pace and remain competitive, we must now concentrate on the middle."

Secure bridges for employees, he says, start with knowledge of "what's out there." Individuals must continually reassess their skills in light of potential career shifts and stay abreast of the demand in the marketplace. Computerized job-listing services, such as those now used by some of the building trades, would be one way to help people track changing supply and demand in the labor market.

Birch is not alone in advocating the need to reexamine and change existing systems of employment support. Pat Choate, senior policy analyst at TRW, advanced the concept of Individual Training Accounts (ITAs) several years ago in *Retooling the American Work Force*, a policy study written for the Northeast-Midwest Congressional Coalition in 1982. Choate's approach mimicks Individual Retirement Accounts. It would create an interest-bearing account to which both employee and employer contribute. Like an IRA, it would be vested in the individual, not the job. Employees who are laid off would be able to draw upon the account to pay for retraining and relocation.

Another essential plank in the new security bridge would be outplacement support for employees who lose their jobs. Judging by the rapid increase in the number of consulting firms offering outplacement services, this one is already in place. The Association of Outplacement Firms has quadrupled its membership since 1982, and the outplacement industry has boosted its revenues from $15 million to $350 million over the past decade. At this point, many companies routinely offer outplacement assistance to managers and professionals; some provide help to lower-level layoff victims as well.

Birch characterizes both outplacement and ITAs as "American" solutions that help employees help themselves between jobs. Rather than the European model of government-funded security—which too frequently amounts to long-term unemployment payments—these are private solutions, he told TRAINING. The jointly funded ITA and the employer-paid outplacement contract are options that form bridges rather than barriers to new jobs.

Nevertheless, says Birch, what it still comes down to is individual effort. "I saw a motorcyclist the other day whose black leather jacket said, 'Yea, though I walk through the valley of the shadow of death, I will fear no evil, for I'm the toughest mother in the valley.' That's what it's all about. Who will get jobs in the future? Those who are well-trained and willing to out-compete others for jobs."

NEW CARROTS FOR NEW WORKERS

BY BEVERLY GEBER

Stories and surveys about lagging American productivity are as common these days as snowflakes in February. Blame is allotted to nearly everyone, not least to the American worker, whose alleged lack of traditional work values makes the manager's job of motivation a lot tougher. Of course, some managers see this simply as a challenge: What kinds of carrots should we dangle before this "new worker?"

Carla O'Dell, a researcher with the American Productivity Center (APC), wanted to find out what companies are doing to create new reward systems that might appeal to the new worker—and whether those systems actually work. She mailed surveys to 4,500 organizations that included members of the APC and the American Compensation Association, as well as an additional sample of firms using gain-sharing plans. The 1,598 surveys she got back represent a 36% response rate.

O'Dell's findings probably don't reflect the prevalence of nontraditional reward systems in American business at large, because her sample was drawn from membership lists of organizations that emphasize innovative ways to get people to produce.

But the value of her research may lie in another statistic: The firms that responded, she says, employ 9 million people, 8% of the work force.

O'Dell found a lot of companies departing from traditional practices because they wanted to tie pay to performance, reduce compensation costs and improve employee commitment. Some plans, such as profit sharing, gain sharing, small-group incentives and individual incentives reflect a shift toward pay for performance. Two-tier plans—in which new employees start at a lower base wage than in the past—attempt to lower payroll costs, while plans such as "pay for knowledge" try to increase flexibility and develop *esprit de corps*.

Among O'Dell's findings:

● *Tremendous recent growth of non-traditional reward systems.* Seventy-five percent of her sample used some form of nontraditional reward, and in the vast majority of cases, the programs started in the last five years. For example, 74% of the companies that offered gain sharing began their programs within that time frame. O'Dell discovered that more systems involving gain sharing, pay for knowledge, small-group incentives, lump-sum bonuses, and two-tier wage plans had been adopted for hourly employees in the past five years than in all of the prior 20. Even among plans that have been used for decades, such as profit sharing and individual incentives, growth accelerated in the past 10 years. Manufacturing firms are most likely to use profit sharing, gain sharing, pay for knowledge, and two-tier wage plans. Earned time off is the only practice more common in the service sector.

● *Nontraditional reward systems are effective.* When O'Dell asked the firms using novel reward systems if they're effective, she heard a chorus of yeses. One exception: Only 30% of the companies using "recognition" as a reward system thought it helped boost production. In the other categories, favorable ratings ranged from 66% of companies that confer lump-sum bonuses on production workers to 89% of those that "pay for knowledge" of hourly workers.

● *Use of traditional reward systems is declining.* Many companies slashed or shelved traditional practices such as cost-of-living adjustments (COLA), merit increases and executive perquisites. For instance, 36% restricted or cut out across-the-board increases; 28% did the same with COLAs. Company cars for executives were junked or curbed at 28% of the companies, and reserved parking suffered the same fate at 12% of the firms.

O'Dell's study also includes statistics on collective bargaining practices. Twelve percent of the respondents were less likely than before to follow the industry standards and 11% eliminated or modified work-rule restrictions.

Reprinted from TRAINING, February 1987

Capitalism, then, is by nature a form or method of economic change and not only never is but never can by stationary."

Joseph Schumpeter
Capitalism, Socialism and Democracy

This year, *Forbes* magazine celebrated its 70th anniversary with a special issue trumpeting the "creative destruction" necessary for progress in our capitalist system. Much of the issue ended up as a tribute of sorts to Schumpeter, a German economist who died in 1950. His theory, *Forbes* explains, rests on the radical notion "that the market perfection of classical economics—in which suppliers are small, numerous and powerless—is less important to prosperity than a society's willingness to change."

Schumpeter's theories have enjoyed a resurgence recently, according to *Forbes*, now that "entrepreneurs, the agents of painful change, are heroes, while bureaucrats and stay-put managers are suspect.... Change, however, is painful to many and disquieting to many more. Democratic governments have to protect the victims of change without stopping the process of economic evolution. The difficult trick is to find ways of treating the unemployed and the underskilled with compassion, without thwarting the wrenching change through which capitalism renews itself."

Whether it's creative destruction or just plain old Brand-X destruction, employers undeniably are in the middle of it. As they ride the current wave of change into the 21st century, many are struggling to balance the requirements for success in a changing economic system against the needs of their employees. Birch outlines the stakes in this high-risk new environment: "However we go about creating security, it must foster—not inhibit—mobility and do so in a way that provides the individual worker with a sense of control over his or her destiny. Moreover, we have to get on with it quickly, for events have a way of overtaking us. As increasing numbers of workers are threatened by the process of change, more will demand that we either slow the pace or create more secure bridges for them to cross. Since we cannot win by slowing down, the alternative is clear enough."

Reprinted from TRAINING, December 1987

REWARDING AND RECOGNIZING PERFORMANCE

REWARDS AND RECOGNITION: YES, THEY REALLY WORK

If you give service workers a paycheck, they'll do the job. If you want them to excel, give them more

BY RON ZEMKE

Money may not make the world go around, but managers in exemplary service-sector organizations firmly believe that recognition and rewards are powerful twin engines for employee motivation. In the eyes of managers from 101 such organizations profiled for a new book on service quality, recognizing and praising employees for a job well done isn't superfluous or magnanimous. It's necessary. It confirms accomplishment and reinforces commitment.

In these organizations there is a positive payoff for employees who meet the service standards, and additional financial rewards and psychic accolades for those who exceed them. Employees who go one step further for the customers become "service heroes." They are held up as role models and rewarded accordingly, because their managers know that the celebration of organizational, group and individual service accomplishments is essential if the delivery of high-quality service is to be the norm, not the exception.

Compensation and motivation

People don't work just for the fun of it. They work mostly for the money they need to buy the necessities and luxuries of life. Money is a powerful motivator—and a generalized one. It is a means to a vast number of ends and makes possible the fulfillment of any number of dreams.

We need to know, first and foremost, that our paychecks will keep the wolf from the door. But as pay rises, so do visibility, prestige, personal pride and self-esteem. Those attributes can be harnessed to motivate continuing good performance. Consequently, great service organizations often pay above-average wages for their industry. They make that distinction a point of internal pride and a prominent feature in their recruiting efforts.

Exemplary companies in the service sector realize that while pay may ensure attendance, it typically doesn't produce strategic alignment, personal enthusiasm or outstanding performance. So many of them use the carrot of monetary incentives as well. Mississippi Management Corp., an extremely successful hotel management company based in Jackson, MS, pays regular bonuses for such mundane tasks as carving prime rib properly or making more beds (correctly, of course) than the norm. Shuttle-bus drivers for Los Angeles-based SuperShuttle Inc. can earn a paid day off, which is compensated according to a variable rate based on their own typical performance. So the more they hustle and the better they serve, the more they earn on the job and the more valuable their time off becomes.

At First Union National Bank of Charlotte, NC, branch employees are "shopped" by a specialized research company up to three times a quarter. The payoff for an employee who scores a perfect "6" is instant cash in hand, as much as $200. According to First Union Corp.'s chairman and CEO Edward E. Crutchfield Jr., instantaneous rewards are crucial. "Recognition and reward have to be done on a very short-interval basis—given immediately after the service has been rendered. It's not something that you'd get in your pension 35 years from now; it's money you can buy bread with on Monday." Federal Express employees, from the couriers on the streets each day to the parcel sorters in the Memphis hub each night, can buy lots of bread. Sorters start at well over $9 an hour, and even part-timers are eligible for profit-sharing bonuses. At Nordstrom Department Stores, salespeople earn about $2 an hour above local retail wages plus a sales commission of 6 percent or more. A top sales associate can gross $50,000 to $60,000 a year, the kind of money usually reserved only for managers in the retail industry.

It's a little puzzling that more companies don't use financial incentives at the front line. Personal pay tied to organizational performance has long been a valued executive perk, generally with sound results. A 1983 McKinsey & Co. study found that in the most profitable companies in the $25 million sales range, for example, 40 percent of CEO compensation and 36 percent of senior management pay is tied to organizational performance. A study conducted in the late 1970s for the National Science Foundation noted that among the 1,100 companies then listed on the New York Stock Exchange, those with formal incentive plans for managers earned an average 43.6 percent more pre-tax profit than companies that did not use incentives.

Executives aren't the only ones who respond well to such programs. The same National Science Foundation report also reviewed 300 studies of productivity, pay and job satisfaction, and concluded that when pay is linked to performance, employees' motivation to work is raised, their productivity is higher, and they're usually more satisfied with their work. One study cited in the report examined 400 companies and found that those that switched from a system that didn't measure work to one that measured work and included performance feedback raised productivity an average of 43 percent. When both performance feedback and *incentives* were instituted, productivity rose 63.8 percent on average.

The study's authors concluded that increased productivity depends on two things. First is motivation: Arousing and maintaining the will to work effectively means having workers who are productive not because they are coerced but because they are committed. Second is reward: Of all the factors that help to create highly motivated and satisfied workers, the principal one appears to be that effective performance is recognized and rewarded in terms that are meaningful to the individual, whether financial, psychological or both.

That message traditionally has been better understood in manufacturing companies than in service organizations. *People, Performance and Pay,* a recent study by the American Productivity Center in Houston and the American Compensation Association, found that 48 percent of manufacturers, but only 19 percent of service companies, use performance incentive systems. In the service businesses that use these compensation tactics, the most successful techniques are reportedly productivity gain-sharing, pay-for-knowledge and small-group incentives.

Incentive systems aren't automatic performance generators, of course. They can even backfire. Sometimes organizations will "readjust" a system when it becomes obvious that salespeople are going to greatly exceed their sales goals. The excuse is always that the program "needs some fine-tuning." The real reason is that someone in senior management has decided it would be unseemly for some of the troops to earn so much more than others "at *their* level." Translation: "Who do they think they are, earning as much for front-line work as I do as a manager?" Invariably, the front-line people get the message and never again do anything remotely productive enough to get them "rate busted."

It's a natural impulse to make sure the troops' wages don't compare too

closely to those of the leaders, says Harvard University's Rosabeth Moss Kanter. "Social psychologists have shown that the maintenance of an authority relationship depends on a degree of inequality," she says. "If the distance between boss and subordinate—social, economic or otherwise—declines, so does automatic deference and respect.

"This is further aided by the existence of objective measures of contribution. Once high performance is established, once the measures are clear and clearly achieved, the subordinate no longer needs the good will of his or her boss quite so much. One more source of dependency is reduced, and power again becomes more equalized. Proven achievement reflected in higher earnings than the boss's produces security. Security produces risk-taking. Risk-taking produces speaking up and pushing back," Kanter concludes.

The instinct to preserve traditional forms of hierarchy and bureaucracy is understandable, but it's worth suppressing when the goal is superior service. Managers are only free to lead when they are able to free their employees to think and act—to understand and do something about the problems encountered in day-to-day business. Nothing signals the sincerity of that message like an incentive for exceptional customer service.

It is vital, however, to think through all the implications of an incentive plan before you institute it. Brokerage houses have long provided incentives to stockbrokers based on their individual performances, typically calculated in terms of sales. Of course, large individual revenues accumulate into large corporate revenues, which can make the organization more hungry for record-breaking quarterly reports than for customer satisfaction.

Even before the October 1987 stock market crash, the business press had begun to question some of the practices in vogue on Wall Street. At some houses, every possible sort of incentive was dangled before the brokers—furs, Mercedes-Benzes, yachts, dinner for two anyplace on the planet, you name it. The question was whether these practices—notable by their absence in firms such as Goldman Sachs and A.G. Edwards & Sons—were causing brokers to work *against* their clients' best interests,

churning accounts and pushing people into questionable ventures because those activities boosted the brokers' own compensation and rewards so remarkably.

To be effective over the long term, incentives must be based on the customer's best interests as well as their effects on the individual's paycheck and the company's quarterly revenues. They should emphasize legitimate customer satisfaction. An incentive program that subordinates an organization's long-term relationship with the customer to an individual's short-term gain—whether that individual is a salesperson, a stockholder or a highly placed executive—is a dangerous narcotic.

Reward and corporate culture

Reward systems are both a product and an influence on an organization's culture. Professor Jeffrey Kerr of the Edwin L. Cox School of Business at Southern Methodist University, believes that "who gets rewarded and why is an unequivocal statement of the corporation's values and beliefs." Kerr and his colleagues suggest that there are two opposite extremes in organizational reward "systems." Those extremes illustrate just how heavily various types of systems can influence an organization's culture and its people's behavior.

The hierarchy-based reward system, as the name implies, is a top-down model. Superiors define and evaluate the performance of subordinates. Performance is defined in both qualitative and quantitative terms, with qualitative performance parameters often as important as—or even more important than—quantitative measures. Evaluation of performance is usually quite subjective. Even in quantifiable areas, superiors sometimes use their own knowledge and experiences to interpret the numbers.

That bare-bones description makes working in an organization with a hierarchy-based reward system sound about as pleasant as being a serf on a medieval estate; any alternative would be an improvement, right? Don't be so sure. Hierarchical structures lead to formal salary systems, like a Hay system, that rewards tenure as well as performance. Bonuses tend to represent only a small slice of compensation and are usually based on group and team performance rather than individual performance. Belonging, cooperation, teamwork and loyalty have high value in the hierarchy system. Activities such as employee training, career development, frequent promotions, lateral movement for developmental purposes and the awarding of special perquisites characterize organizations with these reward systems.

The resulting culture, says Kerr, is very much what *Theory Z* author Bill Ouchi describes as a clan: a familial or fraternal group in which all members acknowledge an obligation beyond the contractual exchange of labor for salary. The individual's long-term commitment to the organization is traded for the organization's long-term commitment to the individual. "The relationship," Kerr explains, "is predicated on mutual interests."

At the other extreme of organizational reward systems, says Kerr, is the "performance-based reward system." Numbers are paramount. The qualitative aspects of performance don't affect evaluations, especially at the managerial level. Performance objectives are precise and tend to be primarily numeric. Results matter, and the methods for achieving them are usually up to the local managers and their subordinates. Performance evaluation and feedback focus on the immediate, not the long term. High levels of autonomy and reward characterize the performance-based organization. Concepts such as mentoring, socialization, development, promotability and career planning play little part in the performance-based organization.

In Ouchi's scheme of things this is a market culture. Relationships are contractual and mutually exploitive. Level of performance and level of reward are the only guarantees in the contract. When a juicy job opens up, the company is as likely to bring in someone from the outside as to promote an insider.

Are there any pluses in this dog-eat-dog culture? Certainly. For instance, earning potential is unlimited. The profit pool is established among a small number of people, usually a division-sized unit, and is independent of the larger organization. Symbols of rank and status are almost non-existent, and being a member of the "right clique" or the right family is not a factor in getting

ahead.

Kerr also points out that the market culture "does generate personal initiative, a strong sense of ownership and responsibility for operations and decisions, and an entrepreneurial approach to management. The individual is free to pursue goals with a minimum of organizational constraints."

The point of making the distinction between the two systems carries more than mere academic interest. When you are thinking about ways to improve performance through reward and recognition, you must be guided not only by the art and science of incentive motivation but also by an understanding of the culture and values of your organization.

Symbolic reward

Money isn't everything—although many continue to insist that it's ahead of whatever is in second place. Still, effective incentive and reward programs can be created from a combination of dollars, trips to exotic locales, merchandise and purely psychological payoffs. American Airlines takes much of the reward methodology of its frequent-flyer program and plugs it into an employee incentive program for individual and small-group service achievements. At Ryder Systems, the Miami-based transportation company, a similar program is in place for rewarding the dealers who rent Ryder's trucks to customers.

Exclusivity can lend appeal to programs whose actual goods range from simple to awe-inspiring. Employees at Southern Bell often ask where they can buy the designer-style jackets and sports apparel the company awards to outstanding service providers. They're told the items aren't for sale—the only way to get a jacket is to earn a jacket. Similarly, executives at Acura's U.S. headquarters in Gardena, CA, can only envy the limited-edition crystal sculptures awarded to the best dealerships; the contract calls for the artist to produce only enough for the winners.

A little spontaneity is often an effective ingredient in choosing an award or making one out of something at hand. With the St. Louis Cardinals playing in the 1987 World Series, a Citicorp manager in that town knew exactly how to reward the service accomplishments of his

branch's people. The cruise-for-two promos accumulated from wholesalers in 1987 by Ukrop's Super Markets in Richmond, VA, became highly sought-after prizes for exceptional front-line performance within the small supermarket chain. Auto mechanics at Don Beyer Volvo, a car dealership in Falls Church, VA, regularly compete for a month's worth of driving around in a luxury model right off the showroom floor.

Little rewards can be as effective as big ones if they're used in the right way. Lapel-style pins and special name tags are tactics common to service leaders such as Federal Express, Citicorp, LensCrafters and First Federal/Osceola. At Citicorp Retail Services in Denver, good suggestions for new or better ways to serve customers warrant a "Bright Ideas" coffee mug or similar keepsake. The employee who submits the month's best idea wins temporary possession of a circulating trophy—a three-foot-high light bulb.

It's a lighthearted approach, but the underlying thought is what's important. According to Lauren O'Connell, Citicorp's assistant vice president of operations, "The point of these contests and recognition programs and service evaluations and checklists is that they make everyone feel that quality service is his or her individual responsibility. That not only leads to better service quality for the customer, it also means higher morale. People do care about their jobs when they know that their managers consider those jobs to be important. And caring about one's job and knowing that it's important is where service quality really starts."

Celebration

Often entwined with recognition and reward is a sense of celebration. That's clearly apparent when American Express assembles its Great Performers in New York City each year so executives and colleagues can glow upon them for a job exceptionally done. BellSouth, parent of Southern Bell and LensCrafters, also brings its service award winners into corporate headquarters at annual meetings to laud their achievements. Pizza Hut and Domino's Pizza do the same for managers and franchisees at national meetings.

Organization-development consultant Cathy DeForest writes that, like the leaders of an army, managers must "recognize that the act of celebrating provides a way to nourish the spirit of an organization as well as create a moment in time when a glimpse of a transformed organization can be seen and felt."

Recognition and celebrations also are ways of reaffirming to people that they are an important part of something that matters. These little ceremonies can be significant motivators for people in any organization, but especially so in a service organization, where "pride in the product" is essentially pride in personal performance. Two recent studies make the point.

In 1987 *Inc.* magazine and the Hay Group consulting company compared opinions and feelings of employees in the relatively small companies that form the "*Inc. 500*" with those of employees in the large corporations that make up the "*Fortune 500.*" Employees in small companies rated their pay and benefits as poorer, their opportunity for advancement as less promising, and company communication as worse than did their counterparts in the larger companies. But surprise! Overall job satisfaction in small companies was significantly, even spectacularly higher.

Why? According to the *Inc.*/Hay survey, employees of the smaller companies tended to believe they were important to their organizations and to feel that their organizations were doing something significant.

More specifically, people in the smaller companies felt their work was more challenging, said their ideas were more likely to be adopted, reported a higher sense of accomplishment from what they did, and thought they were treated with more respect.

Focus group discussions validated the survey findings, *Inc.* reported: "These are employees who talk about the company in first-person plural, as in, 'We can serve our customers faster' or 'We may look like we're disorganized, but we're not.' Said another: 'The quality is personal—the product is us.' "

The second confirmation of the importance of feeling involved in something worthwhile comes from a study done by the Forum Corp., a Boston-based consulting company. Forum found that employees who believed their organizations served customers well were much less likely to say they planned to leave their current jobs within the next year than those who felt they worked for a company that was doing a poor job of serving the customer.

The concept of being part of something valuable, worthwhile and important often is expressed most forcefully by the executives at the top of an organization. Fred Smith, founder of Federal Express, has the iron-jawed, fiery look of the true believer when he tells an interviewer, "Our corporate philosophy is people, service, profit. We do something important. We carry the most impor-

tant commerce in the history of the world." It is no accident that one often hears that sentiment repeated with similar fervor by couriers and managers throughout the FedEx system.

Marriott employees, when asked about their unusual corporate loyalty, say, "We're part of a family here. The name Marriott is a person's name, and it stands for something." That same sense of pride and belonging becomes evident when you talk to people at a lot of organizations that routinely receive high marks from customers for service quality and performance: Lands' End, Dun & Bradstreet, United Van Lines, Southern Bell, CompuServe, Delta Air Lines, Miller Business Systems, Kinder-Care, Chubb, Northwestern Mutual Life Insurance Co., 3M, H.B. Fuller, Beth Israel Hospital, the Mayo Clinic. . .the list could stretch on.

But the most memorable way I have heard it expressed was at Walt Disney World, where I asked a young groundskeeper, "How do you like being a street sweeper in a theme park?" He stepped back, stood up tall, looked me square in the eye, and shot back: "I'm not a street sweeper. I'm in show business. I'm part of the Act."

To front-line workers in any organization with ambitions of providing distinctive service to its customers, the feeling of being a part of something important may be the most important motivational principle of all.

Reprinted from TRAINING, November 1988

THE POWER OF POSITIVE FEEDBACK

Formal performance evaluation meetings can intimidate managers and employees. Suppose these tete-a-tetes were redesigned along less ambitious lines . . .

BY DONALD V. SCHUSTER

In most organizations, performance evaluation creates quite a quandary. Most managers don't know exactly how to carry it off and, consequently, their employees don't have a clue as to what to expect. While all parties generally agree that employers have a *right* to require some kind of performance review, managers are often hesitant—even timid—about conducting the necessary evaluations.

There are a number of performance evaluation systems to choose from, although in reality nearly all of them are minor variations on the same theme. When a company does select an approach, it normally embraces its choice with a notable lack of enthusiasm—nevertheless, the new system becomes "the only game in town."

Employees, too, are left with a sense of ambiguity. They genuinely want to know how they are doing, but their uncertainty about how the meeting will be handled often overwhelms any desire for feedback. As a result, they go into a performance evaluation interview with feelings ranging from mild apprehension to outright dread.

Are such feelings on the part of managers and employees alike simply inherent in the performance evaluation process? Those who say "yes" proceed as if they are as concerned with minimizing "losses" as they are with achieving objectives. And this ambiguity, of course, does not go unnoticed.

Although some management theorists disagree that this type of internal inconsistency is in the nature of the beast and offer useful analysis and insight, they have provided little in the way of workable change models. The whole subject of performance appraisal is on the front burner today, as a quick look at training, industrial relations and personnel literature will demonstrate.

Reevaluating the system

All performance evaluation systems (with the possible exception of MBO which has some unique vulnerabilities to accompany its strengths) have certain difficulties in common. These include rater biases, the fact that evaluation criteria may not be perceived as job-related and management's failure to follow through or support the stated objectives of the performance evaluation.

Proponents of any evaluation system are quick to insist that the most important element is how it is handled by the immediate supervisor. They also stress thorough training in advance, especially when "minimizing losses" is a major consideration. They recognize that a poorly handled evaluation interview may not only fail to deliver the expected benefits, it may work against the company.

If employee sensitivity is a major obstacle to the truly worthwhile objectives of a performance evaluation, then shouldn't you try to eliminate it, rather than just reduce it? Simply improving supervisors' interviewing techniques and sharpening their human relations skills won't do the trick. Why ask a supervisor to compensate for the system's known deficiencies? Why not reevaluate the system itself?

To reevaluate your company's performance appraisal system, the key question to ask is, "What are we really trying to accomplish?" It's unlikely that your organization has reached a consensus on its objectives. It's even more doubtful that you have seriously considered whether your system actually meets those objectives.

Let's take a look at some of the most common goals for performance evaluation:

- Provide a record of performance.
- Provide a basis for wage increases.
- Identify employees' potential for advancement.
- Determine training and development needs.
- Let employees know "where they stand."
- Motivate employees.
- Provide an avenue of communication.

To reach these objectives, organizations generally use one or more of these standard performance evaluation systems:

- Graphic Rating Scale.
- Rank Order Method.
- Forced Distribution Method.
- Critical Incident Method.
- Forced Choice Method.
- Goal-setting Method.

Most performance evaluation systems "fail" because they try to accomplish *too much*—they ask too much of one document (an evaluation form) and one event (a performance interview). Even a glance at the objectives stated above will convince you that the challenge is formidable.

If you accept the "too much" criticism as valid, your options become fairly simple. You must either abandon some of the objectives (which few of us would accept) or consider alternate routes for meeting some of them.

Sacred cows

Let me goad a "sacred cow" here by questioning the validity of one of the traditional objectives of the formal performance evaluation—letting employees know where they stand. Most people consider that objective one of the most important goals of performance evaluation. In practical terms, it means giving employees an unbiased assessment of the good and bad elements of their performance and behavior. Logical enough. Yet it is the single aspect of the performance evaluation interview that most exacerbates sensitivities and is often either unproductive or counterproductive.

Most of us will agree that employees need to know how they are doing on the job. But is the formal interview the best place to deal with the negative points of performance? It's an article of faith among trainers that there is no substitute for ongoing performance evaluation, which is communicated implicitly as well as explicitly. You know employees are getting the message—positive or negative—by the way they respond on the job.

To try to use the formal interview as a net to catch all the cases in which the supervisor failed to give feedback along the way suggests a lack of supervisory skills. If supervisors have not kept their employees informed of performance deficiencies, the delay, from the company's standpoint, is inexcusable.

It's hard to see how formalizing a criticism which the employee already knows about—or at least should know about—can serve a useful purpose, unless terminating the employee is the objective. Behavioral psychologists generally agree that constructive criticism is far more acceptable to the employee and more likely to produce results when it is handled informally, rather than in an episodic, highly judgmental fashion. Positive and complimentary remarks, on the other hand, *do* have a place in the formal performance interview.

Recognition, not evaluation

An interview that fails to give a "balanced" picture of the employee (negatives as well as positives) has little relevance to performance evaluation as we now know it. Instead of *performance evaluation* then, the process I have in mind might better be called *performance recognition*.

In addition to omitting negative evaluations, performance recognition also would exclude most of the other objectives of a typical evaluation and concentrate on just two: *motivation* and *communication*. Splitting off the other objectives doesn't mean abandoning them. They meet real needs, which I'll refer to later.

The totally positive PRO (Performance Recognition Opportunity) approach is designed to motivate employees with meaningful personal recognition and, at the same time, open up an avenue of communication between supervisor and subordinate. I presume that these objectives meet a need in the organization, or at least offer a chance for improvement.

PRO is based upon some ideas that not everyone goes along with. The first is that virtually all (non-pathological) employees would prefer to do good work rather than poor work. We must, of course, add the usual qualifier, "all other things being equal," which they often are not. Trying to eliminate that qualifier as much as possible is one of the practical focuses of PRO.

Another assumption is that employees genuinely value nonmaterial forms of recognition, *if* they are meaningful and fairly administered, and that the opportunity to communicate one-to-one with a superior, in an atmosphere of respect and relaxation, is also highly regarded.

A third assumption is that employees don't perceive any contradictions between the company's and their supervisors' attitudes, policies and procedures and the first two assumptions.

PRO requires a certain type of job description for each employee, like the type we have produced at World Color Press. Clarity and adequate detail are the first two considerations. Almost *anyone* should be able to read the job description and get a good idea of what the person actually does. Generalizations are not tolerated. Each duty or activity in the job description contains (wherever possible) some statement of the level of competence expected for each duty. Job descriptions written in these terms have several additional uses for a company:

• Taken altogether, the job descriptions present an intelligible view of the interrelatedness and various functions of the different departments within the organization.

• They provide an excellent definition of position requirements to aid both interviewer and candidate when new positions open up.

• They are basic training documents for new employees. They also aid the trainer in conducting cross-training between departments.

PRO in action

PRO, which we've defined essentially as a motivation and communication tool (although some of the other evaluation objectives are met indirectly), works like this.

At least once a year, the immediate supervisor invites selected employees to attend a one-to-one PRO meeting. Only those employees whose performance has been deemed minimally acceptable or better are invited for "recognition." Being invited, therefore, constitutes a basic level of recognition, and employees are advised well in advance.

Conversely, the 5% or so of employees who are not invited will interpret this exclusion as a strong comment that their performance level (as they should *already* know) is not acceptable. It's important not to deny an employee this recognition interview without the agreement of the supervisor's manager and the approval of the personnel director. When in doubt—recognize.

The totally positive approach of the program has been communicated in advance, so the meeting begins on an upbeat note. Using the employee's job description as a guide, the supervisor discusses the *job itself*, not the employee. The supervisor must listen carefully to the employee's interpretation of how work is progressing and what help the employee may need to improve performance. Sometimes there are roadblocks to "professional" performance that the supervisor may be able to remove.

The supervisor takes every opportunity to comment favorably on some aspect of the employee's work that is going especially well. The supervisor avoids bringing up any aspect of the employee's performance that is *not* satisfactory. Should the employee voluntarily initiate discussion on a problem or deficiency, the supervisor is free to discuss it. But the supervisor should remain as positive as possible and, in any case, offer to help. If this approach seems a bit subtle, remember that the situation is no more demanding than conventional performance appraisals.

Discriminatory?

Is it discriminatory *not* to interview an unsatisfactory employee? So long as the approach remains completely positive, and the objectives are clearly perceived as performance recognition and improved communications, any union objection should be without merit. Unions, themselves, have long been on record as proponents of recognition for their members.

In any case, there is no known *requirement* for a company to recognize any employee's performance. If the union pressed the issue, however, it wouldn't violate the integrity of PRO to give a candid evaluation of the poor performers, one that includes full disclosure of performance and attitude deficiencies.

As we mentioned before, not recognizing the 5% doesn't mean abandoning or ignoring them. It is important to take pains behind the scenes to find out *why* they don't measure up and then to take appropriate action. If your informed judgment is that the reason is simply lack of concentration or effort, the personnel department should pursue the usual disciplines. When the employee is unsuited to his job, lacks training or has personal problems, these conditions also should be handled appropriately.

Can the union successfully use the fact that an employee has received PRO recognition as a barrier to subsequent discipline and/or termination? Probably not, as long as you stick to the twin objectives of recognition and communication instead of evaluation. But it is a complex question, one better fielded by legal experts.

Clear objectives

The interplay between supervisor and subordinate during the recognition interview will vary as all normal communication varies in tone and style between different people and at different times. Friendliness and informality, to some degree, are necessary to accomplish the objectives. The only imperative is to remain constantly aware of the basic intent of the program.

Employees should perceive that supervisors (and therefore the company) are eager to recognize whatever they are doing right. More importantly, they should understand that the company is validating this goodwill by helping each employee reach professional performance levels and achieve personal self-development goals.

PRO, then, is a way to provide formal recognition as an incentive to superior performance. If PRO succeeds as an incentive, employees become more professional in their work. An added bonus: After a number of "recognition interviews," supervisors get an excellent picture of their employees' attitudes, capabilities and needs.

Further possibilities

Most companies have individuals in each department who are clearly outstanding, an opinion shared by fellow workers and management alike. They generally perform to self-imposed standards and are exemplars of professionalism in their jobs. They aren't perfect, but few managers would hesitate to hire a clone if one could be found. It's not uncommon for fellow workers to complain that these people don't receive their "dues."

One goal of the PRO process might be to single out these people for some sort of special recognition or rewards.

On the other hand, however, the PRO approach should not turn into a competition. Employees, in order to be motivated, need to see that the company wants to recognize *all* good performance. The worth of PRO will be validated to the extent that a significant number of employees value the opportunity for recognition enough to perform accordingly.

Just how well the PRO concept would meet the motivational and communications needs of a given company depends on the unique needs of each organization. Models already exist for the type of job description that is essential to the program. Several years ago, the basic model for the formal performance recognition event (based on the standard of professionalism) was successfully implemented by the space systems division of General Electric Co.

How do you meet the *other* objectives of the conventional performance evaluation interviews? I don't have a final answer to that one. Some of the conventional performance evaluation forms might be useful here, as long as only the job description is used in the performance interview and the inter-

INCENTIVE PAY FOR EVERYBODY AT DU PONT

Employers are always looking for incentives to motivate their people: trips to the Orient, congratulatory dinners and so on. When cold cash is used, it usually takes the form of year-end bonuses for executives, and profit sharing or gain sharing for hourly employees.

Du Pont Co. has devised an incentive pay plan with an egalitarian twist. Beginning Jan. 1, the 20,000 employees in Du Pont's fibers division, from the group vice president down to hourly workers, will switch to a pay plan that ties salaries to the company's profits. Although numerous compensation plans for executives are designed along these lines, Du Pont's plan is one of the first to include all employees, says Steven E. Gross, a Hay Associates consultant who helped devise the plan.

If the plan is accepted by the union and written into the bargaining agreement, a five-year phase-in period will begin next year. After that time, all employees in the fibers division will begin to draw base salaries that are 6 percent below those of Du Pont employees in similar positions in other divisions. If the fibers group reaches 100 percent of its profit goals, the workers gain back that 6 percent difference. If the division hits 80 percent to 99 percent of its goal, they get back only half the difference. Under 80 percent: Workers lose the whole 6 percent. But if the division reaches 150 percent of its profit goal, the employees would earn a bonus that would make their compensation 12 percent more than the earnings of comparable Du Pont employees.

Robert P. McNutt, head of the task force within Du Pont that devised the system, says the plan is different from a traditional profit-sharing program because "this one has some downside as well as upside." Because employees' base pay is 6 percent less than it

normally would be, they have something at risk if the company doesn't meet its goals. "It does a better job motivating people than if you just had a payout when the company reached a certain plateau of earnings," McNutt says.

Unlike some other systems, this one was not instituted because the company was threatened with losses, McNutt says. According to the *Wall Street Journal,* the fibers division is one of Du Pont's most profitable sectors. Last year, its after-tax earnings were $624 million on sales of $5.3 billion.

The fibers division employees will continue to receive increases in base wages, but they will be set to maintain the 6 percent difference from other Du Pont employees.

Gross says the Du Pont plan is an effort to change the culture of the organization and encourage more individual responsibility. "They really wanted to link the employees' performance to results. The years of entitlement are gone," he says.

Reprinted from TRAINING, December 1988

view is kept totally positive. These other forms might be kept on file in the department and/or personnel office, so that employees could have access to them. Is this keeping two sets of books? Not really. They are not (or at least shouldn't be) contradictory. They simply meet different needs in different ways.

The PRO approach is more than a program. Company "programs" are traditionally perceived as extraneous activities that come and go with predictable regularity. PRO should reflect a company's fundamental people-management philosophy and become an integral part of it.

Reprinted from TRAINING, January 1985

REWARDING AND RECOGNIZING TRAINERS

Reward systems are expensive and tough to set up. Recognition systems are easy and cheap. Here's how organizations do both

BY BEVERLY GEBER

There's a big chasm that separates salespeople from trainers, and it's filled with trips, clothes, merchandise and envelopes crammed with cash.

In short, incentives. Like greyhounds straining toward a mechanical rabbit, salespeople go for those special incentives that corporations typically offer: trips to Hawaii, fur jackets, television sets or the Old Reliable—cash. Do those things make trainers go too? Most companies don't know. Common though it is to reward salespeople for quotas met or calls made, it's almost equally uncommon to reward trainers for a job well done.

Do a good job as salesperson and you stand to dip your toes in tropical waters. Do the same as a trainer and you're likely to win little more than a robust slap on the back.

There are reasons for this dichotomy (or discrimination, depending on your point of view) and most of them are quite plausible. For instance, of all professional occupations, the salesperson's job is probably the easiest to measure for productivity. Therefore, it's easy to reward. The salesperson who sells an astounding 560 doohickeys this year gets to spend two weeks on Maui. As a system, it's simple. It's straightforward. And it's a motivating jolt right

between the eyes for the salespeople who sell only 60 doohickeys and have to pay for their own vacations.

But try to set up a reward system for trainers and you'll probably find that it's neither simple nor straightforward. If you follow the sales model and try to reward trainers for the number of doohickeys facilitated, designed or produced, you run into a conundrum: If you reward the kinds of behaviors that are easily measured, you may encourage behaviors that aren't necessarily important to the organization; but if you try to reward crucial behaviors, you often can't figure out good, objective ways to measure them.

That's one reason why few organizations offer tangible rewards to their HRD staffers. It's the reason that most training directors choose instead to recognize their people with inexpensive pats on the back.

Lest we call down a rain of sympathy on the downtrodden trainer, we must add that trainers have a good bit of professional company. The only reward most professionals qualify for is an annual bonus, which often is tied to the performance of the company rather than to the individual's performance. Line managers are more apt to receive rewards than staff employees, such as trainers, in part because it's easier to measure whether that line manager contributed to the organization's bottom line.

The efficacy of rewards and recognition is another matter altogether. Most companies that use them have found they do, indeed, motivate people. (For a complete discussion of the value of rewards and recognition, see "Rewards and Recognition: Yes, They Really Work," TRAINING, November 1988.)

The number of companies that use some kind of pay-for-performance system is rising steadily, according to the 1987 report, "People, Performance and Pay." The survey of 1,598 companies, conducted by the American Productivity Center and the American Compensation Association, found that 75 percent used at least one nontraditional form of reward system for at least one group of employees, and that most of the plans were less than five years old. It cast a wide net in defining nontraditional reward systems, however, including profit sharing, lump-sum bonuses, individual incentives, gainsharing, small-group incentives, pay for knowledge, earned time off and two-tier salary systems.

According to the report, salaried employees are most likely to have profit sharing, lump-sum performance bonuses and individual incentives for performance. Sales and marketing employees are eligible for more incentive plans than any other kinds of employees. As for recognition systems, the survey found that 46 percent of the organizations used recognition systems but only 30 percent reported that the systems are helping to improve performance.

In TRAINING Magazine's Readership Survey, described in this month's cover story, 35.7 percent of our respondents said they were eligible for bonuses this year.

A trip to Paris!

Suppose you decide that tangible rewards for trainers would be swell, and you want to do it as objectively as possible. Fine, but here are some of the thorny issues you'll have to deal with. How would you set up an objective measurement system for the kinds of things trainers must do well in order to succeed? How would you measure the organizational results of a course on giving performance appraisals, and how would you assign credit to the various people who worked to produce and deliver the course?

If you do use quantifiable measures and choose an index such as the number of courses delivered or developed, aren't you inadvertently encouraging quantity instead of quality? Naturally, one could go instead to a system of subjectively measuring accomplishment. But that has its drawbacks, too. When decisions are purely subjective, the training director runs the risk of allegations of favoritism, as well as alienating the unchosen HRD staffers.

Reward systems for trainers that use objective measurements and are tied to individual performance are difficult to set up. Jerry McAdams, vice president for new product development for Maritz Inc. of Fenton, MO, and coauthor of the report, "People, Performance and Pay," says a good reward system must be closely connected to the organization's goals. Yet even if the training function is aligned with the organization's goals, it's hard to pinpoint precisely the effect one instructor or instructional designer will have on the organization.

Michael O'Brien, vice president of the St. Paul, MN, consulting firm McLagan International, says organizations can try to overcome that difficulty by looking for certain indicators. For instance, if managers were recently taught to make better hiring decisions, look for lower turnover. If the corporation wants more employee involvement and managers were trained to encourage it, look for an increase in the number of employee suggestions for improving things. This doesn't imply that training is the sole cause of the change, he says. It's just an indication that training had some effect.

Although O'Brien believes that a purely objective system is a noble goal, he doesn't think it's possible or necessary to create one. Use subjective measurements, too, he says. Collect course evaluations, or sit in on a session to observe an instructor.

"A reward system would need to include both objective and subjective measures because training is both an art and a science," he says.

In the real world, rigorously objective systems don't often exist. Neither O'Brien nor McAdams was familiar with a training department with an exemplary one. Further confusing the issue is the fact that training directors can't agree on what's a reward and what's an act of recognition. Often the terms are used interchangeably. And what a training director sees as a motivational carrot won't necessarily look like one to the trainer who receives it. For instance, is it a reward if a trainer is dispatched to a corporate branch in Paris to deliver training? Depends. The training manager might consider the location a prima facie reward, no matter how hard the trainer has to work there. ("You're going to Paris!") The trainer might not consider it a reward unless he's given a few days afterward to relax and sightsee at company expense.

Tuxes and ball gowns

Reward systems usually don't spring up in training departments unless the corporate culture encourages them. Rare is the maverick training director who starts one up in an organization whose top executives believe that employees ought to do superior work routinely and get rewarded for it with a paycheck. "You don't want to be out of step with the corporation," says Walt Thurn, manager of employee development for Florida Power Corp. of St. Petersburg, FL. "If the corporation doesn't go in for rewards, you don't want to be a red flag."

In companies that are permeated with the philosophy of rewarding employees for exemplary performance, trainers can qualify for companywide rewards as well as departmental rewards for exceptional performance.

Federal Express Corp., the overnight courier based in Memphis, TN, has a formal award system that applies to all employees in the company, as well as a more informal instant reward system in which managers mete out cash awards for small acts of exceptional performance. If you ask training directors to name companies with Cadillac reward systems, Federal Express pops up frequently. Its system is both objective and subjective.

The companywide reward system is available to all employees who are, at minimum, judged satisfactory in their performance reviews. Goal setting is the first step. In cascading order, goals are set for the company, divisions and departments, and end up as individual goals called professional business objectives (PBOs).

For instance, says Peter Addicott, senior manager of training, one of his objectives may be to keep from overspending on his budget. An instructional designer might have a goal of developing five videodisc training programs a year. That's the objective part of the system. But there's also an element of subjectivity, designed to gauge quality as well as quantity. For instance, trainers whose duty it is to keep enhancing the training programs for Federal Express couriers are asked to meet with station managers to gather information. How often? That's up to the trainer. The training director might judge the quality of those meetings by talking to the trainer and the station manager.

Four times a year individual results are compared with objectives and points are given for accomplishment. Twice a year, the rewards flow. Each point is assigned a dollar value, which depends upon how successful the company has been, and employees rake in a cash reward according to the points they've accumulated.

Sounds great, but how does one set up the objective part of that system? How does Addicott, for instance, set goals for the training department that are tied to the business goals, then calculate whether they were accomplished? Addicott says it can be done. "It's difficult to do but if the training function is going to be effective you've got to show the return on investment," he says.

He looks at such measures as the number of students taught and the pass-fail ratio. He has trainers follow up with managers to find out if trainees continue to use the skills they learned. He calculates the money Federal Express saves if couriers can be taught to do their jobs more efficiently. For one course, Addicott says, savings equaled $497,000.

Within his own department, Addicott gooses individual performance through the use of "Bravo Zulu" stickers and cash awards. Bravo Zulu is a U.S. Navy term that entered the FedEx lexicon via founder and Vietnam veteran Fred Smith. Addicott gives the sticker to someone who has committed a small act of good performance. He usually backs it up with a letter of praise for the personnel file and some cash—as much as $300—from a discretionary fund each manager has. He recently gave one to a trainer who did an outstanding job instructing a class of representatives from about 40 area companies on how to package dangerous goods.

Addicott also has an elaborate system of recognition for his trainers. Each year, the training department gives out four awards of excellence. The process starts with a group of instructors and managers who meet and devise the criteria for judging each class of HRD staffer—classroom instructor, instructional designer, whatever. The criteria, which change little each year, are distributed to employees so they know what to strive for.

Then Addicott and other managers accept nominations. They whittle the suggestions down to six or eight names and submit them to a vote by training department employees. The winners are the guests of honor at a formal, black-tie dinner attended by training department employees and senior management.

"We started out just having a nice dinner at a restaurant, but we felt a need to make it really special," Addicott says.

Selling Slurpies

You might expect Maritz Inc., a company that helps other companies set up incentive systems, to have a reward system for its employees. Dead right. "Our business is motivating performance," says Tom Tener, vice president for training and development at Maritz. "Our belief is that all behavior is a function of its consequences, so we reward tangibly the kinds of behavior we want."

That doesn't necessarily mean frequent large cash awards and expensive prizes. More often it means small rewards, in the form of points, that employees can save up and redeem to purchase items from a catalog of merchandise. Tener says there's an item in the catalog for every taste, from barbecue grills and children's toys to mink coats and vacation cruises.

Tener uses the points to reward his trainers for performance beyond the call of duty. He likes to reward them on the spot, when he sees them doing something in a particularly accomplished way. "That's when the award credits blow out of my pocket," he says. "If you believe that behavior is a function of consequences, then consequences should immediately follow

behavior." Tener doesn't use objective measures to decide when to reward. His evaluation is mostly subjective: watching a trainer delivering a course, reading trainee evaluations, overhearing compliments voiced by participants as they walk down the hall.

Every two months or so, managers identify about 50 "peak performers" from across the company, who receive 10,000 award credits and the chance to attend a fancy luncheon with CEO Bill Maritz.

Robert Saunders, vice president and director of corporate training and development for Northern Trust Corp. of Chicago, uses a combination of small rewards and recognition for the trainers in his department. The trainers can qualify for a corporate-wide reward system, through which three trainers have received cash awards in 18 months. At his discretion, Saunders can also draw on a special fund to reward a trainer for such things as putting in long hours voluntarily to finish a project. Sometimes, he hands over cash. Other times, it will be a dinner at a restaurant, tickets to a baseball game or an engraved pewter mug.

To give trainers a little pat on the back, Saunders has built a "wall of fame" just outside the entrance to the corporate training department. It contains the framed covers of internally developed training programs, signed by each person who helped produce them.

At Southland Corp., the company that operates 7-Eleven convenience stores, Tom Roney tried to come up with a reward system that uses purely objective measures, but he couldn't figure out how to do it. Roney, training center manager in Southland's Bethlehem, PA, office, wanted the system because he uses trainers recruited from line management. Former store managers who were rewarded for bottom-line results came into the training function wanting to know exactly what to do to qualify for rewards. Roney couldn't tell them.

"How do you find objective measures and then come up with a dollar amount?" Roney asks. "Do we get a color TV if we train people to sell more Slurpies?"

Reluctantly, he retreated to a subjective system of judging. "I can't define it, but I know it when I see it," he says of the kind of performance he's

inclined to reward. In Roney's budget is an extra cache of money earmarked for rewards, which he likes to bestow with fanfare during staff meetings. Not only does it recognize the outstanding trainer, but it lets the rest of the staff know what kinds of things he's looking for.

In lieu of rewards

In some companies, rewards are nonexistent. Either the organization doesn't condone them or they are forbidden by law. Some training directors instead try to motivate trainers by taking extra pains to recognize them. Recognition dinners, public praise, letters of commendation, inexpensive tokens such as plaques, blazers and T-shirts are all part of this genre. Other training managers take the position that creating the best job environment and encouraging constant self-development are the best motivators for trainers.

Gretchen Redden is training systems manager for Weight Watchers International in Jericho, NY, which doesn't offer its employees a system of rewards. Nor does Redden have discretionary budget money to reward them spontaneously. She relies on little strokes to let her people know they're valued. For instance, she occasionally sends flowers to trainers' hotel rooms when they're delivering instruction out of town.

At Florida Power Corp., Thurn is denied the chance to give his employees money or merchandise; the state won't permit regulated utilities to do it. Instead, Thurn says that when he encourages self-development by sending trainers to professional conferences, it's a form of recognizing and rewarding them. He writes letters of praise and certificates of commendation. And he believes that providing trainers with the right work environment, one where they get the support and resources they need, may do as much to motivate them as any kind of reward.

That's also the attitude of Richard Nerad, managing partner in the professional education division of Arthur Andersen & Co., based in St. Charles, IL. Nerad said it's not part of the company's philosophy to reward any of its employees with special bonuses or gifts. Instead, its career development program is based on the belief that development is the best motivator and the best reward a company can give. "We try to enrich the job as much as possible," he says.

The common denominator in any reward or recognition program is, of course, motivation—or at least an attempt to motivate. That's usually what training directors intend when they give a cash award or a public word of praise. They're hoping that the color television or the valentine of commendation read at a staff meeting will not only spur the individual to even better performance but will encourage the rest of the staff to the same end.

Do these things really lead to more productive trainers? The respondents in the survey "People, Performance and Pay" say that rewards work very well to motivate better performance in their organizations; recognition also works, but not as well.

Addicott believes that Federal Express' reward system has boosted productivity and improved performance. Five years ago, before the company started the system, it was difficult to get people to take on new projects. Now if a new project is announced, Addicott gets plenty of willing volunteers to head it. He also finds that trainers who reap recognition for developing a course tend to feel more attached to it and will follow up later to find out how it's being carried out.

Although some training directors doubt that recognition increases a trainer's performance, plenty believe that trainers are the kind of people who thrive on it, even more than other kinds of employees.

"I think recognition is very important to trainers," says Northern Trust Corp.'s Saunders. "One of the reasons we like being in a classroom is that you get that kind of instantaneous feedback."

Eleanor Hill, director of training and development for General Mills Restaurants Inc. in Orlando, FL, thinks that trainers have a normal need for recognition. Unfortunately, the nature of the job makes that need hard to satisfy. "I think it's harder for them to get recognition because of the intangible nature of the results of their efforts. One of the things I tell people who want to be trainers is that you really need to have some pretty significant internal reward systems. Because often a trainer is a catalyst. We are not in the business of being stars but of being star makers. That is a very, very removed type of reward."

Reprinted from TRAINING, November 1989

WHEN AND HOW TO USE INCENTIVES IN TRAINING

Like those multitalented Renaissance folk who excelled in many areas, you can benefit by increasing your fluency in all areas of performance and motivation

BY DAVID CUSHING

There's a lot of talk about incentive-based performance improvement programs these days, and much of it is just that: talk. But in some organizations the words are translated into action that produces some very real results, both in how people do their jobs and to what extent their organizations succeed. Although situations vary greatly, human resources development professionals often play key roles.

Item: After installing a reward system of free meals and gifts for on-the-job safety at the Quaker Oats pet food plant in Lawrence, KS, the factory's injury record vaulted from the corporation's worst to its best.

Item: A suggestion program through which employees receive recognition from top managers saved the Hughes Aircraft Corporation of Culver City, CA, roughly $175 million last year.

Item: Within 18 months of starting contests in which fast-food employees at Whataburger of Arizona compete for prizes from a menu of choices—like color television sets and space-age telephones—the company's training director noticed rising levels of quality, service and cleanliness in the chain's 25 stores.

At an accelerating rate, HRD people are called upon to investigate and help design and implement productivity improvement systems that revolve around human performance and hinge on motivation. In many cases, these new systems center on a key element: incentive awards for employees who help organizations achieve their aims by cutting the costs of doing business, improving the quality of products and services, making conditions better—and safer—for workers, and generally boosting the results of human labor.

Of all the people in an organization, the trainer is ideally equipped to design incentive programs, according to Thomas D. O'Connor, manager of performance improvement for the pharmaceutical division of Merck, Sharp and Dohme (MS&D) in West Point, PA, and president of the American Society for Performance Improvement (ASPI). "Trainers know how to perform needs analysis, write objectives and do all the things essential to getting a program going," he says. "To my way of thinking, trainers should head up new incentive systems."

O'Connor knows the effect a trainer can have on a company's performance level because he's been coordinating efforts at MS&D for years. The theme of his program is Pride In Quality, a zero-defects style system that focuses on doing the job right the first time and preventing production slip-ups. "When you make a mistake in this business, you find out from the U.S. Food and Drug Administration in a hurry," he says. "It can cost a million dollars if we have to recall a batch of drugs, so our goal is not to let anything out the door that isn't perfect."

The plant's 4,000 employees are all eligible to be nominated for awards by their superiors, based on their performance "above and beyond the average," O'Connor says. At least once a week, O'Connor's staff hands out a prize package which includes a Pennsylvania license plate facsimile that reads "Pride In Quality award winner," a privileged parking space in the company lot, a $50 savings bond, a presentation in the program director's office, a letter of recognition in the personnel file, a special pin, color photos to be posted around the plant, T-shirts, hats and other small personal items.

Although the number of nominations increases every year and O'Connor goes so far as dressing as Santa Claus at Christmastime to keep the program's visibility high, he emphasizes that an incentive program alone isn't enough to maintain the kind of performance MS&D strives for. To O'Connor, the incentive approach is only one of many things trainers should thoroughly understand if they expect to advance.

Integrating your roles

"You can't separate incentives from anything else a trainer does," he says. "You teach more than technical skills; you also teach how to interact with people, and to me that's where motivation steps in. Likewise, you can't separate the training department from the incentive program."

This integrated approach to training shows up in MS&D's sessions with new supervisors. Not only do they receive 40 hours of instruction on technical matters such as filling in time cards, handling complaints and attending to basic supervisory chores, they also get an additional 40 hours of behavior modeling training based on Development Dimensions International's Interaction Management. This program, designed to acquaint supervisors with human relations skills, is taught by the same trainers as the basic skills courses. To O'Connor, it shows how active and versatile trainers should be.

"More and more you have to be a generalist in this field," he declares. "You have to show the organization you know how to train, but you also have to know how to operate suggestion systems, understand motivation, implement incentive programs and function as a consultant from within. It's up to you to broaden your base if you hope to increase your importance."

Suggestion systems

If having an incentive program (or programs) meshes with your approach to HRD, you should make sure that the program permeates all aspects of your operation, O'Connor says. At MS&D, the Pride In Quality program is supplemented by a cost reduction suggestion system. Like many companies, MS&D rewards employees who submit significant ideas. Even though there is no cash involved, employees like the recognition and entertainment packages they can get.

Another aspect of the incentive program involves the company's commitment to quality circles, through which line-level employees design solutions to identifiable problems and present their findings to management. According to O'Connor, the fact that circles even exist is an incentive for workers to participate.

Since cutting the costs of doing business increases net productivity, many organizations welcome—and reward—employee suggestions. At RCA Corporation's television picture tube plant in Marion, IN, for instance, nonwage workers—roughly 10% of the 3,000

employees—compete in their own performance award program, according to Lee Maxcy, standard cost manager. The ideas they submit are evaluated by the plant manager and several other staff members who rank the suggestions and hand out cash awards and merchandise certificates ranging in value from $75 to $150.

Although this is a high priority program for the plant, the training staff hasn't had much to do with it so far, says Milton Schearer, an industrial relations and training specialist there. However, Schearer is working on a manager-supervisor communications program to improve the human climate in the plant. That approach, the ultimate goal of which is to reduce the number of rejected picture tubes through better information flow and awareness of the plant's total production process, does involve the training

staff. If the factory can lower its reject ratio, future plans may include some kind of incentive rewards to keep it down. Thus the trainers will have laid a foundation on which to base such an award system.

Top-down incentives

In many cases, trainers have nothing to do with designing and implementing incentive award programs. When corporate headquarters decrees that a new system will be implemented, trainers at the division level just have to adapt. For example, the General Telephone Company of California recently put in a quality consciousness program in which some employees will win big prizes. But, says training specialist Hal Elliot, the program originated from top management offices in Stamford, CT, leaving

INCENTIVE 'CARROTS': MAKE THEM LARGE AND PLENTIFUL

BY DALE ARCHIBALD

Over the past few years, the methods used for training and for boosting performance have shifted. Stick brandishing has lost favor, while offering carrots has gained ground. But Richard P. Brengel, chief of the incentives awards branch of the U.S. Office of Personnel Management in Washington, feels many organizations are approaching the issue of incentives all wrong. In effect, they're either offering undersized carrots or not enough of them. The result? A bitter taste in workers' mouths.

Brengel explains, "There is much talk and, all too frequently, inadequate action on the part of organizations to enhance individual motivation. Getting the work done on time, within quantity and quality constraints, becomes so important that insufficient attention is devoted to human resources. The individual's needs for a clear statement of the organization's goals, and how his or her work relates to them, often are overlooked."

He agrees there is a steady movement to compensate people for exceptional performance, but he warns that there can be problems.

1. Setting up clear, intelligible

standards for supervisor and employee is difficult and time-consuming.

2. Once standards are set, employees must be confident that the standards will be adhered to, either with rewards or punishments.

3. Rewards must be meaningful. If not, they could actually have an adverse effect.

4. Rewards must be granted and presented promptly, with sincerity.

Since complex forms are often ignored, he suggests that all recognition systems be kept simple. Recommendations (preferably one-pagers) should describe job elements and performance standards and explain how the recommended person has exceeded those standards.

He feels it's also important that supervisors and employees should all be trained in how the system—whether formal or informal—works.

Another area he feels most establishments are weak in is that of suggestion programs. But he does acknowledge that an impressive array of companies have discovered the value of this concept. For those that have, the average return on investment is approximately six to one, excluding second or third year benefits. He says one of every four suggestions is adopted, with an average award of $132 in industry and $109 in government.

As examples of money-saving ideas that originated in the suggestion box, Brengel points to successes at NASA and Kodak.

"Recognizing the problems in designing engines that could be used to test-fly the 75-ton Space Shuttle Orbiter," Brengel recounts, "an employee developed a proposal and then convinced NASA authorities that a modified Boeing 747 could be used as a ferry aircraft and airborne launch platform." This NASA employee at the Johnson Space Center saved the government some $30 million.

At Kodak, an employee felt cameras should be loaded with batteries, film and flash just prior to filling dealers' orders. "As a result," says Brengel, "customers are now provided with the freshest possible batteries and film. And the company realized tremendous cost savings since less storage space is required and the investment in batteries and flash is delayed." The employee won a $50,000 award for the idea.

Human elements— recognition, creativity, a drive for excellence—are becoming more and more important in business and government. Brengel says, "Management is discovering that by developing and communicating standards for job performance and by recognizing and rewarding excellence, employee motivation and productivity are enhanced." Clearly, investments in developing and maintaining active, ongoing reward systems for excellence and suggestions are realizing substantial returns— for all concerned.

Reprinted from TRAINING, February 1981

little room for him to get involved as a trainer. "That bothers me," he says. "We have little to say when the corporation puts on a program like this. We got the notice just like everyone else."

Some trainers, however, are in a position to make the most of that kind of situation. At Whataburger, training director Michael L. Hall shrewdly volunteered to handle the company's performance improvement program, which is based on incentive awards. Even though Hall got the administrative duties for the program from higher up, he has put his HRD skills to work running it. One thing he's done is survey employees about what they think would be good prizes to compete for in interstore contests based on quality, service and cleanliness. Giving employees input into the system should, he thinks, increase the likelihood that they'll work harder to win prizes.

That premise, in fact, forms the core of a doctoral dissertation Hall is planning. Using Whataburger's 300 employees as subjects, he wants to investigate what effect employee involvement has on whether incentive systems work. And because he's a trainer, he'll be basing his experiment around an in-store training course. Employees will be split into three groups, each of which will be asked to complete a self-instruction course. The first group will go through the training with no promise of an incentive. Group two will be told what they'll receive upon course completion. The final group will be allowed to select its own incentive from a list they develop and supervisors approve.

Hall predicts the latter group will finish the course faster and retain the information better than the other two. It sounds logical, but Hall cautions that the research base for incentives systems is still rather slim. "There's a large amount of money spent on incentives," he says. "We tend to assume that incentive awards are good for employees, but we have to recognize that it is a cost. What I want to know is if incentives are worth the money or if we'd do better by spending it another way."

Whether to give cash and merchandise awards to employees for their good performance or ideas is indeed open to debate. Some companies give thousands of dollars to idea-prone workers. For others, that approach doesn't quite fit. For example, electronics giant Hughes Aircraft saved an estimated $175 million in 1980 through its suggestion system, reports Cecil Hill, corporate manager of improvement programs. But, he says, the company gave no monetary awards: "We recognize ideas and make employees feel they're needed. Our motto for the 1980s, in fact, is 'People need to be needed.'" Employees whose suggestions are accepted get a special dinner with high-level managers and a token award, such as a self-contained picnic or a pen-and-pencil set.

Hill sees several problems with cash awards for cost reduction programs. For one thing, such a system can be divisive, he says, with employees guarding their ideas from one another on the chance their suggestions will be ripped off. Moreover, he says, 20% of the work areas at his company would get 80% of the cash because they do many more projects. In addition, many suggestions call for current investments that actually cost the corporation for the first several years. Savings may come eventually, but there's no good way to account for it in a cash award system.

Finally, Hill says, there's an increasing amount of litigation associated with cash award programs. "Companies are getting sued by employees who claim their ideas were stolen," he says. "Anytime you turn down an idea, there's the chance the employee will feel cheated out of money. With us, if their idea is rejected, all they've lost is a pen-and-pencil set."

More companies investigate performance incentive systems than implement them. At Michigan Mutual Insurance Company in Detroit, training director Thomas Hoskinson was all set to go with a cost reduction suggestion program. Most of the firm's 1,200 employees would have been eligible for a percentage of the first year's savings accrued from their ideas. "We were looking for a way to help improve performance," Hoskinson says, "and we were especially interested in getting employees more involved in solving work problems." After checking with similarly sized insurance companies, Hoskinson concluded that the suggestion system would best meet Michigan Mutual's objectives.

To encourage suggestions in the early stages of the program, the company would have awarded pen-and-pencil sets to workers who submitted at least three ideas in a year, whether or not they were accepted. "Our research told us that you have to get employees used to thinking about—and submitting—suggestions," Hoskinson says. "This kind of reward would be one way to do it." Accepted suggestions would have meant 10% to 15% of the first year's savings for the submitter.

But the more Hoskinson thought about this approach, the less it appealed to him. Checking with a few additional companies using suggestion systems revealed that not all that many suggestions were coming in. Moreover, as he considered the time and material costs of administering it, Hoskinson concluded that it would be difficult indeed to justify the program. So it was scrapped.

Instead, the company is now concentrating on supervisory and technical training to boost performance. "We're pushing the philosophy that employee involvement in problem solving is part of the job," Hoskinson told TRAINING. "For now, we see incentive systems as external to the process of getting the job done."

From these examples, it's plain to see that trainers are already involved to varying degrees in many incentive award systems. But there's room for much more, the sales predictions of incentive vendors suggest. As programs developed by these firms come to rest in organizations around the country, the demand for incentive-conscious trainers will increase.

Reprinted from TRAINING, April 1981

SHARING THE WEALTH: HRD'S ROLE IN MAKING INCENTIVE PLANS WORK

When employees hare productivity gains, their goals and views move closer to management's. Here's why some plans succeed—and others fail

BY RON ZEMKE

Employees do a better job when they've got a piece of the business," declares a Chicago and Northwestern Railroad ad in a recent *Business Week*. It goes on to suggest that, since C&NW employees own the business "down to the last spike," they work a little harder, smile a little wider, frown less, take more pride in their jobs, control costs better and are more profitable, innovative and productive than people at other railroads.

Though C&NW is an extreme example, a number of organizations are coming to see the point the C&NW ad makes: Employees *do* perform better when they have a piece of the action.

A recent National Science Foundation study investigating worker motivation, productivity and job satisfaction tends to confirm this growing management belief. The study, conducted by Katzell, Yankelovich, Fein, Oranti and Nash, examined over 300 behavioral science studies dealing with productivity and job satisfaction. It concluded that increased productivity depends on two propositions. First, "...the key to having workers who are both satisfied and productive is *motivation*, that is, arousing and maintaining the will to work effectively—having workers who are productive not because they are coerced but because they are committed." And, second, "Of all of the factors which help to create highly motivated/highly satisfied workers, the principal one appears to be that effective performance be recognized and rewarded— in whatever terms are meaningful to the individual, be it financial or psychological or both."

Engineer Mitchell Fein, Hillsdale, NJ, developer of the Improshare Plan— a productivity improvement system— suggests that the two propositions make complete sense, are irrefutable and yet, by and large, are exactly the opposite of what most managers do. "Managing policies are based on coercion in practically all plants," claims Fein. "Workers are seldom rewarded financially for more effective performance. The realities at the work place diametrically oppose what is needed to raise job satisfaction and motivation. Though unintentionally it works out that most workers are generally penalized for doing a better job, so they oppose management's objectives. Management senses the antagonism, and its managing and control systems are designed to operate in a hostile environment, to apply pressure and coercion to workers, to get them to do more.

"Workers readily see that if they assist in raising productivity, some of them will be penalized; if they improve productivity, reduce delays and waiting time, reduce crew sizes, some will be displaced and the plant will require fewer employees. They receive no financial gains for their efforts, nor are they persuaded that increased company profits will benefit them in the future. What employee will assist in raising productivity, only to be penalized for his diligence?"

The real folly of this "lose-lose" approach to managing productivity improvement is even more apparent when one realizes that such antagonism to productivity improvement is far from endemic to organizations. "Exempt" employees— executives, administrators, professionals and salesmen— are treated differently. A manager does not work himself out of his job by superior performance, nor is a salesman's security threatened because he sells too much. An engineer does not cause the layoff of other engineers by being too creative. Instead, these employees anticipate rewards for their creativity and effectiveness.

"When workers excell and raise productivity, the company benefits and management is pleased, but the workers do not benefit," Fein continues. "On the contrary, in the short term, their economic interests are *threatened*, and some suffer loss of income. When exempt employees are more effective, they are covered with glory; their economic security is *enhanced*, not threatened. Ironically, the relationship between workers and management actually provides workers with the incentive *not* to cooperate in productivity improvement. Without realizing it, all that most companies offer their employees for greater dedication and for raising productivity is the opportunity to reduce their earnings and job security. No wonder workers oppose productivity improvement. The system operates perfectly to *demotivate* workers. A more effective system could not have been designed to cause workers to oppose management's goals."

The NSF study team suggests six critical ingredients of systems that effectively raise job satisfaction and worker motivation. Heading the list is "financial compensation of workers [which] must be linked to their performance and to productivity gains." The NSF study found that when workers' pay is linked to their performance, the motivation to work is raised, productivity is higher and they are likely to be more satisfied with their work.

A study of over 400 plants in the United States found that when these plants instituted work measurement, productivity rose an added 42.9%. The average increase from no-measurement to incentives was 63.8%.

Most managers know that pay tied to productivity will motivate higher performance. From two-thirds to three-quarters of all the sales forces in the United States use incentives. Approximately 78% of manufacturing companies have executive bonus plans; the median bonus for the three top executives averages 42% of their base pay. A study of executive compensation of 1100 companies listed on the New York Stock Exchange found that companies with formal incentive plans for their executives earned on the average 43.6% more pretax profit than did the non-incentive companies.

By any measure, pay tied to productivity is the most powerful motivator of improved work performance. Yet only 26% of United States workers work under financial incentives. In some industries, such as basic steel and sewn products, incentives cover over 80% of the work force; in many industries, no incentives are employed. Few non-manufacturing operations are on incentive.

Why the limited use of financial incentives for workers in the United States? There are several reasons:

- Some managers are concerned that incentives will diminish their ability to control the operations and, over a period of time, that incentives will deteriorate, causing labor problems.
- Some managers believe that productivity improvement is largely created by management efforts; there is no need to share productivity gains.
- Management's-rights advocates believe that improvement is best shared periodically as increases in wages and benefits.

Though there may be some merit to these arguments, it is undeniable that, from floor sweeper to president, all increase their productivity when their pay is tied to performance.

Three how-to's for productivity improvement sharing

C. Jackson Grayson Jr., chairman of the American Productivity Center, talks about the Three Rs of productivity improvement: Reward, Recognition and Responsibility. This simple concept is the basis for many successful productivity improvement plans and programs. Give *recognition*— plaques, company dinners, pats on the back—for accomplishment. Promote *responsibility* by encouraging individual initiative and involvement. And *reward* productivity improvement with bonuses, incentive hard goods, travel or time off.

The real problem with productivity improvement sharing plans is equitable implementation. Often, the result of the most well-meaning PI plan is a complex rat's nest that yields a dismal bottom-line.

Three of the most successful productivity improvement sharing plans are Improshare, the Rucker Plan and the Scanlon Plan. Improshare Plans are reportedly in place in a coal mine, a post office, an airline and a metal fabricating plant.

Rucker plans are used at Universal Cyclops Steel, Teledyne and Amtrak. And Connelly Mirrors, Inc., and the Dana Corporation have successful Scanlon Plans.

The Scanlon Plan is the oldest of the three and has received wide attention in management circles. It is especially

WANT TO KNOW HOW PEOPLE FEEL ABOUT THEIR JOBS? ASK 'EM

For years industrial psychologists have sought clever ways to find out what people *really* think about their jobs. The problem premise has been, of course, that when asked whether they are satisfied with their jobs, most people will lie. And even if they tell the truth, they will not be able to *quantify* their satisfaction in reliable terms.

Flash! According to University of Minnesota researcher John Campbell, simply asking people whether they're satisfied with their jobs may give you answers that reflect their true feelings more meaningfully than do their responses to a whole list of cleverly constructed and statistically mashed questions about a multitude of job factors.

Basically, what Campbell is saying is that the whole is greater than the sum of its parts. He arrived at that conclusion as a result of administering open-ended questions to 185 engineers and technical people to determine what accounted for satisfaction with work. Together with colleague Vida Scarpello of the University of Georgia, Campbell found that many of the determinants of job satisfaction for the people surveyed were factors not usually measured by standardized job-satisfaction instruments.

Campbell and Scarpello found that scheduling flexibility, pleasantness of work interactions, work space, tools and equipment and how much their co-workers helped with work figured prominently in respondent's job satisfaction. None of these factors, they say, are included on most job-satisfaction surveys.

Overall, job satisfaction also seemed to be affected by how content the respondents were with their occupational choices and how they view their jobs in terms of their career goals or other goals. "The objectives people have for working influence how satisfied they think they are with their jobs," says Campbell.

Career objectives were particularly salient with the group of engineers. "If you see a hard or low-paying job as a useful stepping-stone in your career, you may be satisfied with it," Campbell explains. But for another group—blue-collar workers or office workers, for example—this career factor might not be important, and an entirely different factor—perhaps job stability—might be.

A factor such as career motivation is very difficult to determine, and varies not only from occupational group to occupational group but from person to person. And, adds Campbell, "Job-satisfaction surveys, with their standard variables, do not assess the context in which an individual evaluates his or her feelings about a job."

Life off the job also seems to affect a person's overall job satisfaction, Campbell says. While he points out that the question of whether "life-satisfaction" factors compensate for or simply accentuate job-satisfaction factors has never been completely settled, he feels that the evidence supports accentuation. "Happiness or misery in one area tends to spill over into the other."

Obviously, it is as dangerous to draw sweeping conclusions from Campbell's admittedly limited research as from research that points to other "answers." But it ought not be surprising that the sum of the parts rarely equals the whole in job-satisfaction studies, since there are so many elements—some unrelated to the actual work—that affect it.

Campbell's advice to managers of human-relations and personnel functions: Don't despair. "It's true that overall satisfaction is composed of more aspects than are normally measured, and that there are theoretically hundreds of variables," he says. "But you can't divorce the question of how you should assess a job-satisfaction survey with what you'll eventually use the information for, so you might as well only measure what you can manipulate."

Reprinted from TRAINING, April 1984

popular with industrial relations people because of its heavy emphasis on worker involvement. Productivity changes under the Scanlon Plan are measured by the ratio of dollar payroll costs against dollar sales output, compared with the ratio of base period.

The Rucker Plan differs from the Scanlon in that measurement is only of value added—that is, material costs are deducted from sales in the formula. The Rucker Plan is based on economic, not physical, productivity. That, according to Robert C. Scott, vice president, the Eddy-Rucker-Nickels Company, introduces both flexibility and protection, which are not found in programs using physical productivity measurements.

The organization "going Rucker" must be able to calculate the line wage and salary contribution to value produced, which is defined as sales income less the costs of materials, supplies and services purchased. That percentage of contribution becomes the multiplier for calculating bonuses. A typical Rucker bonus calculation is shown at right below.

position than if there had been a severe volume fall-off and work-force reduction.

The company is also in a much stronger position during the next upswing in business. It does not have to try to rehire its previously laid-off skilled people or train replacements for them. Instead of productivity losses, which typically accompany layoff situations, there has been a continuing effort for further productivity gains all during the recessionary period. When prices are restored to normal, the bonus and profitability could rise to the original—or higher—level than before the downturn.

The Improshare plan is based on the following concepts:
• The entire group shares in the gains; the groups can be only plant employees or include those in the office or those at management levels.
• The past average productivity level is used as the measurement base. Product or service standards are established as the average of a base period, preferably the past year.
• Productivity is measured as the

specifically defined. Increased productivity is shared, with no attempt to pinpoint whether employees or management created the savings. Capital equipment is defined as an installation that costs $10,000 or more; when this occurs, 80% of the improvement derived from the capital equipment is deducted from the product standard, and 20% remains to be shared.

• A ceiling on productivity is established at 160% productivity, which yields 30% shared earnings. When productivity rises beyond the ceiling in any week, the excess is banked and made available in future weeks. Should productivity continue to rise and stay above the ceiling, a simple formula provides that management will buy back the standards from the employees for a cash payment equal to one-half of a year's savings. Such buy-back bonuses can easily amount to $1,000 per employee and more.

The HRD role?

What, you may wonder, is the HRD role in establishing a productivity improvement program based on pay bonuses? First, the HRD specialist can work with the finance and compensation people to pick the incentive system that fits the culture of the organization. Secondly, there's lots of training to be done. The Achilles' heel of every productivity improvement program is supervisor and employee understanding of the program. Unless the people affected *understand* the program it soon becomes submarined. Third, there's room for problem solving and small group meeting training. "The best ideas for productivity improvement come from the bottom of the organization, not the top," says APC's C. Jackson Grayson. That process can't happen if supervisors and managers aren't skilled at facilitating employee participation. Fourth, there's work methods and work simplification training; people must learn to look at their work with "a new set of eyes" if they are going to improve current processes.

And, finally, the HRD group is in the best position to sample and monitor employee problems with the system and changes in satisfaction with and attitude toward the program. No doubt about it, there are plenty of critical roles for HRD in the productivity improvement game.

Reprinted from TRAINING, January 1979

	Rucker Calculation with Price Reduction	Basic Situation
Sales Value of Output	$8.000,000	$8,000,000
— Material, Supply & Service Cost	4,100,000	4,000,000
= Production Value Created	$3,900,000	$4,000,000
x 47.4% Standard Share for Payrolls	1,848,600	1,896,000
— Wages, Salaries & Benefits Paid	1,580,000	1,580,000
= Flexible Productivity Bonus	$ 268,000	$ 316,000
Bonus as % of Employment Cost	17.0%	20.0%

Now, suppose a recession comes along, and the company decides a price reduction is necessary to maintain sales at the previous level. The bonus pot would be reduced, but basic salaries— and work-force level— would, or, at least could, go untouched. See above.

The same calculation would apply if a $100,000 increase in benefits were the issue instead of a sales pricing decrease. Such erosions of bonus cannot be sustained year after year without washing out the incentive program. But they are useful as a temporary expedient during business recessions to entice more work into a particular plant, where jobs are much more secure— albeit at the expense of some bonus earnings. Both employees and their company are in a much better

hour value of output against the total hours worked by the group. Money measures are not used. Production is counted only for acceptable pieces packed in a carton and moved into the warehouse. Work in process is not counted.

• Productivity improvement is shared 50-50 between employees and the company. The value of production in hours is matched against the total hours worked, and the difference is shared. To minimize weekly fluctuations, a moving average of four to six weeks often is used.

• Man-hour standards are frozen at the past average. Standards are not changed when operations are changed by either management or the employees, except for capital equipment and technology changes, which are

THE TRAINING/ INCENTIVES CONNECTION

It's still growing in nontraditional areas

BY RON ZEMKE

It is the classic American industrial success story. Through hard work and cleverness, the Tonka Corporation assembly line of 19 women that turned out 14,000 Mighty Dumps® in 1978 is today an assembly group of 17 women producing more than 16,000 of these bright yellow sandbox delights. It is improved productivity in its purest form and the sugarplum dream of every contemporary manager who would be corporate king.

But such success stories are more often dream than reality today. Productivity growth, once the hallmark of American industry, is an endangered species. Journalists, business school professors and social science researchers all have their favorite explanations: too much government or not enough; too little incentive or too much; modern managers unskilled in operations and too skilled in generating short-term profits; modern societal (read: anti-hard work) values.

There is an equally dazzling array of solutions and panaceas on parade. One group touts robots. Another pushes quality of working life solutions. A third promotes anything and everything Japanese, from Quality Control Circles to eating raw fish. But when you stand back and take the long view, there is a remarkably thick thread of commonality among the opinions— and even among the panaceas. Stripped of idiosyncratic vocabulary and emotional appeals,

the experts seem to agree that there are two basic ways to improve productivity at the work-floor level: by increasing the skill, knowledge and motivation of employees and by improving the effectiveness and efficiency of the machines and processes of production. In final analysis, both of these solutions come down to one working assumption: When people learn to do the *right things* and find ways to do them *better, cheaper* and *faster*, productivity is— by definition—improved.

Increasingly, we hear of trainers and other human resource development specialists responding to the challenge of improving employee effectiveness and efficiency by taking on more ambitious responsibilities in productivity improvement efforts. As TRAINING has periodically reported, one of the most fascinating of these for trainers and other HRD specialists is in the incentive motivation arena. Traditionally, incentive motivation has been synonymous with winning toasters and trips to Tahiti for sales excellence. But more and more, incentive motivation is ceasing to be the sole property of the sales division. Performance-based incentive systems are being installed in offices, factories and, yes, even in training rooms. And they are producing results.

In previous reports on the use of incentives in nonsales settings, especially in training-related areas, we have looked at:

• An incentive travel and merchandise program at Eastern Airlines, used to reward a combination of

knowledge retention from refresher training and on-job effectiveness.

• A computerized management training game played for real dollars by management trainees of Ginos, Inc., King of Prussia, PA.

• An oil rig safety program at Noble Drilling Corp., Tulsa, OK, that uses safety training and Green Stamps for an injury-free record.

• A Quality Circle program at Honeywell, Inc., of Minneapolis, MN, that combines problem-solving training, management attention and merchandise for improvements in product quality.

Trainers and incentive motivation specialists still feel their match, if not made in heaven, is at least a relationship worth working at a bit longer. Dr. John Geyer, president of Performax Systems International, Inc., a training company subsidiary of Carlson Marketing and Motivation, Minneapolis, suggests that "we are just learning how really effective the combination of good training and well thought out incentive programs can be. The whole area of adding incentive motivation to Quality Control Circle efforts and other team-building and problem-solving efforts really expands the horizons." Geyer, whose company supplies training programs for Performance Incentives Company (PIC)— the Carlson subsidiary that did much of the pioneering work in the training-plus-incentives area— sees at least a 10% per year growth rate ahead for the 1980s.

William Weller, president of S&H Motivation and Travel Inc., Hillside, IL, echoes Geyer's enthusiasm for the growth of the incentive motivation field in nontraditional areas, but cautions that significant impact will come only when the people using and promoting incentive motivation programs "learn to regard motivation and competence as synergistic and to address competence as well as motivation in their programs." Weller also prophesies that future incentive programs will be more data based, more sophisticated and complex, and as interested in the improvement of competence as in efficiency. "We realize that increasing the efficiency of people with dull or the wrong tools can easily result in a situation where people work harder and produce less," he says.

Duane Christenson of St. Louis-based Maritz Motivation reports that Maritz's nonsales incentive business is doubling yearly and "the company's earlier predictions that nonmarketing applications would comprise 30% of our business by 1985 will be at least met, and probably surpassed.

We are continually impressed by the eagerness with which managers are accepting the total motivation management concept," he adds. "They are very receptive to the idea that goal setting, good communication, recognition and reward are essential in a productivity improvement effort." Maritz is apparently heading into the training-plus-incentives business in a big, aggressive way. Company officials recently announced that Communico, a training subsidiary, will be merged with a new acquisition, Detroit-based Wilding Company, to form Maritz Communications Company.

While no one is suggesting that training programs coupled with incentive motivation plans will cure all the productivity problems besetting American industry, the enthusiasm and impetus to "do more" is there, and the potential for long-term results real. Dr. C. Jackson Grayson, Jr., director of the American Productivity Center (APC), Houston, recently summarized the people and productivity connection for TRAINING:

"They have a motto over at Texas Instruments that goes far toward summing up my views on productivity improvement. They say, 'Assets make things possible, but people make things happen.' They know, and I concur, that assets alone won't solve a productivity problem. You don't solve problems by throwing money at them. Nor will technology solve the shortfall. Technology alone, without the human factor, is sterile. Whether you're making jet engines, computers or automated potato peelers, people must implement and enhance that technology before anything cost-effective can happen. Remember the old Zen riddle, 'What is the sound of one hand clapping?' Without people and human effort in your productivity formula, nothing can really happen. It takes two hands to produce a sound."

Reprinted from TRAINING, December 1981

COMBINE RECOGNITION AND REWARD

An inside look at Honeywell's award winning suggestion system

BY RON ZEMKE

Communications are the key ingredient to the success of the Suggestion System at Honeywell's defense systems and avionics divisions. A six-time winner of the National Association of Suggestions Systems' "Excellence of Performance" award, Honeywell is rightfully proud of their program. Keystones of the program are recognition, reward, visibility and keeping the program fresh.

The Suggestion System generates over 18,000 written suggestions. This creates a significant task to administer, track, follow up and answer. The administrative function is staffed by full-time professional people who coordinate the answering of each ECR (Error Cause Removal, the form used to submit ideas).

According to Robert A. Schwarz, manager of employee motivation programs, the success at Honeywell reflects the combination of careful and thorough administration, dedication of engineering to prompt ECR answering and the use of creative communications to stimulate participation. Two key elements of creative communications are *recognition* and *reward*.

Recognition

In the case of Schwarz's ECR program, recognition is definitely first-class, thorough and creative. To encourage a high volume of suggestions, the names and/or pictures of employees who submit 3, 6, 10, 15 and 25 ECRs are place on "Super Star" charts in their departments. To promote quality of suggestions, individuals who submit high-dollar-award ECRs are singled out for special treatment. Each week, two suggesters' pictures and an explanation of their dollar-award-winning suggestions are made into 11-inch by 17-inch posters and displayed on 160 STEP (Strive Toward Error-Free Performance) bulletin boards located in factory and office facilities around the division. During a given year approximately 80 employees are thus recognized. The award winners receive copies of the photos and posters, most of which are then taken home.

According to Schwarz, this poster idea is fairly expensive, but it has a number of subtle benefits. First, it represents a great "stroke" for those so recognized. And it also performs an important modeling function for other employees; it promises, or models, a potential reinforcement, a sort of "you-too-can-have-your-name-up-in-lights" message. The posters also explain, by example or model, the kind of suggestion that can win recognition and reward. And, finally, the posters communicate specific ideas of the "Hey, that would work here, too" variety. When these same posters are displayed in the winning employees' departments during Employee Open House, employees have an opportunity to be recognized by people outside the normal work setting.

Honeywell's in-house communication vehicles also play an important role in the recognition job. The Honeywell newspaper—*The Honeywell Circulator*—carries articles about winners, winning suggestions and pictures of winners receiving the actual cash awards from members of management at departmental meetings attended by the employees' peers. Twice a year, the paper runs a supplement, the "Suggestion System Special Issue," featuring stories and photos about the system and the winners. Photos of 15 to 30 winners appear in the issue. In addition, stories about individual winners appear in divisional and departmental newsletters. Copy and photos for all this PR came from Schwarz's office.

Each year, three Minneapolis divisions of Honeywell recognize one person as "ECR Suggester of the Year." At Honeywell in Minneapolis, those individuals receive lavish attention. The governor of the State of Minnesota presents winners their Honeywell award, as well as a personal commendation. And, of course, photos of the winners and the governor appear in numerous Honeywell publications, as well as on the STEP bulletin boards.

One final fillip is a sort of semi-perpetual recognition. Each year, Schwarz's office publishes a STEP calendar featuring pictures of seven employee winners per calendar page. Eighteen thousand of these goodies are printed and distributed throughout the company divisions located in Minneapolis, Phoenix, St. Petersburg, Denver and Tampa.

The final recognition opportunity occurs when an employee is due a monetary ward for a suggestion. The employee's supervisor presents the check at a brief meeting attended by appropriate members of management and the employee's co-workers.

Rewards

Both cash and merchandise award possibilities are available to employees under Honeywell's ECR program. Cash awards are made for suggestions that promise to benefit the organization in some fashion; these are calculated on the basis of one-sixth total first year anticipated dollar savings. Merchandise plays an unusual role in the system. The merchandise tends to have low cash value, but Schwarz believes that it considerably enhances the system since it's used to influence both quantity and quality of submissions but has no relationship to the judging of the submissions.

Quantity is influenced by reinforcing numbers of submissions. When an employee has submitted a total of three suggestions, he or she is eligible for a merchandise award. When total submissions reach six, the employee is eligible for another small merchandise hit. At submission levels 10, 15 and 25 of the "Super Stars" subsystem, employees become eligible for additional merchandise available through Honeywell's STEP Certificate and gift catalog system. These suggestion submitters are awarded the STEP Certificates by their supervisor.

Quality of ECR suggestions is influenced by awarding merchandise for the submission of cash bonus winning suggestions. When an employee has his or her first ECR suggestion accepted, he or she receives a small first-aid kit. In addition, when an employee has earned $150 in total suggestion cash awards, he or she receives a Honeywell smoke detector. These two simple merchandise usages, says Schwarz, have promoted "a large flow of good ECRs that provide a favorable level of savings."

Results

The proof of the pudding is, of course, in the evaluation of the "favorable level of savings" Schwarz referred to. And "favorable" they are. As the accompanying chart suggests,

HONEYWELL SUGGESTION SYSTEM PERFORMANCE

	1976	1977	1978	1979
Suggestions per Eligible Employee	2.47	3.17	3.28	3.66
Total Suggestions	8,890	10,136	13,108	18,471
Percent Accepted	49	49	49	49
Savings	$467,722	$440,303	$517,081	$1,304,644

the Honeywell suggestion system is a real "growth stock." Suggestions per employee, at 3.66 per eligible employee, is considered exceptionals and the acceptance rate of 49% is more than double the national average. And, as the 1979 savings figures indicate, quality of suggestions is increasing faster than number of suggestions. Furthermore, the cost of the whole system, from posters and payoffs through administration, runs a cost-to-savings ratio of 20% of first-

year savings.

Earlier, we cited recognition, reward, visibility and freshness as essential ingredients in a prize-winning suggestion system. And that still holds. But we now add one more important element to that formula—first-rate results. It's results that recognize and reinforce the people who run the program and prove that the job of conducting a suggestion system is one worth doing well.

Reprinted from TRAINING, July 1980

HOW AWARDS AND INCENTIVES CAN HELP SPEED UP LEARNING

Incentive programs can be combined
effectively with learning activities so
that training is reinforced and
learned behavior is also practiced

BY ROBERT C. EIMERS,
GEORGE W. BLOMGREN
AND EDWARD GUBMAN

The trainer who is interested only in training will have little interest in incentive programs. However, the trainer who assumes the broader mission of improving organizational and individual *performance* may find incentives an invaluable adjunct to his or her programs. The reason is simple. *Performance* of any task—on the job or off—is a function of two factors, ability and motivation. This may be stated as a simple behavioral equation: Performance = Ability x Motivation. It is important to note that these two factors are related in a multiplicative fashion. To be knowledgeable or skilled at performing a task is not the same as performing it. Nor will desire alone produce actual performance. Management places little value on "trying to" or "knowing how." It's performance that counts.

Several years ago we became interested in the possibility of combining the reward elements of incentive programs with training activities. Our first opportunity to test this interest came in the banking industry, and we have subsequently run a number of programs with both large and small financial institutions across the US.

The results of these programs have been dramatic. In one large bank, over $500 million in new business was produced in a 120-day period, at a total acquisition cost (including the cost of all training and awards) of less than one-half of one percent. While it is difficult to compare the results of similar programs applied to different banks in different markets, our data suggests that performance programs combining motivation and training produce vastly superior results when compared with traditional bank incentive programs dealing only in motivation. The results of two different programs run by the same bank give the reader some idea of the difference (see table).

While our data for these programs does not enable us to actually separate the independent effects of the training and motivation, several processes seem to account for their success. Some, although not directly related to reinforcement, have important implications for performance-oriented learning.

1. Employees are given an incentive (an award) for learning. What is learned becomes worth knowing. The employee can see that skill acquisition will lead to real awards, so even the learning process itself is reinforced. By correctly completing quizzes, employees can immediately earn award points. These are easily cost justifiable because of the enormous program results.

2. Newly acquired skills, such as listening, questioning, or presenting, are reinforced. They have a clear, tangible reward. This reinforcement occurs not in the classroom (correct answers) but on the job or in the marketplace (correct behavior) where the "connections" among behavior, environmental cues, and reinforcement are more realistic.

3. It is peer-oriented training. With the exception of the design of some training material and the initial training of team leaders, there are no experts or training authorities involved in the program. No doubt this somewhat decreases the effectiveness of the teaching process, but it may be more than compensated for by various factors. Learning seems to be enhanced when the learners are also given responsibility for the training. Just as the do-it-yourselfer may devote special care and interest and derive a unique sense of self satisfaction, do-it-yourself training may have some unexamined merit.

4. American industry runs on individual needs for achievement. A group (team) setting for learning introduces group needs for achievement, which we believe are qualitatively different from individual needs for achievement. Among its advantages: it can be created through the formation of teams. By contrast, it is relatively more difficult to effect an individual's need for achievement.

5. Training is, or should be, tied to organizational objectives. Too often, however, the learner is unaware of these objectives; or, if aware, fails to identify with them, thus undermining the personal relevancy of the training. In contrast, when these same objectives are reformulated at the team level, they acquire a personal relevancy, ensuring the meaningfulness of connected training activities.

The ways the trainer effectively can apply incentives are limited only by imagination and organization needs. Whatever the application, the basic

	Incentive Program	Incentive Program with Training
Training costs and promotional material	$ 501	$ 11,773
Awards costs	22,874	54,990
Total costs	$ 23,375	$ 66,763
New business generated	$2,582,202	$11,160,263
Cost as % of new business	.905%	.598%

GIVE AWARDS BEFORE, DURING AND AFTER TRAINING

BY RON ZEMKE

Nearly every employee, sooner or later, attends some sort of training session ostensibly designed to help him or her improve some aspect of job performance. Whether that training actually effects an on-job behavior change depends at least as much on things peripheral to the training as it does on the training itself.

According to a number of trainers and trainees we polled, one of these important peripherals is the matter of RECOGNITION. According to our respondents, there seem to be three critical times to provide recognition to the trainee. Surprisingly, perhaps, the first of these is before training begins.

Pre-attendance recognition. This is really what a salesperson would refer to as positioning.

The best positioning is to take the prospective trainee through the *who, what, when, where, why and how* of his or her selection for this training and to do it well in advance—at least four weeks in advance—of the actual training. The ideal result of this sort of positioning meeting would be the trainee understanding that selection for training is a recognition of both his or her potential worth to the organization and worth as a person.

End of training recognition. Some trainers tend to overlook the importance of recognizing successful completion of a training program in some tangible way. "We [trainers] are pretty blasé about training as a peak or significant event," suggests Sales Trainer Brent Caryle, "but the training event is significant to the trainees and successful completion should be formally recognized."

Another perspective has to do with the end-of-course award as a reminder or stimulus. According to Bob Giorgi, a long-time trainer and manager of National Indirect Distribution, General Electric's Mobile Radio Division, "The end of training diploma or plaque should function to remind the person of the skills he or she acquired in the course. That means it has to end up somewhere the person can see it. And *that* means it has to be classy, just the right piece of merchandise. I want my trainers looking around for a nail to hang it or a shelf to put it on, not wondering where to bury it."

Recognition of accomplishment. People come back from a training program turned on to trying out their newfound skills. But many times they are greeted back on the job as if they had been out with a cold. ' A "the work's been piling up. Get caught up" atmosphere prevails. Most of our respondents suggest that turning the corner from training room to bottom-line benefit is a two-step process.

The first step is another positioning step; recognition that the trainee has had a learning experience and that he or she has developed a new potential which needs some room to be exercised and experienced. Some managers hold an hour or two debriefing with returning trainees. Some require a written report. Many are beginning to go the route of sitting down with the returnee and developing an action plan for trying out new ideas and exercising new skills.

The second recognition step of the "making it happen back on the job" process is the recognition of accomplishments. According to Duane Christensen, vice president of corporate communications at Maritz Motivation, Inc., recognition and reward for using just-learned skills tells the trainee that his or her performance does matter to others and improvement is important enough to be specially recognized.

Christensen and others favor tangible, desired rewards such as merchandise or travel awards because of the validity or earnestness they bring to the recognition of accomplishment. But Christensen also stresses that there are intangible aspects to tangible awards: "There seems to be a more lasting kind of reward that people get. It's the recognition they receive, the 'psychic income' that results when work is well done and goals are achieved. This is a very real thing, although it's tough to put your finger on the lasting impact of the psychological return one gets."

principles of a well-designed incentive program remain constant.

1. The behavior which is to be rewarded must be clearly defined. Any confusion about behavioral standards quickly leads to perceptions of unfairness by the participants. One way to demotivate people quickly is to let them perform certain behaviors and then have them find out that they don't get rewarded because they didn't understand (or you didn't communicate) exactly what was required.

In this sense, target behaviors must not only be measurable and properly defined, but they must also be communicated effectively to program participants. The measurement system assessing performance must also be publicly communicated. The more accurate, specific and behaviorally oriented the measurement system, the less subjective the behavior-reward process will be and the more successful the program will be.

2. Awards should be given as soon as possible after the desired behavior occurred. Bonuses given at the end of the year for a job well done in the beginning, for example, simply lose some of their impact in the intervening months. Why not reward outstanding achievement right away? This strengthens the connection, in everyone's mind, between high performance and management's willingness to reward it. Whereas salaries and other forms of compensation may be rather inflexible in this regard, due to organizational policy and administrative practices, recognition awards and/or merchandise can be given almost immediately.

3. When it comes to awards, one man's meat may be another's poison. We all know that people do things for their own reasons, not for those of someone else. We also know that no' two people are exactly alike in terms of what they value. To maximize the behavioral return on incentive investment, trainers and incentive planners must provide as broad a range of awards as possible. When this is done, participants can then select the award or set of awards that has particular appeal to them. Simple logic dictates that the more highly the reward is valued by people, the greater the likelihood that they will perform the desired behaviors and maintain them over time. Programs that offer only one type of award tend not to influence each participant personally. Broad reward menus, such as merchandise catalogs, typically create greater interest and, consequently, greater effort.

4. Awards should have memorability. One disadvantage of giving cash awards, for example, is that they are

PUT THE PERSONAL TOUCH INTO YOUR RECOGNITION AWARDS

Putting an existing employee recognition program on track or founding one in a growing organization requires feedback best obtained by a "recognition audit," says Robert L. Mathis, professor of management at the University of Nebraska in Omaha.

A proper audit, Mathis says, basically asks simple questions: What are the objectives and methods of the existing or proposed award program? What kind of program do employees think is needed? Which employee groups need and deserve recognition? When should recognition come and what should be recognized?

The first thing to nail down is the objective, says Mathis. Personnel officers need to decide whether longevity, continuous performance (safety, perfect attendance) or outstanding accomplishment (productivity) is to be rewarded. And in setting the award criteria they should rely on a work-force profile.

If a profile reveals a large percentage of young, female, blue-collar workers with more than five years of service, for instance, "one should design a program and offer some awards that will appeal to that employee group," he explains. Similarly, if the analysis discovers that a significant number of workers quit after two or three years, a two-year service recognition award should be established as a step toward the traditional five-year plateau.

Mathis recommends a short, anonymous-response survey to establish criteria for sensible (and tasteful) awards or to assess the effectiveness of existing recognition programs. In a nationwide survey of attitudes toward corporate recognition programs sponsored by Balfour Corp., a manufacturer of customized awards, Mathis found "a definite gap between employees' needs for recognition and employers' understanding of those needs.

"Employees generally felt their contributions were not truly recognized by their employers," he continues. "Also, many expressed dissatisfaction with award presentations. This feeling clearly stemmed from the lack of personal, sincere presentation of awards."

More work on publicity about awards and award programs through newsletters, bulletin boards and local news media is advisable, Mathis suggests. Formal luncheons and banquets should be maintained, he says, but encouraging supervisors to hold impromptu presentations at work sites makes award ceremonies much more personal.

Supervisors who acknowledge accomplishments immediately and in the presence of the employee's peers also aid in promoting the program, Mathis says. The most important part of the event is a personally delivered message of appreciation that focuses on the employee's contributions to departmental and organizational goals.

"What must be stressed is that the thing given, while important, is less important than the manner in which it is given," he says. "All activities connected with a recognition program should stress the personal touch if awards are truly to convey high praise and symbolize real acknowledgment of accomplishment."

Reprinted from TRAINING, March 1983

apt to be melded into household budgets and used for groceries and dental bills. Merchandise, travel, and recognition awards, on the other hand, typically have a more lasting impact, and continue to evoke pleasant associations for the recipient over the years.

5. Effective awards have emotional appeal. They arouse an individual's awareness of his needs and wants, thus motivating him toward achievement and satisfaction of those needs. We have often heard merchandise catalogs described as "wish books," for example. They have a capacity for evoking pleasant images and fantasies of desired life styles. Because merchandise, as well as travel, has such broad and strong emotional appeal, it tends to inspire increased levels of employee performance.

6. Awards should be accompanied by social recognition. Fanfare may be "corny," but you cannot underestimate the value of presenting an award with enthusiasm and dignity. When the company president, for example, presents an award, its impact is doubled. This shows the recipient that his or her efforts are being noted and appreciated at all levels.

Newspaper publicity, even if it is only a "house organ," also enhances the value of an award.

Most trainers recognize and understand the value of verbal reinforcement, recognition and other forms of encouragement. An incentive program provides a valuable opportunity for trainers to tie these social rewards closely to the tangible rewards. Excessive reliance on material awards is just as limiting as their exclusion. Verbal reinforcement is both free and powerful. Recognition and encouragement can be used after the program ends to strengthen the newly learned behaviors. Simple feedback is a powerful motivator, and the results from a behaviorally oriented system of measurement are of special importance. A good performance program taps a vast range of human motivations.

7. Award programs need to be administered fairly if everyone is to participate. Different levels of performance deserve to be rewarded at different value plateaus. When the rewards are too difficult to achieve, effort becomes minimal. Conversely, when rewards are too easily attained, participants are not pushed to excel, to stretch themselves, and generate significant performance increments.

8. Awards must be won if they are going to serve any purpose at all. Winning an award is an energizing process; it creates good feelings about oneself and about the company. Don't be stingy in your award programs. Awards represent an investment in your employees and their performance, an investment which typically pays off handsomely in terms of increased morale and employee effectiveness.

In too many instances, incentives are applied as part of a contest. This typically creates a situation where there are a few winners and many more losers. A number of people approach contests with a negative mental set; their expectations for winning are slim. To avoid this problem, make sure that the program incorporates opportunities for *everyone* to earn according to the amount of effort they're willing to expend or the results they achieve. This dramatically increases participation. An element of competition definitely enhances a performance program, but experience shows that grand awards for winners are best employed as bonuses, rather than as substitutes for programs that allow everyone to earn and win.

9. **While awards can be used to motivate behavior and facilitiate learning, this fact in itself creates real danger.** Just as government excesses in printing money can create economic problems, trainers who print diplomas and buy plaques haphazardly can destroy the motivational value of their awards. Just as "printing press" money loses value, "cheap" awards come to have little motivational value.

10. **Awards stimulate motivation, but we have frequently found that motivation alone is not sufficient.** Performance is actually a function of two factors—motivation and *skill*. Thus, it is often effective to supplement incentive awards with training.

One more point should be made regarding the use of incentives to reinforce behavior. Too often we reward only the *outcome* of the desired behavior, rather than the behavior itself. For example, incentives are often used to reward increased sales. This does increase motivation levels, but the behavioral outcomes are not always under the control of the participant. Whether a person closes a sale is at least partially determined by the customer. If the behaviors leading to the positive outcomes— such as increased prospecting or more sales calls— are rewarded, then we strengthen the desired behavior change. Once this change becomes part of the individual's behavioral repertoire, the desired outcomes will occur naturally and frequently.

The team concept

In general, the use of teams adds a powerful motivational element to any incentive program. Teams satisfy basic social and affiliative needs. Enthusiasm is generated, and, more often than not, this enthusiasm is contagious. Awards based on team performance serve to generate a healthy sense of good-natured competition, which often motivates people who otherwise might not have participated on an individual level. Group achievement, especially when natural work groups are involved, tends to generate lasting organizational benefits, such as improved communication skills, teamwork and leadership training.

Goal-setting

Trainers who truly want to maximize the benefits of using incentives should build a goal-setting component into their programs. This applies to individual goals and to team goals. Research shows that people who set goals tend to perform at higher levels than people who do not. Furthermore, data indicate that individuals who publicly commit themselves to achieving various measurable objectives tend to achieve their objectives more often than those who do not make such a commitment. Thus, it makes good sense for performance program participants to develop their own behavioral contracts, noting the awards they will be shooting for and the specific steps they will take in order to achieve those awards.

The need for improved performance doesn't begin and end during any particular time span. When training is combined with incentives, the goal is to provide a healthy "push" that moves participants toward improved performance and permanent behavior change. The wise incentive user knows that when a performance program ends, performance might well return to pre-program levels. For this reason, it's important to take action to ensure more lasting behavior change. Periodic "booster" skill-building sessions are helpful. So is the continued use of social rewards and feedback. Additional programs, albeit smaller and segmented for specific groups, also can be employed to take advantage of the momentum generated by the effort and success of the initial program.

Reprinted from TRAINING, June 1979

THE 3Rs OF PRODUCTIVITY IMPROVEMENT: RESPONSIBILITY, RECOGNITION, REWARD

Here's why Jack Grayson's prestigious American Productivity Center is gung ho about incentives

BY RON ZEMKE

The American Productivity Center in Houston is described in its promotion literature as "a privately funded, not-for-profit organization dedicated to strengthening the free-enterprise system by developing practical programs to improve productivity and the quality of working life in the United States." A tough manifesto to live up to. But APC's "top dog," Dr. C. Jackson Grayson, Jr., is no stranger to tough assignments. From 1971 through 1973, Grayson served as chairman of the Price Commission (a no-win assignment if there ever was one); served in advisory capacities to the Cost-of-Living Council and the Comptroller General of the United States; and has been dean of the business schools at Southern Methodist University and Tulane.

Grayson is something of a maverick among economists and management gurus. Unlike many leading economists, Grayson does *not* blame the current slump in U.S. productivity growth on such esoteric factors as decreases in technological innovation and research and development (R&D) funding, lagging capital investment in new plants and processing automation, government regulation compliance costs, or blue-collar blues. Though acknowledging the importance of these forces, Grayson firmly believes that the key to renewed productivity growth is the U.S. labor force. In particular, Grayson has some

tough views on the way working people are trained, managed, motivated and involved in their work.

"They have a motto over at Texas Instruments that goes far toward summing up my view," Grayson recently revealed to TRAINING. "They say, 'Assets make things possible, but people make things happen.' *They* know, and I concur, that assets alone won't solve a productivity problem. You don't solve problems by throwing money at them. Nor will technology resolve the shortfall. Technology alone, without the human factor, is sterile. Whether you're making jet engines, computers or automated potato peelers, *people* must implement and enhance that technology before anything cost effective can happen. Remember the old Zen riddle, 'What is the sound of one hand clapping?' Without people and human effort in your productivity formula, nothing can really happen. It takes two hands to produce a sound."

Grayson has been widely quoted and cited for his references to the 3 Rs of productivity improvement,* a formula that emphasizes performance-contingent pay and direct incentives. "One way to get people's attention is through some sort of simple alliterative formula. The 3 Rs certainly have worked well in that regard," says

*In Grayson's formula, people become part of the productivity *solution* when given Responsibility over and Recognition and Reward for productivity improvement.

Grayson. "Actually, I'm fond of alliterations and acronyms. The expanded version of the 3 Rs is 'If you mind your Ps, Qs and Rs, you'll reach greater EPS.' The Ps stand for *Productivity, Participation* and *People*; the Qs for *Quality of Product or Service, Quality of Life* and *Quality of Working Life*. The Rs, of course, are *Responsibility, Recognition* and *Reward*. EPS stands for two things, *Earnings per Share* and *Economic, Political and Social Improvement*. I could do 40 minutes just using those letters. But beyond that, the formula P+Q+R = EPS emphasizes the interrelationships, the integrated viewpoint, one needs in order to understand the human factors in productivity improvement. It emphasizes the personal well-being—the quality of work life people are concerned about—and it emphasizes equally the economic realities and relationships of the world. I really think the factors in this formula are important and that they make sense. They make sense for an individual, for a firm, for an industry and for the nation."

Grayson and the APC staff, composed primarily of executives on loan, recently have been looking closely at applications of the 3 Rs, in general, and incentive systems, in particular, to productivity improvement programs. Their studies of successful applications led them to conclude that a variety of incentives, directly tied to clearly specified performance, can have a high organizational impact. "We're convinced, for example, that recognition for a job well done is extremely important. Plaques, patches, certificates, jackets, mention in internal communications documents— newsletters, magazines, brochures— are all really important to people's sense of well-being. Many management people have chalked off these simple sorts of incentives. They laugh or sneer and say that people are too sophisticated to really care about those things. I think that's dead wrong."

As examples, Grayson points to IBM's P.I.E.* program, a highly successful suggestion program that has as its immediate payoff a *piece of pie*. Equally impressive are the Kodak and Beech Aircraft suggestion programs. At Beech, where early recognition for suggestions is emphasized, they pay $10 net, based on the first review of any suggestion. That quick reward stimulates participation. The base of "winners" is very broad, employees are encouraged to participate by seeing the obvious success of

*Participative Improvement Effort.

others. The ten spot is placed in a special blue envelope and awarded publicly to the employee. According to one APC staffer, Beech employees "wear those envelopes sticking out of their shirt pockets for days." The employee participation rate in the Beech suggestion program is cited as 75%.

Grayson and the APC staff believe that contemporary management development practices and management attitudes contribute to the neglect of recognition and reward programs. "Most managers think their organizations are too sophisticated for these types of programs. And, on top of that, the whole management development process they go through is oriented toward developing managers as critics rather than as facilitators. We train managers to find fault rather than to reward excellence." Another reason incentive reward and recognition programs have been neglected as motivational tools in non-sales parts of organizations concerns job interdependence.

According to Bob Lewis, an APC staffer on loan from Prudential Insurance, "Incentive and recognition plans are the backbone of the sales effort in industry, for example, but the conditions inside an organization, where the bulk of the people work, are quite different from the sales environment. The salesperson is physically detached from other people, his responsibility often tends to be geographically circumscribed, and his relationship to the organizational process is pretty direct and well defined. Most of us, though, are bureaucrats. We're surrounded by people— people to the left, to the right, above and below us, people with dotted-line relationships. And all of these people may have a lot to do with our productivity. It's pretty hard to point out individual key contributors in a bureaucracy."

Lewis suggests that organizations with successful incentive reward and recognition programs have learned to do two things. First, they use group, rather than individual, reward systems. Since most non-sales efforts are group efforts, the work group, not individuals, should be recognized. This allows more people to share in the benefits of effort and also brings helpful group dynamics concepts, such as peer pressure, into play. A group quickly handles nonparticipative members or members who otherwise endanger the payoff opportunity.

The second thing that Lewis believes successful programs have in common is *continuity* or *integration*. "The tendency is for hard-goods incentive programs to be treated as short-run, add-on efforts— contests. The designers rarely integrate the program into the work/pay system as a permanent part of the process. Unless they do, you'll see only short-term results."

Grayson cautions that training and development play an important role in the success of productivity-improvement programs. "For any of these systems to amount to anything, you need real responsibility sharing. First, the people who do the work must believe that their contributions to improvement are wanted, needed and will be rewarded. That could mean a whole re-education for first-line management. Supervisors who aren't comfortable with experimentation have to encourage trial-and-error instead of rule-and-policy following. Supervisors, like parents, dislike "why" questions. But nothing can shut down the process faster than antagonistic supervision. They need to learn to relate to people in new ways.

"Secondly, the working people— those who really put the goods out the door— have to learn *how* to find new ideas, *how* to think improvement, *how* to function in a problem-solving group. If trainers don't provide help to *both* of these groups in the form of idea-generating skills— maybe helping them start Quality Circles,* but definitely in the area of team work— your program is likely to fall short of expected results."

Grayson suggests that there is a third, somewhat risky, responsibility that trainers should assume is within their purview— developing management involvement. General Motors Institute and APC, for example, have collaborated on a video-based program that promotes productivity improvement as a management responsibility. To Grayson, communicating "the message" that productivity can be improved through people may be the trainer's most important task. "We all really must be involved in telling the story that people are the most significant factor in productivity improvement. In return for their efforts, these people need recognition and equitable rewards for the work they do and the ideas they contribute. And they also need and want control, a positive influence over the quality of their work lives. If trainers can help their organizations hear and understand that message, that's a big first step toward solving our national productivity problems."

Obviously, they think big in Texas, and they tackle big tasks as well. But the potential payoff is as Texas-sized as the problem. And both are vitally important to us all.

*QCCs or Quality Control Circles are worker study groups that concentrate on solving job-related quality and productivity problems. The premise is that workers have vital interest and information in Q.C. but are seldom given license to contribute to Q.C. decisions. QCC, a concept started in Japan, attempts to tap that potential.

Reprinted from TRAINING, July 1979

RECOGNITION AWARDS: HOW AND WHY TO USE THEM

When "Thanks" and "Congratulations" aren't enough

BY ROBERT C. EIMERS
AND GEORGE W. BLOMGREN

• *Just two days after he had received a handsome plaque for being the outstanding management trainee in his class, Bill Smith resigned and took a position with one of his company's major competitors.*

• *John Dunn had been the division's leading sales producer for years. During a division-wide sales promotion, featuring merchandise and travel awards, however, he inexplicably failed to bring in any new business.*

• *The company had a long standing policy of offering a $25 savings bond to any employee who could come up with a new and usable idea as to how production could be increased. Surprisingly, few ideas were submitted, and most of these were little more than hastily scribbled afterthoughts.*

• *Elaine Jordan was informed by her boss that she had just been named "Employee of the Month." To her boss's surprise, she seemed rather puzzled and asked, "What for?"*

Do any of these situations sound familiar? If they do, it is not surprising. These cases illustrate a common organizational problem—the failure of awards to serve their intended purpose.

Behavior is shaped by its consequences. This is a fundamental law of human behavior which has been validated through extensive psychological research. It simply means that those behaviors which are rewarded will be strengthened and maintained. In more practical terms, it means that if you want someone to do something, you have to make it worth his while.

Let's look at a work example for a moment. If you want a person to come to work each day and perform up to minimally acceptable standards, then you must provide minimally acceptable rewards (salary benefits, etc.). If on the other hand, you expect that person to perform beyond this level, then you have to offer rewards commensurate with that performance. It is in these situations, where outstanding performance and achievement are desired, that awards can serve a most useful function.

What is an award?

Most of us are familiar with awards to some degree. In fact, awards permeate the very fabric of our achievement-oriented society. From the time we are children, we encounter opportunities to earn awards. The list of awards is virtually endless—plaques, trophies, ribbons, varsity letters, certificates, public recognition, cash bonuses, promotions, etc. What all these awards share in common is that they are intended to promote and reward outstanding performance, i.e., behavior above and beyond that which is ordinarily acceptable.

Awards, especially those that are visibly present in a work environment, take on great importance as *symbols*. They may indicate status (new doctors especially are never without a stethoscope hanging out of their pocket), or symbols may designate levels of achievement within a class or category.

One of the most common uses of awards is for recognition purposes, tapping motivational factors which are deeply ingrained elements of human nature. The stars on the halfback's helmet, for example, indicate touchdowns, and the flags on military aircraft designate "enemy kills." The widespread practice of "President's" clubs and similar achievement societies for salesmen also meets this need for recognition.

A common thread tying all of these various awards together, however, is that their worth is primarily symbolic rather than monetary. Think for a moment about the America's Cup. We have been told that its intrinsic value is worth less than $20, and that it even has a hole in the bottom, so that the winner cannot even drink champagne from it. Nevertheless, people from all over the world have devoted enormous amounts of energy and money to its pursuit.

Although awards have tremendous motivating potential, we too often find that awards fail to stimulate achievement, and in some cases, even "backfire." From our work with organizations and their awards systems, we have identified a set of guidelines which, if observed, can help to promote outstanding performance through the judicious selection and use of awards. These are:

1. **The behavior which is to be rewarded must be clearly defined.** In our example, Elaine Jordan did not have the slightest idea of what she had done to merit being named "Employee of the Month." For this reason, the award really didn't mean very much to her, and for that matter, probably meant even less to her fellow workers. Our point here is simply this: If you want employees to respond positively when you offer awards, you first have to let them know *specifically* what is required to earn those awards.

2. **Awards should be given as soon as possible after the desired behavior occurred.** Bonuses given at the end of the year for a job well done in the beginning, for example, simply lose some of their impact in the intervening months. Why not reward outstanding achievement right away? This strengthens the connec-

tion, in everyone's mind, between high performance and management's willingness to reward it. Whereas salaries and other forms of compensation may be rather inflexible in this regard, due to organizational policy and administrative practices, recognition awards and/or merchandise can be given almost immediately.

3. **When it comes to awards, one man's meat may well be another man's poison.** People have different tastes, preferences, and values. Whereas one salesman may work very hard in order to win an engraved pen and pencil set, another salesman may simply think it's not worth the effort. A solution to this problem is simply to let employees select their own awards. For years, incentive companies have been providing employees with a "menu" of awards, typically in the form of a merchandise catalog. In this way, each individual can select those items which he or she *really* wants.

4. **Awards should have memorability.** One disadvantage of giving cash awards, for example, is that they are apt to be melded into household budgets and used for groceries and dental bills. Merchandise, travel, and recognition awards, on the other hand, typically have a more lasting impact, and continue to evoke pleasant associations for the recipient over the years.

5. **Effective awards have emotional appeal.** They arouse an individual's awareness of his needs and wants, thus motivating him toward achievement and satisfaction of those needs. We have often heard merchandise catalogs described as "wish books," for example. They have a capacity for evoking pleasant images and fantasies of desired life styles. Because merchandise, as well as travel, have such broad and strong emotional appeal, they tend to inspire increased levels of employee performance.

6. **Awards should be accompanied by social recognition.** Fanfare may be "corny," but you cannot underestimate the value of presenting an award with enthusiasm and dignity. When the company presi-

dent, for example, presents an award, its impact is doubled. This shows the recipient that his or her efforts are being noted and appreciated at all levels. Newspaper publicity, even if it is only a "house organ," also enhances the value of an award. High achievers thrive on recognition. You can take advantage of that fact through the ways in which your awards are presented.

7. **Award programs need to be administered fairly if everyone is to participate.** Remember John Dunn, the top sales producer in our example? Well, the incentive program rules were stacked against him and other high producers. Since awards were based on percentage sales increments, those individuals already operating at near maximum efficiency had to work much harder than those people who had more "room for improvement." An effective way to counteract this problem is simply to break employees down into sales *teams* and give awards on that basis. The fun of competing, as well as the desire to be a contributing team member, serves to motivate everyone.

8. **Awards must be won if they are going to serve any purpose at all.** The company with the disappointing suggestion system gave out about one savings bond per year. After a while, employees saw that there wasn't much point to spending time and effort developing new suggestions. Winning an award is an energizing process; it creates good feelings about oneself and about the company. Don't be stingy in your award programs. Awards represent an investment in your employees and their performance, an investment which typically pays off handsomely in terms of increased morale and employee effectiveness.

9. **While awards can be used to motivate behavior and facilitate learning, this fact in itself creates real danger.** Just as government excesses in printing money can create economic problems, trainers who print diplomas and buy plaques haphazardly can destroy the motivational value of their awards. Just as "printing press" money loses value,

"cheap" awards come to have little motivational value.

10. **Awards stimulate motivation, but we have frequently found that motivation alone is not sufficient.** Performance is actually a function of two factors—motivation and *skill*. Thus, it is often effective to supplement incentive awards with training and or skill building. If you want your sales force to sell more, for example, show them *how* to do it. Incidentally, we have found that combining incentive and award programs with training is an excellent way to integrate training and marketing objectives. A well trained employee, effectively motivated by the prospect of winning valued awards, is an employee who is likely to succeed.

As an example, one of the authors once worked with a hospital on effectively combining training with simple recognition awards. The hospital in question experienced enormously high turnover among its housekeeping personnel. Their organizational culture placed a heavy emphasis upon professional status, and the "mop pushers" were far outside the system. Most were members of a minority group or from disadvantaged backgrounds. Training had amounted typically to no more than how to push the mop and scrub down facilities. The training program was changed, however, so that it now emphasized substantive job knowledge and "expertise" in different situations. Training was largely self-instructional, and broken down into two levels of mastery. Certificates of merit were awarded upon satisfactory completion of each training level (vigorous testing standards were maintained). Turnover was decreased quite dramatically, and other measures of performance showed marked improvement.

All in all, awards possess enormous potential for motivating human achievement. If this potential is not to be wasted, however, award programs must be administered in keeping with some fundamental psychological principles.

Reprinted from TRAINING, November 1977

MONEY VERSUS MERCHANDISE: WHICH IS THE BEST MOTIVATOR— AND THE BEST INCENTIVE?

Each has advantages and disadvantages. Here's how to select the one that's best for your organization

BY ROBERT C. EIMERS, GEORGE W. BLOMGREN AND EDWARD GUBMAN

One of the first questions raised in the design of an incentive program is: Which is a more effective motivator, money or merchandise? There are good arguments for both sides, but our experience tells us that merchandise is better in many instances.

The motivational benefits of merchandise awards are psychologically complex and highly symbolic. Money, on the other hand, has direct and understandable appeal as a motivator and reward. Merchandise is the more effective, but the contrast between the two leads to a curious paradox in planning and implementing incentive programs.

Simply put, the paradox results because what people most often say they want is not usually the most energizing award. We recognized this several years ago when we conducted a study of gasoline station retailers. There was a marked discrepancy between how station owners rated the desirability of incentive awards—cash versus merchandise— and the type of awards they recalled having "especially enjoyed." They clearly preferred cash or discounted products over merchandise and travel. However, when asked to recall what awards they particularly enjoyed, had been the most meaningful to them or had provided the greatest motivation, they never mentioned cash or discounts. Station retailers happily recalled the gift items they won and the trips they took, citing them as enjoyable, meaningful and motivating.

Of course, both merchandise and money are useful, depending on the needs and objectives of the organization running the program. Moreover, awards, whether money or merchandise, do not motivate people. Instead, they activate or arouse pre-existing motives or motivational dispositions. The extent of activation depends upon a number of factors, of which the appeal of the particular award is only one. Among the other significant factors are a person's past experiences in other incentive programs, his or her financial needs and wants at a particular time, current levels of satisfaction with the job and the work organization and how the awards are promoted.

It is also dangerously misleading to try to separate the nature of the award from the award program. Incentive programs, whether they involve merchandise, travel or cash, serve as catalysts that call into play a number of other individual or organizational motivators and rewards. For example, a well-planned and executed program will boost morale, enrich jobs, add a little fun to the organization, arouse needs for competition, recognition and achievement and contribute to the personal development of all employees. Thus, to center on the merchandise or money award as the sole motivator is to view an incentive program unrealistically.

In looking at the relative benefits of money and merchandise as incentives, it seems fair to assign certain advantages to money and others to merchandise.

Cash offers the following advantages:

1. Cash has universal appeal. Everyone knows what it is and knows what to do with it. And most people need more of it. People expect that they will be paid more for additional effort or for learning new tasks. A cash incentive program simply confirms this expectation.

2. Often, programs based on cash are easier to administer than programs based on merchandise. There are no shipping charges or problems, and there are no sales taxes to pay. Items never arrive defective or broken, and orders are never filled inaccurately. Money is never out of fashion nor, one hopes, out of stock.

3. Cash offers the program participant complete freedom about how the award can be used. Therefore, people may satisfy many of their own needs and reasons by participating in a cash program. As we will soon point out, however, freedom of usage is not necessarily a motivational benefit because the cash is not always used in an especially satisfying way.

Merchandise awards are more difficult to administer, and their appeal is not as immediately obvious as cash. Yet, for some complex psychological reasons, they are a compelling motivational element in an incentive program:

1. Merchandise or travel awards are more apt to tap emotional needs. While money has universal value, its appeal is rather "cold," nonemotional and diffuse. As economists point out, money has no intrinsic value other then the symbolic meanings that are socially attached to it. On the other hand, merchandise catalogues (often rightly referred to as "wishbooks") afford people the opportunity for instant emotional identification based on existing wants, needs and interests. A picture of a color television set or camping equipment can instantly evoke a rush of pleasurable memories or arouse happy feelings of anticipation. This is not the case with an illustration of a $100 bill.

2. Since merchandise has broader and stronger emotional appeal, greater opportunities exist for program promotion. Money is much more

difficult to promote in a comparable way. A risk inherent in using money is that it so closely parallels compensation, with which it may become psychologically "lumped" even if it is intended only as part of a special program or campaign. It is often difficult to remove money awards without creating negative reactions once the campaign is over.

3. Merchandise awards are memorable. Long after the program is over, they remain a symbol of a person's successful participation in it. Cash awards often become part of the household budget and go toward the grocery or dental bills. Used this way, money isn't very memorable.

4. Merchandise affords many more opportunities for recognition. There's a small but important difference between what you've bought for yourself and what you've been awarded. It is psychologically more appropriate and socially more acceptable to talk about the new patio furniture you've been awarded for special achievement than it is to discuss the furniture that you purchased— even if you did so with award money.

5. Merchandise awards generate familial involvement. When a married person with a family participates in an incentive award program, other family members often select awards they would like or that the household needs. The additional motivation to do something for one's spouse or children is a powerful energizing force for most people. When a bank employee in Utah, who originally opposed performing in an incentive program, became a big winner, his children selected bicycles from the catalog and asked their dad to win them. The employee later recounted proudly how he earned those bicycles for his children.

6. Merchandise awards move people beyond their "comfort level," the point at which they will not expend additional effort for incremental earnings. As evidence, companies using a commission system of compensation find that merchandise and travel awards produce additional sales. This clearly suggests that the qualitative impact of merchandise awards is different than money, partly because of the nature of the awards and partly because of the nature of the organization using the awards. A program that is constant, like a company's compensation system, loses arousal power. A merchandise incentive program that is temporary and novel has greater arousal power because of its newness and uniqueness.

Perhaps, then, the question "Which is more effective— cash or merchandise?" is inappropriately simple. It is far better to ask about the client's organizational structure and climate; to discover its training, motivational and communication needs and objectives; and to assess other structural features, especially the current compensation system. Once these data are gathered and understood, the considerations of each kind of incentive program can be reviewed to determine which are the most productive types of motivational awards.

Reprinted from TRAINING, July 1979

RECOMMENDED RESOURCES FOR MANAGERS

MAIL ORDERS TO:

LAKEWOOD BOOKS
50 South Ninth Street, Minneapolis, MN 55402
800-707-7769 or **612-333-0471**
Or fax your order to 612-340-4819.

UNCONDITIONAL GUARANTEE
Examine and use any of the resources on this form for a full 30 days. If you are not completely satisfied, for any reason whatsoever, simply return and receive a full refund of the purchase price.

Please send me the following publications:

Qty.	Title	$ Amount
	Adult Learning In Your Classroom. $19.95.	
	Creative Training Techniques Handbook, Vol. 2. By Bob Pike. $49.95.	
	Creative Training Tools. By Bob Pike. $14.95.	
	Designing and Delivering Cost-Effective Training—And Measuring the Results. $39.95.	
	Dynamic Openers & Energizers. By Bob Pike. $14.95.	
	Evaluating Training. $19.95.	
	Instructing for Results. By Fredric Margolis and Chip R. Bell. $19.95.	
	Managing the Front-End of Training. By Bob Pike. $14.95.	
	Motivating Your Trainees. By Bob Pike. $14.95.	
	Optimizing Training Transfer. By Bob Pike. $14.95.	
	Powerful Audiovisual Techniques. By Bob Pike. $14.95.	
	Understanding Training: Perspectives and Practices. By Fredric Margolis and Chip R. Bell. $17.95.	
	TRAINING Magazine. 12 issues/yr. $78 U.S., $88 Canada; $99 Other Int'l.	
	Creative Training Techniques Newsletter. 12 issues/yr. $99 U.S.; $109 Canada; $119 Other Int'l.	
	The Lakewood Report Newsletter. 12 issues/yr. $128 U.S.; $138 Canada; $148 Other Int'l.	
	Training Directors' Forum Newsletter. 12 issues/yr. $118 U.S.; $128 Canada; $138 Other Int'l.	

SUBTOTAL

In Canada add 7% GST# 123705485 *(applies to all products)*

In MN add 7% sales tax; in WI add 5% sales tax *(does not apply to newsletters)*

Add $4 for first book; $3 each additional book for shipping & handling.

TOTAL

Subtotal: _____
Add GST: _____
Add Tax: _____
Add S&H: _____
Total Amount Enclosed: _____

☐ Check or money order is enclosed. Check payable to Lakewood Publications. (U.S. Funds)

☐ Please charge: ☐ VISA   ☐ MasterCard   ☐ American Express

Card # _____ Exp. ____/____ Signature _____
(Required for Credit Card use)

NAME _____

TITLE _____

COMPANY _____

ADDRESS (No PO Boxes) _____

CITY _____ STATE _____ ZIP _____

PHONE (_____)_____

H509

ORDER FORM MISSING?
Call 800-328-4329
or 612-333-0471
and ask for up-to-date catalog of
Lakewood books and publications for
managers and human resources professionals.

Mail Your Order Form
and Payment Today To:

Lakewood Books
50 South Ninth Street
Minneapolis, MN 55402